paper love

… ersten Briefe alle? New York …
Und doch, deine letzten Br…
…dings vor unserer kleine…
…er Zeit geschrieben – war…
…ders. – Ich weiß nicht …
…er Liebling, du merkst …
…iben, was du mir dazu …
…u hörst. Ich muß für …
…meine Seele den … Schutz …
…r Kirche, einen festen, ru…
…hen Punkt wissen. In d…
…Wirrwarr müßte es für …
…h, etwas Unumstößliches es …
…, um es ertragen zu kön…
…cht allein unter zu gehen. …
…Du wirst nicht glücklich u…
…wenn du mir schreiben we…
…deine letzten Briefe seltsam be…
…nt deine ersten. Wenn du mi…
…endlich schreiben würdest…
…ab dich sehr lieb! …

paper love

searching for the girl
my grandfather left behind

SARAH WILDMAN

RIVERHEAD BOOKS

A MEMBER OF PENGUIN GROUP (USA)

NEW YORK

2014

RIVERHEAD BOOKS
Published by the Penguin Group
Penguin Group (USA) LLC
375 Hudson Street
New York, New York 10014

USA · Canada · UK · Ireland · Australia
New Zealand · India · South Africa · China

penguin.com
A Penguin Random House Company

Copyright © 2014 by Sarah Wildman
Penguin supports copyright. Copyright fuels creativity, encourages
diverse voices, promotes free speech, and creates a vibrant culture. Thank you
for buying an authorized edition of this book and for complying with copyright
laws by not reproducing, scanning, or distributing any part of it in any
form without permission. You are supporting writers and allowing
Penguin to continue to publish books for every reader.

Portions of this book appeared in different form in *Slate* and *Tablet*.

Grateful acknowledgment is made for permission to
reprint images on the following pages:

Pages 34 and 180: Letter from Dr. Laurence Farmer to Karl Wildmann,
dated May 24, 1938, and letter from Jewish Family Welfare Society,
dated March 6, 1939. Used by permission of the Immigration History
Research Center Archives, University of Minnesota.

Page 249: Index card, Reichsvereinigung der Juden in Deutschland,
Hanna Taube Scheftel, 1.2.4.1/12671976/ITS Digital Archives,
Bad Arolsen. Reprinted by permission.

Library of Congress Cataloging-in-Publication Data

Wildman, Sarah.
Paper love : searching for the girl my grandfather left behind / Sarah Wildman.
p.   cm.
Includes bibliographical references.
ISBN 978-1-59463-155-9
1. Wildman, Karl.   2. Scheftel, Valerie, born 1911.   3. Jews—
Austria—Biography.   4. Jews, Austrian—Massachusetts—Biography.
5. Jewish refugees—Massachusetts—Biography.   6. Holocaust,
Jewish (1939–1945)—Austria.   I. Title.
DS135.A93W55   2014   2014018422
940.53'18092—dc23
[B]

Printed in the United States of America
1   3   5   7   9   10   8   6   4   2

BOOK DESIGN BY AMANDA DEWEY

---

*Penguin is committed to publishing works of quality and integrity.
In that spirit, we are proud to offer this book to our readers; however,
the story, the experiences, and the words
are the author's alone.*

For Orli and Hana,
the two little Jews who grew

and

For Valy and Hans

CONTENTS

paper love

IN THE BEGINNING

In my father's eulogy for my grandfather, he quoted Field Marshal Ferdinand Foch: "Hard pressed on my right; center is yielding; impossible to maneuver. Situation excellent, I shall attack."

———

We called my grandfather *saba*, the modern, muscular Hebrew appellation, rather than the Old World Yiddish, *zeyde*—or German, *Opa*—let alone the (far too) American *grandpa*. Born Chaim, he went by Karl. My grandfather, in my memory and in the hagiography of my family, was a bon vivant, a multilingual, well-traveled émigré doctor who lived with the joie de vivre of a man who had never been oppressed by hardship. Or maybe that's not right: with the joie de vivre of a man who had known *only* hardship, and then emerged from it, phoenixlike, into a problemless promised land. He was dashing, a character out of (Jewish) film noir, with the perfect suit, a jaunty hat, a top note of expensive European aftershave, a bottom whiff of Odol, the German minty mouthwash he imported in bulk for himself each time he returned to the Continent. His appeal was not simply aesthetic—his hair, as his friends teased him, was unruly, wildly curly, clipped close to his head by middle age, always pure white in my memory, long and unkempt as a younger man, so much like my own that my sister and I would joke about our "*saba* hair" when ours would frizz up, above the hairline, beyond our ponytails. His nose was a bit too big, his lips fleshy, and yet he carried himself in the way of men who know they are appealing, who understand women—and men—and how to win over either sex. And swoon they did. His inherent attraction was some combination of pheromones, charisma, charm, actual beauty, mystery.

As much as my grandfather loved America, for what it stood for, for its freedoms, for what it had done for him, he never seemed "of" this country; certainly he stood apart from, or perhaps outside, the town in northwest Massachusetts where he settled and opened a medical practice. His English, though grammatically perfect, had the light, lyrical accent of European sophisticates; he would, biannually, free himself from our idioms entirely for six weeks at a time and find his way back to Europe. The family, at first, remained behind. After a few trips completely alone, by 1952 my grandmother (aware, perhaps, of his attractions) refused to allow him to travel without her. And so they went together, their children left with a babysitter, an Italian-born seamstress musically named Rina DiOrio, whom I remember for her marvelous baskets filled with strips of silks and cottons and tweeds and synthetics, the soft kaleidoscope gleanings of her work that I would tie together into costumes, well into my childhood.

Six weeks they left their kids! Postcards were written to my father and aunt, advising them on where to find their Halloween costumes, to remember to do their homework, to remind them to be in touch by forwarding mail to their next stop, which was, invariably, Munich or Milan or Madrid. It is something I can't quite imagine, but somehow it was just who he was; and, for the most part, it wasn't questioned, he was living a life grander, and more cosmopolitan, than his neighbors in their big but rural Massachusetts town—it was a quest to see the world, to *live* aggressively, that propelled him.

"We have always agreed that life is both grandiose and ridiculous," Karl wrote to his closest friend, Bruno Klein, an old Viennese schoolmate, in December 1979. *"You have always been and still are the master of this concept and this inner certainty. You laugh at the grandiose, the tragic, the heroic, and in the ridiculousness of life, you see grandeur and tragedy and heroism."*

Karl's flight from Vienna—at age twenty-six, six months after the Anschluss, when Hitler swept through the city to throbbing throngs of well-wishers, and Jewish students were expelled from schools across the city, their families banished from work in hospitals, shops, parks, daily life, their world upended—was always described to me in similar grand terms—danger, excitement, fulfillment—nothing short of remarkable. Because he actually finished his medical degree before Jews were stripped of the right to finish school; because he got out at all. And it was complete with a happily-ever-after ending: the entire family, or at least the core of the group, the *essentials*, got out safely. The story of that escape—and the way I understood it—shaped my childhood imaginings, my nightmares, my dreams. The reality of that escape shaped his worldview.

To the same Bruno he wrote in 1983, *"Atheism is utterly incomprehensible to me. It is such a dry, cynical, uninformed, unfeeling and myopic mind that cannot see and feel and imagine the 'beyond oneself.' The energy, the majesty that profuses the cosmos . . . the exhilaration, the joy of life, the infinite of love, call it what you will. Why not God?"*

This was very my grandfather. Everything was *herrlich*, wonderful. Superb. Sublime. He was prone to bold pronouncements, would stand up at family events and command attention with philosophical meanderings. He was a bit prideful, a bit critical, entirely absorbed in the idea of the Jew in History, and where he himself fit into that. I still have my bat mitzvah letter from him, welcoming me to Jewish adulthood. *"As you grow and develop and encounter the world at an ever more meaningful and potent level, your awareness of this endowment will inform you, inspire you, and guide you."* He closed with *Hazak v'ematz*— "Be strong and of good courage," the words that Moses says to Joshua—"Be not afraid!"—when he realizes it will be Joshua who leads the Jews into the Promised Land and Moses will be left behind.

His relationship to Judaism was as much practical—he had his seat in synagogue, in the second row, he held court at Seder—as it was intellectual, philosophical, a game of minds and text study. To Bruno he wrote, *"It is the talent and the destiny of the Jew to have felt and known that there is a beyond, to have pursued it as an idea and principle. . . . The very name Israel is derived from the encounter of Jacob with an angel, a messenger of God. It means to have fought with God and to have prevailed."* To have prevailed! It spoke to the essence of his escape, not to mention his confidence.

———

It was some years after his death when my grandmother casually told me that she had destroyed my grandfather's personal correspondence. We were setting the table for dinner. "They sat in a filing cabinet for sixty-something years," she said. "I decided that was long enough." We fought about it. "They are all in German," she said quietly, derisively. But though I hissed petulantly, *"It's not a dead language,"* really, what was the point? There was no undoing.

"I saved the important things," she said, slyly. "Like our love letters." Emphasis on *our.* What was destroyed? I asked.

"Oh, I don't know. Letters from Shanghai. People you've never met. People who are gone."

Shanghai? People who are gone? It was tantalizing, infuriating. And over time it became clear that the point of her purge was, consciously or not, to preserve the myth of the spotless escape; and, in part, a carefully curated history.

—— ⁓ ——

I'm getting ahead of myself.

A few years after our argument, my grandmother was not well. She sat in my grandfather's old home office, her movements manipulated by some terrible sort of Parkinson's-like disease, as I rooted around in cabinets asking questions about random artifacts. She had always been so meticulous, in her appearance, in her demeanor; the last few years of her life were a blow to that—though there were some constants. She still perfumed herself with Emeraude, a scent that had remained unchanged—like her—since the 1920s; still wore her deep pink and coral lipsticks, still pushed herself into punishing girdles and stockings and heels, her Achilles tendons shortened by decades propped up on wedges. And she hadn't changed the office, or the house, at all since his death, as though she—as though we—believed my grandfather would walk back in at any moment, sit down at his enormous walnut desk, and slice through the mail of the day with the long, sharp letter opener he kept for just that purpose. His marble busts of Schiller and Goethe, of Chaim Weizmann, the first president of Israel, and Theodor Herzl still sat in one windowsill; on the other side of the room, a black marble Apollo flexed his muscles into eternity. Volumes of literature in German lined the shelves. The deep teal blue and green armchair where he pierced my ears with a needle—at the age of five—was still placed exactly where it always sat, beneath a copper flying-saucer-like pendant light. A midcentury Danish daybed, dressed in green and blue wool, hugged the wall; I occasionally slept on it when I would come to visit.

That afternoon, in the cabinets beneath the bay windows where Goethe sat, staring, I came across an old album, the kind with black

*July 1929. On the left, Carl Feldschuh,
my grandfather's brother-in-law; on the
right, Karl Wildman; the girl in the
middle is a friend.*

pages and photo corners cradling black-and-white snapshots with scalloped edges. The photographs ranged from formal—stiff family portraits from the 1910s to the 1930s—to informal—crowds of laughing European teens and twentysomethings in the late 1920s and early 1930s.

There was countryside and friends, attractive girls in old-fashioned swimming costumes, and a cheerful, muscular, incomprehensibly young version of the man I'd known as my grandfather, surrounded in one photo by a dozen girls, the literal focal point, the center of attention.

Among these images were dozens of tiny photos of a young woman. *"Your Valy"* was written on the back of each one, in a feminine hand I didn't recognize. Here she was, laughing, rolling in the grass in Vienna's Augarten—next to my grandfather. Here she was mugging, posed, hands on hips. Another showed the two of them lying on a bed, smiling coyly; it was shot into a mirror. There were photos of him and her in bathing suits, the two of them snuggled up close, laughing. They appeared, in the parlance of teenagers, to be more than friends.

How had I never seen this album before, I wondered, turning the pages, trying not to let the paper crumble. This was his life, I realized, before any of us, before, even, my grandmother. And it was a life so—was there any other word for it?—

carefree. They look so happy, so young, so fresh in the images dated 1932, 1934, 1935. This was his European life, the life—the people, the experiences—he had left behind.

Tucked into the back of the album, folded into a small, tight square, was a piece of paper pasted with a series of photos the girl named Valy had taken of herself. Each square was numbered, 1 through 4. *"I am so sad,"* says the first

(they are all written in German). *"I'm still waiting, but no letter from Karl has come yet!"* Here she makes a serious face. Then in square 2—*"Maybe this will help: '. . . If not, then not'"*—a photo, a wistful face (she is, I learn later, quoting from a popular song of the turn of the last century, "Der Eine Allein"). Square 3: *"But no, it would be so much nicer if he'd write again, the way he used to, the way I endlessly long for it to be! If only he'd write again at last."* Her gaze is now turned away from the camera, into the middle distance. By the fourth image she has turned again to her viewer, with a big smile: *"But maybe a letter will come tomorrow! One will surely come, won't it?!"*

The little note was dated May 5, 1939, about ten months after my grandfather had left Europe.

I held the document up and asked my grandmother who the author was. "Your grandfather's true love," she said, and offered nothing

more. *His what?* My grandmother was not a terribly romantic woman. What a totally peculiar, what a totally devastating thing to say. I tried to press her on it, but she demurred and retired to her room. She refused to comment further; I feared to ask more.

Back at home, I called my grandfather's sister, Cilli. "Who was she?" I asked. *Ah, Valy,* she said, with a sigh, and a moment's hesitation. Valy and

Karl, she explained, studied at the University of Vienna's medical school together. Valy had been desperately in love with him for years, and he had barely noticed her. That lopsided relationship remained true until one summer, partway through his medical degree, when he ran to find her at home—she was from Czechoslovakia—and professed his love for her as well. They had had a few years together. And then he'd escaped to New York. She stayed behind. "She was brilliant. Brilliant! A wonderful girl." *Vonderful.*

Later that week I ran into a prominent Jewish intellectual. Breathlessly I told him of my find: *My grandfather had a lover, he'd left her behind, and who knew what happened. Maybe there was a woman to be found out there, maybe . . .*

"Someday," he said, barely looking up, "you'll pass through Berlin or Vienna. And you'll fuck some German. And then you'll write your story."

Crushed, I thought, *Oh God, this intrigue, this intensity; it's all so horribly banal.* Of course there are these Holocaust stories, of course there were lovers left, of course lives were rerouted, uprooted, destroyed. What new story would I find, really? What more was there to say?

Cilli wrote to me that week. She sent the note by regular mail, to my office. "Maybe you'll write the story of Karl and Valy," she typed, "maybe you're the one to tell it."

But I had already stopped digging.

———

One after the other, my great-aunt, and then my grandmother, died. I had failed to ask more questions, even though I wondered, often, if there was more to the story of the girl in the photographs. I assumed if there was more to know, it had been thrown away, purposely or not, destroyed by my grandmother in her purge of my grandfather's documents. Later, much later, far too late, I went back and listened to an interview I had conducted with Cilli for the United States Holocaust Memorial Museum in the months after I graduated from college. Valy was everywhere in her memories, but I hadn't yet known to listen for her.

"He had a girlfriend who he went to medical school with, she was very bright, and very short, and she was so much in love with him!" Cilli said that long-ago December afternoon. "She would wait every night—until eleven or twelve—while he was out giving lessons to students. She was from Czechoslovakia. . . ." And then, later, the tape mentions her again: "He was making plans with Valy to run away from Austria—this girlfriend—he knew as a foreigner he could not open a medical office in Vienna. Then, instead, he ran away with us."

These sentences hang there on the recording, ready for a follow-up. But each time I listen to it, the outcome is the same: I do not press her to explain further when I hear the name Valy. I do not follow up. Instead, I focus, exclusively, on the five who left—my grandfather, his mother, his sister, his brother-in-law, his nephew—and I push past references to those who did not leave. I was so sure, then, of the important story, so sure of the supreme veracity of what I already held to be true. Now when I listen to the tape, I am haunted by what I might have asked.

But that's now. For a long time, even after I found her photos, and her small notes—even after I knew to wonder about her, when I thought about her, I simply assumed Valy, too, was dead, or, at least, disappeared; a sad, personal addendum among six million catastrophic tales. I didn't even Google her. I simply left it alone. Yet every now and then I wondered: I worried something was missing, some aspect of the grandfather I'd worshipped had been doubly lost by not pursuing the story; I wondered, too, if she somehow might have actually survived.

———

Instead of writing about my own family, I began writing about the other addenda—the small Holocaust stories, little pieces of the puzzle—investigating the narratives at the edges, stories that asked questions of what happened to regular people, the minor stories, the warp and weave of the tragedy.

I didn't find out what was missing for nearly a decade. By then I'd spent some years out of the country, always, quietly, in the back of my mind, searching—though for what, I couldn't have told you. Part of it, I told my closest friends, was an endless foray into my own identity. It felt so arbitrary to be American. If I could better understand my grandfather's story, I kept thinking, as I spent month after month in Europe, I might discover why I could never feel settled, or fully happy, at home, why I felt most alive in transit, moving. A wandering Jew! Just like my grandfather, who fled Europe and then, it seemed, remained on the road for years after. He and my grandmother trav-

Karl and Dorothy Wildman in Switzerland, early 1970s. At some point in his life, he changed the spelling to Carl.

eled endlessly: all across Europe, of course, but also China (just after Nixon), Morocco, over the Atlas Mountains (by car), Hungary, Russia, Peru, Argentina, Ecuador, Brazil, Bolivia, Paraguay, Australia, New Zealand, Thailand, Japan, Israel. I would receive dolls from their journeys, hard-faced toys that weren't meant for play. Stiff geishas in kimonos, with real hair. A Native American woman, doomed to weave her loom forever. A Nordic-looking Swiss mountain lass with eyes that blinked and a stiff crinoline beneath her traditional gown. My sister and I lined them on the shelves in our childhood bedrooms, kept them as dusty reminders of the exotic life my grandparents led.

The more stories I wrote on the period, the more people I met who were grappling with questions of identity—Jew, Austrian, German, Pole—and the more I came to believe that if I was persistent enough, I might discover where my generation—and I—fit into the picture. We were shaped by the stories our grandparents had told us, or not told us, deeply affected by them and yet distanced, unable to figure out how to translate them for our own children and the children yet to come, unable, in some ways, to decide how to talk about this history once the eyewitnesses were gone. The stories were tactile and yet dusty, faded; they were real, and yet totally unfathomable. And if they felt this way to us, what would they feel like to those who came after? We are the last to know and love survivors as who they are—as human, as flawed, as our family. What, now, do we do with that knowledge?

Even as I researched the history of others, I assumed my understanding of my grandfather's story—as well as my knowledge of the sweet girl in the photos—was doomed to remain wholly incomplete.

But then, toward the end of the aughts, something changed. As my parents prepared to sell my grandparents' house, packs of family members visited, culling through papers day after day, selecting, from the acquired detritus of two lives. There wasn't much, there was too much: it was treasure; it was junk. I filled a bag with dresses that had belonged to my great-grandmother from the 1920s, my grandfather's Army-issue pants (he volunteered in 1942 and emerged, after several promotions, as a major three years later), and his University of Vienna medical diploma, stamped with the Nazi insignia.

All the items deemed worth saving were collected and bundled into boxes and brought to basements in New Jersey and New York, where they were promptly forgotten again. Mostly. The ones in my parents' home remained endlessly tempting to me, so much so that, on a visit home a few months later, I couldn't resist and took one apart. It was labeled "C. J. Wildman, Personal," C.J. being the initials for Chaim Judah, my grandfather's given name. Tucked inside was a music box I remembered from childhood, an Alpine house whose roof opens and plucks notes of some long-forgotten Swiss folk song. Next to it, I discovered another carton labeled "Correspondence, Patients A–G."

It was a wide file box with a small metal pull, the sort of thing common in the offices of the 1930s. It had reached the end of its natural life: fibers of its thick paper walls had begun to fray and disintegrate. Inside, there were hundreds of letters held together by rubber bands that had long since lost their snap; they dissolved as they stretched.

They were not from patients.

They were penned before, during, and just after World War II by friends, a half brother (my great-grandfather had married twice and had a son far older than my grandfather and his sister), nieces, uncles, cousins, aunts—many, though not all, strangers to me. The letters, dated from 1938 to 1941, were nearly all from Jews desperate to save themselves, to save one another. The letters dated after 1945 were efforts to reach out to those who had survived, tentative attempts to reconstitute a world after the Nazis were vanquished. Were they purposely placed in this mislabeled box? There *were* a few patients' letters scattered among these papers—was it an innocent mistake? Or had he consciously kept them away from my grandmother's eyes? It was shocking, a collection she had somehow overlooked, never opened; it must have sat in his office on North Street, in Pittsfield, Massachusetts, until the day he could no longer practice. And at that point he brought them home, tucked them away somewhere, and somehow they had missed the purge.

The envelopes boasted a philatelist's dream world of antique foreign stamps, the sheer geographic spread a microcosm of the Holocaust's atomizing impact: Shanghai, Sydney, Prague, Budapest, Vienna, Berlin, Lyon, Warsaw, Brooklyn, San Francisco, Tel Aviv, Haifa. Their thin onionskin pages plotted exit strategies, hailed successes, and rued failures. There was gratitude—a thank-you to my grandfather for an affidavit, for medical advice. But more: there were accusations—why wasn't he rescuing them? Why wasn't he responding? The accusatory tone, the number of angry letters, rankled. This wasn't the history I had known. Where was my lucky family? Where was the story of racing to freedom as the doors were slamming shut, rolling under the gates in the nick of time, and pulling everyone along with him? Here instead were notes like this one:

Vienna, June 19, 1941

To Sarah Wildmann [my great-grandmother]
Dear Aunt,
    I would again try to write you and my sister and my brother perhaps you would after 2.5 years have some emotions for me. And give me an answer.

It is directly a story from heaven, how you left me behind, ill.
You probably know very well—you don't think about asking us if we
are still alive. I am ashamed when other people are asking if I
received letters from you to say I haven't heard anything from you.
And I don't get any sign of life. . . .

The panic, the terror, the anger, and the sheer verbal scrabbling for purchase on the slick wall of Nazi ascendency was so palpable, the sheets of paper themselves seemed to have been handled violently; the ink bleeds through the paper, the pages are crumpled. Here was a world, exploded, over the course of a few months, a collection of people once together who were never again assembled. The letters were as complete a representation of my grandfather's old life as I could have imagined, and yet, reading them, I realized I had never really imagined what he had left behind at all.

In retrospect, the five who fled together to these shores was an enormous number, and, at the same time, not many at all.

Of course, on some level, I had always known my grandfather's story couldn't be neat—that our lives are never neat, never obvious, even when we live in neater times. Of course I had known that there was brutality behind the smooth escape, that nothing was smooth or easy in those years—hadn't I interviewed dozens of survivors? Hadn't I spoken to others who fled Vienna embittered by all they had lost, by all they had seen, by all they had experienced? But grandparents— even more than parents—exist only in relation to ourselves when we are young, when, usually, we know them best. Here, in this box, were dimensions upon dimensions of his story, all of which upended for good the easy ways in which I'd categorized my grandfather as a child.

It was the thing I had questioned the least—my family's successful escape—and it was the thing that changed the most with this discovery. Those letters, dark, angry, dispossessed, seemed to be speaking of another man, another family entirely. What did Karl think of these letters when he received them? Did he worry? Did he put them aside? Did he mourn? Why had he kept them? And did he believe my American-born grandmother would have been—what? Jealous of the experience she did not share?

Who were these people in the box, writing and writing and writing, these close friends, these schoolmates, these relatives, *my* relatives, who'd reached out to my grandfather once he had sailed to safety? Had he tried to help? Or had he spent his life in America burying a past he was ashamed of, or felt guilty about? Had he, with great effort and remorse, set himself to forever look forward and never back, and in that way, and only that way, was he able to go on? Or had he accepted that he had saved whom he could, more, in fact, than was even likely, and that those who had been left behind were not abandoned by him but by their governments, by their nations, by the world?

Either way, what the box showed me didn't square easily with his public persona—which was one of luck and joy and endless good cheer. His photos are cocky and insouciant; he looks, at times, like he is running for office. But this is uncharitable. As I researched his story, and the history of those he had left behind, I came to understand it was not fake, his happiness, his outlook. It was not a veneer. It was the very thing that kept him alive.

That first night, spreading the letters out on my parents' dining room table, I pulled out a folded, crumbling, yellow piece of paper. "Dr. Valerie Scheftel born 4 November 1911" was typed at the top, along with an address outside Berlin: "Bergstrasse 1. Potsdam." Below that, my grandfather's office address, in Pittsfield, Massachusetts. It was dated 1943. Stapled to the top corner was a small square of white paper, with my grandfather's scrawl. *VALY* was written across the top and, beneath it, *HIAS*, the Hebrew Immigrant Aid Society, an organization, I knew, that helped Jews immigrate, and that later searched for survivors and tried to arrange family reunifications.

Two photos emerged out of another envelope. They were staged

for a photographer. The woman in them was clear-faced and smiling slightly, a modest gap between her front teeth, hair cut at her jawline, wavy and thick. Her eyes, in one, looked directly at the camera, under thin, natural eyebrows; she had on what appeared to be a nurse's cap. She wore no make-up, no jewelry, had none of the overly stylized look of other women's photos of the era, and yet had clearly taken care with her appearance. In the second photo, she was bareheaded, looking into the corner away from the camera, her eyes creased like she'd been told a joke. She looked lovely, pretty, without affect, without adornment.

Then a letter:

Berlin, July 6, 1940

My beloved only one, my boy!
  You will be with me in this world! This one sentence in your last letter stays with me all the time, wherever I am; I can hear it, see it and feel it. Always! When I am doing what I've been doing all these days, when I am dressing the children's wounds, when they call out to me at night, when I cannot go back to sleep afterwards and when I am sitting by the window, sick with longing. Always your words—

"you will be with me" are comfort and torture at the same time, because of the question: WHEN will I be with you? Please tell me, beloved, when? I do not know the answer, and the consulate has only a vague idea of 1–2 years, meaning an eternity, unimaginable, inconceivable—equal to a hundred years to me, who must be with you within the shortest imaginable period of time, right now and immediately. Now the third summer without you begins.

She was the girl from my grandfather's photo album. Valy. The two pictures—like the funny folded photo note—were taken when he was already in America; she was writing to him from Germany, she had left Czechoslovakia and made it as far as Potsdam. She was the girl he'd left behind.

My grandfather had kept these papers and photos and letters, mislabeled, away from my grandmother, close to him, a reminder, a memento. Why? Who, really, was this woman? Had she found her way to safety with his help? Or without it? Had he kept her words out of love? Out of guilt? Both? As a quiet means of remembrance?

And then I wondered: Could I find her? Would knowing her explain something of my family's story to me, fill out the myth of my grandfather? Or if I could not find her, if she were lost, murdered among all those murders, could I rescue her from obscurity? Grandiose as it sounded, it also seemed, strangely, achievable in the face of the enormity of the horror. If I could bring one person's name back, wasn't that a small victory? In that moment I decided that, of all the people of the box, it was Valy I wanted to find, Valy I would search for—that I would begin a journey to understand her life, and, in so doing, understand my grandfather as well—I could break through the myth of the perfect, spotless, clean escape and render it a clearer, less idealized picture. It would be dirtier, to be sure, but it would be, ultimately, a purer, truer representation of what he had lost when he had to leave everything behind. It would make more sense, in some ways, to my generation as we grapple with this history, it would allow me to explain the period to my own children, when they came, in a tactile way, with a story of a single person plucked from the enormity.

Valy's letters—there were dozens—were written from 1938 through the end of 1941, and mailed, mostly, from Berlin. Powerful, difficult, they begged, they pleaded, they cried. They were desperate appeals for my grandfather's help. I scanned them and e-mailed them to native German speakers for help with translation. Slowly, they came back, one by one. And each unnerved me more.

I was becoming obsessed with her, and yet what I concretely knew about her was only a handful of things: her birth date, her address, her education at the University of Vienna medical school, her love for my grandfather—and her words. I felt compelled to recover her in some way, to imagine her world, to re-create as much of it as I could, so that she had not simply been disappeared. If I could find her, I believed that I could alter something, change history in some small way, even if only within my own family. In time, Valy came to stand for more; in a way, she represented for me all those other Valys, known and un-known, who had passed into history, if not without a fight, then, at least, without a marker.

My hope was both enormous and very tiny. I wanted to use these small clues, these pieces of paper to rescue Valy's memory—retrace her steps from birth through school through the years she wrote her letters and, perhaps, even find her again.

I wondered: Had Karl and Valy's been a romance of youth—not one, as most of ours are not, made to last a lifetime—or was my grand-mother right: had she been his true love? What did words like "true love"—peacetime words—even mean to the desperate, to the refugees who lost everything, including often, if not always, the loved? Had my grandfather searched for her, reconnected with her? Or grieved his whole life? She was, it was clear, thought of often. In an envelope filled with passport photos—dated, my father guessed for me, in the mid-1950s—there are several small images of Valy tucked in behind them. What had she gone through? What had she experienced in her years in Berlin? Her letters to my grandfather appeared to end in December 1941. What happened to her then?

I asked all my questions impossibly, childishly. Then I set out to find answers.

One

SITUATION EXCELLENT

Here's one of the stories I heard as a child: Lacking a complete set of papers, fleeing Austria, my grandfather and his family traveled from Vienna to Hamburg—through the heart of the German Reich—in September 1938. They arrived at the city's enormous port ready to board a ship armed in part with a set of lies, each prepared to bluff his or her way on board. Yet instead of terror, I heard only of optimism: As his mother and nephew huddled anxiously at the quay, my grandfather and his sister and her husband struck off to see the city in the hours before their scheduled departure. "Who knows when we'll next get the chance to see Hamburg?" Karl purportedly said, blithely refusing to lose this opportunity. He then had to lie, I heard, to get past the border guards (banking on the inability of one to read English). He had, I heard—or perhaps I imagined?—enabled the family to flee.

In truth, he hadn't discussed the escape much with me—or even with my father, for that matter—but that story, shadowy, vague, ultimately triumphant, was what I had always carried. The fall after I graduated from college, I asked my great-aunt Cilli about the stories I had grown up with: *Did my anecdotes leave anything out? Had they, for example, left anyone behind?* Her brother-in-law, she told me, tragically believed Poland would remain untouched—he stayed in Europe. But, beyond him? No, she said, there wasn't really anyone else who might have come with them.

Later, much later, entirely too late, I came to understand my question was all wrong. Like all refugees from the period, he—they—had left an entire world behind, one that seemed to have disappeared behind them entirely, a smooth wall, an unbroken floor, a sinkhole in time—a world rendered so totally lost, it was as though it had never existed at all. It was, I realize now, a reality so discomforting, so unnerving, that none of them ever wanted to fully narrate it for the rest of us, we who couldn't possibly understand, in our relatively carefree world; our own lives having been enabled, after all, by their very ability to leave, by their own success; so to undermine that success by discussing the failures, by fault or not, was simply not done. Only when something mild would go awry would I hear a bit of reproach. *Silver problems*, my grandmother would trill, in response to whatever minor traumas were worrying me, as an adolescent or a twentysomething, at any given moment.

That smooth wall, that vanished world—I had no sense of it, I couldn't grasp it. Even though I knew, from a tender age, of the horror: I cried on Holocaust Memorial Day, gasped at the drawings of the children of Theresienstadt. After all, we often shared our dinner table with women who had been smuggled to England as children, who had lost their parents as a result, who would begin to weep, fifty and sixty years on, when asked about their losses. We kissed the weathered cheeks of the grandparents of our friends, grandparents who hadn't left "in time," grandparents who didn't speak of what they had seen. I would hear whispered fragments among the adults—*her mother never was the same. . . .* Somehow I had always seen my grandfather's story as outside that, happier than that; *easier* than that.

And so, careful obfuscations in place, a blurry filter, Karl became the man with the glossy, glamorous—lucky—past. He came to America at *exactly* the right time, my father would say, admiringly. It was all bold strokes, all perfect. When I was in elementary school, I wrote a short play about his exile—it was all very cinematic to me. It seemed so daring, so devoid of real loss even though, in reality, he had lost everything, and everyone, outside his immediate family. Even though he had lost Valy. But I knew nothing of her then. *I zipped up my valise and sat down upon it. I looked around the room, hugging my knees to my chest. Leaving!* That's how my play began. I played Karl.

And yet, much of it was—not a lie—but a considered construction, a wholesale repackaging, one presented first to the generation before mine, and from there it trickled down to the rest of us.

In the early years after his death, even more than his notes to me, I loved finding the letters between him and Bruno, small windows into his adult mind, his adult relationships. The letters were kept in a manila folder; tissue-thin pages written in half German, half English, the *Gemisch* of a half century lived in a second language, between worlds. By the third quarter of the twentieth century, he decided to keep a copy of all his replies. I can picture him dictating these letters to my grandmother, who spent four decades typing them for him; for that is what he did, usually, either spoken aloud or scrawled, nearly incomprehensibly, onto slips of sheer white unlined featherweight paper that were then patiently translated by the fast clicks of her typewriter keys. Dictation would have been in his study, up the plush, winding stairwell from the formal dining and living rooms below, stairs that allowed him to make an entrance upon greeting guests.

I dream of that grand house still, the textured wallpaper in the formal entryway we hardly ever used (we came in the back) where his outdoor shoes—in the German style—were traded for indoor slippers, his black lambskin hats and heavy coats, my grandmother's furs, hung in a closet a bit further inside. Down a step and under the stairs was a hidden powder room with a plush rose-colored carpet, which, forever, even after their deaths, had treasures in the drawers, a lipstick in a gold-ridged case, a powder compact, a bit of reading. The living room had an enormous hi-fi system, invariably set to a symphony on vinyl, or tuned to classical radio; a large couch with a gold-velvet raised pattern; two camel-colored lamb's-wool side chairs, a brass bare-breasted woman whose arms held up a light; an enormous fireplace with a mirror above it and a mantel where characters wrought by the Spanish porcelain company Lladró were set to waltz, forever, their pale unnatural skin gleaming far from the tiny hands of children. Just beyond was the formal dining room, with its heavy chairs upholstered in a green silk brocade; a large banquette held *kippot* embossed with the slowly fading dates of a thousand weddings and bar mitzvahs, tablecloths, silver platters.

Upstairs, the second floor spread in all directions: straight ahead was their bedroom, with its gold-leaf wallpaper; to the left, my father's childhood room, with its wood-paneled library and ancient encyclopedias, which had largely remained the same over the years; and my aunt's former room, which had not. By my childhood, it had morphed into my grandmother's office, wallpapered in blues and whites, with a white laminate desk and framed artwork from grandchildren carefully aligned on one wall, the latest fiction in the bookshelf. To the right of the stairs was my grandfather's study, its shelves strained by heavy texts, the major works of German literature and Jewish thought, the busts of dead intellectuals. Further still, up yet another stairwell, was the attic, which seemed, always, to reveal some treasure—a wedding gown, a costume, a military uniform, a box of children's toys decades old. And, of course, files upon files of letters.

As I read my grandfather's letters to Bruno, my childhood memories are supplemented and expanded upon by drily witty narrations of medical emergencies (his own quadruple bypass surgery, my grandmother's endless rounds in the hospital for a botched hip operation), his children (my aunt, he writes at one point, has persuaded him to read *Fear of Flying*, which he grudgingly enjoys), his grandchildren (I am stupidly thrilled to discover I am "exceptionally bright and promising"), the world around him, boring summer guests who linger too long, his unadulterated love for his lifelong Viennese friends. He worries about the rise of Communism and the nuclear arms race, believes the Soviet Union to be the death of man's creativity, but also sees Americans as unconscious, unaware, ungrounded. Florida terrifies him, he writes to Bruno in 1977, after investigating retirement homes.

> *What I found is the same one-dimensional man—flat, choked with statistics—lifestyle expressed in two full bathrooms and one half-bath, fulfillment expressed in two bedrooms and emotions, love and interests expressed in fun. I become very melancholy at the pathetic attempts to squeeze some meaning out of 50, 60, or 70 years of living and this grandiose demonstration of the utter futility of life filled to the brim with convenience and nothing else. Where are the storms of curiosity? Where are the tempests and triumphs of the hot pursuit of femininity? Where are the colossal satisfactions of new insights? Where is the grandiose sense of fulfillment that comes from emotional, intellectual, or physical performance? All drowned in instant gratifications and "Bequemlichkeit" [comfort] in an abysmal ocean of ignorance.*

He was a man of great passions who believed passion should fuel all choices. When my cousin Michael, some six years my senior, came to ask him if he, like his father, like my father, like my grandfather, should become a doctor, my grandfather told him to enter medicine only if "nothing else is possible. *Only* become a doctor," he said—they were at another cousin's bar mitzvah reception at the time, and Michael was nearing the end of college—"if there is *nothing* else you can do. If you can picture nothing else of your life but a life in medicine."

"In terms of Valy, I have never heard of her," my father's cousin Shirley (Cilli's daughter) e-mails me, when I start querying family about the story of the girl I discovered in "Correspondence, Patients A–G," the girl who had, far more than any of the other characters that box revealed, winnowed her way into my consciousness. "If Karl was already committed to Dot"—my grandmother Dorothy—"I would imagine there would be much ambivalence about helping his former lover immigrate to the United States.

"Secondly," Shirley writes, "as you know, Karl was an extremely charming, passionate, attractive man—many women loved him and while I recognize Valy may have been one of those women, I wonder what place she really had in his heart."

This sits uncomfortably. If she had a secondary place, would that have made him feel less guilty? What about what my grandmother said about his "true" love? Was that just bitterness at a lifetime of having to share him? Women loved him. When I tell those who knew him, who knew my grandparents, that I'm thinking about him, it's one of the first things people say, with a smile, a wink. *He was a charmer.*

Shirley recommends I go and talk to Tonya Morganstern Warner; she was the first to really meet him in his new world. Literally—she was at an event held by relatives to welcome their European refugee cousins to New York moments after they stepped off the boat in September 1938. When I call her, she is taken aback—*Karl Wildman's granddaughter,* she keeps repeating—and then agrees to see me. Tonya is well into her nineties, and she lives alone on lower Fifth Avenue in Manhattan, near Washington Square Park, in an apartment, lined with oil paintings, that she shared with her husband, Alan, until he died in 1980. They had no children. Tonya has outlived most of her peers, most of her world; there is nearly no one left; even her nieces are dying. She is in excellent health, but like most nonagenarians, she worries life won't continue much longer.

Tonya has always been at the periphery of my family; she was a part of the greater Viennese Diaspora my grandfather cultivated and socialized with, a mix of those he had known in Europe and those his friends had known, a bilingual world Karl held court within. Tonya was in-

vited to every anniversary,
every bar and bat mitzvah,
every wedding. Film-star
gorgeous in her youth, she is
still beautiful now, with clear
skin and the kind of over-
stylized thin brow favored by
women of the 1930s. Born in
Galicia to a wealthy land-
owning farming family, she
was expected to move to
Vienna in adulthood—that's
what one did, it's what her

Tonya Morganstern Warner.

sister did before her; it was the City. She still speaks Polish and German and Yiddish. But instead of Vienna, she came to America with her
parents as a teen, in the early 1930s, when her father became worried
about growing anti-Semitism in the Galician countryside. They were
poor here; Tonya never received the education she was raised to expect.

Younger than my grandfather by a few years, Tonya fell for him
hard, almost immediately after he got off his ship in New York. They
then dated, eventually, briefly, tumultuously. Each time I see her, she
reveals a bit more of an enduring ardor that she has nurtured for over
seventy years. Once, she produces a watercolor painting for me; it is
my grandfather, age twenty-seven or so, circa 1939. She still keeps his
tie, in a drawer by her bed; it is wrapped up in a package he sent to her
in the early 1960s; his handwriting is on the envelope. She explains:
She and her husband were going to Italy on vacation; my grandfather
wanted her to pick up a similar tie for him in Milan. She never returned the prototype, so thrilled was she that this one had once been
around his neck. It is devastating, this love she carries.

Tonya reminds me of my grandparents: she regularly attends the
opera, still schleps uptown to the Jewish Museum, where she was once
a docent; still dresses for her guests. In turn, I feel I have to dress for

her. Her table is always set with several layers of cutlery, a plate for each course; we have to eat a slice of melon, an appetizer, a salad; she would like me to drink a V8, unless we go to Knickerbocker Bar & Grill, around the corner, where she'll push me to eat a steak even though I haven't had meat since I was fifteen. They know her there.

Every time we meet, she wants to tell me that though they were a couple only briefly, Karl really loved her, she really loved him—she wants desperately to be acknowledged as important in his life. Even though the romance ended over sixty years ago. Even though, she rues constantly on one of my visits, all he talked about when he arrived was Valy. Valy, so intelligent, Valy so sexually free; Valy Valy Valy. "If he loved her so much, why didn't he take her with him?" she wonders to me, and then she recoils, worried, horrified she has overstepped. She says, looking skyward, she can't say more, she will upset the dead. She points upward—she doesn't want anyone to be angry with her—"*Turn that off!*" she says again and again into my tape recorder—even though all those who could be legitimately bothered by her consuming love left this world many years ago.

Tonya has all of my grandfather's letters to her, and he, in turn, tucked her replies alongside those of Valy, dozens upon dozens of notes in tiny handwriting, on pages of purple, blue, and white, scattered throughout with photos of Tonya, looking glamorous. These letters are thick with the recriminations of a relationship that never quite worked out. They bickered (and flirted) endlessly, by mail. She suspects he—and his mother—did not find her intellectual enough for him, since she was not able to afford university. She is likely correct.

Tonya tells me that she and her friends tried, for some time, to rescue Jews themselves by writing letters of financial support— affidavits—that showed they held more money than they actually did. The group concocted a scheme to move the same four hundred dollars or so among bank accounts, several times, to show financial viability to immigration authorities. As she explained it: once a refugee had arrived, the money was placed in a different account, under a different name. It was an essential piece to the emigration package; each affidavit provided "proof" that a Jew hoping to come to these shores from Vienna or Poland or Germany would not be a "burden" on the U.S. economy, that if he would not be immediately self-sufficient, he would, at least at first, be supported by an American who had enough money to keep him off the dole. This money—this four hundred dollars, or however much it actually was—might mean the difference to someone stuck in Vienna or Poland. I wonder, when she tells me this, if my grandfather was impressed by the effort, if he explained to her how essential it was, this work. I wonder if he was impressed by the amount of money itself—it was enormous for them—about sixty-five hundred in today's dollars.

After all, he arrived penniless—to a country that was not nearly so much welcoming as it was simply safe. Here was Myth Number Two, a corollary to the myth of escape: *He was a success, always. He was self-made, landed on his feet in this country and was able to work, immediately. He was so fortunate to have his degree already! All he needed was an internship. . . .* This, of course, was in part my own construction, my own fantasy, it wasn't told to me, exactly; it was simply implied, by everyone. It, too, is upended by "Correspondence, Patients A–G." Along with the envelopes from friends, there are cashed checks stapled together—they are loan repayment checks, countersigned by the uncle who provided my grandfather's own affidavit to America—and each green check is itself stapled to a series of tiny yellow notes, painstaking acknowledgment that he paid back, in installments, every penny. The man I knew had been an overnight success. A sheaf of letters detailing the origins of the checks shows how very close he was to losing it all.

Upon closer inspection I realize the loans were not bank loans, but instead came from something called the National Committee for Resettlement of Foreign Physicians, an organization established, I discover, in what appears to be their founding memo, for the "clarification of current misconceptions" regarding foreign physicians. Misconceptions? But that memo, posted online by the University of North Texas, stands lonely and unexplained. Further digging leads me to an article in the *Journal of the American Medical Association*, published in late November 1941 by the founders of the committee that propped up my grandfather. "The National Committee for Resettlement of Foreign Physicians was organized more than two years ago to deal with one of the problems that have arisen out of the present European upheaval," they write. "The task has not been made any easier by the opposition which has arisen in certain quarters. Where once a medical degree from any noted European university was considered proof of outstanding scholarship, now there is a deplorable tendency to swing in the other direction. In incomprehensible isolation, legislators and others build bars around their own small domains, arbitrarily cutting off those valuable immigrants whose professional ability could contribute to the health of the whole nation. It is not the European physician who has changed; it is, at least partially, the American attitude." The committee began a correspondence with my grandfather not long after he arrived in America. He preserved their every letter.

The committee I have stumbled upon was created by a handful of sympathetic (and, interestingly, mostly non-Jewish) physicians in 1939 to combat xenophobic lobbying efforts on the part of the American Medical Association, explains Laurel Leff, a professor at Northeastern University in Massachusetts and best known for her book damning *The New York Times* for burying contemporary reporting of Holocaust-era crimes. She has spent, she tells me, the last few years writing about "the response of American intellectual elites to the pleas coming from Germany and other places in Europe." American doctors, who once venerated their counterparts from the University of Vienna, were nervous about jobs being taken away from U.S. citizens. The AMA appears to have lobbied state governments to block Jewish refugee physicians, like my grandfather, from receiving their medical licenses and finding positions here. State after state, Leff writes in an unpublished article she shared with me, barred graduates of foreign medical schools from taking their medical boards. By 1938, twenty-four states required citizenship in order to take the medical licensing boards—a disaster for those born overseas, who would now be forced to wait the five years to take citizenship tests, five years without an income, without the ability to practice. Twenty-two additional states would require the same by 1943—leaving only two states left to welcome physicians fleeing persecution. Even Massachusetts—safe when my grandfather arrived—would eventually institute rules to make life more difficult for refugee physicians.

Karl's luck held, though—he arrived in time to take his boards, to apply for jobs—in New York, Ohio, and Massachusetts—even as those doors were closing to others. A rolled-up poster I found in his box of "personal" effects applauds him for passing the Massachusetts Board of Registration in Medicine on July 11, 1940. I see my grandfather, endlessly ahead of the rolling boulder of xenophobia, obliterating everyone and everything from his past, and his present. Nazi Germany barred physicians from working beginning in 1933; by September 1938, the month my grandfather boarded his ship in Hamburg, Jewish doctors were allowed to treat only fellow Jews, in Jewish facilities. Then, soon after he received the right to practice, his own American safe harbor became less safe for Jewish émigré physicians.

It was the National Committee for Resettlement of Foreign Physicians that rescued him—and hundreds of his colleagues—from certain impoverishment, from destitution, and from the—I imagine, in his eyes—even worse fate of a life lived without intellect, in a job he was not passionate about, away from the profession he had earned. Created in February 1939, the group was instantly inundated with requests from doctors seeking assistance.

Leff tells me it's unlikely, but if I want to see how my grandfather, specifically, was aided upon arrival in America, there is a chance the Immigration History Research Center and Archives at the University of Minnesota might have him on file. The committee worked as social workers as much as advocates, she explains, and some of the physicians assisted by them have case files documenting both their poverty and their success—or failure—upon receiving assistance. Physicians were screened for competency in their specialties, in medicine in general, for their perceived ability to integrate and work in America. Those files were collected and eventually found their way to Minnesota. In fact, the Immigration History Research Center has collected myriad materials on the immigrant experience, archivist Daniel Necas tells me when I contact him, including a project on love letters between immigrants and those they left behind. He is as interested in my letters between Valy and my grandfather as he is in my grandfather's experience on these shores. But both Necas and Leff warn me that the files are incomplete, so not to expect too much, or anything at all.

Unlikely or not, nearly as soon as he has told me not to hope, Necas writes again to tell me there are some fifty pages in a file about my grandfather. And then, miraculously, in the following days, I receive dozens of scanned pages, mimeographed documentation of the social services that casually determined the course of my family's life. My grandfather, his files show, reached out for help on these shores even before leaving Austria. Three weeks after the Anschluss—

Dr. med Karl Wildmann
Vienna 2nd District
27, Rueppgasse

Vienna, April 4, 1938

Dear Doctor!
By way of a recommendation I got your address and am taking the liberty to ask you, in your capacity as a colleague, to answer the following questions. . . . In 1937 I acquired the degree of a Medical Doctor in Austria. Please let me know the following:
1. Which documents do I need in order to be able to work as a physician in the United States?

2. Which US states require the Official Recognition of Foreign Examinations and what are the underlying conditions?

Let me add that I already do have an affidavit and that I therefore would be most grateful if you could attend to my request as quickly as possible.

Many thanks in advance; obviously, I would also like to compensate you for your troubles.

Looking forward to your esteemed reply, I remain,

with collegial greetings,

Yours faithfully

Dr. K. Wildmann

He arrived in September 1938 and continued to apply for help, even as he took his medical exams and his English language proficiency tests. He had to. He had nothing to live on.

"Dr. Wildman came to this country with his mother, sister and brother-in-law on September 10, 1938," begins one letter from the Jewish Family Welfare Society writing to something called the "Physicians Committee, National Coordinating Committee" regarding my grandfather. It is dated March 6, 1939.

> *His mother is being assisted by a brother in whose home she is staying, and the sister and her husband have made their own arrangements. Dr. Wildman had been living with a cousin but was obliged to move because of this relative's financial pressure, and he therefore took a room in the home of some friends. . . . We have been giving him financial assistance since February 20th. His room rent is $5 a week, and an equal amount weekly is allowed for his living expenses. He speaks English quite fluently. He has passed his language examination and has also taken his State medical board. He has not yet heard about the results. He is looking around for internship [sic] and has been writing to various hospitals and institutions in this city and in out-of-town sections. He has his degree*

*from the University of Vienna, and has very high recommendations
from various professors and physicians in Vienna. I trust it will be
possible for you to see Dr. Wildman within a short time so he can
avail himself of the services of your committee.*

The committee then contacts my grandfather and he writes back.
In the files I have, the committee preserved his own handwritten
notes, as well as a typed—in English!—curriculum vitae; in it, he gently notes he arrived on September 16, not September 10. But otherwise, the documents confirm his degrees, his training, his accolades,
his bona fides. The committee, internally, then arranges for him to be
screened by physicians of their choosing.

May 24th, 1938

Dr. Karl Wildmann
Rueppgasse 27
Vienna 2, Austria

Dear Doctor Wildmann:

I have your letter of May 4th. You would be eligible
to apply for the permission to take your medical state
board examination in the following states if your credentials are acceptable to the Board of Medical
Examiners: Colorado (?), Connecticut, Idaho, Maryland,
Massachusetts, Mississippi, Missouri (?), Nevada, New
Hampshire, New Jersey, New York, North Carolina(?),
Ohio (?), Texas and Virginia. The credentials which
you have to submit to the Board are the following:
Abiturientenzeugnis, Physikumszeugnis, all "Studien-
buecher"(Exmatrikeln), Staatsexamenszeugnis, Certificate
of Medizinalpraktikantenjahr, Approbation and Doctor
Diploma. It might be advisable to have these papers
translated and certified by the American Consulate
in your district.

Sincerely yours,

Laurence Farmer, M. D.
Executive Secretary
LF:CS

Paging ahead, I can see him through the eyes of these Americans:
Here is twenty-seven-year-old Karl, duly assessed—he is, writes one,

unprepossessing, he has a nice disposition; he is not too tall, he is well built, he has exceptional language skills (this was a boon, as the committee could reject physicians for lacking sufficient English). He tells the committee he has trained as an ear, nose, and throat doctor (he had studied for a time in this specialty, in Vienna, at the Rothschild Hospital, the hospital run by the Israelitische Kultusgemeinde Wien, the Jewish community), but the supervising doctor decides that's not what he'll be after all—he'll be a family physician, a generalist. "He has sufficient training under excellent auspices to make him worthwhile. He is not, however, a trained otolaryngologist," he writes. And just like that, a sweep of a pen, or rather, a clatter of typewriter keys, and his professional fate twists: though they tell him he can retrain as an ear, nose, and throat specialist in some years, after he is established, I know he remained a generalist for the rest of his life.

A year will pass before professional life begins for him in earnest. In the meantime, his mother, social workers note, has sold all her jewelry—netting a mere sixty dollars—to support herself. Having exhausted that last resource, she can no longer contribute to her own upkeep. She is on the verge of destitution. Karl will spend that year as an intern in general medicine at St. Luke's Hospital in Pittsfield, Massachusetts. It is that internship that keeps him in Pittsfield, I see from the notes of the committee. He has established himself among the Jews of the town, one document notes. The committee believes he has enough of a reputation at the hospital to start a successful practice there.

In the summer and fall of 1940, the committee internally determines it will enable Karl to establish a practice—without them he would have been completely lost. He could not foot the cost of a single necessary item. They agree to loan him $357, which included money for big-ticket items like office furniture ($75), medical equipment ($80), and a car ($100), as well as smaller ones—food ($35), office rent ($40), and a month in an apartment ($12). The loan is cosigned by my great-grandmother's brother Sam, the same man who issued the affidavits for my grandfather, his mother, his sister, brother-in-law, and young nephew that enabled them to travel from Vienna. Sam was not wealthy, but he had come to this country decades earlier—the irony, my father tells me, was that Sam had been the "unsuccessful" one, in Europe, he had come to America because Europe didn't work for him; he was a "failure" in the old country. And here he became their savior, twice over.

The $357 would help Karl open an office, find a home, bring his mother to live with him under his own roof. There was not a penny of excess in that amount. There was nary a dollar to send to anyone overseas, nor an extra ten beyond what he needed to organize his office, and travel back and forth to see family in New York City. And word from Europe is dire, I'll soon discover. Valy needs hundreds to pay for visas. Money that he has absolutely no access to in those early months, in those early years.

In his initial intake, the social workers indicate my grandfather would welcome a rural practice, but I know from Leff's article, and that *JAMA* piece I discovered, that that is exactly what the physicians' resettlement fund wanted them to say—they were almost exclusively placing these doctors in areas that were lacking medical care so as not to raise the ire of doctors in established urban locations. The loan of $357 came through, and my grandfather's Pittsfield office opened in October 1940, two years and one month after he arrived in America. In a handwritten note, included in his files, my grandfather shyly writes, *"Here I am sitting in my office which you so generously helped establish. More than a week has passed since I started practicing. The local newspaper published a very nice article about me, so everybody knows that a new doctor is in town. . . . So far I had 5 patients and earned $16. Now I am waiting for those patients to get better and to tell their friends about their 'amazing' cure."* He includes the newspaper clipping, and there he is, his face boyish, a hint of a smile.

It was not a smooth start. In the next letter to the committee members—apparently he must write about his expenditures and income each month—my grandfather writes that he has not taken in as much as he'd hoped—in his second month he pulled in eighteen dollars, less than the cost of running an office, let alone rent, let alone supporting his mother.

"Dear Dr. Wildman," they write. "We have your report for the last month and in view of your connections in town are rather surprised it has been so poor. I think you will recall that the arrangement we had made was for supplementation for a three-month period. I wonder whether you might not consider other possible plans in view of the limitations that we have for further loans." And there again he has his luck—they give him just one month to get it right! One month to turn around his finances, his success. He writes back with great anxiety.

December 16, 1940

> *I myself am gravely disappointed about the slow development of my practice. Yet I was told it took people who were born and brought up here in town several months to get started. They know practically everybody in town and had many friends who had confidence in them but they simply had to wait until those friends got sick and after the first few good cases their practice developed rapidly. . . . It is only too understandable that your loans have limitations. Immediately upon receipt of your letter I got in touch with a CCC Camp near Pittsfield trying to get a part-time job there. I hope fervently to get it. That would pay all my expenses. Would you have any other suggestions? May I count on your courtesy in the case of failure?*

The camp he refers to was part of the New Deal work relief program known as the Civilian Conservation Corps—it employed young, unmarried men who worked the land on behalf of their families (for the money they earned) and their country (creating forests and parkland). He seems not to have gotten this job; it was never mentioned again.

The committee reluctantly issues another eighty-four-dollar

loan—the notes in his file are dry and ominous: they can support each physician only for a short amount of time. His time is running out.

And then, somehow, he pulls it out—the money trickles in, the patients start to arrive. The following month he makes seventy-four dollars. It is enough to ensure they will allow him to continue—because he can contribute to his own upkeep, they will give him one more month of support: forty-four dollars more. The notes indicated they would have stopped supporting him if an additional month did not work out—and they would have sought to have him resettled elsewhere, and not in private practice. But with his turn of fortune, they will not cut him off, yet. His mother can come live with him; he can, it appears, support her now. He can, more importantly, be a success here.

Because these were loans in the truest sense, they came due immediately, literally the moment the first patients became regulars and his stationery was printed. Piece by piece Karl begins to repay, forty-four dollars here, a hundred dollars there. He pays and pays and pays, and the committee duly writes to remind him if he is late; to remind him that there are others like him who need the money; that this money is not *his*. His payments continue all the way into the fall of 1942, at which point they write: "We wish to take this occasion to wish you the very best of luck for your service in the armed forces." He has volunteered for the U.S. Army. In all that time, though, I'm now well aware, there was no extra money to purchase freedom for anyone else trying to come over.

As I try to piece together what life was like in those early months, that first year, I call Joseph Feldschuh, my grandfather's nephew who left Vienna with him; he was only three at the time of his passage. He has no personal memory of Valy, at least not from Austria. The name, however, is familiar. He can't give me exactly what I'm looking for; he was too young for crisp memories. It is all broad strokes. "My grandmother, Sarah Wildman," he booms on speakerphone, "had a brother in this country named Sam Feldschuh and he came to this country in sometime like 1900 or 1905 . . . so he left early to get out of being drafted by the Russian army, which was anti-Semitic but was happy to grab soldiers . . . so he got here and he married a woman named Fanny Hollenberg and they had four children."

He proceeds, biblically, to list them all then, and their progeny. I dutifully write it down. "When they finally got the affidavits [from Sam] they were one short." This, I think, must be the story of the incomplete papers in Hamburg. "And my father was the one who interceded somehow with the Nazis. My father was a real charmer, I don't know if you remember him. And he managed to get one more. So there was a visa for my parents and myself. Your grandfather, and your great-grandmother, for five people. You know that movie *Sophie's Choice?* With Meryl Streep? So you know about those kinds of choices." I'm actually not at all sure what he means here, though I read the book and saw the movie years ago. Does he mean Valy? Does he mean the others who don't get to go with them? Who were the others? Whom did they leave behind?

Maybe he means all of it. I'm struck, too, that on his side of the family it was *his father,* not my grandfather, who got them out. Another family's myth? A truth that upends my own version of the story? There is no way to confirm; all those in question are gone.

"I remember that my mother was in communication after the war with a couple of people who had escaped. I've heard there were some letters [before the war] from people needing help, but"— he grows sharper in tone here—"your grandfather was in no position to help anybody. We were very, very lucky that we were accepted into America . . ."

No position to help anybody. This is clear, from the loans I find, from the stomach-tightening fear embedded in Karl's own correspondence with his American saviors.

Some of those rumored European letters I find. They arrived heavy with desperation, at the same time my grandfather was negotiating with the National Committee for Resettlement of Foreign Physicians. At the exact moment the committee is debating his future, my grandfather is receiving requests from half of his former university schoolmates for visa money, for affidavits. At the exact moment it is questionable how he will support himself and his family, his former lover Valy—and her friends, I'll come to realize, and her mother—is reaching out to him and begging him for visas that cost upward of a hundred and a hundred fifty dollars apiece.

He is scrounging for loans that start at *twenty-five dollars*. He cannot pay for his own mother's upkeep. Perhaps, I wonder as I read, the "love" my grandmother spoke of was really guilt: a sense of the horror at how different things might have been, had he not been desperate for another ten dollars here, fifty dollars there, that lingered with him, for a lifetime. By the late 1940s he was successful—later letters show that in the early 1950s, he helped survivor cousins who escaped to Palestine purchase a truck for two thousand dollars, a tremendous amount of money in those years. Was all that largesse in response, consciously or not, to the complete tragedy of his own impoverished years? He was supposed to have been the master of all things—languages, cultures, medicine—and here he was, like so many other émigrés before him, stymied, tripped up, at least temporarily, by a system that was not remotely hospitable, let alone easy to navigate.

Indeed, how could it not have had an effect on him? He was inundated—just like the committee—with requests for money, for affidavits, for passage to the New World. *"News from Europe,"* he writes to Tonya. *"Conditions are terrible."*

"We were unable to stay in Budapest and had to come back here," writes one friend, from Vienna, in mid-December 1938. "We hope, however, to be able to leave from here within 2–3 weeks." The writer wants my grandfather to explain how they can get from Cuba to the United States:

> *Because whatever one hears here is so confusing that it is very difficult to get a clear picture. Some people insist that one may wait*

for the quota in Cuba. . . . Moreover it is still unclear to us how long
the Polish and the Romanian quota must wait. I am convinced that
your creativity and your instincts have researched the shortest and
best options possible. . . . We are allowed to stay [in Vienna] only
until January 10 and hope to have obtained by then the visas in order
to find, as already mentioned, a suitable or tolerable stopover until
we are able to board a ship. The ships that are bound for Cuba are
sold out 2–3 months in advance, but we hope to find a stopover place
with the help of the visas. . . . I do hope, however, that the petition of
Dr. Eisenstein will be met with a positive resolution and that you
together with our noble and much esteemed friend Mr. Klamer will
find ways to help us. While I do not want to cry on your shoulder, I
am quite sure that you do understand us!!

I believe, dear friend, that you are fully in the picture, and I
send you and your loved ones my most cordial regards.

Such a terribly large amount of pressure placed upon him, and so
ridiculously little he could actually do to help—"I do hope . . . that you
together with our noble and much esteemed friend . . . will find ways
to help us." And still the letters keep coming. "Hermann, Lola and
Paul, in addition to their in-laws (all of them Polish quota) already
have received good news from the American consulate and will be able
to travel to the U.S.A. already at the end of September!!" writes another friend, who has made it as far as Prague in August 1939. Were
they still able to leave, once the Germans invaded Poland? This I don't
know. The letter, in any case, continues. "I, my wife and son and
brother-in-law Karl will stay behind. In our case it is even questionable, due to the Romanian quota, whether we will get a chance at all."
Here he gets to where my grandfather could help.

Now I would like to share the following plan and idea for
implementation with you: From here already several general
practitioners (i.e., not clinicians or otherwise prominent scientists)

have traveled to the USA outside the quota to take up hospital or
similar positions or contracts. Since such opportunities could just be
imaginary positions, this should not be too difficult, given your
cleverness! I would herewith like to offer you Dollar 50.00 for your
efforts (and positive outcome) in this regard, and I shall reserve this
amount for you. In this way, I hope to be able to travel quickly with
my wife and son. Our emigration formalities (highly complicated)
have already been initiated here, and we hope to be able to travel via
Italy in about 3 weeks. . . . Let me therefore please ask you not to let
us wait too long. I am sending best regards to you and your family
members.

Laurel Leff confirms for me that this rumor was true, that there were
some who were able to receive appointments at universities, a golden
ticket that allowed them the miracle of bypassing the nearly impossible quota system. But the author of this missive—who writes in formal
German and appears not to be a particularly close friend—is asking
my grandfather to concoct a *fake* appointment, to ensure his family
safe passage by pretending to hire him as a professor: "This should not
be too difficult, given your cleverness!"

So many people need him. And these weren't even the letters from
Valy, for whom, I will discover, he tried to do everything; for whom, I
will discover, the price of survival would climb and climb as 1939
turned into 1940 and 1940 turned into 1941.

A small leatherette address book is stuck into his collection of letters. It was purchased, it seems, in America, as on the cover is written
very faintly in English, "Notes." Inside are listings for dozens of aid
societies, doctors, and friends from Vienna. One after another, ad-
dresses in Vienna were crossed out and new cities, new countries,
written in. These refugees were in good company: some 206,000 Jews
lived in Austria before the Anschluss; from the date of Hitler's arrival
through May 1939, about 130,000 fled.

Everyone is searching for safe passage to another country; or at least passage. "The family is torn without knowing if we will ever be again together in our lives," write close friends who have landed, uncomfortably, in Shanghai. "Only God knows how troubled our hearts are, not to be able to come to you." Vienna is disappearing already, it no longer exists, it is no longer the city of his youth; it is not even the city of the days after the Anschluss. Precious Vienna has scattered into a million tiny pieces across the globe.

Two

THE WONDERFUL CITY

Oh Vienna. My grandfather and his sister pronounced the city's name in a full breath, a sigh, emphasis on the first syllable, and a lilt on the last. The city was the epicenter of my family's fantasy life: it informed the food we ate, the literature we read. It was our destination, and our origin point, literally, figuratively, a sepia-colored lost-promise land. In fourth grade, when we chose country reports, I confidently picked Austria, even though, somehow, carefully tracing the lines of its strange, landlocked borders (shaped, vaguely, I thought, like a cartoon bubble waiting for words), I couldn't see where my family fit there at all.

That Vienna obsession—my grandfather's, Valy's, their friends'—was passed on to me. It was a love affair with geography, an (oft-unrequited) ardor for the history and grandeur of the city. It was an obsession shared across the Jews they knew, these assimilated, ultra-cultured Jews, who remained faithful to the ideal of the perfect city. It was a love that, ultimately, drew me to Vienna as well, that led me, as I began this quest to find Valy, to realize I needed to begin my search there to find what drove them, what shaped them. I wanted to *breathe in a little of this Viennese atmosphere,*" as Valy wrote. "Vienna waits for

Josef Wildmann, my great-grandfather,
in Zaleszczyki, Poland.

you," went the tourism campaign when I began to think of spending time in the city. It was simultaneously passive and enticing.

The truth was, even in Vienna, my grandfather was foreign. He was born in Zaleszczyki, a spa town and Jewish honeymoon destination known as the "Polish Riviera" nestled into a bend in the Dniester River, a waterway that meanders from the Carpathian Mountains until it plunges into the Black Sea. Now in Ukraine, at my grandfather's birth Zaleszczyki was a sunny slice of the Austro-Hungarian Empire; after World War I, it was folded into Poland, rendering him, effectively, stateless. Its nearly twenty-five hundred Jewish residents made up a third of the town's population in 1912, the year of his birth. Of those who remained after World War I, more than eight hundred were murdered on a terrible day in mid-November 1941, when Zaleszczyki Jews were brought to the fields at the edge of town, forced to dig graves for their friends, family, and colleagues, and shot by one of the Nazi mobile killing teams called Einsatzgruppen. Remaining Jews were sent to forced-labor camps and nearby ghettos. No one returned after the war.

But 1941 was nearly three decades after my grandfather's family ran to Vienna while the guns boomed for the Great War; he was barely two years old, it was 1914. The Wildmanns—they then carried an extra *n*, in the Germanic style—arrived in the heart of the second district, on a slip of a street called Rueppgasse, along with other flotsam from the first major upheaval of the twentieth century. A veritable flood of refugees from the east cascaded into Vienna in those war years, overwhelming the capital and reigniting the anti-Semitism that had crept into Austrian politics some twenty years before the end of the previous century. Thousands of them were Kulturjuden, Jews who worshipped the German culture represented by the heart of the empire, Vienna.

Just after college I drove to Cranbury, New Jersey, lugging audio equipment, to interview Cilli Feldschuh, my grandfather's sister. She described that first refugee episode of her life, aged four or so, traveling to Vienna, a journey that began in a wagon filled with straw, until they reached the first train. "It was a very frightening experience, to take this wagon, this covered wagon, it was so dark in this wagon." She never lost her Viennese inflections; the moment I slip on my headset and press Play, I am pulled into the living rooms of my childhood: "wagon" becomes "vagon"; "the" becomes "da." Throughout the tape she stops and laughs at me, so serious with my equipment, and my questions. I looked up the route from Zaleszczyki to Vienna—these days, on modern roads, it would take twelve hours. There were treasures my great-grandparents left behind, she was sure, buried in that resort town—there was silver, there was, possibly, jewelry. Her mother feared being robbed along the way; in any case, she was certain the family would return when the war ended. There was no need to carry it all. But they never did return. There were pogroms in those first years after World War I, both before and after the armistice was signed. Jewish life deteriorated; it simply wasn't safe. And, treasures or not, soon after they arrived, their finances disintegrated, their lives took an abrupt turn for the worse; there wasn't money for a return trip, even if they'd wanted to take one.

"It was 1916. My father was fifty-six and he had an obscure kidney ailment and he was sent to a sanitarium," Cilli told me. "We had money and he didn't have to go to the general hospital. The corridor was surrounded by professors. P.S. In one week he was dead." She pronounces it "dud." "And then I was six years old and it was a *raging* war and then we really didn't have anything to eat, all the money we had saved disappeared, it was inflation, so much so that if you took the electric train to get your savings [at the other end of the line] the savings would have been worth less than the [cost of the] train [trip]. We were without money, at all."

My great-grandfather died and with him went their income, and comfort. They had been relatively well off, Cilli said, and then, suddenly, they were destitute. My great-grandmother, I heard, sold eggs, singly, and pieces of string in the market; some family members tell me she went off to work in a factory; of this I have no record. I know, instead, flashes of their story: that Karl, for example, resoled his shoes, again and again, never able to buy new ones. When he grew older, he tutored other Jewish students for money. Cilli would later tell me, in that first call I made to her after I discovered Valy, that it was Valy who enabled him to do this during school hours—she would attend class and take notes, then give him the lecture, later, late at night. There were always too many people living in their tiny apartment, yet somehow there was always room for one more. Cousin Reuven, whose father was killed in a Ukrainian pogrom, wanted to study in Vienna? He'd come to live there. The only daughter of your old Zaleszczyki neighbors had decided to attend medical school? She could come, too.

This grinding poverty was not much spoken of in America, nor the fact that the people my grandfather emulated for the rest of his life didn't live anywhere near Leopoldstadt, as the second district is called, where Jews from the scattered corners of the Austro-Hungarian Empire settled, nor the fact that the children he tutored lived in apartments six times the size of his. They were Jews, too, but they were Jews with plush couches and servants and ham sandwiches; somehow this *traif* was a sign of their cosmopolitan mien. For the first half of his life in America, my grandfather would associate ham with success.

And yet, despite the family poverty, he was sent first to *Gymnasium*, one of the preparatory upper schools of the German-speaking world whose emphasis on classical education was both arduous and impressive, and then on to medical school, clear, if only in his own mind, that one day he would live like his pupils, ignoring the already virulent anti-Semitism festering around him. "Jew, Jew spit on your head," Cilli remembered neighborhood kids singing when she was seven or eight. "I couldn't

love Vienna," she said, contrary to my grandfather, who very much could, and did. *It doesn't get any better than this,* he would recall thinking, in his rosy recounting of life in Vienna; it was the thought that ran through his mind when he bounded up the steps to his home, aged eighteen, the year 1930, depression everywhere, except in the world of his making. It was all there for him; he just had to scoop it up.

A photo I have from around 1930 shows him on a holiday trip, in a small bathing suit cut like shorts, with the stomach muscles of an athlete, a girl on each arm, two more girls just beyond his reach, laughing in an enormous group of swimsuit-clad friends. Somehow, even nearly penniless, he projected rich; he lived richly. Life was already *herrlich*—marvelous. Superb. Delightful. He would see the theater twice on Sundays—a matinee and then, as soon as that ended, he would line up for the evening opera performance. He took the standing room tickets—it was all he could afford, but who cared? The music didn't change from the front of the theater to the back.

That sense of the *herrlich* world buoyed him throughout his life.

He would kiss the palms of my hands like a Viennese gentleman; he would wax poetic about the wonderful city he'd left behind; he would sing Richard Tauber and Joseph Schmidt, the voices of his youth (never mentioning, of course, that Schmidt had raced from country to country seeking refuge, only to die in a Swiss refugee camp). He would wear the finest that European tailors could provide. He was known for celebrating the best things in life: he owned a Leica because it was the best camera; Italian custom-made ties because they were the best; Head skis, when those were the best. He stayed at the Bristol in Vienna, one of the dowager queen five-star hotels on the Ringstrasse, because it was the best. He and my grandmother went to Vienna for six weeks every other year starting in 1950 because it was still the best, the most cultured place in the world. He returned to study at the university a few years after the war—purportedly because the medical school was still a pillar, still at the height of the field—and perhaps, too, to show that he could.

He never spoke of persecution, not to his children, and certainly not to his grandchildren. He did not tell us of the rumor (surely apocryphal but still telling) that the last time the radical revisionist Zionist Ze'ev Jabotinsky spoke in Vienna, in the winter of my grandfather's graduation from medical school, the speech ended cinematically—with Jabotinsky holding up a suitcase and shouting in the packed Konzerthaus, "Run, Jews, run!" He never talked about the virulent xenophobic wave that drowned his Vienna when Hitler was received like a messiah; he did not speak of leaders of the Jewish community scrubbing the street on their hands and knees, of windows smashed or painted over with the word *Jude*, a word that would come to feel like a curse rather than a description, or an identity. He did not mention that in the heart of the gorgeous first district, amid all those ornate buildings and lovely shops that carried the best of the best, nestled up against the stately Staatsoper, the grand opera house, a massive billboard had gone up promoting a "special edition" of the anti-Semitic rag *Der Stürmer*, festooned with the tag line *Ju-*

dentum ist Verbrechertum—"Judaism is criminality"—and accompanied by the most base, awful caricature of a hook-nose Jew the artist could conjure. He did not mention what it looked like when the Kärtnerstrasse main drag, the Madison Avenue of Vienna, was filled with massive red Nazi banners, or what it felt like to walk those streets the moment that somehow everyone, overnight, had armbands and flags that identified them with the Nazi Party. He did not speak of the terror that the marching hordes brought with them, the bands of men with their arms raised who rode through the streets on trucks, nor the shouting, ecstatic Viennese girls thrilling to the presence of German Nazi officers. Nor did he speak of the looting that began overnight, immediately—the stealing from Jews that ranged from wresting the works of great art held by high families to the pillaging and destruction of humble shops. He neglected to mention that, when he first returned to Vienna in 1950, it was not so much simply to visit, but to look for survivors, if not of people, then of the city itself, to take in the destruction, to contemplate what was left, or really, what, who, was gone.

And to me, at least, he did not mention Valy, the girl with whom he had taken classes, who had pined for him, until he finally noticed her, swept her off her feet, wandered in his city with her, taking in all things they could on their limited funds. He did not speak of this girl who sat in on class for him, took notes for him, freeing up his time so he could tutor other kids and bring in money for his family, for himself. He did not tell us that in those heady, awful, terrifying early weeks of Nazi rule, not only did he lose his freedom, he lost his lover when she ran back to her home country to care for her mother, to plot escape on her own. What would he have said, after all?

Instead, what we heard, what we were schooled in, was the importance, the near perfection, of Vienna's symphony and art and parks, of Goethe and Zweig and Schilling and Schnitzler and Freud. For my grandfather, as Tony Judt wrote in *Postwar*, "in the early years of the twentieth century Vienna *was* Europe: the fertile, edgy, self-deluding hub of a culture and a civilization on the threshold of apocalypse." It was the city of his friendships, his essence, his very being. Only rarely were there hints to what lay beneath. As October turned into November 1956, the year after Vienna finally emerged from occupation by the Allied powers, the year Vienna picked up her head from the curfews that still, to this day, keep shops closing at six in the evening, the Hungarian uprising was suddenly crushed. My grandparents were in Vienna when the Soviet tanks rolled into Budapest; it was the only time, my grandmother told me later, she saw my grandfather panic, the only time she saw a glimpse of whatever had settled into his marrow in 1938. He hustled them, immediately, to Paris, sure, or at least sure enough, that the Soviet tanks would continue to lumber west and engulf them, too; this time he didn't want to wait around to see what happened.

But he was suppressing more than simply a sense of dread in those October weeks. The city Karl cherished already no longer existed when he came back in 1950; the people he had known were entirely scattered—or dead. I suppose I didn't really think this way as a child, it was only later that I came to understand the peculiarity of postwar refugee life: that even if one got out—with a great story and four other family members—you did not necessarily ask what had happened to the man who'd sold you bread, the girl who sat next to you in class, your doctor, your butcher, even your cousins and their wives. You simply did not see them again. And, especially after time passed, you assumed. Any expectations—if you had them—of returning to life as you had once known it had long since dissolved; that life, that community, was no more.

He finally took his children to meet the city in 1963 and again in 1965. Together, both times, they walked through the Innere Stadt to pick up the aboveground tram, line 21, at Schwedenplatz. They sat as the tram made its way up Taborstrasse, winding through the second district, staying on board when the tram turned right on to the boulevard Heinestrasse. They stepped off at tiny Rueppgasse, whose centuries-old buildings look impressive only to the untrained American eye and are, merely, simply, old. A whole trip just to look up at his old home, not even to ring the bell. To his sister, Cilli, he wrote a postcard with a single line in German—*"a backwards look at yesterday."*

——————

It is years after my grandfather's death when I receive a journalism grant to live and work in Vienna at the Institut für die Wissenschaften vom Menschen—the Institute for Human Sciences—a place that sounds both grand and improbable and terribly European. I have vague thoughts of embracing the city as my own. My fellowship is named for Milena Jesenská, Kakfa's lover, a journalist whose opposition to the Nazis landed her in prison after prison from 1939 until 1944, when, in Ravensbrück, her body finally succumbed to the years of deprivation.

My arrival in Vienna is unheralded. I know no one; my plan is completely inchoate, my German limited to the niceties of grandparents. I know nothing of the city after 1938. And really, I don't even know the city of 1938; I know snippets, overheard fantasies; nightmares. I choose my apartment, at random, off Craigslist. It is not the best choice. When the taxi pulls up at the door, in front of a dark nineteenth-century building in the working-class twentieth district, far from the lights and music of downtown, the driver turns to me and says, "Perhaps you've made a mistake." It seems a poor omen.

The woman who answers the door at Wallensteinstrasse 38/40 does not alleviate that concern. She is as cold as the street below, and remarks without cheer, or cheek, that I have brought more bags than things she owns. When I tell her I have a fellowship to write about insiders and outsiders in Europe—Muslims and Jews, immigrants— she murmurs noncommittally. Then she pauses, turns, and asks, almost sheepishly, "Are Jews Muslims?" to which I want to make a joke, but I realize she is serious, and so I try to carefully, briefly, explain the difference. Then she shows me to my spare, spartan room; she has neglected to tell me in advance that to reach my sleeping quarters I have to walk through the bathroom of her (always locked) office. I am in a hidden space. In the morning, after I wake, I discover I have literally been locked into this room accidentally. Panicked, I scream out my enormous fifth-floor window into the freezing air below, *"Hilfe! Hausmeister!"*—Help! Superintendent!—hysterically waving to the Turkish grocer across the street, to various strangers heading to work or running errands, until, after some thirty minutes that feel like hours, I am rescued by the *Hausmeister.* Freed, I walk the streets, lost, off kilter. I entertain my new colleagues again and again with the story of that night; I tell it as farce—*"Hilfe! Hausmeister!"* I'll repeat over and over—though, really, I was terrified, convinced I would have to flee the city immediately.

I am thirty-one and still living in the fantasy spun by Karl. I ride the trams around the cold, marble, glorious Hapsburg architecture of the first district up to the still-poor tenements of the second district where he once lived and a handful of *shtreimel*-wearing ultra-Orthodox Jews now live again, warily, alongside the tattooed young and glamorous and foreigners. I meander through the city—it feels *old*, the demographic average skewing higher, it feels, than sixty, with few baby strollers—and I walk where he walked, attend the opera he loved, squat in the back at the Musikverein with my three-euro standing ticket, sit in the Staatsoper with a cheap ticket and obscured views, gleaning the nearly free music, as he once did. I sit, alone, in the new restaurants nestled in the Museumsquartier. I photograph everything I see and then paw through piles of old photographs in the sprawling Saturday flea market near Kettenbrückengasse; I pick through the images sent home from fathers at war in 1941, men on the wrong side, I can't help thinking, as I look at their Wehrmacht uniforms, their arms slung casually around each other, their beaming faces.

And then, somehow, between the music and the art and the coffees obsessively accompanied with glasses of water, between the streets of the first district, the perfect apricot tarts at Julius Meinl, a food emporium of spices and high-end gastronomy, I, too, start to fall in love with Vienna, enjoy its gray skies and dour ways, carve a space for myself among those people who can't muster even a *guten Morgen* in my chilly, decrepit building, become a regular at certain stalls in the never-ending open market, the Naschmarkt, with its multilingual hawkers and gorgeous food.

It comes in part, this falling for Vienna, because I love, love, *love* everyone at my Institute. They are Germans and Austrians, Norwegians and Canadians. We go out drinking night after night, in clubs and bars tucked into the archways of the Otto Wagner–designed U-Bahn stations of the Gürtel, the "belt" that hugs the city's outer ring, with the elevated trains rushing above our heads. We flirt and dance, we sit in lectures with a relentless series of smart speakers, philosophers and historians and sociologists. We are in love with our lives and our luck; money for nothing; money to sit and think and write. I have a small office in the Institute's building that faces the Donaukanal. I am giddy with lack of sleep and intellectual pretention. My grandfather, I think, would have been proud. In fact, in part, I wonder if I am performing for him, or his memory, when I take the train to Budapest in the snow, when I fly to Paris for a week of reporting, when I walk the streets of Vienna, alone. I have conversations with him in my head; I long to introduce to him my adult self, long to be able to say I am following his model, loving his city.

I've had this feeling before, this sense of performing to his memory. It was in Paris, at the end of my twenties, a different fellowship. An acquaintance introduced me to Jean-Marc Dreyfus, a young historian with a bald pate and an impish mien, who, with sociologist Sarah Gensburger, had just finished an extraordinary book about three forgotten slave labor camps in the heart of the City of Light. One night, over dinner, he explained: The Gestapo wanted not just to eradicate the people who had been sent away, but to erase them, to blot out all memory of these Jews and ensure that no one could reconstruct their

lives going forward. Each camp, tasked with the gruesome responsibility of sorting and redistributing all the useful material goods of the
Jews being sent to their deaths, and burning their personal belongings,
had been fully absorbed back into the city and then, eerily, themselves
forgotten. The task of erasing, of wiping clean the histories of those
who had been here, had been remarkably, horrifyingly, successful.

I returned to Paris again six months after I first learned the story
and sought out for myself each camp—Lévitan was now a gorgeous
advertising agency building in the tenth arrondissement; Bassano was
now an haute-couture atelier near the Champs-Élysées; Austerlitz had
been housed alongside the eponymous train station (and is alluded to
in the book by W. G. Sebald)—now it was a massive construction
site—and listened to the stories of those who had been forced to sort
through the detritus of the deported. Dreyfus's discovery asked a question I had never thought to ask and now contemplated endlessly: What
happened to the goods of regular people, the Sarah Wildmans, if you
will, who were deported? Not wealthy, not poor; Jews who didn't own
great art but certainly had a home filled with the appurtenances of
modern living: A dining room table and chairs. Beds. China. Cutlery.
Notebooks. Photos. Clothing. Cribs. All gone.

The survivors of these Paris camps all had lived out the war under
duress, but protected—most were married to non-Jews, a class of Jew
that, oddly, stymied the Nazi machine, and so were set aside for
later—and when they discovered the truth of the other camps, the
death camps of the east, they settled down to live with a deep shame,
a shame they shouldered as penance for that protection. That modesty
about their own experience—that *pudeur*, as they called it—created a
silence that they broke only at the very last moments of their lives.
And yet within that *pudeur* there was also humanity. One man told me
he was just twenty-four the year he spent in one of these camps; he
was selected to help the Gestapo move the pianos stolen from deported Jews. And he would plot to meet his Catholic wife—not to
escape, but for sex.

There was something about that story—that furtive sex, fast, under the pianos—that seemed so normal. So young. "Come to see me as a human, not as a Jew, as a man," that survivor said. It was a comment that made me think of my grandfather. He, too, had been so young when he left. And what do we want most in life, really, especially as we start out? Intimacy, love. We can't think beyond that. Each man I interviewed—and they were all men—reminded me, in some way, of my grandfather. I missed him, terribly.

———

That hollow sense of loss follows me to Vienna. Even as I fall in love with the obvious bits of this imperial city, the lush cliché of the Belvedere's collection of Klimts, the Leopold's Schieles (all those contested pieces of art that were exposed as former Jewish property), the exacting perfection of the café culture, the smart academics with whom I break bread, I am also, paradoxically, often lonelier than I have ever been, an intense, solitary aloneness, which creeps up on me, unexpectedly, nearly drowning me at night in my strange, empty room, a mattress on the floor, a board over two wood horses as a desk; with enormous double-paned windows that look out upon the electric wires of the tram and the turn-of-the-last-century spire of a building that advertises an ancient pharmacy—APOTHEKE—in gold block letters. A Jewish filmmaker, Mirjam Unger, born and raised at the edge of the tiny postwar Jewish community of the city, flatly sums up the problem: "Everyone is missing here." She is right. It is a city of ghosts.

The truth is, as my new friends at the Institute admit to me, sometime late into our third enormous beer, or walking along the city's inner Ring late at night, or in some deep conversation screamed over the beat of electronic music, Vienna, my grandfather's rosy hagiography aside, had a long history of anti-Semitism, one that had been embodied by its mayor, Dr. Karl Lueger, at the turn of the century. Lueger—whose tenure ran from 1897 to 1910 and whose name, until 2012, graced the Ring itself, much to the shame of my liberal Austrian (young) friends—ran on a platform of political, populist, purposeful anti-Semitism, a new institutionalization of Jew hatred, a political ethnic stirring that had not yet been directed in such a way before he assumed power.

His policies didn't stop Jews from flooding the city. The Jewish population grew exponentially from the middle of the nineteenth century onward; by 1923, Jews numbered some 200,000 out of 2 million. More than half the city's doctors were Jews (a fact that decimated the city's hospitals after Hitler made ethnicity a prerequisite for remaining in the medical profession). By the early 1930s, Jewish lawyers outnumbered their Christian counterparts; Jews also numbered among many artists and journalists of the city, though the majority of them were small shop and business owners.

There were two conflicting impressions of Jews in the prewar period: both come, as do all stereotypes, with some degree of veracity and some degree of falsity: that Jews were penniless scroungers off the welfare state (that image came from the influx of Ostjuden—Eastern Jews—who fed into the city out of Galicia during and after World War I and were often impoverished)—and that Jews controlled large amounts of money, like the Ephrussi banking family, whose palace on the Ringstrasse, the city's grand circular boulevard with glorious statues and figurines on the tops of buildings, where trams run back and forth clicking and sighing on electronic tracks, was immortalized in Edmund de Waal's *The Hare with Amber Eyes*. But while Jews had entered into parts of Austrian society after Emancipation (the extension of citizenship and rights and freedom of movement to Jews, which took place in Austria-Hungary in the mid–nineteenth century, with the benevolence of Franz Joseph I, who didn't hate Jews), anti-Semitism from the turn of the last century until the Anschluss had kept my brethren separate enough, had hardened these conflicting stereotypes, that it obscured the reality—most Jews weren't terribly well off or terribly poor, but were middle- or lower-income, small business owners, or shunted, often, into the professions that were accessible and acceptable for Jews to enter.

One night, early on in my fellowship, Herwig, a Holocaust historian and a Fellow at my Institute, and his Polish girlfriend, Camilla, also an academic, invite me to dinner. I tell Herwig about my childish thrill at riding tramlines my grandfather might have been on, about my grandfather's lifelong, undiminished love for Vienna. "Life in 1938 here would have been awful for him," Herwig says, uncomfortably. "Actually, well before that." I am caught perpetuating the same myth my grandfather liked to sell. I am selling it to myself, to them.

And yet I didn't need to be told this. I know this to be true, I know how Cilli described the city after the Anschluss—as though every non-Jewish neighbor had been merely waiting, their Nazi uniforms pressed and hanging in armoires across the city, ready for the moment Hitler arrived. Unlike her brother, she was quick to describe the prominent men forced to scrub the street as crowds crushed in around them, jeering them on; she expressed the anxiety that rippled through the community. "I saw Nazis march and chant, 'Jewish blood will be on the knife,' and I knew it would be terrible," she said. I have just not chosen to focus on this, yet. Just like my grandfather.

Midway through the meal, emboldened by half a bottle of wine, I ask Herwig why he'd chosen to focus his academic life on the Holocaust. "Well"—he clears his throat, adjusts his glasses—"I suppose it is because of my family. How should I put this . . ." His grandfather, he explains, was a translator for the Gestapo and, likely, participated in the major roundups of Jews in Prague. He doesn't know for sure. He knows, simply, that his grandfather was a Nazi, and that the roundups of Prague required all in town to participate, that Gestapo agents weren't exempted, and even if they were, why would his grandfather have been? He believed in the cause.

Like hundreds of thousands of other ethnic Germans born in Czechoslovakia, Herwig's grandfather was expelled from his hometown after the war; he lived, unrepentant, angry at his own fate, into his nineties. And Herwig loved him, fiercely, but this history always hung in the room nearby, disturbed him, made him wonder how to relate to this grandfather. Herwig called it a *stain* on the family. I love Herwig for telling the story without apology, but at the same time I am at a loss as to what to do with it: Do Herwig and I owe each other something? It feels somehow too intimate, too exposed. I wake the next morning feeling like I have slept with someone wrong for me. I tell him that; it makes it worse.

Such moments contribute to my peculiar sense of self. I feel ghostly in Vienna—transparent, disconnected, unmoored—a feeling exacerbated by my insufficient German, and my very strange roommate, who is often shut behind closed doors. Telling anyone my family left the city in 1938 is an instant identifier. The next words are invariably, "Oh. Sorry." Or "But everyone got out, right?"

I feel, suddenly, very visibly Jewish, which, counterintuitively, makes me push the point. At the Institute, they say, "You're so American." It is not a compliment. It means I am loud. I laugh louder, talk louder, dress louder. Speak of my identity in ways, I know better, that Europeans do not.

———

I walk through the eighteenth-century Augarten, thinking of Karl and Valy. They loved this park; her letters often return to their time there. It is easy to see why: enormously tall cypresslike trees line the path and it feels, vaguely, French; walls keep out the rest of the city. It was not far from where they both lived; it had space, their apartments did not. Plus, in the 1930s, the park didn't yet have the enormous flak towers, stark and bold against the sky, that the Nazis erected in the later part of the war. Those are still there; they were too sturdy, too thick, to be blown up or torn down. In 1946, the year of my father's birth, a group of children found their way inside one; there they discovered a cache of arms and set off a fantastic series of explosions, which terrifically damaged the interior but didn't bring the building down. So the towers continue to stand, ominous and foreboding, marring the sky in this marvelous park otherwise known for a delicate porcelain factory that sits on its grounds and its neatly drawn paths. That mix of beauty with the sad and ugly seems, somehow, appropriate.

One afternoon, I walk through the Augarten with Herwig, and we talk about seduction. He persuades me to go on a ride in the nearby Prater amusement park; we pay to be strapped into a swing that pulls us four hundred feet in the air and then whips us around at thirty-five miles an hour. I agree, unthinkingly, even though I have a terrible fear of being trapped. The city beneath us stretches out in each direction, but I can barely open my eyes in the wind. I panic and grip his hand tightly the entire five minutes we are airborne. *How could I have agreed to do this?* I wonder, breathlessly, upon our descent to earth. "Isn't that the very nature of seduction?" he parries. It is the very way my grandfather and Valy had spoken to each other, and I find myself blushing, despite myself.

I search for my grandfather and Valy everywhere; take their path to school, go hear their Philharmonic, grasp at understanding the obsession with the city. I attend an event at a *Gymnasium* in the ninth district where they invite back old Jews and have the children sing songs they have memorized in Hebrew. *Hashevaynu:* "Return us to you, God, and we shall return. Renew us as in Days of Old." It is a keening, mournful tune. Do they know what they are singing? It's meant for God—in fact it is a line from the Tisha B'av service, Lamentations, which mourns the destruction of the Temple, and it has always felt an almost impudent request on our part—a request that God act first. *Return to us so we can return to you.*

But perhaps, I think as I listen, here in Vienna it has a double meaning. I vacillate, sitting on the floor of the old *Gymnasium*, between boredom and tears. The old Jews, alumni of the school, are asked to stand for applause. "Joseph . . . Escaped in 1938!" Ovation. Relief.

Hannah Lessing is there, that day in the ninth. I see her in the corner. A former banker, since the mid-1990s she has been the secretary-general of the National Fund of the Republic of Austria for Victims of National Socialism, responsible for the reparations payments to Jews who fled after the Anschluss. Glamorous, and Jewish, she is the daughter of Magnum photographer Erich Lessing, who fled the city himself, as a boy, in the 1930s and returned after the war though his own mother had been murdered in Auschwitz. Hannah stands there with her vibrant-beyond-nature sienna-colored hair; an enormous diamond-studded Star of David around her neck, glittering in the afternoon light. It is a purposeful, aggressive *Fuck you* to wear such a symbol here, where everyone pretends the state is secular and not Catholic. She made me cry in her office, once—though to be fair, she was weeping as well. She told me how she won restitution claims for lost Viennese daughters and sons, and she read me a thank-you letter she keeps, folded into fifteenths, in her wallet. Later I am told that this is her thing: she brings journalists in and makes them cry. It is successful, it is brutal; it is smart: we want to cry here.

Hannah has always lived in Vienna. She has always lived in the shadow of death. Her parents insisted she go to the Lycée Français and become fluent in French, lest they need to flee. The Jewish community, after the war, existed here, uncomfortably, quietly, occasionally defiantly. An exhibit at the Jewish Museum of Vienna on the postwar life of Jews in the imperial city is called simply *Leben!* (Life!). It is a strident imperative, a thumbed nose.

The history of expulsion and hatred never sat well in the general community of postwar Vienna. The city, and the country, came late to commemorations, came late to the feeling that they were in some way, or in any way, culpable. There were many who preferred it to just disappear. The first paean to the destroyed Jewish community was a statue of a Jew, on his knees, condemned, Sisyphus-like, to scrub the street in front of the Albertina Museum in perpetuity, his back covered in barbed wire. "This honors us?" my father asks dubiously as we emerge from the museum; my parents have come to visit. Indeed, the monument, erected in 1988, was an immediate source of vexation to the remaining Jews of Vienna; tourists were sitting on it, dogs were peeing on it, others weren't noticing it. Somehow I am not surprised. "Hitler's first victims," as Austrians called themselves for decades, were not quick to reject that label. The memory continues to feel contested, or at least contentious.

And yet Hitler's sweep into Austria in March 1938 was by no means the country's introduction to Nazism. The party hung on the margins of Austrian society for decades, first appearing (with a dismal showing) on the ballot of 1919. Membership grew. Nazis began to show up in city councils, first in Linz, then in the province of Styria. They upended the 1925 World Zionist Congress, filling the streets with vigilante hordes, and began over the next decade to set off small bombs. Surely my grandfather knew of this, by age fifteen or so, surely he had heard of the violence, of the virulence—but perhaps it still seemed (mostly) marginal, almost manageable, not all that different from the casual persistent racism of other political parties. By the early 1930s, political upheaval and economic meltdown made for fertile Nazi recruiting ground. I sit in the library reading books on the period, attend lectures on the history, and begin to understand better that interwar politics in Austria in the post-Hapsburg period was a morass of petty small dictators (first Engelbert Dollfuss, then Kurt von Schuschnigg when the former was assassinated) who espoused a kind of Italian-style fascism that was mildly anti-Semitic. Nazism itself, along with the Social Democratic and Communist parties, was banned in 1933—after Hitler took power next door. But the people did not stop believing. Instead, when the swastika and other Nazi symbols were banned, sympathizers wore long white socks, a symbol to one another.

In the box of letters there was one indication that even my grandfather wasn't so sure of his footing in Austria, far earlier than I had once thought. It is a small note, a flyer, advertising a debate: "How to

Get to Palestine Without Money," it says, in a bold, modern German typeface. "A lecture about the political and economic possibilities of re-settlement of Jews without capital. Speaker: Chaim Wildmann," and then, in tiny letters at the bottom: "Managing editor/publisher: Valerie Scheftel." It is dated June 1933; he was twenty-one.

So, yes, Karl was conscious of the rising xenophobia, of the need to leave—even then. And yet what I hadn't realized was that the crucible of the most aggressive, the most brutal anti-Semitism, and nascent Nazism, was the University of Vienna itself.

Herwig introduces me to Herbert Posch, a young historian at the university. It was Posch who personally pushed the school at last (in 1999!) to formally recognize—and apologize to—all those expelled after the Anschluss. Posch assumed most of those he wanted to commemorate were dead. But he was wrong. Many were still alive, and he rushed to interview as many as he could. Over the next decade and a half, they began to die at an alarming clip. Each man he suggests I talk to is either dead or dies soon after I contact him. It is terribly unnerving.

It is Posch who explains to me, finally, that when my grandfather and Valy enrolled in the University of Vienna medical school in 1931, it had a vibrant Jewish population, and an equally vibrant Nazi faction. The latter was so aggressive that Jews were constantly plotting ways to manage the problem of getting to and from class without incident. Beginning in the 1920s, every Jewish (male) student knew that he was going to be beaten at school. Beaten badly, and often. The school was rabidly, overtly anti-Semitic. Though most of the Jews attending the university weren't visibly religious, it was obvious, immediately, who was who. The Jews took classes from Jews, the Nazis from Nazis. More than half the faculty of the university were Jews, so it wasn't hard to find a class to take.

The school hewed closely to the free ideas of the late-eighteenth- and early-nineteenth-century education philosopher Wilhelm von Humboldt, who believed in a separation of state, church, and university, an entirely free world of education, unencumbered by the government. That might have been a liberal, Enlightenment ideal in theory; in practice it meant the police were barred from the campus until sometime after Engelbert Dollfuss's dictatorship assumed power. After he settled into office, Dollfuss cracked down on the Nazis on campus and installed a police station within the university, to quell the riots—not for any love of Jews but in a brutal attempt to restore order and keep the Nazis away from his own regime.

Before that, Jewish blood ran on the walkways and sidewalks and marble stairwells. In the anatomy school, there is a central staircase, marble and grand. The smell of formaldehyde hangs heavy in the air, the lectures on pumping blood through the heart sounded like every other medical school. Except here the central stairs once denoted a schism in the student body. To one side would go the Jews, to a Jewish adviser. Up the other staircase would go their peers, to study with a Nazi. The staircase revealed each student's identity; battles were fought on the landing.

"In *Gymnasium*," the school years before university, "there was nothing yet, no Hitler yet, but at university we experienced a great deal of anti-Semitism," one of the old alumnae, Dr. Gerda Poll, tells me. She is ninety-seven years old when we meet, frail and white, with the type of skin that's oft described as "papery," wild white hair and a difficult time hearing my questions. But she is still very sharp, still the Freudian scholar—and psychoanalyst—she was trained to be. Dr.

Poll was at the University of Vienna at the same time as my grandfather and Valy, though, as with many other things, she cannot remember them.

"There was a very famous internist," Poll says, referring to one of her professors. "He is written up in books here. Eppinger was his name. He was a big anti-Semite. I was a very good student but for my internal medicine, my oral examination—the *Rigorosum*—he gave me three questions and I couldn't answer a single one. He had researched them purposefully. It was the only subject I ever didn't pass—he flunked me. Because of this I lost three months. When I went back, students demonstrated against him and they all went with me for the second exam—it was a public exam. Oral. Second time he asked normal questions and I passed."

This was typical, I learn. Jews were often taunted this way, given atrociously, conspicuously punishing tests to upend their studies. Poll remembered Eppinger marching alongside Hitler at the Anschluss. I don't know if this is a real memory or a constructed one, but it doesn't much matter. In Valy and my grandfather's school papers, I see that they, too, were studying under Hans Eppinger. And Poll's memory of his brutality was not exaggerated: during the war he went on to conduct gruesome experiments with seawater at Dachau. Roma prisoners were forced to drink salinated water until they literally died of thirst, until they were *licking the floor* hoping for a drop of lifesaving clear water. It was an effort to understand if a man could survive on seawater. Eppinger committed suicide just before his turn at the Nuremberg trials.

Back in Vienna, Posch offers me what he says is the best short narration of the horrific pre-Nazi-period violence against Jews on campus. It is a German adaptation of a chapter in Benno Weiser Varon's book *Professions of a Lucky Jew*. "Louis Pasteur and Madame Curie risked their lives in medical research. I risked mine on the first day I set foot on 'academic territory,'" Varon wrote in the English version of the same. "Aware of the risks of studying as a Jew at Vienna

University, I had, even before matriculating, joined a Jewish self-defense organization named Haganah [defense]." I flip back to the author's name again—Benno. I am shocked, despite myself. I *know* this man: Benno was one of my grandfather's lifelong best friends, one of the buddies he called the Musketeers. I remember seeing the book on my father's shelf. This was no longer a theoretical passage about what my grandfather and Valy might have experienced—this was one of their closest friends, narrating what he and his classmates had actually been subject to.

"We rarely managed to extricate Jewish fellow students who, trapped in a lecture room, were beaten up once the lecture was over," Benno wrote. "But we attacked Nazis who lay in wait outside the lecture halls and we generally gave a good account of ourselves. . . . There was a certain ritual when we entered an institute after being notified the Nazis were preparing a brawl. The Nazis formed a phalanx when they saw us enter, and so did we. First came a verbal exchange." This turned into a brawl, with "injuries on both sides." From February 1934, "Austrofascism came to the rescue. . . . One of the first things the dictatorship did was to abolish the 'inviolability of academic territory.' Dollfuss would not allow the university to remain a Nazi enclave he could not touch. From February 1934, onwards we could concentrate on studying without fear. For once we were beneficiaries of Fascism."

I think, when I am back in the States, I should visit Benno. But when I contact him, I discover I am too late: his wife, Miriam, tells me that Benno can no longer speak—Alzheimer's had taken all but his soul by then. My grandfather's old friend could tell me nothing.

Herbert Posch is dismayed to hear of Benno's condition. Posch is gentle, despite his enormous height and large physical presence. He wears purple the first time we meet, with matching purple Dr. Martens boots. A lightning bolt hangs in one ear; his hair is short, close to his head, the top left a bit long, and what hair there is, is blond. He is fond of large silver rings. There are many like me, he says, trying not to offend me, not to say I'm not original—but he means many seekers who have sought him out since his *Gedenkbuch* (memorial book) project began. We are the relatives of those expelled. We have contacted him and asked him for help filling in what our family members did not tell us about those prewar years. Many of us struggle to understand why anyone would have stayed in Austria at all. It is the eternal question; one of the few we actually asked my grandfather when he was alive. For Karl, it was about the *"best medical education in the world"*; he would tell my father he just wanted his degree, and then a ticket out. When he returned in the 1950s to take more courses, some of the Nazi professors were still there, still teaching, as if nothing had happened at all. But all his fellow Jewish students were gone.

By the time my grandfather and Valy were well ensconced in their studies, those Jewish students were still hanging in, hoping to graduate and then emigrate before Hitler came. But all the while they tried to lead an intellectual life: they took in music, debated philosophy. They were fiercely addicted to cultural life. "They had a very close connection to German culture," says Posch, as bells chime behind us, poetically marking the time. And yet their entire world was Jewish, assimilated or not. They weren't integrated at all. "They were connected to German idealistic romantic culture, with Goethe and Schiller and high culture," Posch continues, "and the idea that, in such a civilized romantic culture, nothing really bad can happen to us." Which of course created a sense of false security and, strangely, adaptation. "They knew Saturdays were bad," he says. It was the day the German Student Union convened; word of mouth kept Jewish students away, for fear of riots and beatings.

Posch has photographed Valy's and my grandfather's files for me inside the archives of the medical school in advance of my visit: a series of yellowed handwritten registrations for school classes over the years. The scrawl is as familiar to me as my own—my grandfather filled out the class cards for Valy. Nationality is filled in as "Jewish," a sign of

Zionist thinking, says Posch. Valy lists no father on her forms. Her mother was alone.

It is a rainy afternoon when Posch and I first meet, cold when it isn't wet, and he and I walk through campus and down the side streets into the anatomy building, home to the university's most brutal anti-Semitic pogroms. We stand on the central landing and contemplate the students in their white coats, rushing in twos and threes up the stairwells that once directed Jewish students and Nazi students to their classes; we duck into a cardiology lecture and stand a moment, watching a professor narrate the valves of the heart as students, silent, scratch notes and glance at us observing them from the corner. Earlier, in his office, Posch showed me photographs of students escaping out the windows, trying to avoid attack at the hands of their classmates. "This is 1933, after a riot," he said, pulling out a photo, "they crawl out the window trying to escape here." He has image after image, from throughout the 1930s, all showing campus oppression.

We leave the anatomy hall and walk over to Berggasse, down the block from Freud's home and museum, and step into a café. Over tea I ask Posch why he started his big project, why he made this effort to honor those expelled during the Anschluss, and the answer is quite simple: Because, in sixty-nine years, no one else had.

————————

"I told a friend I was renting to a Jew," my roommate, Hilke, says to me one morning as she pours her muesli and makes her herbal tea. Around us, crystal prisms dangling on fishing wire projected rainbows onto the yellow kitchen walls. "He said, 'Oh! Don't you feel you shouldn't use that Nazi word, *Jude?*'"

No, I reply, startled, Jew is not a Nazi word. But then other Austrians echoed the sentiment. Yes, says Karin, a friend from dance class, that's how she felt growing up, too. *Jude*, even "race"—those were words not to be used in polite society. It was strange growing up in Austria, agrees Sophie, a glamorous, chain-smoking philosophy student and, eventually, a good friend. For us, Jews were just dead, she says. It was odd to find them, later, in clubs, bars—living normally, unremarkably.

"Yes," says Hilke back at home, impassively. Jews were just victims. And then she adds, as if in explanation: "I dated a skinhead as a teenager." She hung around his crowd, gleaned his hates. "I rented to you because I realized you were Jewish when you said your grandfather had left in 1938. I didn't want to be politically correct anymore. I wanted to ask you all the questions I've never been allowed to ask."

Over lunch at the Institute the next day I blurt the story. The table goes silent, the Germans and Austrians look at one another and sigh. Then each of my dismayed colleagues, in turn, urges me to move. But I go nowhere. I'm curious about her. I think: *I can change her.* I think: *I'll convert her.* So instead, I choose to use her ignorance as cocktail banter; I dip into the cartoon as armor. Vienna offers me a sense of foreignness I haven't felt anywhere else.

Occasionally I walk to my grandfather's old street and look up at its drab exterior. It is not far from my apartment, and not far from the Prater, where I'd gone with Herwig and where Orson Welles's famous giant Ferris wheel looms. Every night Welles's postwar classic *The Third Man* is playing somewhere in Vienna: a metaphor—Vienna, a city stuck in the middle of the twentieth century.

My roommate's fascination with me stretched back years further than our acquaintance. As a teenager, she rebelled against her history-teacher parents, picking up Nazi paraphernalia and acting out in ways both juvenile—an illegal-in-Austria Adolf Hitler T-shirt purchased in London—and disturbing—on a mandatory class trip to the death-camp Mauthausen, she and her boyfriend ripped pages from a commemorative book, filled with photos of piles of dead bodies, and posted them around her bedroom. She told me she hated the "weakness" of the bodies.

"But the bodies didn't start out weak," I complain; even to my ears

I sound plaintive. She shrugs. She hated that Jews got to be the ulti-
mate victims. I promise her that I have no interest in being a victim;
she is unconvinced.

If you were to pass Hilke on the street, you wouldn't notice her.
Straight, unremarkable hair that falls just below her shoulders, the
color of wet sand, close to blond; a kind of hippie-punk Mittel-
European type, with a fondness for skirts worn over pants with hiking
boots, and a kohl-lined eye. A few years back she had a shaved head, a
style she sported until her early thirties as she studied the extreme
Austrian art movement called Aktionism. Born in the 1960s, Aktionism is all about pushing boundaries and norms: it involves blood and
semen and violence. In a film that won her a degree of fame in certain
Viennese art circles, my roommate was hung from her wrists and
beaten until she passed out. She called it *The Sleep of Reason*—after
Goya. When I meet her, she is curating an exhibition called *Abuse*.
One wall highlights an endless video loop of a woman being pene-
trated by a duck. An artist drops out of the exhibition, and Hilke, half
seriously, asks me if I would consider wearing a yellow star as an art
installation. I decline.

———

"There were centuries of persecution," she says one afternoon as I put
away groceries. "Don't you think that means there was something
wrong with Jews?" She wants to find a way to share the guilt between
us, a means to draw a line blaming Jews, at least partly, for their own
destruction. She wants us to be different.

I try to explain that, for centuries, simply not believing in Christ
made Jews suspect, put them at odds with kings and states. This response bores her. "Look," she says, and leads me into her home office,
until now off-limits to me. On her bulletin board are photos of her
grandfathers. Each wears a Nazi uniform, smartly pressed. She tells
me she pinned them there to remind herself—both of what they had
done, and her refusal to be ashamed of her lineage. I am suddenly hot,

and, I find, angry—angry because it is I who feels ashamed standing in front of these long-dead men, doing nothing to convert their grand-daughter. I am ineffective.

The Germans and Austrians at my Institute are bemused by these stories. How, they wonder, have I managed to find a thirty-six-year-old woman who says things long considered unacceptable? Yet when my roommate asks, in one of her strange tirades about the war, wasn't I bored with being obsessed with the Holocaust, it wasn't clear to me that it was only I who was obsessed: Wasn't she obsessed as well? Weren't the others around me? There is Uli, a German who proudly declares that his country deserves to be dissolved for its sins. He is a Marxist and spends his free time translating for me the unsubtly anti-foreigner posters placed by the far-right political parties in the sub-ways. We walk the city together, late at night, around the Ring, once the trams stop running and the Viennese have long since gone home. We mimic my grandfather and his friends as we sit in cafés earnestly discussing history and the state of the world. I wonder, a bit, if my ap-peal is my Jewishness, as though I am somehow a part of a subcon-scious atonement plan. At the same time I don't care. I like it, this strange connection. I like his anger. It feels entirely inappropriate to our generation; it comforts me that I am not the only one still think-ing of these things.

And then there is Thomas, the one other Jewish fellow, a thin, beautiful, Budapest-born philosopher with dolorous eyes, an ever-present pack of Nil cigarettes, and a postcard for the 1924 movie *Die Stadt ohne Juden* (*The City Without Jews*) pinned to his office cork-board. In the film, a city banishes all of its Jews and then falls apart; the city has to invite them all back. It is a comedy. I fall in love, a little bit, with them both, Thomas and Uli; I fall in love, a little bit, with everyone at my Institute.

It is here, in Vienna, when I realize I have always lived with ghosts. I have always sought, in some way, to understand what connects me to my grandfather, to this time. I spend night after night, for months, drinking with Germans and Austrians; we reassure one another that we are disconnected from the war, distanced by more than time, that we are not to blame.

Yet I wonder, even as I collect a group of friends in this town, if I have any place here at all. In Vienna, outside my tight intellectual cohort, when I mention my family, the room turns silent and aggressive, or silent and sad, or silent and annoyed. *God. Another Jew looking for her roots,* they seem to be thinking. *Why must you people always be with your heads in the past?*

<hr />

I think of Valy often as I walk these streets, as I meander down Heinestrasse, the street listed as hers on her school forms, as I visit the places she mentions in her letters. Nowhere is Vienna more idealized than in Valy's letters. *"Unfortunately, I don't have much good to tell you about my work right now,"* she writes in late spring 1941. *"A couple of days ago, alas, I returned from the course I had written to you about. It was quite wonderful! Full of youth, spirit and verve! For the first time, since Vienna, I again felt glad and young! Now it has finally come to an end, unfortunately. I did a lot of teaching there and I believe that I have become a well-respected teaching authority there—your legacy, Karl! Upon my return, I unfortunately had to learn that I no longer can continue my work at the hospital and at the seminary for kindergarten teachers due to a general cut in positions. If I do not succeed in becoming confirmed as an itinerant teacher for various retraining facilities, I will have to start working in a factory before too long."*

Vienna, for Valy, the longer she stays in Berlin, becomes as much a symbol of freedom and life as my grandfather himself. She is a faithful recorder of her time in the city. She writes on it, muses on it, returns to it again and again. She and my grandfather, she writes, spent an *"unspeakably beautiful"* summer together in the Mediterranean-like warmth of Lake Wörthersee, in Carinthia, near the camp for Zionist Jews, swimming alongside the athletes of Hakoah of Vienna, the superstar sportsmen and women of the era, the best swimmers in

Europe. In the winter, they dance at the Medizinerredoute, the medical students' formal ball. They debate how they can be together with no money: it is one thing to travel as students; it is another to live, forever, impoverished. One day, as they walk in the Augarten, my grandfather tells her that she should marry. She doesn't understand what he means—to him? To anyone? Is it to pull her back from her mother, who waits for her in Czechoslovakia? Is it to keep her from focusing only on her work? She wants to know what he meant; she doesn't ask.

The night after she graduates from medical school, they stand on the Ringstrasse, the grand Viennese circular boulevard with its enormous mansions. They are on the stretch of the Ring near Parliament, diagonally across from the lights of stately Café Landtmann. They stand there and discuss the future. I have been on the Ring dozens upon dozens of times, crammed onto trams, talking with friends, walking late at night when the weather turns warm. It is much the same as it was then, and I can see Karl and Valy there, beneath the glorious statues of the parliament, the imposing marble, alongside the electric streetcars with their peculiar distinctive smell of sweat and wood, I can hear the strange way the tram creaks and bends, like an arthritic elbow, the Austrian-accented nasal German of the recorded station-stop announcements, *Stadiongasse/Parlament, Rathausplatz, Schottentor.*

They stand there together, basking in the glory of her degree, and she catches her breath, she has something important to say, she musters her courage: she wants to ask him to stay with her, to be with her, to marry her, to have a life together. But then she doesn't say any of that; she hesitates. The moment passes. She loses her chance.

Four days later Hitler annexes the country, and crowds fill Vienna's Heldenplatz, a pulsating mob with hands held high, palms out. Swastikas fill the city, overnight—there is a run on the flag, there aren't enough to go around.

The crackdown begins immediately. Jews are forced to scrub the streets; the local newspapers run headlines, "Are we German? YES!" Their precious Augarten is taken from them within six weeks. They can no longer sit on benches; they can no longer enter parks. My grandfather joins the endless lines searching for visas, he writes to cousins for an affidavit. Does he try for Valy, too? Does she want him to? "Not all of you have to go!" an acquaintance tells my Aunt Cilli. She scoffs. She says she knew they all must leave.

Violence tilts the city. Jewish stores are sacked. The wealthy students my grandfather tutored are looted; their fathers are arrested and sent to Dachau. Some don't return. Jews are paraded for humiliation. My grandfather pins a Polish eagle to his cap and pretends to be a Pole. He can speak just enough Polish to render his disguise believable. Where did all these Nazis come from? Five years of what had been incrementally imposed anti-Jewish legislation in Germany was put in place in Austria all at once, in a matter of weeks. Restrictive measures were only part of the mortification of the community: the Nazis quickly began to confiscate Jewish property and art, shipping it all immediately into the *Altreich*, the heart of Germany, businesses are "aryanized," taken over by racially pure business owners.

And as my grandfather knocks on doors and cuts the lines at the consulates, Valy takes the train three hours northeast to Troppau, Czechoslovakia, leaving behind her adopted city, and her lover. She can't abandon her mother, in another town, another country. Even if he'd asked. And it does not appear he asked. Plus—at first—returning home *was* an escape. Czechoslovakia was not yet occupied, was ostensibly out of immediate danger.

Somewhere in those weeks of plotting for freedom, my grandfather began to morph into the hero who enabled his sister, brother-in-law, mother, and nephew to escape Vienna *in the nick of time*; the hero that I knew. Valy began to write to him from the moment he set foot on the boat—first from her mother's, and later from Berlin.

*You should know that I bought myself a flute because I am
always so dreadfully lonesome. While I don't think that my musical
productions sound very good at this stage, I am really enjoying it.*

*And I am practicing an awful lot so I will be able to play really
well once you and I are reunited again. You love music so much! And
even though it cannot be piano which you would have wanted—I
don't have the sufficient means for that in more than one respect—
one can make beautiful music on a flute, as well, don't you think?
And you are going to sing along with my playing, in your full-
throated "steam bath" voice. And, whoever does not like it can just
buzz off. We are definitely going to like it!*

She dreams of everything they shared, a dream that she nourishes as
the world around her becomes increasingly nightmarish and the past
becomes the only sharp, clear, beautiful thing she can think of:

*I live through all the different phases of our being together. Do
you remember? The Friday nights. When we went to your Mama's
house. All the other evenings in your place. Everything you did. Do
you remember? Talking. How can we without money . . . ? Skiing
classes . . . The different relationships between us we lived,
together . . . And this time cannot be over yet darling. I beg you . . .
tell me. That this cannot be. It is impossible don't you agree? It
cannot be. Darling?! I think about all those things and I ask myself in
which phase of your life you are right now.*

I show these letters to friends in Vienna and Berlin. One friend
tells me they are too personal to translate. Not only because Valy was
trapped, but also because she did not sound like a woman who fully
believed herself to be loved, to be supported, to be cared for. *"You are
and remain far, far away, out of my reach, you exist only in my memories,
in my wonderful, beautiful 'sunny past.'"*

Even more than emigration, Valy just wants the past to no longer be past. She meanders for pages, she reminds him of the poetry they read together, the books they debated. *"Do you remember? Once, many years ago, we were walking through the Prater, it was in October, and you recited the Oktoberlied for me, talking about the overcast day which we wanted to make golden. . . . We were so happy then, or, at least, I was. With you, I never was quite sure how things were."*

I am struck, seventy years on, by the poignancy of that insecurity. My grandfather was in Pittsfield, Massachusetts, by the time she wrote those lines. It was fall 1941. By then his medical practice had been open a year, he was settling into his new life, he was dating my smart, pretty grandmother, who had gone to Smith College and then transferred—it was still the Depression, after all, and Smith was pricey—to the University of North Carolina at Greensboro. She was the daughter of Jewish immigrants (one Russian, one Latvian) who made a solid living selling wallpaper and paint. Her mother had been a businesswoman in her own right, as a fashion buyer in her early twenties; in all, the Kolmans were a very American, quiet-success story.

In Berlin, in the meantime, Valy was entirely living in the past, comforted only by a phantom version of Karl, a shadow version of their relationship that had long since become as one-dimensional as his photograph.

I discuss all this with Herbert Posch—the life my grandfather created, the life he left behind, the eventual American wife, the girlfriend, the lies, the omissions, the sadness—and he listens, quietly. I wonder aloud about what Karl told my grandmother, and what he knew about where Valy was during the war, and after it. I raise for him the questions that have been consuming me—about my grandfather's lovers, about his guilt, or his lack of guilt.

I tell him that as a teen I made a pilgrimage with my parents to my grandfather's former home, Rueppgasse 27, a street that, to my seventeen-year-old eyes, seemed gray and uninteresting: *poor.* We took the train from Munich to Vienna on that trip—schlepping a million bags from train to train. I remember thinking, I say, *How odd, how disturbing, to be asked for papers and passports in German.* In Vienna, my father went to the bank, to withdraw money. My grandfather, I learned only then, had squirreled away money outside America, should he need to flee again. This was a bewildering thought—Karl had not been sure enough of the United States to entrust our banks with all of what he earned. Instead, he opened accounts in Switzerland, perhaps also elsewhere, in the event that he was once again a refugee, he could enable the family to start over. Not only that—he had also secured a passport for my father when he was born, so the family could make a quick exit if they needed to—little Joseph Wildman is held up in his passport photo by my grandmother. The knowledge altered something for me, even then, opened questions I hadn't known to ask before. That same anxiety that had prompted him to flee the city in 1956— sure that the Soviet army was on his heels—lurked elsewhere in his psyche. He hadn't believed in his success as much as I'd thought.

I suspect Posch is used to this. He gets these same navel-gazing musings from all the others like me who have come to see him, all of us on a pilgrimage to a messenger rather than to a place.

Posch invites me to visit the tiny former synagogue on the medical school campus that is now a memorial site called Marpe Lanefesh— "healing of the soul." For years it stood dormant, decaying, after it was forcibly decommissioned in 1938. By the 1970s, he tells me, no one remembered it had been a synagogue; it briefly became a transformer station, an electricity hub, a center for switches. But a researcher of the architect Max Fleischer, a prolific synagogue designer of the turn of the last century whose work had been entirely destroyed on Kristall- nacht, wondered if, perhaps, the little octagon opposite the campus insane asylum (really) was actually a synagogue. In 2005, a Bulgarian artist—Minna Antova—created the memorial; in it she literally lay- ered the history, placing three glass floors one on top of the other, the first layer a magnification of the 1903 architectural plans of Fleischer;

the next a series of words, a Nazi text calling for the destruction of Jewish holy sites on Kristallnacht; and the top a sketch of the electrical plan of the building. Visitors must put on gray felt clogs to walk on the glass so as not to scratch it; the roof was replaced with a glass cupola so Marpe Lanefesh, even on the gloomiest of days, is filled with light. The feeling is not so much of a synagogue, but of a breathing memory.

In fact, says Posch, it is one of only two standing synagogue structures left in Vienna, though this one is not a functioning chapel. The other is on Seitenstettengasse; that one is gilt and lush, with a soaring ceiling painted like a starry sky and endless names of the dead on the wall, most of whom were killed in the Shoah. All of the other synagogues of Vienna were destroyed on Kristallnacht.

By that terrible night, neither Valy nor my grandfather remained in Vienna. On Kristallnacht, my grandfather was in New York. Valy was preparing to leave Troppau for Berlin. From her letters, I knew it was Berlin where Valy had experienced all of the horror and deprivation that would characterize the ensuing years.

Knowing this, I wondered if the key to finding Valy wasn't in Vienna at all, but Germany itself. I dreamt of finding answers, of understanding some essential truth about her time there, of finding a clue to whether she might have lived through it all; and where she might be now.

Fantastical as my hopes were, I nurtured a belief that there was a place that might actually provide some of that—a complete mapping of her devastation and her path through the war; a final reckoning of the experience through Nazi records. That place was the enormous archives of the International Committee of the Red Cross—the International Tracing Service (ITS)—in Bad Arolsen, deep in the countryside of former West Germany. I had heard rumors about them for years; the problem was, they were not just closed but *barred* to researchers. ITS was created, solely, to reconnect families after the war, to provide answers, to provide an end to stories, happy or not. But so many legal barriers were in place to seeing what was inside, it seemed impossible I would ever get in there. Yet the more difficult it was, the more I wanted to go.

My time in Vienna is ending when I read that the archives in Bad Arolsen would finally be opening to outside researchers.

After months in the imperial city, I finally understand my grandfather's obsession with Vienna. When my fellowship draws to a close, I take a taxi to the airport; the driver takes me circuitously and, strangely, I find myself just at the corner of my grandfather's street. And there, in the back of the taxi, I finally cry. It is, in part, because I have been lonely here, I have missed those who have been gone from my life for years now, but I have made my own connections in Vienna; I have complicated my relationship to this geography with my own friendships, my own intellectual curiosity. I open a book that Thomas and Andrea, my friends from the Institute, gave me as a parting gift. "Vienna loves you, little Wildman," Thomas has written on the inside flap.

I call Herwig and weep to him that I feel ridiculous for these tears, that I feel a part of me *is* here in this city, even though my German is not good enough, my time so superficial, that I have not found enough out, that I have not done what I came to do.

"You'll come back," he says.

Three

SEARCH NUMBER
557 584

The chaos that was Europe in 1945 was of an unfathomable, un-precedented scale. Berlin, like other flattened cities in Germany, is not an urban center at the end of the war; it is a mouth full of rotted teeth, buildings shorn in half; once-lush living rooms are open to the elements alongside twisted metal and brick—they appear, in news-reels, to be held up by twigs; glassless windows offer vistas of burned piles of wood and brick; dust mountains three times higher than the average man; city streets are pocked, lined with the burned-out shells of formerly grandiose architecture—museums, churches, monuments, train stations. Populations are shell-shocked, shoeless, dirty; hard-ened. It is a nearly uninhabitable postapocalyptic world of destruction. The task of reconstruction must have seemed insurmountable. In America, and elsewhere, those waiting for word of cousins, brothers, parents, girlfriends, saw those destroyed cities and began to hear the stories of the camps opening, saw the images of the striped pajamas, the corpselike survivors, the devastation of the cities, and panicked for news of those they'd left behind.

After six long years of conflict, there were some thirty-six and a half million dead, and millions more displaced persons, whole populations residing, temporarily, uncomfortably, within the borders of their former persecutors, their former tormentors. By 1947, the United Nations Relief and Rehabilitation Administration (UNRRA) was running 762 displaced persons camps and centers in the West, most in Germany. Nearly seven million liberated civilians were receiving aid. Orphans had gathered in major cities by the tens of thousands, forlorn, malnourished kids, smaller than their age, lean and hungry and educated only in the strange wartime school of wits. Millions of forced laborers, the cogs of the Nazi wheel, were suddenly free to return home, if their return countries would take them, if they wanted to actually return, if they could find a means of getting there. Communication among countries, among sectors controlled by Allied nations was tortured.

Civilians everywhere were desperate to reunite with lost family members—or to know they might begin to mourn their passing. The essential human need for what we, lately, call closure—that which makes us want to know the end of the story, to bury those we have lost, to find those who remain—meant that efforts to trace the lost began before peace was declared, before the cleanup. Requests for assistance in finding loved ones came from every country touched by the war and from the far-flung shores that took in refugees before Hitler invaded Poland. UNRRA helped, at first, and then when that was dismantled, the International Refugee Organization took over the task of trying to find organization in the chaos.

As the war ended, the collection of documents used to trace the living, the missing, and the dead was centralized. Eventually, the offices officially became known as the International Tracing Service (ITS); by 1952, almost everything had found its way to the small western German village of Arolsen (the town name was changed sometime later to add "Bad" before "Arolsen"—Arolsen Spa). Three years after that, the management of the files was taken over by the International Committee of the Red Cross and the doors were closed to outside researchers, the collections available for one task and one task alone: tracing the path of victims.

I first learned about these archives at an off-the-record meeting at the United States Holocaust Memorial Museum a few years before my Vienna fellowship. It was 2004 and I had just written about the forgotten camps of Paris, proving, I suppose, that I had an interest in buried stories. Could I write about the archives? wondered directors of research at the museum. They wanted the popular press to raise awareness that these documents existed but that they were locked up—there were answers out there, they said, answers to questions we didn't yet know how to ask, and that early decision to keep ITS exclusively for survivor reunification, or searching for victims by family members, had had a chilling effect on scholarship. (Ostensibly closed, at first, to keep the focus on reconnecting families, the archives had remained closed in part due to stringent privacy laws in Germany.) The State Department, they said, wasn't taking the issue seriously enough, and survivors were dying without knowing the end of their own stories.

I agreed to dig into it. It was, after all, a good story. And somewhere in those files, I thought, might be something on the girl I had learned of so long before. Somewhere in there might be more to understanding what had happened to Valy.

———

Exactly what was in the ITS collections was a bit unclear. Some I spoke to maintained that it was just a place of lists: names on lists, places on lists, lists begetting lists; a dusty assemblage of boring German efficiency. The truth was a bit stranger than that. The basic facts were these: As the Allies crossed Europe, liberating concentration and labor camps, cities, villages, and towns, they collected documents left behind by the Nazis, and over time, these collections were deposited— sometimes haphazardly, sometimes methodically—in Arolsen. The holdings were immense, and uncatalogued. Biographical cards from displaced persons camps ended up here, as did millions of files on forced labor, concentration camp inmates, the Nuremberg trials, Nazi activity, and gruesome medical experiments—along with correspondence between Nazi officers, files on the dead, transport lists, sick lists, crime lists, and so on. The material covered political prisoners from across Europe, deported Jews, incarcerated gay men, Roma, millions of forced laborers, and displaced persons—Jews who had survived the ghettos and camps, as well as Eastern Europeans in flight from the Red Army. There were also prewar and postwar photos and "personal effects"—rings, watches, photos—taken from prisoners. There were reams of postwar documents that followed the paths survivors took after the war.

When the Red Cross took over, eleven countries—Belgium, Britain, France, Germany, Greece, Israel, Italy, Luxembourg, the Netherlands, Poland, and the United States—created a strict, official policy for the next half century: the ITS documents were exclusively to be used to trace survivors and victims—and to help families seeking restitution from the West German government. Under West Germany's (and, later, unified Germany's) indemnity laws, victims had the right to pursue economic grievances against the German government for everything from being forced to wear the yellow star to death in a concentration camp. But to obtain compensation, they had to somehow provide evidence of their experience—like a documentation file from ITS. Those who could make claims included Jews, of course, but also thousands of non-Jewish forced laborers (from Eastern as well as Western European countries) who served brutal years in factories and on farms; slave laborers in concentration camps, political prisoners, gay men and lesbians who were persecuted for their sexuality, and those who experienced the horror of the Nazi medical experimentation projects.

In the 1960s, the Holocaust Museum directors told me, ITS puttered along; historians hadn't yet begun to agitate to see what they had inside. But eventually the archive began to falter at its only task—

tracing victims. People said problems began with the arrival of Charles-Claude Biedermann, a Red Cross official appointed to take over ITS in 1985, who ruled the barracks at Arolsen like a fiefdom. He hired only locals to staff the more than three hundred stations inside the archives; they became (and remained) curiously specific experts in parceled areas of research—deportations to the extermination camps, say, or displaced persons but never both. The different departments didn't speak to one another; the department heads knew nothing of the other areas of research. Almost nothing was digitized.

In 1989, when the Iron Curtain fell, hundreds of thousands of new demands for information came pouring in and—it was said—a backlog of requests piled up. The wait for information began to stretch out over years; victims were dying before they found the information they sought on themselves, in order to receive long-overdue restitution payments, or their loved ones. Some survivors had never discovered the fate of siblings, parents, or spouses. Angry families and survivor organizations agitated for the archives to be opened to public scrutiny. Rumors began to swirl that there were secrets hidden there; secrets that Germany, and German companies in particular, didn't want revealed. Germany countered that opening the doors to research would violate the strict privacy laws that protected, they said, the rights of the victims.

In 2001, representatives of the United States Holocaust Memorial Museum requested access to the files. Paul Shapiro, the director of the Center for Advanced Holocaust Studies, and Jürgen Matthäus, the director of Applied Research Scholars, traveled to Bad Arolsen; they were made to sit in an anteroom for hours—after which they were denied entry to the collections. Frustrated, they began an intensive campaign to get inside—and to bring the files to Washington.

After my meeting at the museum, I, too, tried to get into the archives, with no luck. And yet, though several years would then pass, I couldn't let it go.

Now and then I'd ask historians what they thought about the

black box of ITS. Half of those I spoke to were reverential about what they believed was hidden in Bad Arolsen—there was a belief we'd find, perhaps, more companies that had used slave labor, the role of the churches under the Reich, the paths victims took and how they lived their lives during the war—an essential truth that had thus far remained elusive. For my part, I wondered if it would show me the path that Valy took, walk me through the work she did, and if, or how, she might have lived through the war. When I told this to the naysayers, the period experts who believed the myths were just that—trumped-up stories and rumors, a search for a gun that had long since stopped smoking, a search for narrative where there was only dry chronology—most shook their head and cautioned me not to hope for too much. Yet despite that, I fell somewhere closer to those who hoped for revelations. I wanted to know if the Gestapo had kept track of Valy's life after 1939 and, especially, her experiences after 1941, when her letters to my grandfather stop. And if there was material on her, I wondered, what would it reveal?

I began telling the story of Valy to all who will listen, to all who might give me a glimpse into how best to search for her—to all those who might agree that Bad Arolsen is the key to understanding what happened to her, after her letters end. I wanted to know if she was the key to Arolsen, as much as Arolsen was the key to her. How important, I wondered, was one individual story? Was this long-closed archive the key to the individual story as much as the group?

———

I write to Jean-Marc Dreyfus, the author of the book on the Paris camps, and tell him I believe Bad Arolsen is the key to my search. He immediately cautions against my enthusiasm—my conspiracy theories—and directs me to read Éric Conan and Henry Rousso's *Vichy: An Ever-Present Past.* Rousso is an expert on Vichy, the French state during the Nazi years—but also on the myth and reality of the French relationship to the past. I met with him while investigating the

Paris camps to discuss whether their quiet presence in the city was due to the French inability to face its past. (Rousso was quite sure it was not; he was adamant that the word "taboo," so often assigned to the French regarding the war years, was a misnomer.) Conan and Rousso present the problem of opening historical material to a public that does not exactly know what to do with it, and the creation of scandal where there is, occasionally, merely bureaucracy.

Scandal was exactly how the closure of the ITS archives was described to me. It was the Largest Unopened Holocaust Archives in the World (capital letters intended). It was Kept Closed for a Reason. What that reason was, no one knew. Obviously, many said, there was something we weren't supposed to see. As for me—I was less concerned with slave labor at big companies like BMW (though I found it fascinating) and more interested in what the archives could reveal about how Valy fared as she navigated the waves of deprivations that characterized life for a Jewish woman in the Reich.

It is 2008 by the time Jean-Marc writes to tell me that the museum has finally gotten permission to bring the first group of scholars to ITS—four years after my first meeting with the U.S. Holocaust Memorial Museum, two years after my Vienna fellowship (though, by then I had, as Herwig had predicted, been back several times to the city of my grandfather). I ask to accompany the museum's group, and in early June, I arrange with editors to write the story of the archives, apply for grants to support my work, and then fly to Berlin to begin talking to people about the myth of Arolsen—and Valy—with a plan to meet up with the scholars by train a week into my trip. Though I have often traveled alone, this time I am actually accompanied—I am at the very beginning of a pregnancy, carrying a little Jew in search of the fate of old Jews.

Before I left the States, I got in touch with Aubrey Pomerance, the immensely busy chief archivist of the Jewish Museum Berlin, the

Daniel Libeskind architectural marvel in the center of the city, to discuss the impact of the ITS archives opening, and Valy's story.

Pomerance is a permanent expat. A Canadian by birth, he has lived in Germany for more than a quarter century. He is the first of many who urge me to consider donating Valy's letters to his team, or to other teams of researchers. When I mention that her story is frustratingly incomplete, he waves a hand. "Be careful when you say 'incomplete,'" he says. "There is no collection that documents a person's life from moment of birth to moment of death. But you can cull a lot of information from one single document."

We discuss whether it may have been possible for Valy to survive in Germany, in hiding, and for how long. Pomerance doesn't rule it out. He muses aloud about Valy's case, and others like her, as well as the most spectacular example of survival—"The Jewish Hospital in Berlin survived to the end of the war because it was the hospital for Jews in mixed marriages, that couldn't be treated in normal hospitals," he reminds me when I tell him she worked there for a time. "We have a collection of a family, he was a pharmacist, and he survived [at the hospital] with his wife and child." All three were "full *Juden*." In other words: among those with two Jewish parents there were a few exceptions. But very few.

Pomerance is very thin and never lost his Canadian "ehs" and "abouts." He is balding; the hair left may once have been a vibrant red, but it has faded into a very, very slight shade of strawberry. He is nearly paler than white, and he is wearing a pale blue shirt, as though he is attempting to blend into the fading bits of paper he works with.

In fact, he continues, there were a hundred sixty-five full *Juden* who survived at the hospital, eight hundred in all who survived in Berlin. Later I will read books on the hospital, and try to talk to those who worked there. Valy worked in the children's ward of the hospital, when there were still children in Berlin. But, slowly, the Jewish kids in the city emigrate or are sent away. *"The children's group was discontinued, and I became superfluous and left,"* Valy writes in April 1940. *"Three*

afternoons a week I now teach health and nutrition issues. . . . In this man-
ner I am able to make some money without taking on work in the after-
noons. During the mornings I go to the hospital where I do not learn a whole
lot, but still something. I lead my life the way I've been doing for the past 2
years: In a spirit of waiting, without much joy or hope. But, my darling,
don't feel sad for me; I want you to know that I have people around me—
women,—you know that only women are left here?!"

Among the survivors, I will find no one who remembers the name
Valerie Scheftel.

Like a handful of other academics, Pomerance had already been to
the archives in Bad Arolsen once, but on a very tightly controlled tour
with no opportunity to explore on his own. "Up until now, it has
served the purpose of what its title is—the International Tracing
Service—in other words, finding out fates," Pomerance says. After the
war, he continues, "descendants were left without really knowing exactly how or where their relatives died. People need a sense of finality,
and that's what the ITS has been offering people—family members—
for decades."

Pomerance mentions that he was shown a book in Arolsen that I
might see there, too; it documents the number of lice on the heads of
individual prisoners. "When you see those documents," he says, "you
think, 'My goodness, there are people counting the number of lice on
inmates' heads.' It's part of the whole, greater picture. It kind of adds
to the incomprehensibility of it all." Even such a small mention in this
type of file was enough to secure for a former prisoner the postwar
indemnity payments. Or it might simply be the only evidence that a
person lived at all.

"It is incredible what still can, all of a sudden, be discovered," he
remarks, musing on the discovery, in 2000, by the Jewish community
of Vienna of a trove of files documenting the wartime history of the
community that had languished, unattended to, in an attic for more
than sixty years: all that yearning, all those efforts to escape, docu-
mented on curling paper, stuffed into filing cabinets, forgotten. Part

of that wealth of information was uploaded to the Web, waiting for those with names to search for. I tell him that at the Documentation Center of Austrian Resistance, I found the Gestapo mug shots for my grandfather's older half brother and his wife—Manele and Chaja Wildmann. It will be years before I realize that the trove of files we spoke of that day included a number that directly affected my family—that gave both reassurance and finality to Manele's story.

But I don't have that information yet.

Instead, what we speak of is this: Nearly seventy years on, many believe that there are few "new" Holocaust discoveries to be found at Arolsen. Revelations, if they can be called that, are more likely to be of the kind I found in my parents' basement, in the words of the victims preserved for seven decades, the pleas for help. There is great interest in the large body of letters, relatively intact, written by Jews trapped in Europe to those outside. They give texture to the destruction, depth to the history, a personal understanding of something so massive, so incomprehensible, it can otherwise seem too fantastic to absorb.

The night before I interview Pomerance, I meet with Dr. Andrea Löw from the Institute of Contemporary History at a trendy little waffle shop filled with purposely mismatched flea market furniture and attractive, hip twenty- and thirtysomethings in the Prenzlauer Berg neighborhood of former East Berlin. She is thirty-four, and she is the first person I tell on this journey that I am pregnant. I blurt it out, perhaps because we are surrounded, crushed in, by baby carriages; perhaps because she is only slightly older than I; and perhaps because, as always when I start on a Holocaust project, I feel very conscious of my own Jewishness. I tell her I am growing a little Jew. I am not sure she finds this amusing.

For Andrea's work, Valy's letters are just as important as any lists or new information she might come across at ITS. She thinks she might be able to include a few in a multivolume collection of wartime documents she is helping to compile—her hope is to use the voices of the persecuted to humanize the stiff bureaucratic decrees that bloodlessly lay out, day after day, the orders to discriminate against and separate Jews from German society. Andrea reads a few of my photocopied letters as we eat our waffles. They are fairly typical of this type of correspondence, she says, looking for visas, affidavits, for exit doors. We see Valy's fear rise from June 1940 when she writes, *"Darling, I have inquired repeatedly when my number will come up. All I get in response is some vague indication of one to two years."* To the desperation of October 1941: *"Even if there were a possibility to do the expensive detour via Cuba, it would be too late because, meanwhile, German citizens between the ages of 18 and 45 are no longer allowed to emigrate. I cannot tell you how desperately unhappy I am about this!!!! What did you try to do, my darling? Oh, but I am afraid that it all will be to no avail. And I need you so badly! I need to be with you so much. My beloved, you can do so much, why can't you take me to you? But I know that it will not be possible."*

But Andrea also prods me to consider how my grandfather handled the demands of dozens of cousins and friends, desperate and angry that he got out and they didn't. It is the first time I discuss this idea of his guilt with someone else. She is sure it would have been awful, and she is also quite certain he was not alone in shouldering this burden, that everyone like him, every single refugee who made it to calmer shores, was engulfed by the burden of having left others behind. We both agree that the weight would have been too much to bear, it was so heavy, it couldn't be processed daily, it had to be let go of—perhaps that spoke to his idea of *herrlich*, the marvelous, the need to make the world brighter in the midst of all that was so very dark.

We talk about the moral ambiguities of the period: What did my grandfather owe these cousins and friends? Why didn't he take Valy with him? She herself never says that he left her, exactly, nor that he purposely didn't take her; I suspect she would not have left her mother

Mein Liebling,

es ist Nacht — 3ʰ ist es — ich kann nicht schlafen, ich muß immer u. immer wieder daran denken, daß Du mir nicht schreibst u. warum das wohl so ist.

Liebling ich muß dich etwas fragen u. Du mußt mir bitte antworten, ja?: Du weißt, daß ich mich 'als völlig dir-gehörig' betrachte, Du weißt, daß ich mich voll u. ganz Dir verbunden u. gebunden fühle! Sag mir aber bitte, willst Du es eigentlich, daß es so ist? Ich weiß das so gar nicht, wenn ich an unsere Gespräche, in den letzten gemeinsamen Tagen u. an

Mit Luftpost nach Nordamerika

Dr. Ch. Hildman
3010 Beverly Road
Brooklyn - New York
U.S.A.

MIT LUFTPOST
PAR AVION
BY AIR MAIL

behind, in Czechoslovakia. And once she decided to come and join him, he was in no position to help—I tell Andrea about the receipts I found in the box of letters, which showed my grandfather was in the process of paying down loans from the National Committee for Resettlement of Foreign Physicians, in amounts so low he couldn't possibly have had any extra cash to send abroad. He was quite poor in Vienna to begin with—and, like many refugees, he arrived with barely enough to start his own life. In turn, she tells me the story of refugees who tried, unsuccessfully, for years, to get parents out of Germany. They never forgave themselves, she says, though they exhausted every means they had at their disposal. It is a reminder that these stories, so often, have no happy ending, are unhappy at their core.

Our waffles finished, we stand to leave. It seems somehow incongruous, our conversation, set against the brilliance of a June day in Berlin, the city in full bloom, so warm and inviting and hip and cool. Everyone is on a bicycle, there are dozens of children running and playing in the streets of Prenzlauer Berg, and I walk to meet a German friend at an outdoor Vietnamese restaurant with massive paper lanterns that sway above our heads as we eat from terra-cotta bowls; we banter as though I haven't spent the day immersed in the past. The juxtaposition is jarring. It couldn't be more different from the postwar newsreel images, and not only because the streets, in many places of this incredible town, bear little resemblance to what was before. The city of Berlin was so incredibly damaged, and so much of what is here is new—though throughout the former East, there remain gaping holes where bombings took out whole buildings. It is a sharp contrast from Vienna, so perfectly preserved or reconstructed it is a museum.

I'm eager to get going. I want to ask people about who Valy might have been and what she might have experienced. But I also want to know what the popular—and academic—expectations are for the Bad Arolsen ITS archives. I want to know, so to speak, whether there is anything in that bag for me.

Before I get to Arolsen, I have two more stops to make. The first is to Wolfgang Benz, one of the preeminent scholars in the field of Holocaust studies and director of the Center for Research on Anti-Semitism, deep in former West Berlin. He was born in 1941, and when he is asked why he is a Holocaust historian, he parries with, "Why do you use a pencil?" He believes ITS is much ballyhoo about nothing—stirred up largely by misinformed Americans. "This was the campaign," he says, running his hands through wildly unkempt white hair. *"The greatest archives of the Holocaust!"* He makes his voice deep and mean. *"And the Germans! They will not show us! Terrible!* It's garbage." He slumps back in his chair. The archives are just "lists," he tells me. The only "scandal" of Arolsen, he says, is when the "eighty-two-year-old Ukrainian man" asks for compensation for being a forced laborer, and the archive staff is not fast enough with information to ensure he receives payment in his lifetime.

"For normal people, ninety-five percent of the material in Arolsen is extremely dull. It's just working papers. No decisions. No secrets of the Nazi state . . . Maybe some journalists picture archives as a dark room and you come in and *here lies Hitler's personal testimony* and here the archivist is like a magician and says, 'Oh! You cannot read this!'" He makes a face. "It is an *archive* with material concerning German camps. Camps of all types."

I switch subjects and ask him again about Valy. Are small stories important? His entire manner shifts. "Yes," he says, immediately. "As historians we can describe what happened. Where it happened. But we cannot exactly describe *why* it happened. The historian cannot describe the suffering of the individuals. Therefore we *need* the memorials. We need the letters, the diaries, the memories of the individuals. As the main part of the picture of what happened."

It will humanize the story, I say.

"Yes. It is the only way for younger people to understand." Benz lectures in schools. The number "six million," he tells me, means nothing to kids. "I say, 'I will tell you the story of my friend Richard.' Richard was a young man from Czechoslovakia. Jewish. When they brought him to Theresienstadt, he was seventeen or eighteen years old, and from Theresienstadt he was sent to Treblinka. He was one of about forty people who escaped from Treblinka. And then I tell young people the story how Richard went with a friend, two inmates from Treblinka, and they hid *in a lake*. When the SS looked for the escapees after the uprising, Richard and Carl were *underwater* in a lake near the camp Treblinka. For six or seven hours."

"How did they breathe?" I ask, horrified. "With a straw?"

"Yes. With a straw. And then they proceeded. And he tells it—he was a very humorous man—they proceeded through Poland a little right, a little left, on to Germany, and in Germany at the end of 1943, they said, 'We are foreign, we are foreign workers from Czechoslovakia, we lost our papers in the last air raid.' And they were [given factory work] and survived."

Benz pauses, collects, goes on. "When I tell the story to young people, I continue here: We were on a walk near Berlin years ago, it was a very hot summer day, we came along a lake. And Richard trembled. He trembled and he had this"—he demonstrates a terrible shaking—"and he says his body is doing this, the body is remembering the situation in Treblinka. . . . He said, 'This always happens when I am walking around the sea.' And the young people? Now they can understand that this is happening for a person . . . remembering *against his will*. . . . That this is not statistics, that this is not politics from a dark time sixty years ago, that this is not touching them personally. Now it is a story of *my friend*.

"And then they are asking, 'Why was he brought to Theresienstadt? Why was he brought to Treblinka?' And I say, 'Because he was a Jew. That's the only criminal fact, since he was a Jew and therefore he was there.'"

Richard was seventeen, eighteen, twenty years old during the war.

Valy was thirty-one when her letters end. Was that old, I want to know?

Benz sighs. "A lady of forty-six or forty-eight coming in this time may be young. And a lady of twenty-seven may be old. They decided in seconds on the fate, and it was not rational, the decision. Thirty-one is very, very young. I can't—I cannot, of course, I cannot really imagine."

I show him a letter. I ask, "Is one woman's story a tragedy but six million too hard to understand?"

He dismisses that. "No. In this, in this great tragedy there are millions of individual tragedies. And, as a historian, I must see both. I cannot reduce the Holocaust to the history of Anne Frank.

"But Arolsen? Again! I say it again and again. Arolsen is not the ordinance of Hitler, *'Now we kill the Jews.'* There are no personal records to declare what happened to any one person. Archives are dusty rooms for historians." He sighs. "What is the importance of an archive?"

The next morning, I board a slick InterCity-Express train bound for Weimar and then take a bus down what was once nicknamed the "Blood Road," to Buchenwald, the concentration camp ten minutes outside the city of Goethe. I am visiting Volkhard Knigge, director of the camp memorial foundation. Knigge is dressed like an art-gallery owner—black jacket, black button-down shirt, black jeans, white hair. He teaches cultural studies and the history of memory in Jena. Knigge rejects Benz's idea that there is nothing to be found at ITS. "There is material from all the camps," he says, as well as DP (displaced persons) camp material and all the postwar trial materials. Before this year, he says, "more than ninety percent of the Buchenwald records were in Bad Arolsen. We could see meters and meters and meters [of documents], but we didn't have the right to look in."

Yet now that he's had a look inside, Knigge cautions that opening ITS doesn't mean rewriting the history of the Holocaust. Rather, "it is a bit like completing a mosaic: you had some stones before; now you have many more, and the picture becomes much more clear." He thinks there is more there for laypeople than Benz believes. "For survivor families, we can reconstruct much more precisely, with much more detail, the biographies of prisoners." That's what I want to know, I say—I want to know if I can discover exactly what happened for Valy during the war.

He nods. Knigge also has an answer to Benz's rhetorical question about the importance of archives. "I think archives are kind of . . . living monuments. They are more important than monuments. A monument is just a monument, a symbol. But an archive is an original, authentic expression of what happened in history. It is, in a way, living history." He is very earnest, despite his generally dry demeanor. "It is something like a bridge to the past." He sees Arolsen as an important pedagogical tool—giving students new and tangible materials to understand people who existed and were extinguished.

I am eager to get there. At my request, ITS has already pulled Valy's files, as well as the files of a few cousins. I will find them on arrival.

———

For most of the hour-long journey from Kassel to Bad Arolsen, I was the only person on the train. It was, for all intents and purposes, a milk train, but since this is Germany, it was souped-up and sleek with a bullet nose. The train conductor and I pass through bucolic villages, miles of farmland, rolling hills, everything short of shepherds in lederhosen. It's painfully gorgeous, lush in its early summer greenery, a beauty that makes the past's horror that much more bewildering.

The night before my journey to Bad Arolsen, after Buchenwald, I stayed in Kassel with my old friend from Vienna, Uli, and his partner, Urte. Uli is a sociologist; Urte, a scholar of feminist literature. Uli likes it very much when I tell him I'm growing a little Jew. He will ask me now, endlessly, how the "little Jew" is doing. The transgressive nature of the description suits him.

Urte—who is as petite as Uli is tall, and has a face filled with freckles framed by a sheet of chin-length coppery brown hair—has family from the agricultural region outside Kassel. During World War II, as with most farming families who sent a man off to the front, the Reich gave Urte's family a forced laborer, a Russian, probably a POW from the Eastern Front, who was forbidden to socialize with the family. Years ago, Urte came across a photo of her grandmother's first husband with the SS symbol on his collar scratched out; he was killed at the front.

We three tell these stories freely, of our grandparents; it is a relief, somehow, to be able to discuss our relationship to the past with no pretense, no artificial idea that it has no impact upon us, and yet, at the same time, no burden that we are in some ways responsible. Uli reads some of Valy's letters. Immediately, he highlights a question I have asked myself again and again reading her words: Is Valy driven by love alone? *"It is so sad that by now our correspondence has come down to an exchange of letters only on certain occasions,"* she writes; it is June 1941. *"It is much, much more than just sad. You don't know how awful this is for me. But, my darling, do not think that I am reproaching you. I know that three years is an awfully long time! So much can happen during that time!"*

Uli believes that she no longer loves my grandfather but that my grandfather simply provided her with her only path out; he was a rope to the other side. I am not sure in her mind there was a distinction: her love for him was intermingled with her need to leave, her need—really, her desperation—to leave seemed to hinge entirely on her love for my grandfather and whether that love was returned. She seems, at times, to believe that if their love is sufficiently strong, it will allow her to weather the indignities and the deprivations; at the very least it will find her a visa and a passage out of Germany. *"A long, long time ago you wrote to me from Vienna, when I was supposed to go to Prague, that one should not be so small-minded to sacrifice the present to the phantom of the future. You wrote these words in a completely different context at the time. But you were so right then! And maybe that's your thinking right now as well. And maybe you are right in not wanting to sacrifice your present either to the past or to the future. It is, however, so terribly sad for me because I live almost without a present, and I can live only for the past and for the future! . . . The immediate reason for today's letter, however, is our emigration."*

———

As the train pulls into the station, I see that the outskirts of Bad Arolsen are filled with gingerbread houses, low-slung neat cottages with sharp sloping red roofs and flower boxes overflowing with the fecundity of early summer. German flags are hung everywhere—on cars, in windows, in the street. The UEFA European Championship is in midswing and Germany is doing well. Some nights into my stay, I run into Kathrin Flor, the enormously tall ITS communications director. She is wearing two-inch-long fake eyelashes, in the colors of the German flag.

Bad Arolsen is strangely dreamy. The center of the village is baroque, plucked out of a fairy tale—a Prince (Wittekind of Waldeck and Pyrmont) rules over the town; he resides in a wedding cake of a country palace, Schloss Arolsen, a miniature Versailles built in the early eighteenth century, whose land abuts the hotel I'm staying in. His godfather was Heinrich Himmler, the Gestapo overseer; his biological father was given a life sentence at the Buchenwald war crime trials for his role there as an SS officer. The sentence was eventually reduced to twenty years, and then reduced further still for health reasons. In the end, war criminal or not, he died a free man.

Down the lane and across the street are a row of whitewashed late-nineteenth- and early-twentieth-century buildings. The grounds in front of each building are neatly manicured; a flag from the International Committee of the Red Cross flies above a low-slung office building, one of the newer structures. Villagers loaded down with groceries pedal along a paved bicycle lane. The setting is so rosy, so collegiate-bucolic, it could be a university campus in New England.

*Piles and piles of paper: searching for survivors at the
International Tracing Service in Bad Arolsen, Germany.*

Instead, some of these well-kept buildings are former SS barracks
filled with clues to the fates of 17.5 million victims of the Nazis.

At my hotel I am given a very comfortable duplex room with a
kitchenette; there is also a pool. In the morning I do yoga, at night I
pretend to swim laps. Mostly I stand at the shallow end and chat with
Jean-Marc. My pregnancy is, for the most part, still a secret, though
now, in a bathing suit, I see the swell of my belly and I feel self-
conscious.

It is a strange juxtaposition, the lush fecundity of the setting and
my own body, with my search. I am here to see if Valy's medical work
counted as slave labor or if she went on, after her letters to my grandfather stop, to work in a factory—in either case, ITS might have her
work files. I am here to see if somewhere in these pretty streets, in one
of these lovely buildings that house Arolsen's meticulous yet enormous
holdings, Valy's story will unfold before me and the gaps in my knowledge, left by the abrupt ending of her letter-writing campaign, will be
filled in by the hard facts of her Gestapo files and her relationship to
the Nazi state. More than that I do not know what to expect, or to
hope for.

Here is what it feels like upon entering the archives at Bad Arolsen: like a Steven Spielberg movie about an American lawyer of the 1950s, desperately searching for information on an escaped Nazi but with no computers, no modern technology, nothing but boxes and paper. It's like that scene at the end of the first Indiana Jones movie with the Ark of the Covenant tucked away in a warehouse. There might be treasures here, amid a sea of seventy-year-old cardboard, but who would know?

To be fair, the staff at ITS were busily scanning documents when I came to town. By summer's end, they would digitize 6.7 million documents on forced labor in the Third Reich. Soon, nearly all of it will be pixelated. But this was not the case when I arrived. Instead, the scholars I was with had the task of approaching the material and asking each box, each guardian of these massive rooms of paper what these holdings might reveal, and how the materials should be understood and integrated into greater Holocaust research.

The areas of ITS were divided into sections labeled vaguely "General Documents," "Concentration Camps," "Displaced Persons," "Tracing and Documentation," "Forced Labor." In the general documents alone—a loose assemblage of items that were deemed worthy of saving, but unclear on their immediate category—there were 1,786 cardboard boxes filled with, among other things, documents on Heinrich Himmler's Lebensborn experiment (the quest to populate Europe with Aryan children, using wombs from Germany to Norway and kidnapping children with Aryan features from Eastern Europe for adoption in the Reich), medical experiments, persecution outside Germany, maps, court cases, letters between members of the SS, the institutional history of ITS, mass graves, and exhumations. There are more than sixteen miles of files, with faded, neatly typewritten labels. Book after book of death lists, tied up with string. Typed documents drily, methodically explaining how, exactly, to turn a normal van into a murderous gas van—an early and, ultimately, unwieldy method of mass killing.

An entire maze of basement rooms is devoted to thousands of *Arbeitsbücher*—little green books that document each forced laborer's time. The faint smell of paper decay and dust hangs everywhere. In the hallways, hand-drawn maps of the Nazi advance and concentration camp system are framed and hung as art.

On my first full day in town, I join the scholars on a field trip to the Bergen-Belsen concentration camp, a three-hour bus ride through Germany's glorious western countryside, past villages so tranquil and storybook-like, it was easy to be boggled by what they had been witness to. It is almost grotesquely beautiful—all cows and fields of wheat and rye and oats and grass. The former camp is now home to a modern museum cast from concrete, glass, and steel; it is smooth-walled and suspended, as if floating, as the ground beneath is hallowed, and filled with corpses. The architects, KSP Jürgen Engel Architekten, won a prize for the design, which is purposely, almost completely, absent of all color. The museum soberly, and carefully, details the fate of prisoners and tells the stories buried in the fields that surround it: mass graves that now look like nothing more than empty, grassy knolls which can be strolled for hours on end. There is a gravestone marking the loss of Anne and Margot Frank, who died there, but it is placed arbitrarily. No one knows, really, where the girls were buried; and the camp barracks were, for the most part, burned to the ground at the end of the war to stymie the virulent typhus epidemic that killed the sisters and continued to claim victims long after their jailers had fled. Some fourteen thousand inmates died after liberation by the British. Many of those souls who had survived so long only to die in the transition to freedom were Jews.

It is Bergen-Belsen that shaped the world's collective mental images of the horror that was the Nazi concentration camps. It was from here that American moviegoing audiences saw the horrific piles of naked, lifeless bodies pushed by bulldozers, as well as the images of the opening of the camp by the British, and the emaciated walking dead they encountered, the skeletal remains of humans whose eyes blinked enormously from their skulls.

On the drive, Jean-Marc tells me that Marlene Dietrich's sister had lived in the town of Bergen. When the actress toured Germany after the war, she came upon her sister, who revealed that she had run a movie theater for the SS guards of the camp; she maintained no interest in distancing herself from her Nazi past. Marlene, disgusted, eventually denied the sister existed. Some said the two never spoke to each other again.

When we arrive at Bergen-Belsen, hordes of German soldiers mill about the entrance. One of the scholars sees me gaping and explains that we are near one of the largest military training grounds in Europe and they are there for training—in sensitivity? In history? Perhaps both. It is stupidly unnerving to see them there; the soldiers are a part of a different story now, though not disconnected from this history. Yet toggling back and forth between the past and present makes my vision blurry. Fatigues and army boots feel disconcerting here.

Bergen-Belsen is, otherwise, strangely sanitized. It is beautiful, all that concrete so favored by architects and interior designers lately, with miles of texts and horrific videos, all arranged and presented in a way that feels as smooth as the walls, not easy—the subject matter is too heavy for easy—but not hard either. You can avoid the worst films if you're weak of stomach; they are shown in mini-theaters hung with heavy velvet curtains. Survivors speak out from television screens, but they are many years past the point of their experience, and their testimonies are softly lit, their voices audible only once you pick up headphones.

It is far more modern than what we will see back in Bad Arolsen. Somehow the ITS archives, their condition, their presentation, pulls us all backward in time, to a pre-digital era, draws back the curtain, to some degree, on the breakdown in communication between cities and countries—let alone families—that delayed survivors of the Nazi era from finding one another to begin with. ITS, when I see it first, is a hodgepodge of disconnected papers, each recording at length the difficulty the Allies had, the Red Cross had, the refugee organizations had, in tracking down survivors, in reuniting families, in finding places for the displaced to go. In Bad Arolsen, wartime confusion still feels palpable, the number of those affected is so immense, and the inability to search for anything—other than by the sheer legwork and real-time reading that marked research in the postwar era—makes all work cumbersome and paced in a manner completely contrary to the way we live now. "We need a very detailed inventory," Jean-Marc says of these messy archives. "For the moment we don't even know exactly what's new."

In my fantasy version of discovery, Valy's file at Arolsen is filled with everything from handwritten notes (hers, her mother's, friends', lovers') to details of her work assignments, to her path after deportation, to—and this was, in retrospect, the most fantastical—clues as to whether she survived. Perhaps, I think, as I tour the grounds, there is an *Arbeitsbuch* with her name on it, a detailing of the work she did in the Jewish Hospital, a record of the old-age home she wrote from in 1941. Perhaps she had to fill out a request to emigrate, and this, I hope, will be here as well.

Yet, as Wolfgang Benz had warned me might be the case, none of that is here. There is, however, a small stack of papers including a copy of her name on a deportation list and a last-known address typed neatly at the top of an official-looking Red Cross missing persons report.

But, no. There is more than that. Linked to her file is a similarly thin folder with information on a much younger man named Hans Fabisch, born April 29, 1921, in Breslau. Below his name, on his card file, I see Valerie, *geborene* (née) Scheftel. *Ehefrau.* She is listed as his wife.

At some point after her letters to my grandfather had stopped, sometime, it seemed, around the same time my grandfather met my grandmother, Valy not only met another man—she *married* him. Hans Fabisch. I say the name aloud, the first syllables of both names so round and patrician and Germanic, though I note he was—obviously— also a Jew. How did it happen that a thirty-one-year-old intellectual married a twenty-one-year-old boy from Breslau? Did she love him? Was this a happy ending? Was it a marriage of convenience? Was this a means of survival? Here I had imagined Valy pining away, desperate, despairing, when war cuts off mail between Germany and the United States. I had imagined her shrinking away without the lifeline my grandfather's hope gave her, desperately in love, and desperately angry, filled with recriminations, and waffling endlessly between those—I realize now—overly romantic sentiments. Was she instead curled up in bed next to a man a decade younger than my grandfather? It is strangely comforting, this thought, the idea that perhaps Valy finally understood there was little my grandfather could do for her from afar, that to deny herself human contact was a punishment she needn't inflict upon herself, especially in a time of great punishment. Here was a glimmer of hope, or of resistance. To marry so late—clearly sometime in 1942, as my final letter closes out 1941, possibly as late as 1943—was, perhaps, a sign she believed in the future, or, at the very least, was no longer exclusively living in the past, no longer mooning over Vienna, but trying to find a path forward, a way of surviving, if only mentally, if only emotionally. The file is simultaneously enormously exciting and incredibly disappointing—I can merely guess at these things. I can't know how they met. I can't understand her motivations. I don't know if she was in love, if this was impetuous, or exciting, or wonderful. Or was this merely a symptom of the persecution? Instead of finding answers, now I have only more questions.

Most of the scholars on this trip keep me at arm's length. They distrust journalists, I am told; they think we will be too superficial in our analysis, or think we will scoop their scholarship, or think we will be too blithe in the way we cover this material—or all of the above. They will not be convinced otherwise. Most refuse to be on the record with me, or speak much with me at all.

But one of the other USHMM-sponsored scholars doesn't mind me; he is a jocular Aussie academic (by way of Holland and Germany) named Konrad Kwiet. I tell him about my grandfather and Valy, and of my discomfort with what seems to be my grandfather's inability to help her. "I think one should not impose any moral verdicts on behavior," he cautions. Konrad has a bald pate, a fringe of nearly fully gray hair, and a bit of a Falstaffian air. He is considered the foremost scholar on the Holocaust in Australia; it is a position of some renown: half of the country's Jewish population descends from survivors, people who, mostly, tried to leave fetid Europe for the United States or Palestine and were thwarted. Konrad Kwiet was himself war flotsam. During the war, his Christian father and Jewish mother would have divorced but stayed together to protect her. Such *Mischehen*, as mixed marriages were called, were life rafts, preserving, often, the non-Aryan partner. After the war his parents, finally, broke up. But the good deed was done. All survived and Konrad, eventually, landed on the other side of the world.

"There are documents here of utmost significance, but it depends on the questions you ask the document," Kwiet tells me. We are sitting in a mediocre café across from the archives; I am perpetually hungry reading about starvation. "It's not a Holy Grail," he says, "but it will change the direction of research. It's not revolutionary—it's not Hitler's order to kill the Jews." Again that phrase! "But it will become a place of institutionalized memory."

———

I am curious if anyone from my family has ever searched for anyone here. It is one of the oddities of ITS that I might actually know that. A former NATO driving school houses an annex where the requests from families—called "Tracing and Documentation" files—are stored; it is a few miles outside town. The building has the feel of an abandoned elementary school: banging metal doors, wide stairwells, dusty halls. Everything is on paper. Piles and piles of paper. Stack after stack of desperation. The pages aren't protected, merely preserved in the sense of not thrown away—set aside, open to the air. Dust motes hang in the air; each breath I draw brings with it the sweet smell of aging paper. I wander, overwhelmed, around the aisles, each delineated by metal shelves of the sort people use in basements, or rec rooms. The earliest files are yellow and crumbling, filled with tracing paper sheets in triplicate, missives sent among the American, French, and British zones after the war. Visitors can touch what they want. Loose reams of paper are piled in chronological order. Room after room with a thousand files per shelf. About three million requests for information, sixty-two years of desperate pleas to find family members; all are lost, endless suffering on paper. "Unsolved," they are stamped with a special rubber stamp created just for this; or "Auschwitz, no further information." I get lost for a time reading the story of a boy named Louis Clerc, whose mother, left all alone, her husband dead, searched in vain for her son for years. He had been seen, the file said, after the war, on the road to Ulm, he had been in the hospital, he had been released, his trail had run cold. His mother wrote every Allied country, begging for information. The file is in three languages. There is no end to his story. It simply trails off.

"When I am falling victim to routine," Udo Jost, for many years Arolsen's chief archivist, tells me, "I take out folders to read, and then I am angry again. I need this furiousness to be committed." He takes a drag on his cigarette. One year, the federal archive of Germany requested that Bad Arolsen begin microfilming and then destroying the original records. Jost lost his temper. "I say no! These are victims! They lost their names! They were given numbers! And in a few years, there will be no survivors, and then the victims will only be numbers!"

I first met Jost on a tour of the archives; he is a bearded, portly, unkempt man with a gentle, genial manner. We began that first day in an anteroom of the archives. He gestures behind him toward a plate-glass window protecting a sea of library-card files. "What you see here is the main key to the International Tracing Service," he says, speaking in German and pausing for translation, though he speaks English nearly fluently. "This is the Central Names Index—CNI—which covers three rooms and includes fifty million references for seventeen-point-five million victims."

Jost flips open an encyclopedia-heavy tome that explains an arcane alphabetic-phonetic formula developed in 1945 for researching Nazi victims' names: in World War II prison camps, names changed from Cyrillic spellings to Germanic, Germanic to Francophone, Francophone to Polish, depending on who wrote down a prisoner's details upon arrival in a work, concentration, or annihilation camp. In practical terms, that means there were 848 ways to spell the name Abramowitz, 156 versions of Schwartz. There are not nearly so many options for Scheftel, but the point is well understood. "ITS was not structured like an archive," Jost continues. "The task was searching for victims and clarifying their fate. That's why the documents could not be structured according to geographic or national criteria. Families searching for relatives generally did not know to which place their loved one had been deported."

"There is so much that it is difficult to get a handle on where to begin," explains Paul Shapiro, of the Holocaust Museum—arguably the person who took the archives' closing most personally, who worked hardest, and who might take the most credit for its opening.

"It is very difficult to overcome sixty years during which the material was never seen as a resource for understanding or teaching, it was only seen as a resource from which one could find a name." He went on: "The most common description of the documentation at ITS that was used for fifty years was they are 'lists of victims'—lists of prisoners, lists of names. But in the first place, it is more diverse material than that. And second, a list of names takes on a different meaning when it is observed through the eyes of a researcher or someone who knows the history, or through the eyes of someone who wants to understand the dynamic among populations, or what brought survival rather than death. Here you can sample different kinds of people as they made their way through—or failed to survive—the Nazi system. . . . The first challenge is having people understand that there is a broader significance to this material, and the material has to be mobilized and integrated into the way we understand the Holocaust."

With Shapiro's words in mind, I continue to comb the archives, hoping there is something more for me. I try different routes through the material, and one morning I find cousins in the "Displaced Persons" files—they list my immediate family as contacts in the United States when they try to emigrate: Henryka and Benzion Feldschuh, denied access to Palestine and the United States, request to emigrate to Sydney, Australia. Their exit interview with DP officials details their war years, from time in the Lodz ghetto through camp after camp, a bizarro résumé required for refugee status listed by date: 1936–1940, Lodz; 1940–1944, Lodz ghetto; 1944, Auschwitz; 1944, Bergen-Belsen. Similarly, jobs are listed—"teacher" gives way to "farmer" at a work camp—and the reason for termination is "liberation." In their interview, they expressed a desire to *never return* to Poland (reason? "anti-Semitism") or stay in Germany even if it meant settling three quarters of the way around the world.

Konrad Kwiet connects me to a genealogist in Sydney, who, I discovered, not only knew my cousins personally but had worked alongside Henryka in the 1960s. He tells me both died many years ago—news that I shouldn't be shocked by, but which nevertheless depresses me immensely. I am so terribly late to be contacting these people; I had had such an—I know—unreasonable hope that one of them would be alive, that one of them could tell me what my far-flung family looked like, that one of them could tell me how the family members contacted one another before the war, how they related to one another before the apocalypse and how they communicated after. Instead, the genealogist puts me in touch with their son, Michael, who is somewhere near my father's age and thus too young to have known those for whom I search.

"A source," Kwiet tells me, echoing the Jewish Museum's Aubrey Pomerance, as I despair over the sketchy paperwork I have been given on Valy, "is only important by what you ask of it." I go back to the desk that ITS gave me for my stay and look again at the files prepared for me upon my arrival. The best clue, the most dramatic and tantalizing lead, I finally see, is in the file connected to Valy's. Hans Fabisch and Valy Scheftel share the same Tracing and Documentation file number—557 584. Their files also share a date: a request for information on Valy—and Hans—was first made in 1956. The query did not come from my grandfather.

Someone else had come looking for Valy, I realize with a shock, and long before me. My grandiose idea of rescuing Valy's story from obscurity was trumped two decades before my birth. A search for her had begun not long after the war, a desire to know her fate—and that of Hans—had been worried over, considered, *imagined,* more than a half century before I ever heard her name. The card stapled to the top of Hans's file offers more: A woman, Ilse Charlotte Mayer, née Fabisch, had made the inquiry. The notation is very short, very dry: "Nationality: Stateless. Relationship: sister." She had a London address.

I show this to Konrad Kwiet. He explains that the files likely represented the beginning of a restitution case. Germany paid monies to descendants and families of victims and survivors if the claimant could establish that the relative was, in actuality, lost or had survived a ghetto or camp or forced-labor factory—or had not survived at all. He points to a line: "Valy was a Jewess. But they don't have any [death] certificate." He went on: "She left Berlin on the twenty-ninth of January, 1943, on the 'twenty-seventh Ost-transport.' It does not say here where she ended up. But 'Ost-transport' equals Auschwitz."

January 1943 was a terrible time. As Wolfgang Benz had explained to me, back in Berlin, the killing machinery was fully up and running; the Final Solution had been agreed upon—"liquidation" had been announced—a full year before. Its effects were well under way; no longer were Jews being resettled; gas chambers efficiently extinguished the lives of men, women, children, day after day; a *system* was in place; there was nothing haphazard about it, there were none of the vagaries of bullets still being used in the east, there was none of the uncertainty of other means of death. Of the transports arriving, each day, from the west and elsewhere, some seventy percent of the people on each train were chosen for immediate death. It had been a full year since the SS had officially decided to liquidate the Jews. Rare was it, at that point, to be chosen for work.

It was also a terribly, horribly cold month, which hindered hiding in Berlin itself, if one was called for deportations; the cold further diminished the reserves of those who had already been diminished after months of malnourishment and deprivation. Had Valy tried to go into hiding? Nothing in Bad Arolsen could tell me. All I knew was that on January 29 she was headed east.

But before I even got to the circumstances of Valy's deportation, I realized that if Ilse Mayer was searching for Valy, it meant that Hans's family knew they had married. In other words: correspondence had been received from Hans and Valy, well after the last letters she had sent my grandfather. And, as Kwiet had explained, Ilse Mayer had possibly filed restitution claims on behalf of her brother and Valy. Would those files, those restitution claims, tell me what had happened to them both? Would those files have more information about what the two of them had done in Germany, what they'd been forced to do, and how much of their lives they had been able to preserve in the time before they were sent to the camps?

As I read and reread Valy's letters, I keep thinking back to Volkhard Knigge's comment that the ITS archives are a kind of living memorial, a breathing, endless loop of representation, a witness of the individuals lost, forgotten, or displaced by the war. And of their relatives who wrote for decades—and, like me, are still writing.

Late at night, exhausted from pregnancy and walking the Bad Arolsen campus, I ask Jean-Marc to also read Valy's letters. He finds them incredibly depressing, which is striking, as, of course, this is the work he does all the time. He reminds me that Valy's luck was against her at the outset if she had waited to try to get out until after Kristallnacht; the numbers clamoring for entrance to the United States had far outpaced what the country was willing to accept.

I am keenly aware that even if I am to find Valy, she will be well into her nineties. I am late. Very late. One night I announce to Jean-Marc that I will continue to look for her—but also, I will look for those who knew her. I wonder if, if no one else, perhaps Ilse Mayer might just still be alive. He thinks this is a terrible, and terribly unlikely, idea. A search for ninety-year-olds, he says, will disappoint me. Whom will I still find, after all? If I had started this search a decade ago there might have been witnesses, but now? And if I do find anyone—will they have hardened in their memories? Will they share any more than they have already shared? Better, he says, to retrace her footsteps—to find where she'd lived and try to see if there are still traces of her there, if there is something that can tie her back to each location, even as she was scrubbed from the history. You must, he says, start by going back to Troppau, the Czech town where she was born.

Four

WHO SHE WAS

This much I know: On the fourth of November, 1911, Valy was born in what was then called Troppau, a Moravian Sudetenland town so far east that, these days, it practically brushes up against what is now the Czech–Polish border. By the time she was thirty, the town had flown three national flags: but at her birth, Troppau was part of the Austrian empire; it became Czech after World War I— "Sudetenland" being the German appellation for these slices of land, largely German ethnic and German-speaking, that were among the first parcels of territory Hitler would claim for the Reich; locals call it "Czech Silesia." (Historians sometimes refer to the "Czech lands"— Bohemia, Moravia, Silesia.) In any case, the geography is unnecessarily confusing because Valy came into this world at a moment of political and geographic upheaval. Today Troppau is known as Opava, and it is uncontroversially Czech. The joke among Jews in the interwar period, when the villages of their childhoods seemed to change nationalities every few years, was that they didn't emigrate, their towns did.

Valy's birth came two weeks after what would be the last major Hapsburg wedding—Princess Zita of Bourbon-Parma and Karl I, whose lush ceremony, at the Renaissance-era Schwarzau Castle, was

actually *filmed* for newsreels. Pretty, teenage Zita is coquettish in a lace column, the new slim-line dress that for the first time allowed women to drop the bustle, step out of the unnatural corseted styles of their mothers, and really move; she looks happy and innocent and fresh.

Zita and Karl got immediately to work having children—one, nearly, for every year of their marriage—and enjoying their relatively minor royal roles, until the 1914 assassination of Archduke Franz Ferdinand in Sarajevo bumped Karl up to heir presumptive behind the aging Franz Joseph I. Two years later, upon the emperor's death, suddenly Karl and Zita were emperor and empress. It wouldn't last long. Exiled in 1919, as eight-year-old Valy frolicked in Troppau's main square, Karl and Zita ran from rapidly dissolving Austria-Hungary to Switzerland (by train; Stefan Zweig described the weeping masses at their processionals) and then, forced to flee again, to the Portuguese island of Madeira. Dragging an entourage of staff for her seven children, and heavily pregnant, Zita watched her husband die of pneumonia (he had a bad heart) and then took the entire clan to Spain, on to Belgium, and eventually to Quebec, where they lived out the war years before returning to Europe. Zita, who lived well into her nineties, never wore a color other than black after she was widowed at age twenty-nine. Her eldest son, Otto, lived until 2011—long enough to be able to publicly declare, on the seventieth anniversary of the Anschluss, that the Austrians were the first victims of Hitler.

When Valy was born, Troppau was still Hapsburg-controlled; the town was Austrian, and Zita and Karl weren't yet in power.

Her mother, Toni, I will eventually learn, was twenty-six; Valy was her first and only child. The marriage wasn't happy: her father, Franz, I will discover in the town's archives, was gone before Valy was even a year old (Valy doesn't acknowledge that he's even alive in her school forms), and Toni set to work, running a shoe store in the center of town. She raised her daughter alone, and the two were entwined in the way mothers and daughters can be when there is no sibling, no father, and no relatives nearby. Valy's letters worry about her mother, endlessly, and about her grandparents, her uncles and aunts—but they make no mention of a father at all. It's not clear she ever heard from him again.

But before the worry: what a highlight it would have been, for Toni, who sent her only child to the most important school in the world, after all that work. Her single motherhood paid off, her daughter achieving all she'd hoped for her; more.

After all, Troppau was closer to Vienna than Prague, both geographically and culturally. Although, as the guns of World War I fell silent, the flag raised above the town was Czech, no one in Troppau seemed to acknowledge the switch: Valy, and pretty much everyone else in the city, spoke, dreamt, and wrote in German; it was only in the villages surrounding this little city that Czech was spoken.

And with or without the Hapsburgs, life was steadily improving, for Jews at least. With the emancipation of the Jews of the empire in 1867, centuries-long legal barriers crumbled; the Czech lands allowed the Jews out of the ghettos, and suddenly professions that had been barred—and areas to live that had been forbidden—opened to the Jewish community. In 1905, a gorgeous domed Moorish revival–style synagogue was inaugurated in the heart of town. It was an arrival announcement, made with a building so pretty that local postcards used it to promote the city. *"Hugs from Troppau!"* the cards read cheerily. Toni and Valy lived upstairs in one of the buildings on the grand main square, facing the opera house.

Toni herself wasn't a Troppau native; she was born in Borszczow, in 1885, which is now in Ukraine but had once been Polish, and at her birth was Austrian (what wasn't then?). More than a quarter of her birthplace was Jewish at the time. Borszczow—now called Borschiv— was one of those towns decimated by German occupation after 1941. Jews were murdered in batches of several hundred, or sent to the concentration camp Belzec; only a handful would survive; none would return to live in the town after the war. But all that was decades after Toni left.

Troppau was country, but it was cosmopolitan—it was the seat of the regional Silesian government, with a small representative parliament, and a strong bourgeois core of merchants and a sort of rural high society. It was—it still is—lovely. There is a meandering park that winds its way around the center of the old inner city, with a pagoda up on a hill that once boasted musicians each Sunday, and plenty of flowers and trees, perfect for walks for women in their *grands chapeaux* and their dresses, modeled like Zita's at her wedding, slim and long, with a small train. The buildings are Beaux-Arts and eclectic, grand on a small scale—an Epcot Center version of Vienna, with wide-open piazzas.

As if to cement its status as a worldly city, and its link to Vienna, there was also the theater and opera house, built in 1805 in the model favored by Emanuel Schikaneder (librettist for *The Magic Flute* and founder of Vienna's lavish Theater an der Wien) and renovated, after a fire, just before Valy's birth, in the style of Louis XIV by Viennese theater artist Ferdinand Maser. It is as plush and as ornate as any opera house of Europe, decorated with gold leaf and red velvet and carved-marble mythological figures. Briefly, after the war, the Communists encased the opera house in a concrete block, temporarily obscuring the ornate exterior that so reminded them of the dominating Germans. By the time I saw the opera house, it had been turned back in time; the grudge against capitalism had subsided, its original majesty restored. The night I sneaked in, there was a premiere. Everyone else was in black-tie finery; I was in jeans and carrying a backpack. The performance was *Nabucco*, which seemed oddly appropriate— Verdi's interpretation of the expulsion of Babylonian Jews from Jerusalem. An incongruously nice usher allowed me to stand in the back of the uppermost tier. She spoke to me in broken German, knowing no English, and me no Czech. "Only stand," she said, awkwardly, "no sit." So I did, closing my eyes, listening to Abigaille's aria, and feeling, for a moment, I could picture Valy and my grandfather there, across the street from her apartment, caught up in the music they had adored, and I started to well up with tears despite myself.

———

It is also, perhaps, hormones that make my emotions rise so quickly to the surface. The faintly fluish feeling of the beginning of pregnancy will infuse my entire Czech experience, which is made even more peculiar by my choice of guide, a young Czech from Krnov, one of the industrial towns nearby. His name is Pavel, and on paper he is perfect: he is obsessed with the Jewish history of his region, he is a registered tour guide in Prague, he is in his thirties. And he is thrilled to help me—a Jew! with a genuine connection to the region! But, over the course of five days, we spar over our generation's role in this history, to whom this history belongs, who has more at stake in what I find.

I come looking for Valy, but instead, I find a population of young Czechs who are either grappling with the history—some with a better grasp than others—or who have turned their backs on it completely, if they ever considered it at all.

Krnov is one of the few towns in Czech Silesia that still has an original synagogue—it was saved, Pavel tells me, by an entrepreneurial mayor who promised the Germans he would destroy the building on Kristallnacht, but instead burned down a funeral hall alongside the cemetery. He later used the synagogue as a market, so perhaps his salvation was for his own economic gain, but no matter: it preserved the shell. Because it is Pavel's town, and because the synagogue, or at least its frame, still stands, he convinces me that sleeping in Krnov is the right choice, rather than Troppau. We will travel the area from here, he tells me, by e-mails and dropped Skype calls, and so I, not really understanding the distances, nor how I will get around in this region, agree.

At one time, these towns were bustling with industry—it was once known as the "Silesian Manchester," with dozens of factories for textiles (Krnov) and sugar beets (Troppau) and plenty of work, and plenty of money. Later, in Prague, a British historian will tell me that the "sugar beet barons" were Jews, mostly, but this I don't know when I'm in the area. I just see those plants, still belching smoke. And I'll see the former textile factories, a booming industry from the nineteenth century through the middle of the twentieth—most of which are now shuttered, a product of post-Communism, or, as Pavel says each time we pass a boarded-up factory, "There's your capitalism at work." They are closed partly because of globalization, and they are closed partly because they were terribly polluting and unsafe. Strangely, the region is akin to the now-defunct textile-mill towns near my grandparents' home in Massachusetts. The similarity extends further: the countryside, too, is all rolling green hills, low and inviting, not unlike the Berkshires or southern Vermont. Work here is scarce now. There is a large factory run by Teva, the Israeli pharmaceutical giant, but unemployment in the area is at least twice that of the rest of the country, and has been since the end of the 1980s. Krnov is particularly bad. Pavel's mother is a pediatrician in town and there are fewer and fewer children to see—locals either aren't having them, or they're moving away.

The night we arrive in town it is terribly late, rainy and freezing. Pavel had insisted we spend the day in Třebíč, a town about three hours from Krnov, in the shadow of a nuclear power plant, reachable by three local Communist-era trains, and about two and a half hours from Prague. It is one of the most well-preserved Jewish ghettos in the world, Pavel tells me proudly—a UNESCO heritage site. Mostly it feels like an open-air museum to the dead. At the one hotel, the front-desk clerk eagerly explains, "It used to be Jews who lived here, and, then, normal people." The synagogue, lovingly restored, with gorgeous frescoes detailing prayers from the daily service, serves no one. There is a small house, kitted out for a Jewish mercantile family (antique cash register, dry goods) who never returns, circa 1930: a hardened challah on the table, hamantaschen on the counter, matzah in the pantry; a menorah in the bedroom. It is Colonial Williamsburg for Jews. The tiny homes, in these crooked streets, are now filled with artists who hawk tiny ceramic golem and take pride in the history. But there aren't any Jews. "You need to see this," Pavel had assured me, in Prague, "these are your *roots*. This is what your family was *from*."

What he meant was the shtetl, but really, even though there's truth to that, no one in my family would ever have admitted to—or celebrated—a time before Vienna, and if they did, it wasn't here, it wasn't Czech, it was deeper into the past; it was Galicia. So many of the Jews of Vienna—and so many of my grandfather's friends—were, by origin, what the German Jews called *Ostjuden*—Eastern Jews from the shtetls scattered across what is now Ukraine and Romania and Poland, small-town Jews whose manner of dress, work, and way of life seemed backward to the big-city *Yekken*, or German Jews.

The day prior, we had spent ten hours together, my first day in Prague, running from place to place—from the fortified, tiny Jewish archives (like nearly everywhere in Europe that caters to Jews, to enter one has to pass through a series of hermetically sealed rooms, show a passport, submit to a bomb-detecting wand), on to the Jewish community center, where I listened, ineffectually, to a group of frail former resistance fighters chat in Czech, and then a lecture, from Pavel, to a group of former hidden children also in Czech, about a Jewish newsletter he edits, and then struggled still further as a woman named Judita Matyášová gave a talk about a forgotten Kindertransport of a hundred fifty Czech teens to Denmark in 1939. Judita told the crowd she had spent the last two years trying to track down these "kids" and document their story, before they are gone. To me she wondered about American funders: Where were they? How to find them? She was upset.

The day had been frustrating—I'd felt the keen stress of a short research trip and lost time. There was no one, among these aging Czechs, from Troppau. And therefore, unsurprisingly, no one had ever heard the name "Valerie Scheftel." But then a woman, she called herself Mária Engelová, a formerly "hidden child" who spoke English, shyly approached me, after Pavel explained to the group my project, and asked me if I had been to Bad Arolsen. "That's where this search began," I tell her. With that she explained that she had spent years trying to get into the International Tracing Service. I asked what she was looking for. "I don't know," she said then, earnestly, with a strange half smile on her pillowy, moon-shaped face, "if I am I." She was a large woman, wearing a wool, midnight-blue pea-coat and a man's paper boy's–style cap pulled low over short gray hair.

I don't understand, I said. And she explained: She was born in 1943, hidden as an infant. And then everyone else was murdered. Everyone. Her parents. Her sister. Uncles. Aunts. Grandparents. After the war, the only two surviving relatives of this once-proud family—an uncle, a grandmother—stumbled back to their hometown and found each other. A local farmer, soon after, asked her uncle—*Didn't you have a brother? With two girls?* He told the uncle the baby, he believed, was on a nearby farm. "I was found," she continued, "in 1946." The family who hid her didn't want to give her up. But, eventually, she was brought to live with this uncle and this grandmother. Yet the grandmother, perhaps, never quite trusted that this little girl was the lost baby tucked away. When she was bad, or did something deserving, in the grandmother's eyes, the elderly woman would murmur: "I don't know . . . Are you, you? I think you are not you." It was a seed of distrust, a fundamental undoing of the structure of her own identity that the girl—turned woman before me (she was a nuclear physicist, she mentioned casually, in addition to a searcher of her own past)—had internalized, swallowed whole. When I asked what she knew of the parents, the nuclear family, she had had only for moments before they were sent away, she faintly shouted, "I was a small child! I don't remember anything! I don't know!"

And so, after Communism, she crisscrossed the globe, from Jerusalem to Brazil, looking for anyone who might have a memory, a photo, a link that would unpack for her her own identity. "You find one document after another, you collect—like an analyst!" She became animated. "When you are looking for information on only one person, is it not so difficult! But to look for a whole family?" She made a face that read: *impossible.* "I didn't know who was my grandfather! I didn't know anything about my mother!" A relative in Brasília gave her a photograph of her and her lost sister. She has no others. Once, she tells me, as a much younger woman, in the years when she was a university student, she was on a tram in Prague, holding on to the standing strap above her head, and a man seated below her asked her, suddenly, if she might, by chance, be related to a woman he remembered from before the war. And then, "He named my mother's name. Maiden name, not married name. I met him one time—we went to a coffeehouse and we spent about two hours speaking together and we arranged to meet again. But he didn't show up."

It was a living nightmare, her story; a true-life *Twilight Zone.* The search I was on at least had the players in place, at least I knew for whom I was looking. I thought of how my own identity was shaped by knowing the experience of my grandfather, my parents, and how this search was about finding more pieces to the mosaic to reveal the bigger picture, as Volkhard Knigge, the Buchenwald director, had said to me of Bad Arolsen. Finding Valy was, in part, about fleshing out the person of my grandfather, in part about telling her story. I can't stop thinking about this identityless woman, as Pavel, Judita, and I walk away, and then settle in for expensive cakes at Café Slavia, where once Kafka's lover Milena Jesenská held court.

That night my friends in Prague, an American expat and her

Czech husband, find it amusing that I'm spending so little time in the capital and then rushing away to Troppau. "It's as though," says my friend's husband, "someone arrived in New York and said with a great flourish, 'But I'm really here to go to the hinterlands of Iowa!'"

The following morning, in Třebíč, Pavel and I run from place to place, visiting people he knows and picking up promotional pamphlets about the town that he will bring with him to Israel the following week. He is not tall, but he has the thickset look of a frequent gym-goer, with a slightly receding hairline and a line of stubble around his face; he wears a leather jacket and an enormous backpack filled with copies of the Jewish newsletter he edits. I am a burden; I can't communicate at all, I'm totally dependent, bewildered. He insists we hike up above the town to take in the vista of the claustrophobic little shtetl streets, barely wide enough for a single car, the sloping red-roofed homes beneath us, the twelfth-century basilica in the distance, the nuclear plant further on. No matter how high I climb, it is not enough. Pavel eggs me further on, though I am wearing the wrong shoes, and we are not on any sort of path and I keep slipping, and though I am, I whisper feebly, pregnant.

On our way out of town, I tell Pavel I am mostly interested in Troppau, not Třebíč, nor in some of his other suggestions—like a Polish town on the other side of the border that once had a major Jewish family (now long gone) that the town has (belatedly) come to celebrate through an exhibition that he has arranged for me to see. I tell him, given my limited time in the country, I think we should skip our day in Poland, so I can be, simply, in Troppau, wander there, maybe run into elderly people, maybe catch some glimpse of the life of the late 1930s, navigate the city. But I have misjudged our relationship, and Pavel gets angry that I have questioned his judgment, his arrangements. "What will you find there?" he nearly shouts at me, exasperated with my singular focus, over the rattle and wheeze of the ancient train hurtling somewhere through the Czech Moravian countryside once we depart Třebíč. "Nothing! It was bombed! There is nothing to see there! I will take you to see what you need to see." I sputter a bit, mumble about just sitting in town, and walking; taking it in. Even as I say it, I realize it sounds vague at best; ridiculous. And so I agree, perhaps there isn't much to see, but it doesn't matter, I just want to be there, in Troppau, I repeat, *taking it in.* Pavel sighs and looks away, then picks up his phone and scrolls through his messages.

The trip from Třebíč to Krnov is exhausting, a dash from train to train, with a long pause in Ostrava, a cold industrial city at the edge of the country known, says Pavel, for "Gypsies, skinheads, and unemployment." On the last train, a single car packed with Teva factory workers at 11:30 at night, it is a hundred degrees on board and the windows are badly fogged with condensation. I am exhausted. I had half assumed there would be nothing to be found about Jews in the regional archives, but, thinking aloud, I realize this can't be true: Valy's mother ran a shop. Surely that would be in the secular archive.

It is past midnight when we finally arrive in Krnov; and it is freezing, and wet. Pavel's mother fetches us in a small lipstick-red Volkswagen. She is a tiny, plump woman with boyishly cropped hair dyed a deep red-brown. She speaks no English, but proudly shows me she wears a large silver Star of David around her neck bought, says Pavel, in Israel. She drives us, through abandoned streets, to a large nineteenth-century building behind a massive iron gate. You'll be sleeping here, Pavel tells me, indicating the building, a pediatric medical clinic; it is his mother's office, she is the pediatrician. And I realize they mean to leave me at this clinic, alone, to sleep on a pull-out couch in the attic, a room with a skylight for a window and a mirrorless bathroom with a refrigerator full of tetanus shots and walls covered with posters on baby development that look vaguely familiar but are all written in a language indiscernible to me. I'm in a full, sweaty panic as Pavel's sweet mother, using sign language and simple words, shows me how to lock myself in—into the gate, the front door, the middle door, the upstairs door—and all the food she has brought to keep me fed while they are gone. As she unpacks—soup, bread, cheese, apples, oranges—and mimes using the microwave, I cry out, stupidly, "But I can't even say the name of this street!" looking out into the cold, wet night, the abandoned buildings all around, and I know I am irrational, and I know I will be fine, but I am hyperventilating. They leave me anyway—there really is no alternative—and I cannot close my eyes, I turn on every light, every sound in the marble halls echoes around me; I cannot even read, I don't fall asleep until nearly five a.m. and I am a wreck and I don't know why I'm there, traipsing the former Communist industrial corridor, so far from the story I am trying to tell.

As my terror subsides into general insomnia, I lie awake and wonder: *Am I closer to Valy in Krnov, this strange post-Communist town? Is this trip for nothing?* Thus far it feels like a vanity project, a chance to feel ill and foreign, but having nothing to do with my search. People ask me if I've read Jonathan Safran Foer's *Everything Is Illuminated*, and I feel the question implies the search is redundant, the story has been told. The trip to the shtetl, hours in transit, hours walking these long-empty streets, feels gratuitous. I am reminded of my roommate in Vienna who returned home one evening as rain pelted the windows outside. "Two Jews on a rainy night in Vienna watching a Holocaust documentary," she exclaimed, upon finding me and my partner watching a movie on television. "It's like the beginning of a joke!"

Valy was not in Krnov. Is it absurd to be here?

⁓

The next morning Pavel and his mother are late to get me; I am strung out and overtired as we set out into a beautiful morning, into the Czech countryside with a brilliant blue sky, driving down country roads past farms and gentle rolling hills, green as far as the eye can see, a kind of Eastern European Vermont, on our way to Karlsbrunn, now called Karlova Studánka, a spa town in the Jeseníky Mountains, built in the nineteenth century, favored by the bourgeois of Troppau during the interwar period. I am eager to get there, as it's actually a place Valy might have gone—but Pavel insists that we first stop at the home of

Valy Scheftel and her mother, Hanna (also called Toni, Antonie) Scheftel,
in the Czech mountains.

some friends, a stained-glass maker, who is helping to recast the glass for the semi-destroyed Krnov synagogue, and her husband. The husband wears a silver Jewish star around his neck; on his mantel he has a small shrine to Jews—a slice of Jerusalem stone, a photo of Jerusalem, Shabbat candlesticks, and a menorah. *"Baruch ata adonai!"* he sings to me as I walk in, and then, with a flourish, he shows me his necklace. On the wall is a poster of the Yiddish alphabet. They are kind, though, and offer cake and Nescafé, and I buy a pair of earrings wrought out of stained glass, as I assume I was brought here to do. The stained-glass maker, who seems lovely, despite our language barrier, comes up to me and, to my horror, rubs my stomach. She whispers, conspiratorially, "You will have many children, as the *Hebräisch* do?" Pavel, I realize, with chagrin, has shared with them the fact of my early pregnancy. I don't know what to make of these judeophiles. They are all obsessed with the idea of us, but they seem to have met few actual Jews. We are like fairies, good-luck charms, surreal, unreal.

Finally we continue to Karlsbrunn, where the first bathhouse was built by Maximilian, the youngest son of Empress Maria Theresa, in the 1780s. It is warm in the valley but it gets cooler and fresher as we climb. During Valy's childhood, Troppau natives would escape the smog that blanketed the valleys in the years after the Industrial Revolution by visiting Karlsbrunn. These roads haven't changed much since the 1930s, other than that these days they are paved, and navigable by cars; in Valy's childhood, the area was reachable by a two-part journey: train followed by horse and buggy. The Jeseníky mountain waters are said to have curative powers. Sure enough, there are people bottling the water in massive jugs as we arrive, filling up at public taps. Pavel tells me, proudly, that Václav Havel took a cure here, for many months. During Communism, he says, the spa went from being the playground of the rich to a worker's retreat. Now it is something in between the two.

———

Valy writes to my grandfather, reminding him of times they hiked and swam and skied together in the Austrian and Czech countryside, and elsewhere; in his album there are photos of her, in a dirndl, on the mountainside. She returns to these moments, often, in her letters.

June 7, 1940

. . . *Now the third summer without you begins. Instead of going swimming or boating, hiking in the woods and sharing all the beautiful things with you, as it should be, I am sitting here, pounding insanely, madly and full of sadness at the typewriter.*

I pay a small fee and go into the pools, alone. I feel completely dislocated as I bounce around, looking for the jets. There are several saunas, but pregnancy keeps me out of their warmth, so I opt instead for the "photo therapy" room, which turns out to be a floor of white smooth stones, like a driveway, in a faux-hut, walls pasted with images of some distant tropical isles like a tanning salon and what look to be hamburger lights above. Czech women of various sizes lie on the ground wheezily gossiping and I join them, baking for a few minutes. I come out and see that Pavel is huddled over Facebook, updating his status.

For two days Pavel schleps me to places I don't want to go. I feel childish and angry and stuck and spoiled. And I can't explain exactly why it is, but I am deeply uncomfortable traveling with him to see Jewish graves from the interwar period, maintained or unmaintained, cemeteries that have large empty spaces where graves were disinterred, disturbed, destroyed, or large empty spaces where the rest of the community was supposed to have been buried but whose lives were cut short, who were never given the honor of a cemetery burial. He finds it fascinating, sad, but also, ultimately, anthropological. He photographs the gravestones, wanders among them. I find it terrifying, these whole stretches of land that have long since lost their original purpose—but remain empty, marked off, set aside. They are as good a representation of the loss of life as I've ever seen, and yet to be here with Pavel means I cannot express my sorrow without feeling like I am acting out the part he has created for me.

We are met, one morning, at the Krnov synagogue by a group of Poles who want to show me their town, Głubczyce, which once had a prominent Jewish family named Hollaender. I have lost my battle with Pavel over this Polish side journey.

We are, I start to realize, fighting over the rights to this story—he believes it is his to show me, his to explicate—the Polish Hollaender family, for example, as model Jews—because this is *his* region—his lost history, his current history, his past. He believes that understanding the story of this once-Prussian, now-Polish town, the past of the Jews there, will provide insight into what Valy's family experienced. While that may be true to some degree (Valy's family were transplants to the region, from Galicia, and then remained residents for less than a full generation, after all), I am looking for something beyond what he can reveal. The moments I find illuminating aren't those that Pavel anticipates, or provides: it is in the side story, the human interest, the individual experience of loss. I want to know what the cities feel like now, and what they felt like then—who the neighbors were and what they thought when a quarter of their population was destroyed. What happened to their shop? What happened to their lives? Towns like Troppau were strongly pro-Nazi and then aggressively anti-Semitic when Hitler came to power, especially after the Sudetenland was "returned" to Germany under the Munich agreement—but what was life like? What did it feel like to walk down the street? And how did it change under Communism? And how did it change after that? Did the memory of these people linger? Or was it just suppressed? I don't want a faux-Jewish home in a once-Jewish town. I want the real thing. I want the moments like I had with that identityless survivor woman in Prague. They are not constructed moments, they can't be orchestrated; they operate on a kind of serendipity that is very difficult for me to explain to Pavel.

One of the Poles, for example, out of the blue asks if I can help with his family's search: he had one Jewish grandmother, he said, who believed she was the only one of her family to survive—she had been married to a non-Jew, which gave her a privileged status, protected her from deportation. But after Communism ended, he discovered that one of her sisters had survived, in the United States. In 1978, that sister provided testimony for Yad Vashem, the Holocaust Martyrs' and Heroes' Remembrance Authority, that explained *she* was the only survivor, that she had searched and found no one. The two sisters had each lived half a century past the war, always assuming they were alone in the world. They both died before the end of Communism might have led them to find each other. He would like to find that sister's family, in New York, he tells me, hoping I can help him. I promise to try.

Of course his story provides nothing concrete about Valy or her experiences specifically, but it does draw again, and clearly, how many of these not only unhappy but *end-less* endings exist; how possible it was for two sisters—let alone lovers—to live out the rest of their lives never knowing each had survived. It is another illustration of how these stories that have no ending extend for generations, permeate the edges of normal life with the tragedy of what came before, infuse the following generations with their *tristesse*. It makes me wonder, wildly, improbably, if perhaps Valy had the same experience—if she were stuck behind the Iron Curtain, could she have remained there, alive, after the war without my grandfather knowing? It's a bit unlikely, but not totally impossible.

In the meantime, Pavel and I are at an impasse, which only worsens when we finally arrive in Troppau.

The peculiar thing about Troppau is that, at first blush, there seems to be nothing at all to connect the modern city—now called Opava—with the town that was before. At surface, today, you could easily never know its past: the Jews were expelled or murdered, and then, postwar, the rest of the Sudeten Germans were expelled and the city's name changed. In the late 1940s, Opava washed itself clean of its German roots, started again with a new Czech life, and turned its back on the past, ending centuries of speaking, writing, reading, and using German in the town. It reminds me, when I first arrive, of something the late professor Fouad Ajami once said of the Turks under Atatürk: that by putting the language into Latin letters, and out of Arabic, the country no longer allowed itself to access the past. In Troppau, too, there is little access to the past: no one speaks or reads or grasps German at all, let alone remembers much of a time when there were Jews running half the city's businesses. Troppau—especially Troppau's Jews—was always oriented more toward Vienna than Warsaw or Prague. The town's history is told in German, the town's Jews were obsessed with German culture—which means this past is nearly inaccessible to most of the Czech youth I meet. Pavel can read and speak German; he is an exception.

In the Jewish archives of Prague, page after page in stacks tied together with ribbon testify to the relationship between the Jewish communities of Troppau and Vienna, stretching well back into the nineteenth century. By the early 1930s, smart girls like Valy were sent to Vienna to study. When she enrolled in the medical school in 1932, she was part of a second wave, a group of women who believed in their place as doctors, not nurses, and saw their enrollment as entirely normal, entirely obvious: feminists without using the term. There were dozens of women in the medical school in Valy's year—and of those, more than half were Jewish.

She was a German aesthete—no money, but rich in the poems and music of the city she adopted. Her time in Vienna was a shelter for her, mentally, emotionally, a respite that she would return to, in her letters, in her mind, when life began to morph and twist into the horror of the Nazi period. When she graduated, five days before the Nazis took the city, she held in her hand one of the last degrees from the university given to a Jew before the Anschluss deprived her classmates of that privilege.

For some time I couldn't understand why Valy hadn't stayed in Vienna, or rather, why she hadn't stayed long enough to flee with my grandfather. I assumed—I still assume—it was in part because she felt she must return to her mother, alone in Troppau. That sense of loyalty surely played a tremendous role. In her later letters she does nothing without her mother.

> *My mother is again with me. She was supposed to take on the management of a local home, but was not approved by the labor department, alas. Now she will probably have to take on a completely subordinate job—household or cleaning. It has to be that way. We are greatly saddened by this, because we fear that she will not be up to it physically. I just hope that it is not going to be too hard. We now live together in a furnished room and are truly happy to be together.*

But it was also, I realized in the Czech Republic, because in March 1938, Troppau was a way of fleeing Vienna without having to go very far. It was free. It was (relatively) safe. It was, she thought, they all thought, enough out of reach of the Nazi arm that they had time to collect themselves, to consider their options, before emigration. So she went to Troppau to organize her life, to escape the Anschluss, to reunite with her mother; and—maybe—to wait for a marriage proposal. And Karl continued on his path to emigration.

Valy began to write to him from the moment he set foot on the boat from Hamburg to New York.

Troppau. September 13, 1938

Beloved boy,
    A warm welcome to America!
    Europe and I send you greetings. We both grieve for you! . . .
    When your card arrived, I wanted to fly to Hamburg. I simply could not fathom that you were leaving and that I had to stay back here by myself. It was inconceivable no longer to have you here within reach. Finally, I comprehended that you had actually taken the step you had been contemplating for months and that I must be happy.
    Do you remember, darling, how you would console me when I used to be so unhappy at the onset of the long summer break because we had to separate for such a long time? "Be sensible, there are only six weeks that separate us; neither you nor I go to America!". . . And now, many weeks and sky-high obstacles, an entire world history is between us! Isn't that so sad that one might want to die? . . .

                                       Valy

Her uncle, she writes him, is worse off than she—he is now considered stateless and is wandering from place to place, using up time in each country till he can find safe passage to a place he might actually stay in. Statelessness was suddenly a massive problem affecting Jews across the German-speaking world. Jews were increasingly deprived of citizenship, taken in by no one, wandering from border to border, illegal, hungry, fearing their own incarceration. Erich Marie Remarque wrote a whole forgotten book on the phenomenon—*Flotsam*, on the unlucky ones (in his book, they are not only Jews) shunted across borders, never taken in, doomed to wander just like their stereotypes. The book appeared before things turned even darker; it was 1939 and the characters of Remarque's imagination consider Paris. And Mexico. Valy does not immediately consider traveling toward France or South America; she wants only to meet my grandfather in New York. Her mother suggests Palestine; Valy doesn't want that either.

The week Valy's letter was sent, Chamberlain flew to visit Hitler. "The Third Reich will win again—whether by bluff or by force," wrote Dresden diarist Victor Klemperer on the twentieth of September. So: poor Valy. Only months after she is out of suffocating Vienna, and days after her lover has fled the Continent, her hometown is handed to Hitler; the Munich agreement gives him Sudetenland, and thousands of Jews flee into the Czech interior. But not Valy and her mother; they stay, with her mother's shop, with their smothering surroundings. Even as early as September 1938, the small towns were oppressive for Jews. It got worse and worse. Kristallnacht was particularly brutal in the Sudetenland, an eager proof to the Nazi government that the newest citizens cheered the Nazis' racialized violence: that night Troppau's gorgeous synagogue burned, the fire department stood back, keeping the crowds, and the lifesaving water, at bay. Almost every synagogue, for miles around, was turned to ash.

When Pavel and I finally arrive in town, we walk immediately over to see where the synagogue had been. There is no plaque. The square it once stood upon is just a stretch of lawn, with trees and grass, a leafy traffic island. Nothing was built to stand in its place, and nothing marks that anything once stood here. But next to it, the brick rabbi's house still stands, and we peer in the windows where photos of the once-magnificent synagogue are hung. *Okay, let's go,* says Pavel, but I say, *No, let's go in.* So we do. There is a Roma evangelical revival meeting taking place—boisterous praises of Jesus and the Lord in Czech. Pavel sits in the corner, plugging his phone into the wall, while his mother and I chat with the leaders of the meeting, the pastor and a bouncy, tall woman named Blanca, with an open, young face. Her "half Gypsy" daughters are in the meeting and she hopes to bring me to Jesus. She speaks impressive, if quirky, English—and Spanish from years of living in the Canary Islands.

"Here was the most beautiful synagogue in Czech Republic, here in Opava," says Blanca, using the modern Czech name of the town. "Here we pray to say 'We are sorry' to the Jewish people for what happened in Opava because they were killing many Jewish people." Eventually the pastor joins us. His skin is ruddy, and expressive, and he looks fit, more like a gym teacher than a spiritual leader. The pastor adds, "We were just talking about this yesterday—in this city it was once only Jews and Germans who lived in the center of town; Czechs lived in the surrounding towns." He runs and brings me a photo of the synagogue's famous cupolas, burning. But when I ask if they were aware of this history growing up, they demur. "It was Communist, so they didn't teach us these things," says Blanca.

Blanca prevails upon me to come into the revival meeting. One very young woman standing near Blanca's older daughter is openly weeping; Blanca whispers that the woman's daughter has just accepted Jesus. Her own daughter is a head taller than her "full Gypsy" friends, she has dreadlocked hair pulled back in a ponytail tied low at her neck; she wears a—yet another!—large silver Star of David around her neck. The girl grasps her friends around the shoulders and sings with gusto along with every song. Blanca signals to the keyboardist and then stands in front of the room; the music begins to slow and then, finally, peter out. Blanca tells the group that I am Jewish (a woman in the crowd gasps, another begins to cry) and that my family lost family members—*just like you, just like the Gypsies*—in the Holocaust. There is much nodding; many eyes are moist. The keyboardist stands up and announces, in halting but clear English: You have been sent by Jesus. Pavel has finally come to join us and whispers, "What the hell are we doing with these Gypsies?" But his mother, at least, looks happy, and when the music starts up again, she begins dancing, merrily, arm in arm, with various members of the crowd. She hooks an elbow into mine and suddenly we are square-dancing with the evangelicals.

The next day, when I arrive at the archives, I will discover Blanca and the "Christians of Opava" have preceded me—leaving a Gideon's Bible at the front desk, inscribed to me; wishing me well on my journey to Christ. "We find the mesia [*sic*] is there and we wish you will find Him as well. We pray for you. Read John 1:42–43." They were so very sure that my stumbling upon them was about them; so clear that it was Jesus who brought us together, not Valy. But before that, Pavel, his mother, and I wander the town, in the dark, and come to the opera house where *Nabucco* is onstage and I am—momentarily—transported seventy years into the past. As we arrive, Pavel is telling me how he put on a production of *Brundibár* on this stage—the children's opera by Czech Hans Krása, staged at Theresienstadt and recently restaged, in New York, by Tony Kushner and the late Maurice Sendak. I slip away from him for a moment into the warm theater and stand there, imagining Valy and Karl taking in the same arias seventy-five years before me, finally feeling like I can grasp them a little bit, see them walking down the hall, giggling together, see them in their lives together, and finally feel a bit closer to her.

When I come back downstairs, Pavel and his mother are drinking sweet pink sparkling wine with an usher they know. We wander on, trying to determine which home on the inner ring was Valy's. There are several old buildings still standing—in fact, contrary to our argument on the train a few days prior, the entire city was not bombed, just pieces, like missing teeth, which were filled in Communist-bloc style, so the effect is that of a home misarranged, mismatched, that was once a grand estate.

One of the standing buildings, from the late nineteenth century, reminds me of Paris apartment buildings of the Haussmann era. It is a grand presence, all large windows and carved sills; I am sure it was Valy and her mother's building, it is the same number! It is the right period! I want so badly for it to be so, I want to know that I have found the markers of the beginning of her life. Beneath it, on the ground floor, there is a small depressing casino, filled with slot machines and the kind of dead-eyed gamblers of small, poor towns the world over. The workers in the casino look at me dispassionately. They have no idea if number 43 from 1940 has anything to do with a building numbered 43 in 2012; the street name, not to mention the numbers, is different today. We leave with no answers.

As dawn breaks the following morning, I am picked up by Aron, a friend of Pavel's who is a bond officer in Opava. I am bleary with exhaustion, and in my sleepy haze, I decide Aron looks like he's playing the part of Tevye in a school play: a scraggly beard, a belly, enormously tall, a wool paper-boy cap, he drives a creaky old black Mercedes that needs a great deal of love to keep it moving. Like Pavel, Aron is not Jewish but is deeply involved in the recovery of the area's history, and we talk about what it was like growing up, the jokes that were told about Jews (most involving gas—"Why did Hitler kill himself? He got the bill for the gas"), how he long believed—or perhaps hoped—himself to be Jewish—his grandparents were descendants of ethnic Czechs who spoke the language peculiarly, and with an accent. He was sure they were hidden Jews—it seems, like many here who have taken an interest in the history, to some degree he *wanted* them to have been hidden Jews—but, he now knows, they were not. He grew up near one of the abandoned Jewish cemeteries and taught himself basic Hebrew reading the tombstones; now he is the president of the Krnov synagogue association.

Pavel and Aron are curious corollaries to my strange roommate in Vienna—for them, as rebellious teens, as outsiders, Jewishness was a bit interesting, but unlike Hilke they went toward it rather than against it. Judaism was in some ways a means of embracing a world-view different from, perhaps more exotic than, what they knew. It feels at times like searching for Native American roots in the United States.

Aron drives us into Troppau and we go up to his office for coffee. There he tells us a bit about the history of the town—"It was high society," he says, meaning haute bourgeoisie—and he and Pavel discuss the rise of anti-Semitism here.

After being kept from living downtown until the mid-nineteenth century, restrictions against Jews were lifted and, suddenly, by the turn of the twentieth, they were flooding into the professional classes. As in Vienna, in Troppau they made up a quarter of all doctors, a fifth of all lawyers. And they started to buy up houses in the main squares. "People had the feeling that every second house in the center of town was Jewish. And every second shop." Tensions rose between Jews and non-Jews over perceived Semitic success.

Aron is due at the prison, so Pavel and I walk on, through the city's parks and around the center. Finally, we arrive at the former Silesian parliament building, now the home of the regional archives. It looks a bit, as many of these buildings do, like a medieval hospital, a miniature version of the Reina Sofía museum in Madrid; the floors are wide-planked wood or massive ceramic tile, there are high plaster archways everywhere, and the walls are filled with photos of old military men. The archivist speaks no English and Pavel translates. We tell him that we are trying to establish where Valy and her mother lived—Oberring 43—and together with the archivist we scan the 1938 town address book, and pull up map after ancient map on the archivist's computer. Finally we see it. The building we had walked into last night, the small, sad slot-machine casino building, nestled into the ornate apartment house that I was so sure had been theirs, was not Valy's home. Their building was directly across from the opera house; the old number 43 was leveled by bombs and postwar cleanup. I am sad to know it, sad to know that I cannot touch what she touched, see what she saw—what they saw together.

Then the archivist asks if I want to know why they left Troppau. I say I think I know: anti-Semitism was terrible in these small towns, and I hear Pavel, translating me, and I get the sense he is making fun my assurance. "She says she *knows already*," he says, in a falsetto voice. Perhaps his words were different; I can hear the tone, I don't understand the words. The men in the room laugh. "Are you mocking me?" I ask, shrill, I have it on my tape, my exhaustion, my near tears. Everyone sobers. *Perhaps,* the archivist asks, *you would like to see the forced aryanization papers?* We all stop talking for a moment. "That's a possibility?" I ask. I would very, very much like to see that. And, suddenly, before us is a book; halfway through it we see that Toni Sara Scheftel, Valy's mother, has a file. Pavel and I both are taken aback, thrilled even, to have a chance to see its terrible contents.

The introduction to the book is entirely in Czech, but I photograph it and take it with me to send on for translation. "On 26 April 1938 Regulation came into force regarding registering Jewish property in the whole territory of the former Germany." April 1938 was one month after Valy returned to her mother; the regulation applied, after September, to the Sudetenland. "In that regulation, it was ordered that every Jew . . . must register all their domestic and foreign property as of the date on which this Regulation came into force. . . . Intentionally falsely reported data subjected the [false] reporting person a subject of criminal prosecution, with the maximum penalty up to ten years in jail." By November 12, 1938, a few days after Kristallnacht, the Reich announced "the exclusion of Jews from German economic life." Effective two months later, on January 1, 1939, "Jews were forbidden to operate stores, shipping or ordering companies, as well as to be self-employed in business. In addition, from November 12 they were prohibited to offer goods for sale in markets of all kinds, and exhibitions, nor were they allowed to advertise goods. Jewish businesses operated in spite of this regulation could be closed by the police. From January 1, 1939 a Jew was also not allowed to lead any company." All membership in professional organizations was also stripped. All Jewish property, including investments, was taken away, and Jews were not allowed to own gold, silver, platinum, or jewels.

———

And then we are presented with Valy's mother's file, antique pages we spread out on the floor to see them more clearly, ancient pages detailing the careful dismantling of her business, her life, her livelihood. "What lengths did they go to," marvels Pavel, "to despoil the Jews!"

The pages look like this:

LIST OF ASSETS OF JEWISH PERSONS

with the effective date of ~~April 27 1938~~ December I, I939

for Ms. Toni Scheftel
Business woman (shoe store)

in Troppau
Adolf Hitler Ring 43

Personal Data

I was born on December 27, I885

I am Jewish (Paragraph 5 of the First Regulation of the
Reichsbürgergesetz (Citizenship Law of the Reich of Nov.
I4, I935, Reichs Gazette P. I333) and German citizen . . .

~~stateless~~

Since I am Jewish and a citizen of Germany ~~stateless Jew~~
I have enumerated and valuated all my assets, both
domestic and foreign in this list.

I was married to Franz Scheftel, and have been divorced
since I9I2. Franz Scheftel was born in I883 in Berlin.

My husband belongs to the Jewish race and is an adherent
of the Jewish religion.

VI Remarks

In accordance with the Aryanization purchasing
contract of OI-3I-I939, my shoe store at 43, Adolf Hitler

Ring, Troppau, was sold for a total price of RM IO,800.
The purchasing contract is with the Regierungspräsident
for approval.

Troppau, January 3I I939

Toni Scheftel

All other assets are also listed. All bank account information and life insurance, all are listed to be despoiled; methodically she is stripped of all she owns. Here, then, was the disassembling of twenty-eight years of work, in ten sheets of paper, the undermining of all that Valy's mother had built since her divorce. It is here, actually, that I discover that she was a divorcée and not a widow, as I'd originally believed. It is here I see that their street name—once Oberring—had become, like so many streets across the greater Reich, Adolf Hitler Ring.

The archivist and Pavel are both very pleased with our discovery. Pavel implies that if I pay the archivist a bit, perhaps under the table, he will likely be happy to help me going forward. Waiting for us all this time, in the corner of the archives entrance, is a woman named Katka, who runs the "Lost Neighbors" program here in Opava, which aims to acquaint local youth with their lost Jewish past. She began it in part because members of her family witnessed the destruction of the Troppau Jewish community.

Katka, who speaks only Czech, has that kind of deep-red-dyed hair favored in countries of Eastern Europe and in parts of Israel; she wears it up in a ponytail, with heavy bangs and dark, thick-rimmed glasses. The three of us walk through town to a restaurant Katka recommended. As we sit she tells me—as Pavel translates—her mother-in-law was here, in town, the night of the synagogue burning, and they both want to know if I'd like to meet her. *Far more than eating!* I say. Katka nods and we abandon the restaurant and get into a cab. As we travel to the village where her mother-in-law lives, Katka rubs my shoulders and explains that she does energy healing; she thinks I could use it.

Just beyond the city limits of Opava is a small village filled with bungalows. This is where we find Katka's mother-in-law, Mrs. Havlásková; she seems pleased to see us. Her parents, she says, as she limps around the kitchen, setting up cookies and tea, were dairy farmers. This is the house she was born in, she explains, sitting down heavily and placing fruit tea and chocolate cookies in front of me. She has deep wrinkles and a head of curls that may once have been blond but have faded to an ashy gray. "My mother had come to town with milk to sell and she said, 'Come have a look! The synagogue is on fire!'" Mrs. Havlásková says in Czech, and Pavel slowly translates into English. "And we saw the smoke from it. And two Germans were standing there protecting it and they hadn't allowed anyone to approach the fire. The synagogue was on fire. The Germans were standing at a distance and not allowing anyone to go to the synagogue because they didn't want anyone to put it out." Mrs. Havlásková's mother had a soft spot for the Jews: she had worked for a Jewish family herself, before she had children: a bourgeois family named Meyer, German speakers, who were good to her, who paid her well, and gave her gifts on Christmas and made her feel a part of the family. Mrs. Havlásková insists she and her mother went to visit the Meyers, later, under the occupation, and that she was in the apartment, as a ten-year-old, and heard an argument between her mother and Mrs. Meyer. "The old lady Meyer said to my mother, 'We have to go, they are moving us somewhere else,' and my mother said, 'No, hide somewhere!' and Mrs. Meyer said, 'It's not possible. We have had Germans in the apartment already, and they ordered us to prepare our luggage, and pack things . . .'"

I am suspicious of the story, though it is fascinating. I think Mrs. Havlásková wants to believe she heard this, she wants to feel good about her mother, about the woman her mother—she thinks—tried to help, but I also think it is possibly too fantastic to be true, that these dairy-delivering villagers happened to be delivering in Troppau on the very day of the deportation of her mother's former employers.

It doesn't really matter anyway, Mrs. Havlásková is one of very few people not only still living but still living near Troppau who remembers the synagogue at all, who remembers the night when it burned, when Valy and her mother must have huddled together—just two blocks away—wondering how they were going to survive. Where could they go? What would they do? When Valy must have realized, immediately, that not leaving with my grandfather was a much graver, much more difficult choice to have made than simply losing a boyfriend.

Sudeten Germans were expelled at the end of the war, so eyewitnesses, as old as they would be, were scattered far and wide. There are only the Czech elderly, who were children then, who remember the burning of the synagogues; few speak of it. That's why Katka worked on this "Lost Neighbors" project—to tell the children of Opava who once shared these streets. Otherwise it would be very, very easy to forget. So few returned after the war.

Katka's son has joined us at this point. He is young, nineteen, twenty, and his English is better than his mother's. The two of them take me back to Troppau in a taxi and straight to the train. I want to stay and walk in town a bit more, but they are insistent that the time to travel is that moment, and so I obey, getting on a train to Ostrava, and then another to Prague. It takes five hours, and in the end, I am grateful to finally be back on my own, and grateful that they insisted I make the journey rather than push on to another interview.

The following day I go to the Terezín Initiative Institute, a project dedicated to the history of the Final Solution in Bohemia. Its headquarters are in Prague. I show up unannounced, but there I meet Tereza Štěpková, the director. She sees nothing in her files on Valy, but she sees that Valy's father was deported to Theresienstadt in 1943. He died there. As she has not much more to offer me, we find ourselves talking about children. She has two, and she's involved in this work because of them. "I think it's better when the child knows very early in his life" about the war, she says. "It is better than if he or she comes to school and at ten years old, along comes the Holocaust and he or she

knows nothing about it. I think for the child it is . . . a shock. And it
is not good for them." I tell her I wonder if it is different, though, for
Jews. Jews know from such an early age about their own persecution,
perhaps we learn too early and too much about victimization. How
can we navigate their relationship to the material? She considers that,
but it is far from her own experience. For her, it is important that kids
recognize ordinariness. The arbitrary. That those who were lost were
their neighbors. Were kids like them. Otherwise they can be too distanced from the material.

And it is true, to some degree Valy sought ordinariness. She and
her mother left Troppau—where everyone knew them as Jews, where
her mother's business had just been destroyed—and sought shelter in
the most contrary place I could imagine—Berlin. In Troppau's archives, I see what I know from my own collection of letters—by 1940,
if not earlier, both women are ensconced in Berlin, in the process of
being "retrained" for emigration.

Berlin had more work to offer Jews, and the city, counterintuitively, was less overtly anti-Semitic than the small towns. Their move
to the bigger cities was part of a larger migration that began in 1933:
Jews seeking anonymity away from the stifling villages. Valy was fortunate, to a degree: she was hired by the Reich's major Jewish organization, the Reichsvereinigung—the Council of Jews organized and
manipulated by the Nazis in Germany to control the Jewish population. It was organized, first, to push Jews out the door through legal
emigration. It morphed into a macabre temp agency, putting Jews to
work until they were sent to their deaths. Eventually, the organization
helped the Nazi machine keep the deportations orderly. They thought
if they did so, some would be saved.

Valy writes my grandfather that she desperately wanted to stay in
medicine, not be sent to work in a factory, not have her mind shut
down; and for a long time, she did that—she worked as a nurse, she
taught, she saw patients. She ached for my grandfather more and more
as time went by. He was not just her old boyfriend, of course—he was

freedom, he was the real world, and he was the difference between terror and normal life. She was endlessly, endlessly trying to emigrate. She was thwarted at every turn. When Germany invades Poland, Europe is again at war, and outlets for emigration—few to begin with— close day after day. At first, life in Berlin is easier than Troppau, but only marginally—the restrictions confining Jewish life come week after week. I want to find a listing of all the restrictions, to know what her days were like, to know how her liberties were stripped from her. I want to know if I can find more about what she actually experienced there. To follow her path, I will go back to Berlin.

Five

BERLIN

B erlin is a peculiar time for me. Pregnant, I feel vulnerable wandering these streets, looking for ghosts. I rent a room on Huse-
mannstrasse in Prenzlauer Berg, in one of the late-nineteenth- and
early-twentieth-century buildings reclaimed and rehabbed after Communism by young Westerners drawn to the opportunities (and kitsch)
offered by the old East. The building itself is older than so much of
this rebuilt city, but the neighborhood is very new Berlin. On the
ground floor is a center for ayurveda and wellness; the central courtyard is packed full of bicycles and baby carriages; the back garden is
lush and green. My flatmate is a taciturn British artist who spends his
days tutoring English and his evenings sketching eerie images of
women whose faces he then purposely blurs out; he makes barely
enough money to pay the rent and hardly ever goes out. The others in
the building are far better-off; there are dozens of small children.

Among most of the people I meet in Berlin, there is more conversation about the Cold War than World War II. Unlike the ghosts I am
chasing, the Wall is still a part of recent memory, still raw, especially
here in the old East. For me, the Wall is further away, less tangible.

Even so, unlike in Vienna, the Holocaust is not subtext here, it is contextual; it is so present, it is almost absent, part of the texture of the streets, part of the culpability on behalf of grandparents easily acknowledged by those of my generation. If anything, it is overacknowledged, often apologized for. I am reminded constantly of the penitent prayers we say on Rosh Hashanah and Yom Kippur—*Ashamnu, Bagadnu*, "We have become desolate," "We have betrayed." Memorials abound. One night a group of expat acquaintances and I troop around the corner to the Rykestrasse Synagogue; the building survived Kristallnacht (locals feared fire would take down the neighborhood), the war, and Communism. The Israeli singer Idan Raichel was performing there that night. As the musicians took the stage, Raichel began to speak to the audience. His grandmother, he said, had been a Berliner; she fled, in the 1930s, for Palestine. Before he came to Berlin, he told the crowd, she urged him not to go—"Who will come see a Jew perform?" she said. The sold-out synagogue applauded and cheered. I began to cry.

So there are memorials, verbal, physical. But it's for the *un*-memorialized that I've come here. So I begin to walk where Valy walked, go where she went. I request materials from the archives that might have information on Valy's life, work, and residences during the war. There was careful documentation of all property looted by the Gestapo from Jews, notes on their restricted movements, their work, their highly observed and constrained lives. For Valy and others in Berlin, these, largely, remain on file at the Landesarchiv Berlin (the Berlin state archive) and the Brandenburgisches Landeshauptarchiv in Potsdam (the Brandenburg state archive), and they include the notes of the Oberfinanzpräsident Berlin-Brandenburg, the financial tallying of all those looted by the Nazis before deportation or expulsion. I send away, too, a request to the Compensation Authorities—the Entschädigungsbehörde—at the state agency that facilitated indemnity requests for those who had been forced laborers or concentration camp inmates, indeed for all German Jews who had been persecuted; compensation was paid for having to wear the yellow star, for loss of professional advancement, for loss of family members, for physical damages (and psychological ones).

I want to know if anyone filed a request on Valy's behalf for monetary damages—or for any compensation—or on behalf of Hans Fabisch, the man mysteriously linked to her name at ITS. I hope I might find whether Valy survived the war, or, at least, gain some larger understanding of her experience under the Reich. In the meantime, I begin to visit all the places Valy wrote from—there are at least a half-dozen, she moved a lot—and I finally start to parse the letters more fully, as the key to understanding Valy best is her own words, and those of people she knew slowly making their way out of the Reich.

I have never actively craved motherhood, I realize, yet somehow this pregnancy makes my journey much less lonely. I talk to my belly as it grows; I photograph it. I am suddenly desexed; men do not notice me. I am often alone on an old bike that I bought in Mauerpark, the flea market in the Cold War–era no-man's-land where the Wall (*Mauer*) once ran, from a Swiss kid who sold it to me for twenty-four euros and later wrote to me, worried that he had sold me a lemon in my condition. I try to picture Valy writing to my grandfather. She never speaks of motherhood, though the years of her letters bring her into her early thirties, late by the standards of her day, and she is working with kids.

The children in Valy's care are patients, or they are work; they are both darling and a nuisance—or they are leaving, in droves. They are not a source of wistful imagining. Perhaps the hope of emigration was enough wistfulness. Perhaps Valy hadn't wanted children. In truth she wasn't in a terribly good position to have them—pregnant women and women with small children did not fare well under the Reich, not in the time of deprivation—as children become, intentionally, aggressively, more and more malnourished—and certainly not by the time of deportation. Children were not useful to the Nazis; so they were, eventually, destroyed, murdered in ways I can barely stand to read about. I feel ravaged by story after story, especially knowing I am growing my own child.

But Valy doesn't speak of motherhood in part because she is still more engaged with her role as a daughter. Valy leaves her mother in Troppau while Toni grapples with the forced closing of her business, to see if—away from the stifling, virulent, small-town racism that had engulfed them since Valy returned from studying in Vienna— the two women will find a path to emigration together in Berlin. With her mother's source of income taken over by the Gestapo, Valy now needs to find work, to support them both. All around her, the once-affluent Jewish community is disintegrating—from 1933 to 1939, the Jewish population of Berlin halved, from 160,000 to 80,000 Jews; those who are not able to leave are progressively, purposely, poverty-stricken.

It is mid-1939 and, outside the Jewish community, there is virtu-ally no work available to Valy; she and her mother are teetering on destitution. They are in good company. Factory owners and business-men have been forced to give up their businesses, or sell at purposely ludicrous fire-sale prices—even the wealthiest soon have little to nothing, their assets tied up in blocked bank accounts, their meager stores of cash left to ransom themselves or their family members, if they are lucky. There is no social safety net left for Jews—they have been stripped from the rolls of welfare, even as the number of Jews needing welfare climbs higher by the day; about one in three German Jews will need assistance by the time Valy arrives in Berlin.

Valy registers with, and begins to work for, the Reich's main orga-nization for Jews—the Reichsvereinigung. This wasn't simply smart; it was compulsory. Work was the only way to scrape together funds for day-to-day life, and registration with the community was mandatory (eventually this would be a helpful way of organizing the Jewish com-munity for deportation). By the end of the 1930s, over a third of Jew-ish social welfare institutions had been shuttered because of lack of funds, lack of staff, or by police—and the Reichsvereinigung was

scrambling to staff up the remaining Jewish institutions
serving the poor, the elderly, the
youngest, the ill. Before my
grandfather had even left Europe, some sixty thousand Jews
were out of work, but there was
a need for women like Valy, for
nurses and caregivers and doctors and those who could take
over old-age homes and kindergartens.

Though the Reichsvereini-
gung was formed officially in
1939, and was, by then, controlled by the Gestapo, the
bones of the organization had
been created by the community

*Valy in Berlin. The photo was enclosed
in a letter dated August 8, 1940.*

itself; the structure dated back to Hitler's takeover in 1933. The first
incarnation was known as the Reichsvertretung, and it gave the diverse Jewish community a loosely unifying structure in which to pursue emigration out of Germany, and to lobby for the needs of the
community with the Nazi leadership. Its leader was Rabbi Leo Baeck.
His, and the organization's, independence was increasingly compro-
mised, until the original body was ostensibly dissolved and then re-
formed as the Reichsvereinigung, at the behest of the Gestapo.
(Confusingly, Baeck remained the head of the organization, many of
the leaders remained the same, and, similarly, the Reichsvereinigung's
putative raison d'être remained getting Jews out of the Reich, though
it did so with far less agency and mobility, constrained by the ever
more oppressive regime.)

So the new organization that Valy joined, the Reichsvereinigung,
served both the Jewish community (for good, mostly, as much as it

could, trying to reorganize and keep fed and clothed a steadily more destitute Jewish community) and the Gestapo (first by pushing Jews to emigrate and, later, by organizing deportations). Early on, Valy was assigned to work with children and to teach in what was called the Kindergartenseminar, one of the last ways for young Jewish women to find an education and certification that (they believed) was transferrable, even useful, should they secure a job and a visa to go abroad. As anxious as Valy was to get out of Germany, the seminar was an oasis in an ever more worried city, a source of intellectual stimulation, of a (Jewish) social life. She was, at first, not terribly unhappy:

August 3, 1939

My Darling,

For such a terribly long time I've wanted to write you, and it was so totally impossible until today—and actually it's impossible today too, because in a moment the children will be awake, they'll cry and ask for their "Auntie Doctor," and they'll need to be washed, dressed, tended to, and supervised; they need me so badly to play, to pester, to not-obey, and to love. You see, I'm employed—really employed, Darling (me!!) and I'm earning money (!) (50RM [Reichsmark] plus board and lodging); I'm in a training college for kindergarten teachers, where some children (the number changes, at the moment there are 6) are housed as well! I'm with these children right now, and in addition I'm in charge of the trainees; they're young girls from the big city, exuberant, sassy, in some cases very smart (in some cases not so smart!), who naturally don't have a glimmer of respect for me and do whatever they want to. A few of them are nice and smart and don't exploit the friendly relationship that I emphasized right at the outset (to my great disadvantage). But most of them do! And they honestly try to prevent me from "being happy" here. But on the whole, things are wonderful for me here (relatively speaking, of course!). We live in a gorgeous mansion in

Grunewald [an upper-class Berlin neighborhood], with a garden,
balconies and all the trimmings. I have a small, very charming (at
noon, very (!) hot!!) attic room with such a lovely, charming, peaceful
view over the treetops and mansion roofs. I greatly enjoy sitting at
this window! And dreaming. And I so enjoy dreaming, only I have so
very little time to do so!

Valy's school was at Wangenheimstrasse 36, a stately villa in a
neighborhood of villas in the lush Grunewald neighborhood deep in
the far western half of Berlin. I take two overland S-Bahn trains out
to this edge of the city and wander the streets until I find it. There are
mansions all around, most built at the turn of the last century. But
"36," when I find it, looks all wrong. It doesn't seem terribly old and I
cannot tell if it is the right address—hers was supposed to have been
built in 1909—but there is no one to ask, on the street, or around the
building. On a Sunday, this suburb-within-the-city is leafy and green,
and totally bereft of foot traffic. It might be that it is one of the grand
houses across the street, one with turrets and small attic rooms, as
Valy and others who recalled the seminar described. Though number
36 looks as though it may have been torn down and rebuilt, the rest of
the area looks as though it has not changed at all since the turn of the
last century. But I don't know. There are no markers, no suggestions
of the upheaval witnessed here. I linger as long as I can, wondering if
anyone knows that this neighborhood was where Jewish girls came for
their last hope of a good education as the 1930s drew to a close. Some
long suburban blocks away, there is a small café where I order tea and
Käsekuchen. But the waitress there appears to be in her twenties; she
has no idea what the neighborhood once held.

———

The coordinators of Valy's school, the rank and file of the prominent
Jews remaining in Berlin, morphed into a new role as 1938 turned to
1939. With so many new regulations, there was a need for an inter-

locutor between Jews and the Reich leadership—so that Jews would understand how to navigate those rules, and know how to remain on the right side of the ever-shifting bounds of the law. The Reichsvereinigung filled that role, too. As I stir my tea and look out over this calm suburb, I wonder if Valy knew that, when she took her position at the seminar.

When Valy came to live in Grunewald, more and more indigent people were on the streets of Berlin; the desperation for emigration was becoming ever more frantic, as the funds necessary to leave were elusive, nearly impossible to come by—for tickets, of course, but also for the onerous system of fleeing and "taxation" imposed upon Jews who wanted to flee. Unfortunately for Valy, women were often seen as having needs secondary to those of men, as men had already experienced the brutalities of camps like Dachau and Sachsenhausen, where some thirty thousand were sent during the widespread pogroms of Kristallnacht. There was some trepidation about letting women leave alone, that they wouldn't be able to provide for themselves, or live honorably. Men were privileged with the chance to leave first.

"The emigration problem demanded our greatest labors," wrote Alfred Schwerin in 1944, after his escape to Basel, Switzerland, in a manuscript published, in part, in the book *Jewish Life in Germany: Memoirs from Three Centuries*. Schwerin, a Reichsvereinigung worker, had himself been sent to Dachau after Kristallnacht, though he was released within a few months. "We registered children and adults with the emigration aid agencies, filled out the endless questionnaires, wrote testimonials, and took care of providing funds for the journey and the purchases needed for it. This often entailed quite considerable sums. . . . The Reichsvereinigung did not approve immediately and readily, because it wanted to help as many people as possible and tried to avoid spending too great an amount for any one person." Jews lingering in the Reich made the Nazi authorities angry; yet as angry as the delay in expelling the population made them, they did everything they could to make the process of emigration arduous, ruining, demoralizing.

The Kindergartenseminar at Wangenheimstrasse opened in 1934, the brainchild of the women of the Jüdischer Frauenbund (the League of Jewish Women, a remarkable feminist organization that lobbied for women's suffrage and against prostitution before 1933; after the anti-Jewish laws came into effect, it became an advocate for Jewish women in the Reich) and the Reichsvertretung—the earlier representative body of Jews of the Reich. The idea was a school to train teachers, a place where girls could go after high school, or even just before graduation, and receive an education in pedagogy. It remained open as Jews were dismissed from all other areas of Aryan life. Students studied education theory, psychology, history, literature—as well as hygiene, civics, "gymnastics," drawing, and music. There was also Hebrew, Judaism, and Jewish history.

Marianne Strauss was nearly sixteen and among the youngest of some thirty girls when she enrolled at the Kindergartenseminar in April 1939. Wangenheimstrasse 36, she told historian Mark Roseman, whose book about Strauss's astonishing underground life is called *A Past in Hiding*, was a "very good address, like The Bishops Avenue," in the Hampstead Heath neighborhood in London, "enormous, with I don't know how many really splendid 1920s [era] bathrooms." The building, previously the home of a Jewish banker, had been donated for use by the Jewish community in the mid-1930s. Number 36 housed the Seminar as well as a boardinghouse with space, at the outset, for fifteen girls and women who had come from other parts of the Reich. Strauss told Roseman that that attic room—perhaps the very one Valy claimed for herself—for a time, was the "plum," the room everyone wanted, tiny, but with a fantastic view down Wangenheimstrasse through one window, and Lynarstrasse through the other.

Writes Roseman, "The elimination of opportunities elsewhere"—the closing of doors to Jews across the Reich and into Austria—"was a boon for the school as a glittering array of intellectuals and inspired teachers had joined the teaching staff. Aware that in different circumstances many of the students would have sought a more academic education, the college offered a far more intellectual and wide-ranging course than was usual for kindergarten teachers." Rabbi Leo Baeck, the head of the Reichsvereinigung, was on the school's board.

The Jewish community of Berlin provided not just education but also social and cultural services. With an eye to the needs of a people accustomed to steeping in opera and art, plays and concerts were arranged by the Jüdischer Kulturbund, employing the suddenly out-of-work Jewish actors and musicians in the big cities; tours were set up for the areas beyond. Only works by Jews could be performed, and each performance was vetted by Nazi henchmen; the Gestapo attended each event. The image is bizarre; I daydream about a room full of once-prominent Jews, a nefarious character in the back, out of *Indiana Jones*, taking notes in a small leather-bound notebook with a silver pen, a swastika armband gleaming in the darkened theater. These performances kept the girls of Wangenheimstrasse 36 culturally engaged for as long as they were allowed. The Kulturbund was dissolved in 1941, well after Valy had left the Kindergartenseminar.

The girls in the Kindergartenseminar—many on their own for the first time—felt liberated, emboldened, thrilled to have briefly slipped away from their parents, to be studying with the best Jewish teachers left in the Reich from across the German-speaking world. The population they worked with, however, was miserable, babies born from and in terrible situations—made worse by the growing number of harsh covenants against Jews. Already in 1938, Jews had been banned from soup kitchens; throughout that year and into 1939, all remaining social services were, one by one, stripped away. They would be banned that winter from "warming rooms" for those who couldn't afford heat. Jews found themselves running afoul of the law as well—traffic stings had been set up to charge Jews with jaywalking, giving them fines of fifty Reichsmark (Valy's monthly salary!) for what would normally be a five RM fine.

At the same time, the population of young German Jews was diminishing rapidly: Marion Kaplan's excellent account of life in

Germany under the Reich, *Between Dignity and Despair*, notes that between June 1933 and September 1939, the population of Jews under age thirty-nine decreased by nearly eighty percent. It was a stark contrast to the still-rich world of the Kindergartenseminar, the bubble Valy lived in, in which, Marianne Strauss told Roseman, "you forgot really what was going on outside," as there was "always something interesting going on. There were lots of interesting people still living ordinary lives in Berlin—very public well-known figures. . . . Musicians would come and give concerts; we'd have get-togethers . . . folk singing, lectures . . . wonderful social things going on all the time."

So despite the increasingly difficult life outside the walls of Wangenheimstrasse 36, despite her mother's rapid and bewildering, race-based impoverishment at home in Troppau, Valy's time in Grunewald was, intellectually at least, peculiarly, and temporarily, not unlike her life in Vienna—and far, far better than it had been in her claustrophobic hometown.

On the other side of Berlin, near touristy Checkpoint Charlie, I stop at the Topography of Terror, an indoor-outdoor permanent exhibition situated on the land where the Gestapo and SS headquarters were located during the Reich. The museum narrates the Gestapo's work over dozens of architecturally lovely panels; it is all Plexiglas and chrome, like an architect's loft, incongruously pleasant to wander through. It's an excellent exhibition, if a bit wordy, but I find myself inordinately annoyed that out of some, say, fifty panels, two are devoted to the "Jew catchers," those Jews whom the Gestapo used as their sniffer dogs to ferret out other Jews in hiding. Granted, these *Greifer*, as they were called in German, did horrific work, but there were so few, in comparison to the minions of the Gestapo. There was debate, after the war, about the role of the Jewish councils, and Jewish organizations like the Reichsvereinigung—but the *Greifer* were in a whole other category of moral turpitude. They were tasked specifically with flushing out their co-religionists. To put so much emphasis on such an aberration here seems peculiar, as though there is a spreading of guilt in a way that seems, at least to me, grossly imbalanced.

In the small shop at the front of the museum, I pick up historian Wolf Gruner's book *Judenverfolgung [Jewish Persecution] in Berlin, 1933–1945*, which lists the restrictions on Jews, day by day, for Berlin alone. Here I can match the dates of Valy's private letters to what her public life was like. Every month—nearly every day—comes degradation, making her time in the Kindergartenseminar that much more precious. The restrictions range from the onerous and burdensome (throughout January 1939, for example, children were continuously deprived: first of the right to foster care, then to special-needs schools) to the humiliating (in March, Jews were denied access to city libraries, a blow to those like Valy who no longer had money to buy books). The children's reading rooms were now barred to Jews as well, making those who cared for children stuck with trying to creatively entertain and educate kids in a world that seemed to contract, daily, around them.

Yet despite the intensity of the deprivation, despite the cruelty and randomness of the things barred to her, in August 1939, Valy still has a heartbreaking amount of hope that she, too, can leave. She's sure of it, and so is everyone else around her.

> *I'm the acknowledged favorite of the director [a woman], and I'm addressed as "golden child" (people easily and often forget my [academic] title here). I am quite evidently being protected and favored by a female senior official . . . of the Reichsvertretung.*

The director was Margarethe Fraenkel, a forty-year-old "Aryan" woman and mother of five who was married to a Jewish man. Fraenkel eventually joined the anti-Nazi resistance. Her extended family was able to emigrate, while she tried to "overcome her great loneliness by helping others," as her colleagues described her. But it is Valy's loneliness that engulfs, and propels, her to promise—herself, my grandfather—continuously, that she will leave soon:

These two women—they are quite extraordinarily smart and good (not only because they are nice to me)—shudder at the thought of the moment when I receive a Permit and leave. It defies all explanation, I think, because I never do anything at all exceptional, of course, and I am totally replaceable. But as far as I'm concerned, of course, they can just continue to "shudder." I am so terribly busy here; my day starts at 6 a.m. and ends at 8 p.m. (theoretically, a few days off are envisaged, but there aren't enough suitable supervisors . . . on the "theoretical" days off). In the evenings I'm very tired and in no way able to do anything for myself or to write. My mother is still in Troppau and busy shutting down the household, and after that she too is supposed to come here for the time being, and I hope she surely will find someplace to stay.

My prospects for England were quite good until recently, but the day before yesterday I received a letter informing me that my Permit can't be granted for the present; I'm afraid that physicians aren't getting [necessary] Permits. . . . Lonka Schlüssel had a very nice job for me as a lady's companion, but I would have to be there soon, and with these new complications that is hardly possible. I'm really quite worn out, but that's really not what I want to write you about!

Valy's loss—the permit problem—is enormous. In fact, my grandfather already knew about her England prospects; Lonka had written him earlier that month, assuring him—he seems to have asked—that she had found a place for Valy. August 1939 was early enough that in Lonka's letter, written in English, she worries more for herself than for Valy, even though Lonka is already safe in London. In her letter Lonka explains she had just been told her quota number had come up, she could meet her family in America, and then, just as quickly, she learned the consulate had made a mistake—her number was a ways off. "I fainted in the street," she tells him, "and two people had to carry me into a shop nearby." Later she gets to the subject of Valy. "Yes, I hear from Valy," she says, and "I managed a post for her as a companion." She, too, tells him about the Kindergartenseminar.

But permits to England would not get easier to receive. Valy's lost window, in a few weeks, will be cemented over into a fully sealed wall. But even as she worries about her prospects for emigration, Valy is still racked by the feeling of loss from the forced end of their affair:

> *I was so delighted to get your letter; so very, very delighted! About everything. And it is just impossible to describe how much I miss you! I really didn't mean to write you about this subject either, because it is scarcely possible to describe to you this feeling of emptiness, this dismal feeling of not being able to be with you, the catastrophic feeling of having lost something irreplaceable, and this out-and-out longing for you. It is indeed possible that someday I can come to you again, but the 3 or 4 years it will take until then seem hardly bearable to me, and very often I lack the courage to believe in this possible Later on . . .*
>
> *Goodbye, Darling! I would be happy to hear from you again soon. Please don't forget to write! There is so little that brings me joy.*
>
> *Lots of love and all imaginable good wishes to you, and thousands and thousands of kisses,*
>
>

Yours,

Valy
>

> *The letter was written in installments. I was very frequently interrupted while writing.*

"There is so little that brings me joy." Such a small line, but so much— and it is only summer 1939, the world has not yet completely narrowed, it still seems possible to leave; the distances are still merely about time, not life and death.

To understand Valy's experiences better, I seek out authorities on the Reichsvereinigung. I meet Gudrun Maierhof, a professor of politics and social science at the University of Applied Sciences in Erfurt, at a small café in front of the Charlottenburg S-Bahn station. She looks Israeli, Gudrun, from her dyed red-purple hair to the Hebrew *chai* (life) and *ahava* (love) necklaces she wears, a small nod to her immersion in Jewish history, or a flag of affiliation with Jews. She skims one or two of the letters I have brought along and then gives out a little yelp when she sees Valy worked for most of 1939 and part of 1940 in the Kindergartenseminar. Part of her dissertation was on the seminar, so she sends me a section of that (unpublished) text, to help me better understand the opportunity, the optimism the school represented. From 1938, she explains, one-year and six-month intro courses in child care and kindergarten teaching were offered. The hope was the girls enrolled would move on to exactly the kind of position Valy sought in the United Kingdom. In the end, though, dozens of the girls would be called to service in Berlin itself as more and more parents— and mothers of small children—would be pulled into forced labor by 1941, leaving thousands of unschooled kids in need of care, instruction, and supervision. It was a well-educated, if temporary, workforce, a high-end finishing school in the anteroom to hell.

Maierhof also tells me, with huge excitement, she knows someone in Berlin who studied at the Kindergartenseminar—perhaps, she wonders, with some awe, she was even Valy's student: her name is Inge Deutschkron, and she's a local celebrity in the world of survivor-speakers. She was the Israeli daily *Ma'ariv* correspondent in Frankfurt during the Auschwitz trials and she later wrote a book—called *Outcast* in English—about her experiences under the Nazis; the book was made into a play that is still regularly performed by school groups in Germany. She speaks often to children's and women's groups.

Deutschkron, Maierhof says, was saved by a man named Otto Weidt, a kind of small-time Oskar Schindler. Weidt, who was himself legally blind, ran a small broom and brush factory that employed blind and deaf Jews, alongside a handful of sighted ones—like Deutschkron. He insisted, for years, that his staff was essential and couldn't be deported; he rescued them from roundups again and again. Eventually, his efforts to keep them aboveground exhausted, he helped some, including Deutschkron, secure new identities. Once, Weidt traveled from Berlin to Auschwitz itself to rescue one woman, a former worker and—it was rumored—his lover. She survived, but not all his workers were so lucky: he kept a family of four, stashed behind the wall of an armoire, all hiding from the Gestapo until they were denounced by one of the *Greifer*, the Jew-catchers.

The week I meet Gudrun, my friend Baruc Corazón is visiting from Madrid. I tell him these stories and he parries with an anecdote he had recently heard of similar reverberations, into our generation, in Spain. A contemporary of his was in the process of researching her grandfather's death, he says, a killing that took place decades before her birth at the end of the Spanish Civil War. The grandfather had been exposed—and then, in the final moments of the war, was summarily shot, without trial, for being a Republican. Baruc's friend looked up the grandfather's records and discovered the name of his denouncer; all involved lived in a small town on the Costa Brava, the beautiful swath of coastal Catalonia just above Barcelona. The granddaughter called the house, and a family member told her the denouncer had died the week before. The man on the phone said, tearily, "He was a wonderful man, he just died." And Baruc's friend said, "He may have been a wonderful person, but he denounced my grandfather, and ruined my family." We sit with that for a moment, stunned even in the retelling.

Weidt's former factory is now the Museum Blindenwerkstatt Otto Weidt; it is at Rosenthaler Strasse 39, down a graffitied alleyway in Hackescher Markt, the heart of the old East. These days, there is a Starbucks just in front of the alley, and, next door, an art-house cinema; dozens upon dozens of bikes are always parked there—the area has become known for boutiques and eateries. The museum itself is up a small flight of stairs, easily missed unless you're searching for it.

Deutschkron's and Otto Weidt's stories are marvelous, even cinematic, but when I meet her, Deutschkron is unsentimental to the point of caustic. She is a compact woman, with short-cropped hair, a similar color to Gudrun's, that unnaturally red-purple; her eyes are lined in kohl and she looks younger than her near century of living. When we meet, she is dressed in a way that reminds me of my grandparents— put-together: a leaf-green sweater and a bouclé tweed skirt, pearls, stockings, and orthopedic shoes. She has the brusque deportment of someone who has relied on herself for her entire life; she makes it clear before I come that, at nearly ninety, she hasn't time for small talk, long interviews, or second visits. (This is nonnegotiable, I find. Upon arrival, I see I have forgotten my camera, and she insists she will absolutely not allow me to return for a portrait. I show up, instead, some days later at the Blindenwerkstatt, where Deutschkron is lecturing to a group of immigrant women. She grumbles, "None will have heard of me there," meaning America, but then submits to my camera.)

Deutschkron's tenure with Otto Weidt came well after her experience at the Kindergartenseminar—she was in the school only for a year, and then was pressed into forced labor, standing for some twelve hours a day in a factory. Eventually, she got herself the (relatively) easier job as secretary in Weidt's factory by purposely screwing up her right knee; it never properly healed.

I show her a photo of Valy; she barely looks at it, and scoffs when I say, quietly, perhaps she might have known her. It is uncomfortably warm in her apartment; we are sitting in a small, sunny, enclosed porch that amplifies the effects of the sun. Then I make the mistake of saying that Valy might have survived, being young; that I am hoping I might discover she outlived the war. "Why should she have survived?" she nearly shouts at me. I start to cry. I want Valy to have survived, I say, aware, immediately, how ridiculous, how childish, it sounds. I'm so close to the idea—the fantasy?—of Valy, I almost want to will her into being, into finding her.

Deutschkron sighs heavily at this. She is unimpressed by Americans. She is unimpressed, particularly, by young American Jews who

Inge Deutschkron lecturing at Museum Blindenwerkstatt Otto Weidt. Behind her is a photo of her from the early 1940s.

come to weep with her, or who weep at all. She feels Jews in the States did nothing and come back now, seventy years on, to express their sadness. She doesn't want it. "The Germans forbid immigration in October 1941, so, until then, everyone knew in the world—if they wanted to know—what was happening to us. And the Americans could have helped us! They could have helped us to get affidavits! *Ach*," she practically spits the words. "Disgusting! I think this is really disgusting and they are the ones to shout at the Germans *ahahahaha!*" She jabs a finger in the air, accusatorily. "You know what happened to me in the States? I had two lectures there, in both of them [people said], 'What you are telling us can't be true! Germans didn't help Jews!' in that fashion. Thank you very much! *They* didn't help us! Ach! I could tell you after the war how many American soldiers opened parcels that we got, and took out coffee and things like that, but that's perhaps human, but it was unbelievable.

"What do you mean, 'should have survived?" she asks, switching back to Valy. "Were they not masters over lives and deaths, these people, these Nazis? Why would she have survived? Just she?" She laughs, bitterly. "There is no 'should.' You see what I mean. I was helped by *twenty* Berlin families who helped us to survive. This was a dictatorship of the worst sort and whoever was found helping Jews was taken to a concentration camp. The Americans! Their immigration quotas were from 1918 or something. They didn't change these quotas. I

think they allowed a certain number of people in." I tell her Valy writes
to my grandfather that, at best, her number on the quota list was two
years off. "Exactly!" she says. "Disgusting! Honestly. That's how I feel
about it. Especially when Jews from America come along and tell me,
Oh, how hard. The Americans didn't help us!"

Deutschkron is also unimpressed with me because I have not yet
read her book (I will, upon returning to the States, but that is some
months away, and I hadn't heard of her before meeting Gudrun). And
she is busy. "I have so much work to do! I'm eighty-six, you see. And I
don't have much time! . . . Incidentally, what you should see is the
play," she adds, meaning the play that was made from her book. She
tells me it has been performed more than three hundred times in Berlin alone, but no one in America has interest in it. "I have an agent
who says it is hopeless. They are interested in Jewish victims but not
in those who survived with the help of Germans."

I disagree, but I don't want to fight with her. I can't say exactly
why one story is picked up over another. And, to her greater point, I
think there, too, she is mistaken: Americans are obsessed with the
exceptions, the defiance, to the detriment of the bigger picture, the
bigger loss, the norm of death. We are always looking for the happy
Holocaust story. Even me, here, I realize. Though I am busily break-
ing down the myth perpetuated by my grandfather—his own defiance, his own happy story—I am clinging to the hope that, somehow,
Valy could have survived the trauma, the vicissitudes, the cruelty, of
Nazi Berlin, until the end.

We sit, for a moment, in miserable silence. Hoping to make the
most of a visit that has been, at best, uncomfortable, and at worst a
waste of her time, I ask Deutschkron if she wouldn't mind telling me
her story anyway. So, after some grumbling, she does, in great detail,
over the course of the next two hours. And of course, as with all such
stories, it is shocking, and it is amazing. She lived in hiding spots
that ranged from the temporary and uncomfortable to the distinctly
miserable—including a wet and cold goat shed whose only benefit was

its relative safety. She pretended to be a refugee from bombing raids—first in the east, then in Berlin itself—lying directly to Hitler youth, using false identities and claiming her papers had been destroyed, along with her possessions, by British bombers. And yet hearing her tale gets me no closer to knowing more of what happened to Valy—other than to know that Deutschkron and her mother, both of whom survived in hiding, did so with the help of many, many friends and acquaintances who had known them before the war. In listening, I am reminded that Valy had no such network. She was foreign in Berlin, alone, save her mother.

"We couldn't get an entry permit into Great Britain," Deutschkron says. Immediately after the November pogrom, Deutschkron's father fled to England at a time when many believed men were at greater risk than women. And she—like Valy—had missed a chance to serve as a maid in the United Kingdom.

"Immigration wasn't easy, because countries didn't want us. It was the same with Great Britain [as America]: they asked for bank guarantees or rich relatives who would take us in. Well, my father had a cousin in England who was really British, and though we didn't know her very well, she offered to help, to provide a . . . bank guarantee. For one person. She couldn't provide three. So we thought it was best for my father to go. Men were going to concentration camps, and besides, my father was an active Social Democrat and he was dismissed from service, not because he was Jewish but because he was a politician. We thought it would be easier, once he was there, to get us out, and he looked into us being [maids]. And indeed he found a family that would take [my mother and me] as a cook and an assistant. But this didn't work because we had to fulfill so many things—like paying Reichsfluchtsteuer [the tax charged by the Reich to leave; it was twenty percent in 1933, and by the end of the 1930s it would fleece a family of all they had] and all the strange boxes Jews had to check off in order to leave! We had to list all the things we wanted to take with us, like handkerchiefs and underwear and so on. Someone came from the [tax office] and the finance office, and they checked whether it was all correct and so on, and it took a lot of time and then the war broke out." And so they were stuck, much like Valy.

By October 1939, the world tipping into war, Valy toggles between hope—that she may yet be rescued—and despair—her chances, she fears, are already lost. To get to America, she has applied too late, she is thousands of names down the list and the quota system is capped and truncated, it is keeping not just her but thousands of her compatriots, and her co-religionists, out of the United States. By the following spring, even those most reluctant to leave had applied to place their names on these lists. "My registration number is very high; I applied too late. I am number 77,454 under the German quota, which means I will have to wait at least five to six years," teacher Hertha Feiner wrote her half-Jewish daughters, who were already safe in Switzerland.

But those who had applied—like Valy—earlier still held out hope a window would open for them. Even as Valy struggles for a way around these emigration problems, life in Germany itself is getting more and more surreal—on September 6, a curfew is imposed on Jews, making it illegal for them to be out past eight p.m; they are also no longer allowed radios and other such small comforts. Her mother, at last, has made it from Troppau. She has work, food. The Seminar girls were even given gas masks, as the Reich was still protecting Jews in the event of chemical warfare. She can see the deprivation all around her, she knows her position is fortunate—for now. But Valy is so very, very lonely. And so very, very sad.

Berlin, October 12, 1939

My dearest, very dearest boy,
    Today, finally, after an interminably long time, a letter from you arrived. How I waited for it, how I yearned for it, how I rejoiced . . . and how much I would love to be with you again. And since it seems to be absolutely impossible that we will see each other soon again, so

hopelessly long, that I am sometimes completely desperate and feel that I cannot take it, although, speaking from a purely external viewpoint, I am, relatively speaking, well off: I continue to be in the seminar and I am making money, and I am able to have my mother with me; together we live in this, the most beautiful room of the villa; mother has been a "guest" of the Reichsvereinigung for the past three weeks; over the next few days, she will begin a "retraining" course / housekeeping, and we hope that she will obtain a relatively good position here. They like me here and they are fantastically nice to my mama; most of the people here are nice and good to me, the children adore me, and there are surely many who are deeply envious of me. . . . Still and all, I am absolutely not happy with this life I am forced to lead, devoid of intellect, friends and love. I work a lot,—15 hours a day; every third day I have nightshift; that does not leave a lot of time for intellect, joy . . . [or] love . . . and I long so much to do something other than wiping children's derrieres and struggling with unruly kids and tidying up children's rooms—that, however, hardly ever are really tidy, and that, just like today, time and again cause interminable fights. But I must be quiet and seemingly content because I must earn money, and, as I said before, I am really, relatively speaking, rather well off.

Isiu got a summons to the Consul for November 6th, and hopes to be able to travel soon thereafter. Hermann is in Trieste on his way to Shanghai. My grandparents and Berta are in the interior, and we worry a lot about their livelihoods.

Oh my darling, how much I would like to hear your supposedly poor German—something I really cannot imagine and how terribly sad it is that even you consider it questionable if and when this may be possible—although you always were such an optimist in these matters. But let us not give ourselves headaches over this now; somehow or other it will work out, and it is impossible to make plans since all decisions are being taken away from one. Unfortunately,

*however, one can't help but feel miserable at times, but that, too,
shall pass.*

*Darling, are you now the "top banana" or close to it, at the St.
Luke's Hospital? Do you like it, and do you feel good about things,
everything told. Lonka was wonderfully kind and nice. And it
almost did work out. Unfortunately, I no longer can write to her
now. Please give her my very best regards!*

*I want to write to you very soon again, my darling. But, please,
you must do so as well. I do not know how much longer I will stay
here; maybe my own disorderliness is my undoing. Now you see—
that's what you get for always calling my sloppiness largesse and
geniality (but only when you were in a good mood). But, surely, there
is much positive about my work here, and the people do like me.
Maybe I will even stay.*

*Goodbye, my beloved boy. Give my regards to Mama, Cilli and
Karl (what are they doing???) and countless kisses (if I still master
this technique) from your*

Valy

Lonka remained Valy's contact in London. *"Unfortunately, I can no
longer write to her now"*— Germany has invaded Poland. Another route
to salvation has closed. Karl and Lonka continued to write back and
forth about Valy, until Lonka could no longer offer much hope at all.
Lonka writes to this effect in September:

17.9.1939

My Dear,

*How very nice of you to think of me in your prayers. What is
a pity is that they've not had the effect you wanted for though your
intentions were good, things don't look too cheerful just now. . . . The
American consulate is closed for emigration for an indefinite period as*

they have got too much to do with repatriating their own people. So only God knows when we shall be there, provided we shall be able to go at all. Have you been in New York for the high festivals [Rosh Hashanah and Yom Kippur] and have you, by any chance, seen my sisters? It really seems absence makes the heart grow fonder for the last two weeks I have been longing for my sisters and brother more than I ever did before. Talking about high festivals, I forgot: a very happy new year to you.

And how is the world treating you except that you have to work 24 hours a day in your hospital? . . . I have not heard from Valy and I don't suppose I will now as I have not got friends in neutral countries on the continent who would forward my letters to her. I feel so sorry for her, poor girl, in occupation. I am so lucky to be here. . . .

Valy's own "disorderliness," I can only imagine, meant her delay—at least compared with Karl—in joining those who were lobbying for visas to America, in putting her name on those interminable quota lists. The problem facing Valy extended back decades—quotas were instituted during and at the end of World War I, a nativist response in the United States to an influx of immigrants. Germany's numbers, officially, weren't actually all that low—just over 25,000 a year—but there was never a year that immigration actually reached those heights. And then it dropped to a minuscule percentage of that number, as the Great Depression engulfed the States in the late 1920s and early 1930s. Quietly, as the American economy teetered, President Herbert Hoover pushed American consulates to reinterpret and enforce the clause for keeping out immigrants. A line in the law which read if an immigrant was "likely to become a public charge" was reread to mean essentially "needed work," a move that reduced immigration beginning in 1930 by ninety percent, limiting those coming in to the independently wealthy. By the late 1930s, the numbers had climbed a bit again, but the actual numbers remained well below 10,000 people per year. The

U.S. Holocaust Memorial Museum in Washington estimates that something like 300,000 Jews applied to immigrate to America between 1933 and 1939, and some 90,000 were accepted. It was a battle at the State Department between those who believed that the United States was, for most intents and purposes, full, and those who saw it as a haven of some kind.

Valy is in despair. But instead of focusing on her miserable visa status, or her inability to get herself out of this hell, she worries, instead, about my grandfather. He comes to symbolize everything. Even in the early letters, she feels like she is losing him, and she can't lose him because losing him means losing hope. She sees him everywhere, in everything she does. She sees her world shrinking—everyone seems to be getting to safety but her, everyone seems to be moving on. Her world is caving in; it is stifling.

And so, instead, she lies in bed at night and imagines a time when he was in her bed beside her, when their only bit of necessary resistance was to defy their mothers—oh, how normal to defy a mother! These two fatherless Jews with their small rebellion—and Valy unlocked her bedroom door and let him in.

Berlin, 12-16-39

My darling:

Your last letter with the really fantastical date of August 27—and nothing since then, not even one syllable—is before me. And I always thought it had to be that way,—that the mail simply did not work. Then, all of a sudden, I met Paula Holländer's sister. I am happy about this meeting and am anxiously breathing in this little bit of Viennese atmosphere. She told me that she is getting letters from Paula every week. . . .

Do you know, my darling, when I think of you? For example: In the evenings, after my room, overflowing with students who, enthusiastically smoking, spend their leisure time with me, finally gets emptied out and I, after making my evening rounds (when I have nightshift) finally return to my abode that greets me in total disarray and reeking of smoke—just like it was at Mandels, Spieler, Hirschfeld's, etc. after I unlocked the door for you and quietly sneaked back into the room with you—then I lie down with the absolutely wonderful feeling that I will meet you somewhere tomorrow and will be able to talk about everything again and be with you. Or: I am standing in the laboratory and boiling urine samples . . . and dream of our chemistry course. Do you remember the time, Karl, when we showed up with our sausage sandwiches at this elegant restaurant—I think it was called something like Libig—and were so terribly embarrassed?

And then I think of you when we work at the hospital the way you don't like it, and every time I pass a newsstand where they sell entertainment journals; when I read something you would love; when I put on a dress you would like; whenever the word "America" is mentioned; when there is talk of love.

Otherwise,—I am doing quite well: I continue to work afternoons in the infants' group (that meanwhile has shrunk quite considerably) against free room and board. During the mornings I sit in at the children's ward in the hospital. The "Reichsvertretung" may grant me a Stipendium of Reichsmark 60.00 per month, which I would need urgently for my mama, as the position unfortunately did not materialize for her. Alas, she is again in Troppau, and, of course, without any kind of income.

Life here is nice and much more carefree than elsewhere. Last week we had a beautiful Chanukah celebration during which I received generous presents from everyone and, among other things, got a medal with the following inscription: "And then there came a little person in a white coat. You already know her. And our little ones, in particular, do. When she enters the room, they all shout:

'Auntie Doctor, are you free today?' And then there is a lot of ruckus.
And the students, or so I hear, love and respect her as well—that's the
reason we give her this medal." . . .

Goodbye, my beloved boy

In the meantime, her life is in flux. The Kindergartenseminar has suddenly lost the building at Wangenheimstrasse; it will soon be aryanized and the school will be absorbed into a different part of the city, a smaller building, forcing Valy to seek work elsewhere. She treads water, and works and tries to make sure the reason she stayed behind—her mother—can actually be with her. Without her, none of it seems worth it at all. Worse still, she feels abandoned by everyone, forgotten.

He is not writing. It has been three months of silence. In America, he is still banging on doors, trying to pick up the pieces of his life, doctors are writing about him—the executive secretary of the Emergency Committee in Aid of Displaced Foreign Medical Scientists, a doctor he has met only once, is busily determining his future. "Dr. Wildman is a person who would most likely fit into a smaller hospital. His appearance is not very prepossessing, though he is of medium height and quite well built," a letter in his National Committee for Resettlement of Foreign Physicians file notes. "His manner is reserved and his English is fair." Another, a typed card, simply says "Single. Nice Personality." He is a specimen.

Perhaps the letters really do not arrive. Perhaps he writes and they disappear. Or perhaps he does not write to Valy, because he has nothing to say or because he is ashamed of what he would say if he did write. He has no real *news* yet. No way to prove he has mastered this country. He has his own survival story, after all. He is busy trying to keep from drowning in America.

He was uncomfortable, but his discomfort, he can't have yet fully understood, was nothing compared to hers. There seems never a mo-

ment when she can relax, never a moment when anything is a given.
Life is constantly shifting, and she has to be on guard.

December 31, 1939

*My beloved boy! This time, my day off came and went, and I
was not able to write to you, my dear. Therefore, I am writing to you
now while I am on duty, watching the sleeping children. I hope they
won't disturb me too often. There is one boy, an unruly lad, who is
incredibly attached to me. He has caresses that remind me of yours. He
strokes my hair and my face, loves to kiss my eyes and looks dearly and
deeply into my eyes—not really in a childlike manner. I always have
to think of you and you may have sent me this three-year-old boy and
with him your kisses and caresses.*

*All of a sudden it has become quite questionable how much longer
I will be able to stay here. The day before yesterday we received a
termination notice for this house, which we now must vacate within
2 months. Therefore, I will also lose my position. But, my darling, do
not be concerned for me: 2 months is a long time and somehow I'll get
along.*

There are still no letters from Karl. And as life becomes more
burdensome, this lack of contact with him weighs her down. It is bitterly cold and, in January, the Gestapo announces Jews can no longer
purchase new clothing or shoes. The central office of the Reichsvereinigung will now begin to take used items from fleeing Jews and
carefully distribute them to those who reluctantly remain. Even passing clothing from Jew to Jew is forbidden without special permissions.
And so Valy huddles in all her clothing, and waits for word. Karl is
Valy's only outside link, her only chance.

Six

THREE HUNDRED
DOLLARS

As 1939 turns to 1940, Valy's pleas for help are joined by a chorus of pleas from others who lobby my grandfather on her behalf. They push my grandfather not to forget Valy, to help her, to *do something*. As they do, they narrate again and again the problems faced by the refugees on these shores, who were scrambling to pull those left behind across the Atlantic. "Dear Karl, I arrived in New York on October 15th," writes Paula Holländer in early 1940. She is an old schoolmate from Vienna. "My entire family is still in Germany." The letter is dated January 18, one day after Karl's twenty-eighth birthday. Paula continues:

> *I was able to scrape up a little money that I sent to Switzerland in order to pay for transferring my parents (illegally) to Palestine. I am so clueless that I did not even succeed in getting an affidavit for my sister, who is living with her husband (27 years) and child (1 year) in Berlin. She . . . asks that $3000 be transferred in the name of my brother-in-law. If we were able to document the existence of this account, my sister and her family could come right away. However, who would be able to put up this kind of account? So far, I*

was not able to find this kind of benefactor. I also have a 25-year-old brother, a dear guy, who fled from Poland to Lithuania; he was born in Vienna, has been registered for a long time, and I don't even have an affidavit for him either. Don't you think I am really incapable? With all these worries I have relatively little time to think about myself. I have thought of you often. . . . I could imagine that you would complain a bit about my clumsiness and that you would smile and give me advice on what to do.

Do write to me—that would really please me. By the way, Valy has not had any mail from you in a long time. I don't have Valy's address, but she sees my sister often.

Later that year, Paula writes that she has succeeded: "My sister and her family arrived from Berlin . . . and brought me greetings from Valy. While she is doing quite all right, she would very much like to come over here. She is working at the Jewish Hospital, but you probably already know everything."

Valy knew others were getting their loved ones out, and my grandfather knew, and that knowledge hangs heavy in the letters. The anguish was already intolerable. What had they done that he hadn't? What had they accomplished that he could not?

In the meantime, bits and pieces of the degradation and humiliation now defining life in Germany were trickling out, exposing Karl to some of the horror. Even strangers implore him to help Valy.

February 24, 1940

Dear Dr. Wildman,

I do not know whether Dr. Valy Scheftel in her letters to you ever mentioned my name. Until March of 1939 I was a rabbi in Berlin, where the Gestapo had tasked me with the care of the Jews in the occupied Sudetenland. It was in this context that I met Dr. Scheftel in Troppau.

*I am writing to you in order to inquire whether and to what
extent you may be in a position to do anything for the emigration of
Dr. Scheftel, and possibly also her mother. I do know that you sent
affidavits about a year ago that were submitted to the consulate in
Prague. In the best case scenario, the waiting period for Valy would
be at least two years and even longer for her mother. Before my own
emigration, I tried to do something for the two women, at least
economically. As you surely know, V. has been working in a children's
home of the Reichsvertretung. It was my hope that this work would
at least feed the two women until they can come here.*

*The events that unfolded during the past weeks, however, and
especially the beginning deportation of the Jews . . . let me fear the
worst. I would be only too happy to help them to immigrate to an
interim country, where they could wait until their US number gets
called up. Only a few weeks ago, my parents-in-law immigrated to
Chile. At the moment I am working on the emigration of other
relatives whom Valy often sees, from Berlin to Chile. (This is the only
country for which it was possible to find visas for the past several
weeks. Brazilian visas, for example, are no longer affordable, at least
for my means.) Do you think that you or others might be able to do
the same for Valy and her mother? A Chilean visa for one person cost
me US $150.00, and a confidential source has written to me that
additional visas would cost about the same amount. While the visas
appear legitimate, they seem to have been issued illegally. In any
event, they enable immigration to Chile, as the case of my in-laws,
who arrived in Chile on January 3rd, proves. My confidante, a
former physician from Breslau, who now is in Santiago, is absolutely
trustworthy.*

*I beg you not to misunderstand me. I only write to you because of
my concern as a friend for Dr. Scheftel, who again wrote to me a few
days ago. I would be most grateful if you could write to me soon what
your position on this issue is, and, above all—something I am unable
to decide on my own—whether you consider this solution, interim*

country with further immigration to the USA, as feasible, as far as
Valy is concerned. As far as I know her and her mother, I believe that
they would be capable of feeding themselves in Chile until they can
come here. And, although it may be difficult in Chile, a hard life in
physical safety is preferable to an easier life in constant danger.

With kind regards,

Sincerely,

Alfred Jospe

"The events that unfolded during the past weeks, however, and especially the beginning deportation of the Jews . . . let me fear the worst."
Jospe is referring to the deportation of the Jews of Stettin, which took
place earlier that month. Stettin—now known as Szczecin—is a Baltic
seaport; in early 1940, the Germans violently expulsed Stettin's Jews.
They were rounded up, brutally, aggressively, robbed of their possessions, and then sent on to Lublin, Poland, to "clean" the area, to make
room for the *Volksdeutschen*—the ethnic Germans—who wanted their
homes. The entire community, from children as young as two to octo-
genarians, were roused from their homes, some forced into a former
mortuary under conditions so crowded that many died there on the
spot, foreshadowing what would come for the rest of Europe's Jews.

But unlike what happened later, this deportation was handled so
baldly that Jews across the Reich learned of it and panicked. Even the
foreign press got wind of it. On February 19, 1940, the Jewish Telegraphic Agency reported from Paris that fifteen hundred "men,
women, children and even the inmates of the local Jewish home for
the aged were piled on a cattle train to be shipped to an unknown
destination. . . . Those too old or sick to walk had to be carried to the
train by others. . . . Nazi storm troopers visited Jewish homes on two
successive nights, told the occupants to prepare to leave, forced them
to file inventories of their possessions and then confiscated all valuables after requiring them to sign statements renouncing this property.

The expulsion took place at three o'clock on a bitterly cold morning. Two storm troopers called at every Jewish house to see that the deportees took no silverware or other valuables. They were permitted to take only a small valise each containing necessary articles. Bank accounts were confiscated." A month later, more news trickled out: the Jews of Stettin were dying, in droves.

Foreign diplomats clamored to know what was happening. Germans grumbled to one another in official documents that the United States would get involved if they weren't more careful. They were anxious to keep neutral America—and Roosevelt—disinterested.

So Jospe knows this—and he assumes my grandfather does as well. But—how awful—the hundred fifty dollars he proposes for a visa was an inconceivably large amount of money for Karl. Astronomical. Three hundred dollars to rescue the two women wasn't simply large, it was nearly the entire amount that the National Committee for Resettlement of Foreign Physicians would lend my grandfather later that spring to start his career. It was a fantasy sum.

So when Jospe says the Brazilian visas are too high, but Chile is accessible, he doesn't know that what he is asking is completely out of reach, and not simply because none of these schemes was fail-safe. These illegal visas—if discovered as false—could simply lose all value on a moment's notice, leaving the women stranded, and any funds scraped together for them would disappear.

And yet despite this, Jospe's admonition seems to have spurred Valy's Uncle Julius, already here in America, and my grandfather into some kind of action:

New York, March 25, 1940

Dear Karl,
Enclosed is a letter from Dr. J. . . . Before I answer the letter, I want to write you a few lines, make my opinion known to you, and

*ask you to what extent you could be (materially) helpful to me, that is,
what sum of money you could scrape up. Of course, it would be
considered a loan to me. Forgive me for bothering you with such
matters. The possibility that both women could be rescued sounds
much too good to be true. It goes without saying that dear Valy would
not leave without her mother, and I think that things mustn't come to
naught over the sum of $300. I could round up $50 at most and
pledge to pay back $20 a month over the course of six months. The
remainder I would repay later, when I'm able.*

*I would be very happy to be able to write and tell Dr. J. to
initiate the necessary steps. I anticipate that the relief committee
[Hilfskom.] will take care of the tickets for the ship (Dr. J.'s
intervention regarding the tickets will surely be successful). Please
write me immediately so that we don't lose any time, and I would be
very grateful to you for a reply in the affirmative. . . .*

Warmest regards,

Julius

Reading this, I am horrified. A three-hundred-dollar missed opportunity. In February 1940, Karl was mired in debt and taking on
more debt each month. An internal memorandum of the National
Refuge Service, written in June 1940 and now held in the files at the
University of Minnesota, discussed the case of the Wildman family as
a whole: he could not help with the upkeep of his mother, let alone
anyone else.

*The following information refers to our telephone conversation
of 6/17, in connection with Dr. Chayim Wildman [sic]. . . . Mr.
Wildman's mother Sara, 75 years old, arrived in New York 9/10/38.
She lived with her brother, Sam Feldschuh, an upholstery
salesman. . . . Mr. Sam earns $15 a week and therefore, when he was
unable to continue maintaining his sister, she went to live with her
daughter Celia F. She sold her remaining jewels for $60 and thus*

*paid for her upkeep for sometime. When this was exhausted she
applied to us for help on 2/2/40.*

*Financial assistance has been given since 4/12 at the rate of $23
a month. I was not aware of the fact that Chayim earned anything at
all, or I should have gone into the possibility of his helping his mother
to some extent. His sister, Celia, tells me Chayim is not able to
contribute anything at all. . . .*

There was no money for visas to Chile. There was nearly nothing
to eat. He is embarrassed. I find a draft of a letter he wrote to Tonya
Morganstern Warner, dated December 14, 1940, months later. *"I regret to have to tell you that I am not getting on so 'very' well as you seem to
believe. I am probably doing much better than anybody else who has been
practicing for 6 weeks, but it is still far from being satisfactory."* He is not
yet in control of this new country—him! The one who mastered everything, the one for whom everything came easily—languages, affidavits, visas, jobs. Here he was failing Valy, not by his own accord, but
what did that matter? He couldn't win. He had nothing to offer her
beyond the affidavits he had already issued, the affidavits that would
soon wither and expire. And here he was, shamed by outsiders, by his
old school friend Paula, by Valy's Uncle Julius, by this stranger, Rabbi
Jospe—all of them underlining for him that he is failing her. It is
simply awful. It is unfair. He seems unwilling to let that be the case,
and yet neither can he realistically offer much in the way of material
support.

New York, April 19, 1940

Dear Karl,

*Forgive me for not answering your kind letter until now. I
couldn't get around to it sooner. Thanks very much for your aim and
intention to help my sister and Valy. But I can't ask it of you, because
you're in the phase of establishing your livelihood, so that material*

[handwritten: make card send my for]

JEWISH FAMILY WELFARE SOCIETY
80 WILLOUGHBY ST.
~~1095 MYRTLE AVENUE~~ BROOKLYN, N. Y.
TRIANGLE 5-9128
TELEPHONE — ~~EVERGREEN 5-0000~~
Borough Hall District

MORTIMER SCHWAGER
PRESIDENT
MICHAEL G. APPEL
VICE-PRESIDENT
WALTER A. MILLER
VICE-PRESIDENT
JACK WARSHAUER
VICE-PRESIDENT

CHARLES I. MANDEL
TREASURER
DR. HARRY KOSTER
SECRETARY
—
GERTRUDE R. DAVIS
EXECUTIVE DIRECTOR

March 6,1939.

Mr. Charles Jordan,
Physicians Committee,
National Coordinating Committee,
165 West 46th Street,
New York City.

Re:Dr. Wildman, Chaim -1912
2125 Pacific St. %
Stolzenberg.

My dear Mr.Jordan:-

      Dr. Wildman came to this country with his mother, sister and brother-in-law on September 10, 1938. His mother is being assisted by a brother in whose home she is staying, and the sister and her husband have made their own arrangements. Dr. Wildman had been living with a cousin but was obliged to move because of this relative's financial pressure, and he therefore took a room in the home of some friends. It was at the point where he needed financial assistance that he applied to our agency, coming the first time on February 10th. We have been giving him financial assistance since February 20th. His room rent is $5.00 a week, and an equal amount weekly is allowed for his living expenses.

      He speaks English quite fluently. He has passed his language examination and has also taken his State medical board. He has not yet heard about the results. He is looking around for interneship and has been writing to various hospitals and institutions in this city and in out-of-town sections. He has his medical degree from the University of Vienna, and very high recommendations from various professors and physicians in Vienna.

      I trust it will be possible for you to see Dr. Wildman within a short time so that he can avail himself of the services of your Committee.

Sincerely,

Fanny Slutsky

DISTRICT WORKER.

FS:DL

obligations on your part are impossible. Besides, I doubt that the
[option] proposed by Dr. Jospe will become definite/official.

Warm regards,
Julius

I want to know more about what Julius and my grandfather did, about what they tried to do. And more about what Jospe could realistically offer. But I have no one to ask but the letters. Alfred Jospe lived in Washington, D.C., until his death in 1994—he was the national director of B'nai Brith Hillel. I know that I cannot be searching for Valy's contemporaries, I know I will not find them, but it feels so desperate and awful to know he was *right here* and that I missed him. Jospe saw Valy in Troppau and knew her choices, knew why she had gone to Berlin and knew about her mother, her quota number, her inability to get to a third country.

Perhaps my grandfather's own misery made him silent; how helpless he must have felt, how incompetent. And so, instead of writing her, he trucks along, trying to make his life on these shores make sense. And she is angry.

Berlin, 04-13-1940

My dear, dear boy

The many unanswered letters I have written to you meanwhile have become a legion! . . . All I can do is to hope that my letters will reach you one day and you will write to me. . . .

I am no longer in the seminar for kindergarten teachers. The children's group was discontinued, and I became superfluous and left. Three afternoons a week I now teach health and nutrition issues and was thus "retained for the institute" through this ingenious idea of the leader of the seminar, a woman who feels very well toward me. That's what they say in the home, and they seem happy with it. So am I, very much. In this manner I am able to make some money without taking on work in the afternoons. During the mornings I go to the hospital where I do not learn a whole lot, but still something.

I lead my life the way I've been doing for the past 2 years: In a spirit of waiting, without much joy or hope. But, my darling, don't feel sad for me; I want you to know that I have people around me— women,—you know that only women are left here?!, who still have something to say, who like me, who help me and who want to make life pleasant for me. But I do not succeed very often, and they never will be able to replace you, my boy! You are and remain far, far away, out of my reach, you exist only in my memories, wonderful, beautiful "sunny past." . . . You are no longer even a letter, such as tiny, modest piece of the present. Why don't you write?? . . .

Now I have again finished a letter to you. Will this one also be lost or read perfunctorily and then forgotten, and, in any case, remain without answer? I am so very tired and sad. Even in the most positive of circumstances it will be such a long time before I hear anything from you. Please write me lots about you! It will not be long now that you will have gone through your hospital residency year. What will you do then?

Farewell, my darling, many, many thousand kisses and WRITE IMMEDIATELY!!!!!!!!!!!

Your Valy

And then, a postscript:

04-14-1940

Darling: Mrs. Jurmann, Paula's sister, told me today that Paula has written and reported about you. She says that you don't know where I am and that you did not have any news from me and that you are "upset with me." I am so happy—as ridiculous as this may sound. I am so happy that this worrisome silence of yours has a natural explanation. Naturally, our letters do get lost! They always

*used to get lost when it was particularly important that they would
reach their destination on time. And, of course, it is also natural that
you after sending an exploratory letter into the world—exhausted
from this effort and very pleased with yourself—were "waiting" a
bit. Well, my one and only, beloved boy: I am still alive, currently
residing at Berlin, Rombergstrasse 2. That's where I am awaiting
your letters. Maybe it is better if you send your letters to
Wangenheimstrasse 36, Berlin Grunewald. It is possible that we
won't stay at Rombergstrasse very long, and somehow I always get
mail in Grunewald.*

*And now, in closing, the upshot of my letters from yesterday and
today: I am waiting, waiting, waiting for letters from you.*

Your Valy

Is it true that he hasn't heard from her? It's possible some letters were
lost—among those I found, there are enormous gaps in time. But it is
also possible that she has seized on this, chosen to believe he hasn't
heard from her, rather than think he has forgotten, or turned away, or
has become inured to their plight. I wonder: Was he was too sad to
write her? Too chagrined that for three hundred dollars, he would be
of no help? Julius doesn't feel sorry for him, though. He writes again,
angry now:

N.Y., 05-06-1940

*I just received a card from dear Valy from 04-19. She writes:
". . . The last letter I have from Karl is dated August 27, and I got it
in mid October. Since then I have written a lot, but never got a
reply." At the end she wishes you would write. Could it be that your
cards and letters, in particular, did get lost for the past 7 months!?
Please, pull yourself together and set aside at least once every few
weeks 5 minutes to write a couple of lines to poor Valy. She also
writes that it will be her turn only in about a year (and her mother*

in a few years' time); she is working at the children's ward at the local
hospital and also teaches hygiene at a seminar. Her address: c/o Mrs.
Levy, Berlin, N.O., Romberg Str. 2
  Otherwise, everything unfortunately unchanged.

                                                          Regards,
                                                          Julius

But then something does change. My grandfather writes again, giving
her hope. Her letters in June 1940 are suddenly buoyed, even happy,
all fueled by his returning to her, at least in writing.

It's a good moment for hope, because the Jews of Berlin have been
suffering, increasingly. Berlin in the first half of 1940 is claustrophobic; it is grinding oppression, a dangerous cocktail of malnourishment,
social exclusion, and, early that year, freezing temperatures. They are
prisoners in their homes, in their lives. In January, Jews had been denied legumes, most fruit, and meat.

They are now being forced into *Judenhäuser*—Jew houses—
clutches of people forced to live on top of one another, all in one space,
desperate for resolution. It is the end of privacy. Jews no longer have a
moment to think, to be alone. Inge Deutschkron described the time to
me like this: "Every day there was a new law. A new something: One
day they took the telephone from us; then they asked us to hand in
wages, then we weren't allowed to sit on public transport. [Then] public transport itself was totally forbidden, except for going to work, and
only if the workplace was seven kilometers away."

For a time, there was still the Jewish newspaper. "And then of
course they stopped that too. By then we were all forced to live together in a *Judenhaus.* . . . We lived on Bamberger Strasse at the corner
of Guntherstrasse. Bamberger Strasse 22. . . . The *Judenhaus* was
owned by a Jew, and two people always had to share one room. That
meant one five-and-a-half-room apartment was shared by eleven people. There was one toilet and, of course, one kitchen. You can imagine
what was going on there. All of us wanted to get to work on time—we

were sure we would be in danger if we weren't on time—and if someone was sitting too long in the toilet? You can imagine! *Bang! Bang!
Bang!* at the door. And so on. And the same would happen in the
kitchen. Everyone came from work at five o'clock, and everyone always wanted to cook as soon as possible. They were always hungry.
Because we didn't get eggs, we didn't get anything! They had laws that
said *Jews are not allowed to buy eggs or buy a cake*! It was unbelievable the
ideas that these people had! There must have been somebody special
who thought every day, 'How can I punish the Jews?' It was impossible
to follow all these rules."

As time passes and Valy's work changes from the oasis-like Kindergartenseminar in Grunewald, with its lovely private attic room, to
the more tedious Jüdisches Krankenhaus, the Jewish Hospital, her letters are no longer sent from Wangenheimstrasse 36; they are now
posted from all over Berlin. Each return address indicates that she has
been added on to a new household, she sleeps in a new bed, or on a
new couch, always in someone else's space. Perhaps, as she hopes, my
grandfather is writing to one address, and she has already left. It is
possible: from Ostender Strasse, near the Jewish Hospital in the Wedding district, her address is listed "care of Schwartz." From Rombergstrasse at the bottom of Prenzlauer Berg, not far from Alexanderplatz,
it is "care of Levy." Who are these people with whom she now shares
a bathroom, a kitchen, a living space? She does not say. She is a wan-
derer in the city; she lives like a ghost, a shadow, unseen, almost unknown.

I go in search of these small markers in her journey, but I often
find nothing when I arrive, no trace of what she knew or saw. That is
the case in Rombergstrasse—in fact there is no building there; the
entire block was destroyed during the war and rebuilt, decades later,
into large, Mondrian-style apartment blocks, with shiny bits of blue
and red. Even the name of the street has changed. Now—as it was
before the Third Reich—it is named Mendelssohnstrasse, after the
composer Felix, who, like all Jewish artists, was forbidden and smeared

by the Nazi propaganda machine during the war. (Mendelssohn had been the focus of an anti-Semitic tirade by Richard Wagner at the end of the nineteenth century. In his vitriolic essay "Judaism in Music," Wagner wrote of the "involuntary repellence possessed for us by the nature and personality of the Jews" and singled out Mendelssohn, then a star of modern music.) The street name was changed in 1938; it was restored to honor the composer well after the war.

Of those transient homes, Valy writes nearly nothing—other than that she has found herself a furnished room—for the first time, on her own, but not on her own terms because it is not with my grandfather, not with friends, and not even with her mother. It is a symbol of her own transience, her loneliness, her plight, her own sense of distance from the rest of the world, from her friends, her former life.

About her fourth home Valy writes much more. That is the house in Babelsberg, the village within Potsdam, an area known as Germany's Hollywood—its film production output, especially in the 1920s and 1930s, rivaled that of California. Valy's mother has finally found work—suitable work, work that befits a woman of skill, a businesswoman, a woman who had once held a position of high regard in her community. She is now the director of an old-age home, located in a villa. It is calm here, and so beautiful Valy feels almost as though she and her mother might have actually chosen this spot. Best of all, letters from Karl reach her here, and the combination of her reinvigorated correspondence and the sudden, if relative, comfort gives her a new burst of optimism.

This letter, from June, is perhaps the most poignant, the most hopeful, the most vivid letter of her whole oeuvre.

Berlin, 06-07-40

My beloved only one, my boy!
You will be with me in this world! *This one sentence in your last letter stays with me all the time, wherever I am; I can hear it, see*

*it and feel it. Always! When I am doing what I've been doing all
these days, when I am dressing the children's wounds, when they call
out to me at night, when I cannot go back to sleep afterwards and
when I am sitting by the window, sick with longing. Always your
words—"you will be with me" are comfort and torture at the same
time, because of the question: when will I be with you? Please tell me,
beloved, when? I do not know the answer, and the consulate has only
a vague idea of 1–2 years, meaning an eternity, unimaginable,
inconceivable—equal to a hundred years to me, who must be with
you within the shortest imaginable period of time, right now and
immediately.*

*Now the third summer without you begins. Instead of going
swimming or boating, hiking in the woods and sharing all the
beautiful things with you, as it should be, I am sitting here, pounding
insanely, madly and full of sadness at the typewriter. And the
summer is so beautiful this year! But there is much else I need to tell
you. Mama has been asked to manage an old people's home in
Babelsberg near Potsdam, one hour from Berlin that is housed in the
villa of a former Russian diplomat. The house has a dreamy location!
It sits at the highest point of the town, next to the university's
observatory and is surrounded by an enormous, completely
overgrown, jungle-like fairy tale kind of garden. The house itself
looks like a castle [Burg] and everyone here calls me "Burgfräulein"
[damsel of the castle]. There is a large cupola at the very top and a
blue room with lots and lots of little windows. Earlier on, this was
the music room, and that's my favorite spot where I love to spend
time. Here I am singing "Solveig's Song" and all the other songs you
used to love. I am spending a lot of time sitting here and dreaming of
you. And then I sometimes climb up on the roof or I go all the way up
to the very top of the cupola. The view from here is absolutely
spectacular—one can see villas, woods and lakes. It is simply
unbelievably beautiful. It hurts so much that I have to see all of this
by myself and that I cannot show it to you. I will have to bring people*

out here. Maybe, when I am not so alone and all by myself, I will be able to forget from time to time that it is not you who can be here with me.

Objectively speaking, the fact that my mother was asked to run the home here is a wonderful solution. Although mama makes only a very modest salary, it frees us from the most pressing and sometimes almost dramatic existential needs. Most importantly, however, my mother now is doing work that corresponds to her qualifications. She is again able to manage, to organize and to direct. As always she is rising magnificently to the task, is up to both ears in work and does not have any time. That is wonderful! There is so much work to be done here, and I can only hope that she will not exhaust herself. During her, admittedly, very sparse leisure time she has the use of the balconies and of the garden. I am incredibly pleased and grateful that everything turned out this way and that my mother got this position.

Unfortunately, however, I am not able to live in Babelsberg. I had to rent a small furnished room near the hospital—the first furnished room without you, all by myself. I am coming out here every weekend and sometimes even during the week.

Professionally speaking, things are going well for me. During the past two weeks I had the sole responsibility of leading the Children's Ward at the hospital. One of the women physicians was on holiday, and the other one fell sick. During that time I was living at the hospital. Unfortunately, this is over now. There was an incredible lot of work during the time when I substituted. . . . This was a real test of strength and I never thought I would pass it. But I did pass it quite well! Naturally, the head of the Ward would make his daily rounds and spend one hour every time. He did not spend any more time or stay any longer than when the physicians were around. The nurses, however, were the most difficult problem for me. They are a particular breed of people, especially in the Children's Ward. While

*they may be quite agreeable in private, in the Ward, the head nurse
has the say, then comes nothing, and then, after a long while, come
the nurses and then maybe, just maybe we come. One day, they may
almost die from their own sense of importance, these nurses!*

*Darling, I have inquired repeatedly when my number will come
up. All I get in response is some vague indication of one to two
years. . . . I will, however, go to the consulate one more time in order
to try and get more information.*

Please write to me soon and write a lot. . . .

And now goodbye for today; I am kissing you many, many times.

Your Valy

*Darling, I just learned from Mr. Jurmann, Paula's brother-in-
law, that our affidavits must be separated, i.e., one for me and one
for my mother and that this must be initiated in the USA.
Additionally, he thinks that several supportive affidavits from
relatives naturally would improve the chances. Would you please tell
me the exact degree of relationship for the issuers of my affidavit, as I
do not know these relatives particularly well and one is required to
give exact information about the degree of relationship? Please, be so
kind and initiate the separation of our affidavits, if necessary.
Much love.*

Your Valy

I look up "Solveig's Song," originally part of the incidental music
for Ibsen's play *Peer Gynt*: the music, by Edvard Grieg, is haunting,
beautiful. The lyrics, translated from the Norwegian:

*Both winter and spring might pass, perhaps
and next summer too, and the whole year,
but sometime you will come, I know for sure,
and I shall wait, as I promised before.*

I cry, listening to it. I imagine Valy hoped my grandfather would take out a recording of this song and think of her in the countryside. My father, when I tell him of the song, gives a start. "*Peer Gynt?*" he says. "How odd. It was on often in the house."

Perhaps Valy and my grandfather sang it to each other once, perhaps they saw the play together. But now the words "and I shall wait, as I promised before" have so much more weight to them. Later the song promises—she will wait alone, even if it is in the world to come. Its promise of a deathly meeting, if not on the earth itself, is both beautiful and terrible. I can see her, the *Burgfräulein*, in her cupola, looking out over the wooded glen, wishing terribly she could share the moment with Karl, wishing she could abandon even this oasis for the uncertainty of the road, or the sea, with a valid passport, affidavit, and visa in hand.

There is so much Valy does not include, or at least is not explicit about. It is beneath the surface, if my grandfather had known to look for it. The importance of her mother's position, her delight in simply having a room—they are clues to the privations of the *Judenhäuser*. The scramble for papers—the reevaluation of the affidavits—as Jews are even more panicked now that Western Europe is rapidly falling to Germany. Diarist Victor Klemperer, the month earlier, expressed the doom of the period in his journals: "The successes in the West are prodigious, and the nation is intoxicated. All Holland, half of Belgium taken . . . in the market hall they're saying Hitler will speak in London on May 26."

France falls in June, and in Berlin, Jews are banned from the major parks; the Nazis have stolen their homes, their clothing, their liveli-hoods, and now, it seems, they are stealing the very air around them, their ability to breathe, to walk, to be outdoors. By autumn, London will not fall, but be pummeled with bombs.

For Valy, her losses—freedom and love—compound each other. We have all had this yearning, I think, as I read and reread her letters. We have all been desperate for love, felt love was lost before we were ready to let it go. We have all felt that sense of—stupidity and child-ishness, rage and hopelessness—around love. But for Valy it becomes the only thing left, so she draws it carefully, underscores it, writes around it, highlights it, again and again. She still loves him, but she is uncertain of him, she wants him to know what she is going through, but more than anything, she wants to know she has something to look forward to, to live for—with everything in her world upended, she needs him to remain a constant.

08-08-40

My darling,

It is 3.00 am and I am unable to go to sleep. I keep thinking why it is that you do not write to me.

Dearest one, I must ask you something and you will respond, won't you? You do know that I consider myself as belonging to you wholly and entirely and that I feel that I am bound to you. But please, do tell me if you want it to be so. I am really not sure when I am reflecting on our talks during our last days together and on your first letters from New York and now on your lengthy silence.

And yet, your last letters—admittedly written a long, long time ago—were different.

I don't know how to go on, darling, you must write to me and tell me what you have to say about this. I must have support and some kind of a fixed point of reference for all my thoughts and feelings. In order to endure all this confusion and not to be swallowed up by it I would need something incontrovertible.

You will make me happy if you will write to me that your last letters are the ones that count,—and not your first ones. If you only would finally write to me!

I do love you very much! Good night.

Your Valy

It's devastating, her need for him. And surely his lack of response is a mix of things—his insecurity about his professional position in America, his love affairs, his uncertainty about his connection to a girl he hasn't seen now in two years. And yet something draws him back time and again, he never quite lets her go, never wants her to give up hope in him, never can quite sever that relationship—for himself, I suspect, as much as for her own sense of security. So each time she starts to pull away, to question him, he writes again, so that each time she hears from him it is proof, in some way, that he still loves her, and she extrapolates that to mean that there is still something good in the world.

He writes to her that he has opened his practice. It is so fresh, it is so shaky, his establishment on these shores, but he tells her, immediately, that he has begun—finally—to really live here.

Berlin, 11-08-1940

My beloved boy

You can't imagine how happy your picture and your letter made me. The picture is so wonderful, so good, so beautiful the likes of which I never saw before. I can't possibly describe to you how much you have pleased me by sending it. And then there is the news that you have opened your practice! I am all puffed up with pride! O my

*darling, I wish from the bottom of my heart that everything is going
to work out beautifully for you. I am so happy for you and for your
dear mama that you can have her with you. Are you spending your
mornings at the hospital? How are you living? Do you have a nice
room? What does it look like? O darling, I am so curious and would
so love to experience all these new and exciting things with you.
What did I do to deserve that I cannot be with you?!? But, before I
start to bawl, let me write about other things: My birthday was very
nice. Everyone in my station was delightful. The children had small
presents for me. They were all excited to give them to me. Everyone,
including my boss, got to see your picture. It is standing on a small
table, right next to my bed, surrounded by flowers. All I have to do is
to look at it in order not to feel so terribly lonesome. I have to write
about your picture, again and again. It makes me so indescribably
happy. Thanks a million, my beloved.*

*But now you surely will want to know something about me. You
do know that I am working as a trainee in the children's ward,
thanks to a stipend I was granted by the "Reichsvereinigung."
Moreover, I have in the meanwhile passed the federal exam as
Registered Nurse. Now they want to take away the stipend unless I
agree to work for two months as a nursing trainee and then to take
on medical care. Since I have my RN exam, the people there think
that I do not need any further specialized training to become a
physician. Lots of problems, but I don't want to trouble you with that
stuff. The upshot of all of this is that my boss, who earlier on was one
of Berlin's leading pediatricians, with whom I am on very good terms
and whose family has visited us often—advised me to work for two
months, but not as general nurse, but rather as nurse for infants in
the children's ward, which I have been doing since the beginning of
this week. He considers this type of practical work very important for
a pediatrician and did it himself during his time as a young assistant
physician. Now I spend the time between 7.00 AM and 7.00 PM,
and sometimes 8.00 PM, at the infant nursing ward, examine the*

stools of the little darlings, keep popping food into their little mouths, which they sometimes spit out again. Meanwhile, I am developing something of a "nurse's soul," with all the customary meal breaks etc. In the evenings, I am totally exhausted. While I think all of this is quite useful from a practical standpoint, I also feel it is overly taxing and I hope sincerely that the two months will pass quickly. I don't know what will follow. It is possible that my boss will be appointed the director of a large infants' hospital. If that happens, he may try to hire me as assistant pediatrician. However, this is a purely speculative matter at this point.

My mother is much beloved and appreciated in her nursing home. She is really doing a fantastic job. I believe that her nursing home is the best managed institution, and most definitely has the best kitchen. I am so very glad to have her nearby and that she has found a relatively good position. Nevertheless, I am constantly thinking about emigration. My mother would dearly love to go to Palestine, but that is particularly difficult at the moment. I, on the other hand, cannot make up my mind to go there, because I feel that this would remove me even further from you and from the possibility to see you again. No emigration in the world would be worth that sacrifice.

My darling, please forgive my terrible scribbles. Most of this letter was written in bed, because I am so tired at the end of the day that I find it hard to sit upright at the table. . . .

You cannot possibly imagine how very important your letters are to me!! My beloved, I beg you—don't let me wait so long again!!!!!!

I love you and I am forever

Your Valy

Such a long letter in which she gives him nothing, no indication of what she knows. And yet there is this chilling line: *"No emigration in the world would be worth that sacrifice."* It makes me wonder: Did she pass up an opportunity to go to Palestine, her mother's first choice? Earlier that spring, I read in one survivor's testimony, it seems thirty

thousand people had applied for "illegal" ship passage to Palestine—
illegal only to the British, who were not thrilled to have more Jews
trying to upset the balance in Palestine; the Gestapo knew everything.
Five hundred were chosen. An astronomical twenty thousand dollars
was contributed by the passengers to cover the cost of the passage;
among those on board were known active Zionists. In the end, three
hundred fifty "young people" under the age of thirty were chosen, a
hundred fifty older people. The ship sailed in August 1940. Valy and
her mother were not on it.

Later that fall Valy wrote again—this was, I realize as I begin to
stack them chronologically for myself, one of the first letters I had
read, when I discovered the collection. The idea of her alone, with her
flute, dreaming of her time with him in summers, on mountains, in
their city, haunts me.

Babelsberg, 11-18-40

My Darling!

*I've come up here to see my mother for a couple of days. I am
waiting out an infection. . . . In any case, I finagled to get myself a
couple of days off, which I love. Despite all my sense of duty etc. I was
able to pull a fast one on my superiors. I am in a splendid mood! Now
I'm just curious whom the poor babes will make wet when they're
being fed. They used to do that exclusively when I had them in my
lap! The poor things will have to wean themselves from doing any of
this (pooping and wetting) entirely. And tons of dirty diapers surely
will await my return. And here I am sniffling, using up oodles of
handkerchiefs, resting on my mother's couch. I am catching up on my
serious sleep deficits and am playing the flute, much to the
disgruntlement of the home's denizens.*

*You should know that I bought myself a flute because I am
always so dreadfully lonesome. While I don't think that my musical
productions sound very good at this stage, I am really enjoying it.*

And I am practicing an awful lot so I will be able to play really well once you and I are reunited again. You love music so much! And even though it cannot be piano which you would have wanted—I don't have the sufficient means for that in more than one respect— one can make beautiful music on a flute, as well, don't you think? And you are going to sing along with my playing, in your full-throated "steam bath" voice. And, whoever does not like it can just buzz off. We are definitely going to like it!

And thus I constantly dream of how things will be when I am with you again, my darling, and how incredibly happy I shall be. In such moments I let our entire past life together pass in front of my inner eyes and live through all the different phases of our times together. There was the era of Mrs. Mandl, the "Medizinerredoute" [the Viennese medical students' ball], Dr. Krügerheim, the chemical laboratory, the clinic, the exams, and the unspeakably beautiful summer at the Wörthersee, Dalmatia, Prein, the Rax mountain, Karlsthal, Professor Morino, Italy; and then there was a summer's day in the Augarten park when you told me that I should get married, and other things that I absolutely did not understand; the evenings at Frau Hirschfeld's, when you kept repeating these things to me; the night after my graduation when you, on the Ringstraße, between the Parliament and the Rathaus spoke of my future. Do you remember? . . . Friday evenings at your mama's, the other evenings at your place; your undertakings/courier of pleasure . . . ski courses . . . Heinestraße etc. etc. A whole array of different relationships to one another which we lived and experienced together; this time simply cannot have passed, darling, I beseech you, that cannot be! My beloved, isn't it true that it cannot be so?! I am thinking of all these things and I ask myself what phase you find yourself in at this point. Dr. Krügerheim? Or the Rax? Or the Augarten? Or Karlsthal?

My darling, I shall again write a letter to you every week as far as I am able to. Karl, please give your mama my most cordial regards; I think of her so often with great love.

*Farewell for today, my darling. Please, please write soon and
about the many things that keep you occupied. A thousand kisses,*

Your Valy

She is living only in the past. She has no present and no clear picture
of the future. She is so terribly lonely, she is hungry, she is sad. His
present isn't one she can remotely imagine. And thus, between the
notes from those who urge him to get her to safety, from her own
commentary on the chaos that has engulfed her life, my grandfather
would have known as well that there was nothing to return to. And
this is without him knowing the minor indignities that eat away at
her, that she is not even allowed to be called a doctor—even if her
training is complete. She is a *Krankenbehandler*—a Nazi term for Jews
with medical degrees, "a caretaker for the sick."

She is, sometimes at least, at the Jüdisches Krankenhaus, a strange
oasis of normalcy at the corner of the Wedding district in northern
Berlin. It is the only place that Jewish and half-Jewish patients can be
treated, and it continues—throughout the entire war—to function as a
hospital. I decide to go up there and see if there is anything to be
found. And then I also turn to the last year of the letters, 1941. If 1940
was depressing and urgent, then 1941 was sheer desperation.

Seven

THE VISE

I am six months pregnant and round. I have started to wear stock-ings that compress my legs to better their circulation. I am con-scious of what I eat, and more conscious still of the rations—or lack of rations—that restricted how women and children ate and dressed during Valy's time in this city.

In January 1941, Jews are denied the right to repair their shoes, to keep their typewriters; by February, milk is all but unavailable. As the year progresses, the restrictions become legion: No longer can Jews have telephones, bicycles, fish, coffee, fruit, chocolate, alcohol, or jam. Jews are limited to one hour a day to shop; if they reach the top of the long queue when the time is up, they have lost their chance to purchase anything at all. On public transport, Jews are forbidden to sit. By 1942, they will be denied access to trams and trains entirely, unless they have a seven-kilometer commute to their labor assignment. Special rail permits will be issued for this "privilege." Meat and butter and eggs will be gone by then as well.

Three quarters of a century later, I mull over pastries and cheeses, handcut ravioli, and fresh, dark seeded bread from the organic Saturday outdoor market in Kollwitzplatz, in the center of Prenzlauer Berg; I feel sheepish, almost ashamed.

In the collection I found, there are more letters in 1941 than any other year. It is this year that Valy both gives up on Karl and clings to him, it is the year that my *saba* turns deeper into his new life and yet can't quite let her go. In Germany, morale among Jews sinks ever lower; Hitler appears unstoppable, new deprivations, new humiliations, malnutrition, and ever-greater amounts of unremunerated work mount weekly. Terror has begun to creep in around the edges of life; desperation is rising. The segregation of Jews is nearly complete. People do not look at one another, their heads are bowed; eyes never meet. Loneliness seeps.

Babelsberg, 01-03-41

Dearest,

How much I had wished to be with you, finally, on this birthday of yours. Darling, I want so badly to s a y to you, how I wish you all the very best from the bottom of my heart. I yearn to tell you finally everything that is written only on paper, so dead, so empty and so boring. How I wish I could see you, behold your dear face and your beloved hands. . . .

I haven't written to you in over a month because I was quite ill in the meantime. I had a terrible angina, clinically speaking referred to as serious diphtheria, but without any bacterial findings. I still have not fully recovered. Until a few days ago I had a fever, I feel miserable. . . . The doctor who is running the station insists that I should have my lungs checked.

Moreover, I had awful troubles with a lady from the . . . association who absolutely insists that I should start a nursing career because this, according to her, would be my only way of earning a living. She feels she has a right to make this decision since she got me a scholarship from the "Reichsvereinigung" and that I therefore must abide by her decisions. You can easily imagine how much I resist this type of "rape" and how much my resistance upsets her. By now, we have become sworn enemies, and she does her best to discredit me whenever possible. Luckily, nobody believes her,—at least not yet, and my boss is trying to put things right. Hopefully, he'll succeed. Even my participation in this leadership course has now been drawn into question as she has raised objections. I did write to you once that only especially chosen people are supposed to participate in these courses, i.e. the elite of the young people still remaining here. And, in the eyes of this lady, I no longer belong to this elite group since I do not want to submit to her wishes and become a nurse. Forgive me, dearest, for bothering you with these things, but I am so preoccupied by this injustice that I have to tell you about it. I do want you to know what is happening to me, just as I so would like to know everything about you!

Darling, I have not had a letter from you since the beginning of November. Haven't you written to me? Did you get my pictures? Receiving a letter from you would make me indescribably happy. I keep on writing and writing letters that remain without an answer. It is almost as though I am writing into an empty space. It is too sad!

Farewell, dearest! Your Valy kisses you many times.

Please do not send registered letters as I do not know where I will be during the next period of time; due to the signature requirements, this would only mean delaying the mail.

Please write soon! Please!

It sounds ridiculous, perhaps, now, to our ears, to say it was a "rape" to be forced into nursing, but it was, indeed, yet another indignity. Valy had spent most of the prior decade studying medicine. Now she is being pushed into what she saw as an inferior profession, or at least one that did not acknowledge her years of training. Young women, nineteen, twenty, with almost no schooling at all, are being sent into nursing, churned out in a year or two. None of them are nearly as qualified as she, none of them had taken their oral exams in Vienna as she had, none of them had spent half a decade in the lecture halls of the world's best medical school, as she had. And yet she is expected to toil alongside them, learn to empty bedpans, to take the temperature of the children in her ward, to endlessly defer to those around her. It is an indignity, among all the other indignities she is suffering, and she cannot fully explain how this blow, issued, it seems, by the Jewish community itself, is in and of itself so demoralizing as to sap her strength. And yet this work is drastically better than her alternative, the mindless drudgery of forced labor; the backbreaking work her peers are struggling under. She has the audacity to want to be respected at a moment when such luxuries are no longer afforded to anyone.

Valy's letters are always opened; they have been opened since the beginning. *Geöffnet*—they are stamped, across the back—"Opened." Everything is read before it is sent along; an official makes small unintelligible notes in pencil at the top of the page and then forwards on the missive. Because of this, everything on her pages that is not about her longing comes as subtext, allusion. *"The elite of the young people still remaining here,"* she says, a nod to the fact that the vast majority of those under forty are gone, fled, in safety, or relative safety in the United Kingdom or the United States or Canada or Palestine or, only temporarily safer, in France.

There are so many things that Valy does not say: That the nursing program is really her sole option for staying in medicine. That her days are marked by a gnawing sense of persistent hunger. That she has been imposed upon with an extra name, "Valerie 'Sara' Scheftel"—that "Sara" stuck in under an August 1938 law; by January 1, 1939, all Jews whose names were not immediately identifiable as Jewish were forced to add Jewish monikers—"Sara" for women, "Israel" for men—to ensure they could not pass as Aryan even on paper. Valy just places that "Sara" there, quietly, it simply shows up, a stain; it is illegal not to use it. It rankled, it erased—pushing everyone into one category, denying

her, and every other woman, the dignity of their own individuality. In Berlin I meet Hanni Levy, a survivor, who reacts to my name with a start, with a sigh—"Ah, Sarah," she says with a small smile, a little shrug; "for too long I was Sarah." I have always liked my name, but this gives me pause.

The weight on Valy comes from everything. The children in her charge are denied parks, they are forbidden to walk in the forest, they are forbidden to walk on the major streets of the city; and so they take to playing in the Jewish cemetery in Weissensee, the only place left that Jews are allowed to walk freely outside. Air among the dead, as there is no air left in the streets for the living. I visit the cemetery with my parents when they arrive for a week. Weissensee is lush and enormous—the largest Jewish burial ground in Europe. These days it is overgrown, at least in summer, but the grounds are well kept, the paths are neat; the graves appear unharmed. It is a respite, strangely. Perhaps also because those buried here died, for the most part, of natural causes.

Jews are no longer dying naturally; they are taking their own lives week after week, at an alarming clip. When they don't succeed in killing themselves, they are taken, ill, to the Jewish Hospital, where Valy works.

Gerda Haas, giving testimony to the Holocaust Museum decades after the war, explained the horror of it: Beginning in the fall of 1941, people were "disappearing every day to go on transports. And then many people made secret plans to go underground. That was a big deal. And many people made secret plans to go across the border into Switzerland, and many were caught. . . . The patients we got, most of them were suicides that we had to get back to life in order so we could ship them to the collection center to be going to transports. And you know we sat and agonized over that. Is it really our duty to bring those people back to life? But, yes, it was, or we were punished ourselves. The SS were always there to supervise us and do this. It was a very unnatural time, and always the fear that we would be the next ones to have the transport notice."

I contact Gerda Haas's family; she is still alive, and living near Boston. She is not well, they tell me. They show her, on my behalf, Valy's name and photo. She does not remember. She does not know what happened to her. So she cannot tell me if Valy is alive or if she lived beyond the war at all.

Everyone left in Berlin is scrambling. In the city, Elisabeth Freund writes, "we are convinced that in reality America wants to help . . . but they do not know there how difficult the situation is; otherwise they would permit these poor and tortured people to get there quickly, while it is still possible. They could lock them up in a camp there until the situation of every individual is clarified, and the relief committees could bear the costs for it. But we had better get away from here, and as quickly as possible; otherwise we will meet the same fate as the unfortunate people who were deported from Stettin to Poland, or as the Jews from Baden, who were sent to France and who are being held captive there in the Pyrenees."

I understand from reading Freund, and flipping back to the letter from Alfred Jospe, dated February 1940, that the destruction of daily life through restrictions on living and shopping and eating and walking was made all the more terrifying by the small bits the Jewish community knew of what was happening in the east. The Jews of Stettin who didn't die during deportation were sent into what was known as the "Lublin Reservation," the marshy area set aside as a reservation for Jews, part of the so-called Nisko plan dreamed up by Hitler himself, as well as Alfred Rosenberg, Heinrich Himmler, and Adolf Eichmann, the *Obersturmbannführer*, and formally the architect of the forced emigration of the Jews of Vienna.

Similarly, the Jews of Baden, Germany, near the French border, were deported west, into France, only to be interned by the Vichy government in Gurs, the camp in the Pyrenees, where life was freezing and muddy, and, later, in Rivesaltes, the camp in Languedoc-Roussillon, originally created for Spanish refugees, and then eventually housing foreign Jews, Roma, and other "undesirables." Rivesaltes is a brutal slice of land—in summer it is hot and unprotected, in winter it is freezing and the same. It still stands as a camp today, dusty and cracked, with the walls of the barracks marked with the slashes of prisoners, and bullet casings still in the ground. I visited once, two summers after I left Vienna, and the dust seemed to cling to me for hours after I fled that terrible place and headed out toward the beautiful sea, the Mediterranean that the Jews interned at Rivesaltes likely never saw. Eventually so many of those ill-fated Jews were sent directly to Drancy, the camp outside Paris, and then on to Auschwitz. Most were murdered.

But in part, at least, because her letters are opened, instead of deprivation, and certainly instead of deportations, Valy speaks of loneliness, of desire, of human need.

Reading her words against the restrictions she is under, against the contemporary accounts of the walls closing in around her, I have to constantly remind myself that, unlike me, she doesn't—can't—know it will get worse.

As Jewish hospitals closed across the Reich, and doctors fled, the Jewish Hospital in Berlin, founded in 1756, was kept open because there was nowhere else for Jews—or anyone considered Jewish under the Nuremberg racial laws—to go. Aryan doctors would not touch them. The hospital continued to train nurses (the program Valy so resisted) long after the right to carry the title Doctor was gone.

The Jewish Hospital still runs today, and, bizarrely, is still called the Jewish Hospital of Berlin, though it is in no way segregated now.

The hospital is perched in the district called Wedding, at the edge of Berlin, midway between Tegel airport and downtown; the streets around it are filled with kebab places and phone card stands; immigrants. I take a tram from Prenzlauer Berg up and then transfer to another, and am promptly lost. I wander in the bright sunshine and finally come across it. A friend of a friend has arranged for me to meet a colleague there—a cardiologist. He in turn connects me to Dr. Richard Stern, one of the remaining Jewish doctors on staff—if not the only one. Stern's specialty, poetically, is heart failure.

Dr. Stern was born in Romania and immigrated to Germany in 1975, when he was twenty-four. His own father survived Auschwitz as a teen and would never speak of the experience; his paternal grandmother and aunt survived, but his grandfather and uncle were murdered.

"I've heard some stories from my father," says Dr. Stern. We are sitting in a second-floor doctor's lounge with brightly colored faux-leather seats. "But there are these experiences, they went so very deep and were so intense that—you know when you cook a soup with a pressure cooker? And if you open it when it's boiling—well, you can't. You have to wait till it cools down so there is no explosion. I'm convinced these experiences went on boiling in these people—but it was possible for them to go on living by keeping closed down. Because if you were to open it would be a kind of an emotional explosion that would sap you of your strength to live. But his second wife told me that he woke at night—sweating and shouting. He never told us what was in those dreams."

Stern explains some of what I already know from reading. "The Jewish Hospital was the only Jewish institution in Germany when all other institutions were closed. This hospital never stopped work as a hospital; and during the war, all during the war, there were still Jewish doctors treating patients. . . . They weren't called doctors, they were called 'Jew healers.' It was a multifunctional place, this hospital. It worked as a hospital but also as a deportation camp."

He means a transit camp. When the deportations began, he says, from the train station in Grunewald, "those Jews who were sick or couldn't travel" were set aside. The Gestapo, of course, "didn't tell them they would be deported to be murdered. It was said it was deportation for work." But if people told the Gestapo they were sick, they were investigated by doctors or nurses at the Grunewald train station. If a person was sick enough, he would be taken for treatment and brief convalescence at the Jewish Hospital "to make him fit for the next journey." The doctors and nurses would *cure* people in order to murder them later.

The Gestapo had a station at the hospital. "It was part of the hospital," Stern says. "It was a prison." The Gestapo would come and ask the doctors for a list of who was fit enough to go to the camp. "And if the doctor said, 'I'm sorry, they are not fit enough,' or 'I have nobody,' [what people told me was] the Gestapo would then say, 'Okay, maybe I take your uncle or your aunt or someone of your relatives.'"

After the war, the hospital became the center of the remaining Jewish community. The first postwar bar mitzvah was held here. Stern tells me that in 2006, at the 250th anniversary of the hospital, a handful of nurses who worked through the war came back. They told the current hospital staff stories of work under occupation—and about Dr. Walter Lustig, the Jewish director of the hospital, who ruled like a little king. He has been described as having been something of a pig,

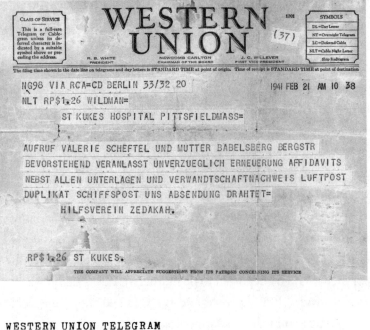

WESTERN UNION TELEGRAM
FEBRUARY 21, 1941
TO: WILDMAN, [ST. LUKE'S] HOSPITAL, PITTSFIELD, MASS.
TELEPHONE CALL VALERIE SCHEFTEL AND MOTHER
BABELSBERG
BERGSTR. IMPENDING—INITIATE IMMEDIATELY RENEWAL
OF
AFFIDAVITS PLUS OTHER DOCUMENTATION AND PROOF OF
RELATIONSHIP AIR MAIL DUPLICATE SHIP MAIL—CABLE TO
US RE
SHIPMENT
AID ORGANIZATION ZEDAKAH

Lustig; he regularly took nurses to bed, controlling, as he did, everyone's destiny, so that few felt they could refuse. ("We called him the *Schlächter*. The slaughterer," Inge Deutschkron told me, indicating that everyone in the remaining Jewish community knew of him. She, too, spoke, with disgust, of his sexual exploits.) Eventually he took the helm of the Reichsvereinigung. At the end of the war, he disappeared.

It was rumored that he was killed by the Soviets for collaboration. In truth, no one knows.

These days, unlike when Valy worked there, the hospital no longer has a children's ward. When I ask to see what still exists, and operates, in the same manner as it did when she was here, Stern suggests we walk over to the small chapel on the campus of the hospital. It is a synagogue, nominally; there are cardboard-bound slim prayer books and small *kippot* waiting for those who would like to pray, though there is no longer a Torah scroll here: the *aron kodesh*, the small cupboard that keeps the Torah, is empty and the ceiling is peeling in places. It is no longer specifically Jewish, I suppose, more like those "prayer rooms" one sees in hospitals everywhere, or in airports. What remains is the shape of the room, a hint of its former life; on the wall there is a Jewish star, and the shape and structure and texts of a Jewish prayer hall.

In the early months of 1941, people were still leaving the hospital nearly daily, fleeing on the last trains and boats out of Germany; it was a scramble, it was awful, but it still seemed—however remotely— possible that emigration could happen. Valy clings to the hope of boarding a ship and sailing away from this nightmare.

[Spring 1941]

Dear, dear boy,

Today I have to write to you again. It is so sad that by now our correspondence has come down to an exchange of letters only on certain occasions. It is much, much more than just sad. You don't know how awful this is for me. But, my darling, do not think that I am reproaching you. I know that three years is an awfully long time! So much can happen during that time! And one can have so many experiences! A long, long time ago you wrote to me from Vienna, when I was supposed to go to Prague, that one should not be so small–

minded to sacrifice the present to the phantom of the future. You wrote these words in a completely different context at the time. But you were so right then! And maybe that's your thinking right now as well. And maybe you are right in not wanting to sacrifice your present either to the past or to the future. It is, however, so terribly sad for me because I live almost without a present, and I can live only for the past and for the future!

But, darling, I can understand! Especially right now I really can understand as I have just had a passing experience that showed me how strongly the present can demand its right from us. But, as I said, this experience touched me only lightly and everything was nipped in the bud. It was a man who often reminded me of you. He was a bit like you, somewhat older, quieter, a little less genial, but perhaps a bit kinder. But he is not free and I, too, still do not feel free enough and therefore we did not live the experience to the fullest. Therefore, Karl, I could understand everything, although it would make me incredibly sad! What I find almost impossible to understand, however, is the fact that you don't write about anything at all!

I have wanted to write this to you for a long time.

The immediate reason for today's letter, however, is our emigration. As you will have learned from the cable that was sent three months ago, the matter now has become current, thankfully. Whether it will be doable, however, is another, far less simple matter. A couple of days ago we received another affidavit from Dr. Feldschuh that we will pass on immediately. Hopefully, it will suffice for the two of us! Because we do hope that dear mama and I will be able to emigrate together. Now the additional, very important question of the passage arises. It is of the utmost importance that two passages be booked on a certain vessel and for a certain date to the U.S.A. It would be possible to deposit a down payment from the US; the rest could be taken care of from here. What is really important, however, is that they be reserved and secure places! From here I cannot judge which shipping company would be feasible. I have learned that the American line is sold out until February of 42. Starting from September, there may be places available with the Spanish–Portuguese line, but I don't know whether this is certain. If there is a possibility via Sweden, I think this would be best, although it supposedly is very expensive. Please contact Uncle Isiu and Dolfi Feldschuh from Vienna. We have also written to both of them/please make it possible for us to get out of here, as well. Maybe you could also consult with Alfred Jospe. He cannot do anything financially, but maybe he has some good advice. He is currently trying to get some of his relatives out, and maybe he has already got some experience. I will also write to him. Darling, many, many thanks for all your effort and please, please do not get tired and let up on your efforts! . . .

Unfortunately, I don't have much good to tell you about my work right now. A couple of days ago, alas, I returned from the course I had written to you about. It was quite wonderful! Full of youth, spirit and verve! For the first time, since Vienna, I again felt glad and young! Now it has finally come to an end, unfortunately. I did a lot of teaching there and I believe that I have become a well-respected teaching authority there—your legacy, Karl! Upon my return, I unfortunately had to learn that I no longer can continue my work at the hospital and at the seminary for kindergarten teachers due to a general cut in positions. If I do not succeed in becoming confirmed as an itinerant teacher for various retraining facilities, I will have to start working in a factory before too long.

Well, darling, this letter was not too exhaustive, was it? Now you know everything about me—really everything and honestly told. Just the way you always wanted it! And I don't know a thing about you! Don't you think I should know of the things that matter to you and thus also to me?! . . .

> *Farewell, darling! And many, many kisses from*
> *Your Valy*

This letter lays me low every time I read it, both in its devastatingly perfect mimicry of my grandfather's manner of speech—*one should not be so small-minded to sacrifice the present to the phantom of the future*—and in its stark narration of a moment of pleasure she denies herself. Valy had a passing—what? Infatuation? Dalliance? It's hard to say exactly: she had a passing love interest—a crush!—that she let pass in part because the man was married, in part because of Karl. I read and reread, trying to decide if Valy is still in love with Karl, or if Karl is simply the only lifeline she has, and therefore she mistakes desperation for love.

When I read it with a German journalist, Katrin, she sighs; she is sure of Valy's intentions. "Because I still love you—that's what she means here clearly, she's still in love, so nothing came of the man she met." I tell her that I've shown this letter to other native German speakers and some disagree—my friend Uli in Kassel, for example, thinks this is not a love letter at all, that it is merely her means of trying to free herself from the Nazi yoke, that my grandfather was nothing more than a life preserver by this point. Katrin scoffs at that; she thinks my grandfather has given up on Valy, but the reverse is not true. "I think she knows it's over. Obviously Uli has never received a love letter. This is the sort of letter you write when you're trying to revive memories. This is something you do when you want to win someone back. These are not the words of a lady who feels she is loved back. She is unsure. . . ."

It has been three years now since Karl has seen Valy; three years since he last heard her voice. He is twenty-nine years old; they had not made a commitment to each other; he has dated other women. But somehow I wished for him to be a bit purer, perhaps. It is unfair, and unrealistic. She is twenty-nine, too, but she is so much older than that now. As she tells him: *"I again felt glad and young"*—they have aged rapidly, the young people left in the Reich.

But worse, even, than Valy denying herself the chance to be with someone else is her belief that the waiting has not been in vain. The possibility of emigrating grows dimmer and dimmer. But it is the only option. Valy and her mother request additional papers from my grand-father. They ask for more and more. She has no sense of what my grandfather can, or can't, do—money-wise, influence-wise. But she implies her quota number had come due, that her affidavits—requested multiple times and sent, somehow, by members of my grandfather's extended family—were in order. The only thing left was to secure seats on a ship. Just tickets! Just seats! The problem was: that in and of itself was nearly impossible. And neither she nor my grandfather knew just how difficult it would be.

Even if everything else had been in order, the challenges facing my grandfather and Valy went far beyond the sorry state of his finances, or even the status of her affidavits; they were diplomatic and policy driven, and they came from the other side of the world from where she sat, desperate, in her room.

———

I contact Professor Richard Breitman at American University; he has spent years unpacking how the U.S. State Department and the Roose-velt administration handled the question of would-be Jewish emi-grants into America. Breitman patiently walks me through the policies that left many visa quotas undersubscribed and many would-be refu-gees trapped. Then he recommends I go further and match my grand-father's and Valy's efforts with the documents he collected while working on several of the books he has coedited; these cover the dia-ries and papers of James G. McDonald, who served as high commis-sioner for refugees to the League of Nations and then as a leader of President Franklin D. Roosevelt's Advisory Committee on Political Refugees. McDonald was an early, vocal, and often lonely advocate in Washington on behalf of those caught in the maw of the Reich.

Already in June 1940, I discover, the U.S. State Department had cracked down on visas: factions in the State Department and consular systems were convinced would-be refugees were just as likely to be potential spies and fifth column infiltrators as genuinely persecuted victims of Hitler's policies. Consulates were advised to assure Washington they had "no doubt whatsoever concerning the alien."

Advising the Roosevelt administration in Washington were two wildly conflicting points of view—that of those who shared the pro-refugee sympathies of James McDonald, and that of those who believed the entire idea of refugee desperation was a sham, a means of infiltrating the United States, of using humanitarian efforts as a path to overthrow democracy. In the latter camp fell Assistant Secretary of State Breckinridge Long, Avra Warren, head of the Visas Division, and, unfortunately, the ambassador to the Soviet Union, Laurence Steinhardt, whose own Jewish identity was often trotted out as a proof of sorts, verification that the Jews trying to leave Europe were swindlers because if he, as a Jew, believed it, then it must be so. (Steinhardt would later have a change of heart about his Jewish cousins; as ambassador to Turkey, his post after Moscow, he helped save thousands of Balkan Jews who fled in the direction of Istanbul.)

Breckinridge Long outlined a way for the State Department to stop the already very slow flow of immigrants. "We can delay and effectively stop for a temporary period of indefinite length the number of immigrants into the United States," Long wrote. "We could do this by simply advising our consuls to put every obstacle in the way and to require additional evidence and to resort to various administrative devices which would postpone and postpone and postpone the granting of the visas." In August 1940, a representative of the American Friends Service Committee in Vienna had already written, "There is absolutely no chance for *anyone*, except in most unusual cases. FDR doesn't want any more aliens from Europe—refugees have been implicated in espionage. . . . All part of the spy hysteria . . . Day after day, men and women just sat at my desk and sobbed. They are caught and crushed, and they know it." The following month, James G. McDonald wrote, "Unfortunately the prospect of anyone being admitted at the present time to this country, who cannot prove that he is an eminent scholar or distinguished labor leader and is in imminent danger, is very slight."

The internal State Department directives purposely produced confusion, and massive delays. By the time Valy is writing in mid-1941, no clear path had been drawn for those attempting to flee persecution from Germany or occupied countries; consulates were willy-nilly asking for extras in the means of guarantees needed to be presented by anxious would-be immigrants (trust funds, guarantors in the United States), and there were so many obstacles thrown up for German nationals that between July 1, 1940, and March 31, 1941, the full immigration quota for Germany—27,370—did not come close to being met: only 2,126 visas were issued from Germany itself. For Germans already outside Germany—that is, German nationals who had made it to a second or third or fourth country—an additional 10,020 visas were granted. But Valy, of course, is still inside the Reich.

The visa was not the only additional hurdle. Eleanor Roosevelt's secretary, Malvina Thompson, wrote to James McDonald on February 3, 1941, echoing some of Valy's concerns: Even if they had a visa, how the hell did refugees get passage across? Through Sweden? Spain? Portugal? Morocco? By May, McDonald wrote, discouraged, to the acting governor of the Virgin Islands, "In fact, after an American visa has been granted, there will still be the more and more difficult problem of getting transit visas through Spain and Portugal. Then following that, the present facilities for transportation out of the Portuguese capital give no promise of facilities for newcomers within a year and a half or two years. Meanwhile, the boats which formerly cleared intermittently from Marseilles have, with rare exception, discontinued service from that port."

In June, the cause of stopping the (supposedly nefarious) refugees had been taken up on the floor of the Senate by the severely isolationist senator from North Carolina, Robert Reynolds: "I wish to say . . . that if I had my way about it at this hour I would today build a wall about the United States so high and so secure that not a single alien or foreign refugee from any country upon the face of this earth could possibly scale or ascend it." A new obstacle had been raised that month as well, and transit problems were now to be mixed with an additional, disastrous holdup: anyone with a relative left behind in a totalitarian country was now suspect and would be denied a visa, or find visas they had already been issued suddenly canceled. That meant even if Valy would have been able—let alone willing—to travel out without her mother, they were now forced to travel as a pair: her mother would now be considered a potential means of espionage or blackmail.

On June 19, 1941, *The New York Times* published a front-page story blaring "U.S. Ruling Cuts Off Means of Escape for Many in Reich—Many Visas to Be Voided." The piece went on to say that American Export, one of the shipping lines out of Lisbon, "has assigned space to alien refugees for sailings from Lisbon well into 1942, and the majority of these prospective passengers may be rejected by United States authorities." Restrictions would be expected to "increase rather than relax," and there was no point in searching for additional ships to bring out refugees, as seats on board wouldn't be filled and "refugees' prospects, already slender, would be reduced further."

Editorial pages filled with vitriol, lambasting the new stipulations. In *The New Republic*, editors criticized the State Department for "persecuting the refugee": "Bars have now been raised making it almost impossible for political refugees to get out of Europe at all," they wrote, pointing a finger at "anti-Semitic, and pro-Nazi forces in the State Department," and went on to accuse the system of becoming needlessly impossible to navigate. "The Department is now demanding proof that the refugee can get an exit permit and a transit visa before it will give an American visa; yet our officials know very well that no papers can be obtained in Europe unless the American visa already exists. People trying to help refugees come out have found it almost impossible to get copies of the new application." Thousands who might have gotten out to safer shores were denied claim.

Otto Frank, Anne's father, was tripped up by the same State Department purposeful backlog. From April to December 1941, Frank begged for immigration aid from relatives abroad. The U.S. consulate in the Netherlands was no longer operational—and, like Valy, Otto

Frank tried to see about visas to Cuba, to Spain, to Portugal. On April 30, 1941, around the time of Valy's telegram to Karl, Mr. Frank wrote to Nathan Straus, Jr., an old university friend and a very wealthy New Yorker. Straus was heir to the Macy's department store fortune, and director of the New York City Housing Authority. "I would not ask if conditions here would not force me to do all I can in time to be able to avoid worse," Frank wrote, as *The New York Times* quoted in 2007 after the letters were discovered. "Perhaps you remember that we have two girls. It is for the sake of the children mainly that we have to care for. Our own fate is of less importance." Frank's needs were enormous: five thousand dollars, exit visas from the Netherlands, entrance visas to one of the remaining European countries that still had a consular relationship to the United States—and then passage for every other member of his family so that none could be used to demonstrate the Frank family's potential to be coerced or co-opted by the enemy. Even knowing some of the most powerful people in the States didn't help them. The requests were not met. Straus couldn't do it. Frank briefly procured a Cuban visa—on December 1, 1941—but Pearl Harbor and the escalation of hostilities prompted Cuba to cancel his papers.

Valy's inability to emigrate and her increasing feeling of abandonment by Karl are tied up together, the failures are intermingled, they cause each other—they diminish her, they snuff out the bits of hope she still holds. She hints that failure may mean failure to see each other ever again, not just a separation of years, but a separation of a lifetime.

July 22, 1941

Dearest boy,

I no longer want to be so small to wait with my letters for your reply, to wait for a response to my questions. I will write to you, as often and as long as I am able to and will keep on telling you that I, despite everything, believe in you and will always believe in you and that I feel, time and time again, that I am your "creature," now and

always.—Maybe you are not even interested in all this right now,
but I want you to know it. Maybe you will want to know one day
and then it might not be so easy anymore for me to tell you. I am not
at all sure why I am thinking of you so much again right now and
why I feel that I am one with you. It was not always like that during
the interminably long time of our separation. But now it is like that
and I feel a great desire to tell you.

These lines are amazing to me. Is she saying goodbye? She seems unsure even to whom she is writing anymore—*"I am not at all sure why I*
am thinking of you so much again right now." It is a heightened version of
so many love stories, in normal, less pressured, times: a love affair has
ended, but the ghost of the lost person reappears, becomes present
again, a triggered memory, a phantom limb of love, that tingles long
after the relationship is over. Yet this is what gives me greater pause:
"Maybe you will want to know one day and then it might not be so easy
anymore for me to tell you"—does she mean because she, too, will be
sent to the east? Or does she believe, more benignly, that one day she,
too, will be in a relationship and, at that point, it will no longer be appropriate to share her feelings?

Above all I want you to know about the man whom I believed
I loved, and maybe I even did love. I wrote to you about it in my
last letter. You know, that he and I decided to forsake each other out
of consideration for his bond with his wife and my relationship
with you. It was not always easy for us. There were hours when I
thought this was meaningless self-torture, making our poor, joyless
lives even poorer and more devoid of joy. And you made it so hard for
me to believe in you and in a future together. But maybe you—I—we
did remain victorious in the end; and this makes me indescribably
happy. And the fact that you remained victorious remains now
undisputed!
I simply had to tell you these things, even if you might find them

sentimental or uninteresting. I believe that we, or at the very least, I cannot afford to bypass or keep secret matters that concern us deeply.

And now, a brief report:

As far as my work is concerned, I am doing quite well at the moment. I work both as a nurse and as a doctor in a baby home—as a volunteer. I am probably going to write you more about this next time. Now I have to start preparing for the course I will present tomorrow.

Karl, I don't think I have to tell you how much I am waiting for a letter from you! I no longer can write about this.

Many, many thousand kisses and warm regards to your dear mama.

Your Valy

Valy reaches out to relatives and friends, asking them to intercede on her behalf for emigration—and to shake my grandfather out of his writing torpor. Her Uncle Julius, who was struggling, though safe, in America, wrote to my grandfather in some anger:

New York, August 19, 1941

Karl . . . Assuming that you will be interested to know how our dear Valy is faring, I am attaching her letter. Unfortunately, emigration to the USA is currently out of the question, only to Cuba (ca. $ 1,400 per person including the ship passage). Even though she would love nothing better than to leave this hell, she is unfortunately forced to stay there. I am so sorry that I am unable to find a way out. Hopefully, she will be spared the "Arbeitsdienst" [the Reich Labor Service].

As you will see from the attached letter, she is inquiring about your well being; it is difficult to imagine that it is exactly only your letters that do get lost. . . .

Let me ask you to write her a few lines (surely you will be able to

spare a few minutes of your time). I am convinced that you, too, do
not approve of your own writing hiatuses. . . .
    Best regards to you and your dear mother.

Your Julius

The letter included was the following:

Dr. Julius Flamm
522 W. 112 St. Apt. 41
N.Y.C.

From: Toni Sara Scheftel,
Babelsberg [Valy's mother, though Valy is the author]
1, Bergstrasse Babelsberg, 07-27-41

My beloved Little Uncle [in Yiddish, Onkele] and dearest Rozia,
    We were overjoyed to hear from you and, in particular, to learn
that you, dearest Rozia, are completely restored to good health. We
were also terribly pleased to receive the greetings of Isiu Mann and
Dr. Friedmann. We were so happy, but especially that you all live
close to each other and manage to get together from time to time. I
wonder whether a "half nine" will ever be possible again? I fear not,
for a long time to come. Chances of emigration are, for the time being,
almost nil. You cannot imagine how sad and disappointing this is for
us. Supposedly, the entire immigration/emigration matter is now to
be processed from Washington, and one would need people who are
able to deal extensively with this issue and who also are in a position
to make financial sacrifices. If you should be able at all to intervene
in this regard with Dr. Feldschuh or if you could gain the interest of
other people to do so, please do so. I cannot express how much we
would love to be with you. Please let us know if there is anything you
can do.

*For the time being, we are doing relatively well. My mama
continues to work very hard—but she does love it—and very
successfully and with a lot of recognition, in her home; it is a "home"
in the truest sense of the word. Not only for the patients and me, but
also for many different people who find peace, quiet, hospitality and a
loving reception here for many days. Two ladies from the RV
[Reichsvereinigung] are, for example, spending their holidays with us
and are extremely delighted and happy here.*

*For the past 6 weeks or so I am working in a large home
for children and infants, functioning as both nurse and doctor.
I have to take care of a ward with 4 children and, in addition, to
discharge all medical duties. There is really a lot to do, but I am
extremely happy to do it, and I am so fortunate to have this job.
Unfortunately, the end is in sight, however, as we must leave
the home. I do not know yet when this will happen and what will
follow thereafter. My superior, who also was my boss at the
Children's Ward, continues to try very hard to retain me in the
medical field. I am so grateful to him. Hopefully, it will also be
possible in the future. I really do like my work; my children are so,
so cute and I have become an almost perfect infant nurse. What
I thought impossible in the past, namely to be able to keep a ward
clean and orderly all by myself, I am now managing quite well;
my dear mama is overjoyed that I, as a consequence, am becoming
familiar with some housework and thus will become somewhat
"domesticated."*

Let me close for now. . . .

*Please also write to Karl on occasion and find out a little more
about how he is doing, what he is up to and let me know. It should
really be possible to find out what is going on with him.—And now,
let me close, finally!*

Thousands and thousands of warmest regards and kisses.

Your Valy

Please write to us very soon!

My dear Ones:

Valy has written everything already that is worth knowing. Let me ask you from the bottom of my heart, as well, not to leave any stone unturned to try and help. . . .

I will write more very soon. Please give my warm regards to Dr. Friedmann.

Toni.

Between this letter and the next, Valy's angriest, most bitter, something finally gives.

To:
Dr. Ch. J. Wildman
St. Luke's Hospital
Pittsfield, Mass. U.S.A.

From:
Dr. Valy Sara Scheftel
Potsdam—Babelsberg 2
1, Bergstrasse

09-03-41

Tell me, Karl, what is going on? Who am I to believe? You and my notions of you as my friend, my companion, the man, the most important person in my life, who will remain as such even though he may, in the firm confidence of my deep bond with him, not bother with me for a long time, for whatever reason? There may be so very many different reasons and I can understand them all. Or should I believe the people around me who keep telling me that your silence could have only one reason, namely that you have forgotten me a long time ago and probably even married and—that I simply cannot *fathom—did not even think it necessary to tell me about it. One of them, however, is not all that convinced, although he, logically speaking, should be convinced, as he says. He thinks—forgive me, if this sounds somewhat vainglorious—that you are* my *friend and therefore incapable of acting in this manner.*

Karl, I ask that you *tell me what I should believe. I beg you to finally wake up and remember and understand that it is simply intolerable for me to live in this state of uncertainty. Do tell me everything. Do not let yourself be influenced by pity, nor by a temporary situation or fleeting mood that may pass. Only do write to me and don't let me believe that I meant so little to you that it is unnecessary to let me share what is happening in your life. Karl,* where *are you?! I beg you to write to me and let me know.*

I don't want to write anymore today. Not today and not again— until I have news from you. Maybe these letters make you tired?! And I *must* know first how things are with you!

Farewell! I am forever your

Valy

This—this last missive—this seems to have done something. The response her threat to stop writing inspires is the only response I have in all of my grandfather's papers; it is a draft of the letter he sends back to her, handwritten, complete with cross-outs and false starts:

09-17-1941

My only beloved!

How can I explain that I did not answer your letters? Your letters! Your sacred letters!

Beloved, I believe that you once read a book that begins with the words: "I want to write of a generation that was destroyed by war, although it may have escaped its cannons" and want to refer to this book. This is the only explanation I can give you.—I am dead because I have died—mentally and morally. I cannot remember having laughed even once during the past three years.

Shall I tell you that I have been terribly busy? Surely, I was terribly busy, but is this a reason for not writing to you?

Shall I tell you that I had so many cares and worries that I did not find the calm and concentration to write to you? Certainly, this is true as well, but is it a good reason?

Shall I tell you that I no longer love you enough in order to write to you? How could I when I feel every moment of my life how much I miss you, how much I long for you, how dear you are to me, how much I need you—your words, your laughter and your tears ~~your hot temper~~, the inspiration of your great good and innocent character. . . . When you come here, little one, you will meet so many friends whom you haven't met before and who have not seen you before, but know you so well through my talking of you, dearest one. . . .

Why did you not threaten earlier that you would not write to me any longer? I think, it is your fault!

Darling girl, I have not neglected anything regarding your immigration, nothing at all, and I am taking all possible steps to speed up the matter. ~~I have just received a letter from Isiu (??) and shall reply immediately.~~

I am a very successful physician. I have two practices, one in Pittsfield, and one in a smaller town nearby. . . . I see ca. 25–35 patients on a daily basis, I have two ~~assistants~~ secretaries; but, my little one, I am not happy at all! ~~I certainly did have girlfriends and more or less serious relationships.~~

Darling, will you answer right away? Please write immediately and I will write to you, every time and immediately, about everything you want to know.

Beloved, I kiss you a thousand times

Karl

He is, to put it kindly, telling only part of his story. He certainly has had girlfriends. Two who were quite serious—there was Tonya Morganstern Warner, in those early days in the United States. And then he met my grandmother, Dorothy, whom he would marry in the fall of 1942—surely there were others, but those are the ones I know of. Does he love Valy? I think he does. I think she was the love of his youth, the love of his Vienna years, the years that shaped him, and he loves her as much for what she stands for as for who she is. But his inability to get her out of the Reich makes her also a source of pain, of guilt, and this makes it hard for him to know how to relate, let alone how to write, to her. What will he say, after all? That he went boating with the woman who would become my grandmother? Or that he is worried about not bringing in enough money from one month to the next? By now he knows it does not compare to what she is facing.

So he doesn't share his women, or his real woes, with Valy. Why? Does he want Valy to keep her hopes up? To keep believing in something? He is not lying—he has done everything he could do to aid her emigration—but he hadn't the money or the connections he needed early enough. The one window of opportunity—if it even was that— for the hundred-fifty-dollar visas, twice over, to Chile came in 1940, at a time he could not afford his own rent, when his mother was selling her last possessions. He may be established, finally—but barely. And by 1941, connections and money simply weren't enough. It doesn't matter—the letter he sends picks her up, lifts her spirits. At her worst moment, so far, it gives her hope.

There's not much to be hopeful for. Though the refugees have advocates in Washington—James McDonald and Rabbi Stephen Wise met with FDR the first week of September—their detractors prevail. Breckinridge Long wrote in his diary on September 4, "Rabbi Wise always assumes such a sanctimonious air and pleads for the 'intellectuals and brave spirits, refugees from the tortures of the dictators' or words to that effect. . . . Of course only an infinitesimal fraction of the immigrants are of that category." Soon the visa wranglings in Washington are no longer the problem: the Nazis substitute forced retention for expulsion.

On the first of September, 1941, Valy is forced to sew a yellow star to her coat and clothing, to stitch it carefully, to ensure it was not obscured, and that it would not fall off. A hidden star was considered sabotage, grounds for arrest. No longer could she walk unimpeded; she was now marked. Jews were being picked up in the streets. There is panic everywhere.

Tuesday evening, September 30, as they had for centuries Jews began to celebrate Yom Kippur with the Kol Nidre service.

It would be the last Yom Kippur celebrated aboveground. Hundreds gathered at the Levetzowstrasse Synagogue in the Charlottenburg district of western Berlin, words from Isaiah were carved in Hebrew over the doorway: "O, House of Jacob, Come ye, and let us walk in the light of the lord." At the end of the services, the Gestapo confiscated the synagogue and turned it from a place of refuge and worship into a place of devastation and horror: a transit camp.

No longer was Germany interested in simply expelling Jews to other lands, now German Jewry would be forcibly relocated to the east. October 1941 began a push into ghettos, into an impoverished, bare existence that would make the deprivations experienced thus far seem almost minor in comparison. The east was something fearsome. The Warsaw Ghetto had already been open for a year; in the fall of 1941, the Einsatzgruppen, the special mobile military killing units, were endlessly mowing down Jews in Russia and across the Ukraine, in what would, decades later, come to be called in French the *shoah par balles*—the Holocaust of bullets. Vans retrofitted to pump exhaust inside, rather than out, pulled the breath from groups of Jews stuffed inside. German soldiers on leave were told not to speak of what they witnessed, but some did: the black stories then trickled into the Jewish community. Rumors abounded.

Legal immigration out of the Reich is officially cut off in October.

Valy knew that the Gestapo had begun to gather people to send them out of the Reich, but she felt protected by her work and her mother's position. She was buoyed by my grandfather's renewed attentions. His letter sends her into a dizzy spell of love and memory, and she takes out their experiences together like a crushed photograph, smooths out her memories, and gushes to him that their time together was beautiful, even though it—apparently—was confusing to her even in times of peace and togetherness:

Dr. Valy Sara Scheftel
Potsdam-Babelsberg 2
1, Bergstraße

To: C.J. Wildman, MD
74 North Street
Pittsfield, Mass.

10-10-41

Beloved, I did know that I could believe in you and that I was doing the right thing—despite all the skeptical people and their common sense! I am indescribably happy that I did not listen to them who thought that my clinging to you was utterly ridiculous and almost humiliating. Those who judged you like this cannot help it. They did not know you the way I know you. Dearest one, most beloved, each line and each word of your letter made me so unbelievably happy. At first, I simply could not believe that I actually did hold a letter from you, from you, in my hand! I was speechless, almost in shock! And then, everything turned bright and light and so

wonderfully joyous. And I remembered Storm's "Oktoberlied"
["October Song"]:

Do you remember? Once, many years ago, we were walking
through the Prater, it was in October, and you recited the Oktoberlied
for me, talking about the overcast day which we wanted to make
golden. . . . We were so happy then, or, at least, I was. With you, I
never was quite sure how things were. . . . This morning, when I
saw this overcast, ugly, utterly depressing day, I thought in my
despair that one should gild it! And just a few hours later, your letter
arrived and made this day golden—as ever a day was turned golden.
More than the most wonderful wines of this world could make a day
golden. This is just my own little modification of Storm's "recipe"
which you applied, but the result was so overwhelming that he,
Theodor Storm, surely would have been happy with your effort. Just
as Professor Biener was happy with your "Matura Arbeit" [written
graduation exam at the Gymnasium *in Vienna] "Schiller's Cultural*
and Philosophical World View."

You are a successful physician, my darling! That, too, had to come
to pass. I never doubted it even for a second. The fact that it all
happened so relatively quickly, makes me especially grateful and
happy. You must tell me everything about it. How do you at this
stage view medicine in general and your work in this field, in
particular? You write that you are not happy. Does that mean that
you do not view your work and your role in a positive way? Beloved,
do write me about your life, including your outer circumstances, how
and where you live. Tell me about your friends and keep on telling
me that you need me. I cannot hear it often enough, I've been missing
hearing it much too long!

I am now with my mother at the home in Babelsberg. I cannot
go to Berlin. Due to health reasons, however, it is good that I should
be here and not in Berlin. Several weeks ago I was quite sick. I had
abscessed tonsils with everything that goes with it. My overall state
was pretty poor, and recovery took a long time [handwritten, on the

side] *(But I am already doing very well again). My former station physician (a woman) with whom I am very friendly, thinks that the reason for my low resistance is all the drudgery in the baby home where I worked before—you do know about that? She is delighted that I have been forced to stop this work. I, on the other hand, am not particularly pleased as I, despite all of the hard grind, had the opportunity to do some medical work—something that means a lot to me. My boss had outfitted a small laboratory for me, which made me really happy. Maybe I'll manage to get a travel permit, after all, for which I did apply. Right now, I am by and large quite content in this beautiful, quiet, secluded house—I did describe it to you earlier on, right? I read a lot, I help out a bit, and have recently begun to take English classes again. As you can see, I have not given up the hope to join you some day, although right now the situation in this respect seems very, very sad, even impossible.

Even if there were a possibility to do the expensive detour via Cuba, it would be too late because, meanwhile, German citizens between the ages of 18 and 45 are no longer allowed to emigrate. I cannot tell you how desperately unhappy I am about this!!!!

What did you try to do, my darling? Oh, but I am afraid that it all will be to no avail. And I need you so badly! I need to be with you so much. My beloved, you can do so much, why can't you take me to you? But I know that it will not be possible.

My mother is well, considering the circumstances. She continues in her role as highly competent manager of the home. She is ubiquitous and makes the impossible possible. A few months ago it seemed that our home was filled to capacity. Then, another 10 people had to be accommodated. Over the next couple of days, new people will be arriving. She makes all of this that seems impossible, possible, and is much adored by everyone. I think this is the right place for her, as far as work is concerned, although she, too, yearns to emigrate.

My darling, I will write to you soon, as you did promise me to respond to each of my letters. Nothing could be more precious to me

than your letters! You do have so many things to talk about. Please tell me everything you experienced in America. I want to live it all vicariously with you again. How I longed to be with you during all this time!

My beloved, I kiss you many, many times! You made me very happy today with your letter! A thousand thanks. I am sending you a small picture from our garden today. Don't you have any pictures you could send me?

I love you so much! Farewell!

Your Valy

There is, of course, so much Valy wants to make golden, beyond the gray skies. Her diminished resistance to infection, surely worsened by malnutrition, her daily life "in drudgery." On Kurfürstendamm, the main thoroughfare in Berlin, shop after shop bears the sign banning Jews. Butchers, bakers, vegetable hawkers—they, too, ban Jews now. Her joy, her desire to live vicariously through my grandfather's successes, it's as though she takes it all as a sign, a rainbow: despite all of the restrictions, despite the very colorless life they are leading, there is some hope. And yet even here she chides a bit, recognizes that beneath her fantasy Karl, there was a more complicated relationship—*"We were so happy then, or, at least, I was. With you, I never was quite sure how things were. . . ."*

Still, as happy as she is that he has recognized her once more, she is starting to believe she will never be reunited with him after all, that it is all for naught—her begging, her hope of emigration, her efforts and his. I go back to her letter from the beginning of the spring: *"Now the additional, very important question of the passage arises. It is of the utmost importance that two passages be booked on a certain vessel and for a certain date to the U.S.A. . . . . What is really important, however, is that they be reserved and secure places! From here I cannot judge which shipping company would be feasible. I have learned that the American line is sold out until February of 42. Starting from September, there may be places available with the Spanish–Portuguese line, but I don't know whether this is certain. If there is a possibility via Sweden, I think this would be best, although it supposedly is very expensive."* The stalling of the State Department, the constantly shifting requirements, the affidavits, the monies, all met up with the lack of ships, the lack of places to go to, the inability of this group of people to buy these two seats, two berths to get these two women out of Europe. Sold out through February 1942? September 1941 was the last chance, really, to escape legally.

The first group of Jews is deported from Berlin to the Lodz Ghetto on October 18, 1941. The last train left the same day for Paris, with the last group of legal emigrants on it. It wasn't a secret. Washington *knew.* An internal diplomatic memo from October 25, 1941, read: "Word has come through from Berlin to the effect that before the end of this month about 20,000 Jews are to be deported from German cities to German-occupied Poland, principally to the ghetto of Lodz."

Valy was now in Babelsberg full-time. She is spared the factory once again and is allowed to come and serve the elderly in her mother's home.

10-20-41

My beloved, surely you are waiting for news from me. I do hope that you received my last letter!

Darling, if you only knew how happy your letter made me and how important it was that it should arrive just now! It gave me 100% more stability and poise, and life is no longer all that

meaningless. Especially now, I do have an obligation to be upright
and courageous, right?! Yes, my darling, I know that you, your letter
and your attitude towards me, mean an obligation for me. But I also
have to confess to you that I desperately long, for a change, not to have
"poise" and simply to be happy! And, also that I now, after receiving
your letter, am even much, much more impatient to come to you! You
must never forget that, my darling!

My dearest one, a few days ago I began to work here as a nurse.
Surely, that will please you! . . . Today was my first full day of work,
and I am actually pretty much wiped out. . . . But, my darling, you
must not think that I am working myself to death here. We have an
especially nice patient here—although he looks just terrible—who
helps me with my nursing duties and who looks after the patients
during the night so they don't have to wake me up. He is really
extremely touching! . . .

It is possible that we may travel, you will hear from us then. For
today, I am kissing you a thousand times.

Your Valy

The deportations are ominous, but in the general population no
one can confirm what they really mean. "I have the impression even
the Jewish Council [the Reichsvereinigung] did not know because,
even later when I was arrested, they supplied us with soap and pieces
of clothing, since we were taken from work and had nothing with us
except the things on our person," explained a boy identified as "Jürgen
B" in an interview he gave at a displaced persons camp just after the
war. "The Jewish Community Council had supplied us with six slices
of bread, margarine and cheese. In each [train] car they had placed a
can with water, a large vessel." Men, women, and children were locked
fifty people to their car, with no toilet.

Somehow Valy is still relatively happy, she has some hope—something has come through for them. At least she has been reassigned to
work in her mother's home; this is huge, it means she can stay with her

mother, it means she is still "relevant" to the war effort. "It is possible we may travel" is a code phrase; many of these would-be emigrants used it to imply escape.

But when emigration is finally, fully, cut off on the twenty-third of October, desperation returns to Valy's letters, the path to normalcy seems fully blocked now. She now shreds the last bits of her dignity and begs my grandfather to marry her, hoping that might help bring her out of Germany. It is a last-ditch effort—but even if he could have, even if he wanted to, what could he do now that the legal wormhole to leave had been filled in with dirt? Valy refuses to believe it, she has read it, she has heard it from her colleagues, from her mother, but she will not accept it.

10-27-41

My beloved,

I would like to tell you so much about me, but when I start thinking I find that, most of the time, my life is so poor as far as inner content is concerned, and thereby I mean positive experiences, that it hardly makes sense to talk a lot about it. It was and continues to be some kind of stupor, a type of hibernation, an eternal waiting for you.

Somebody once said that the best and most tolerable way of dealing with a long wait is to fill the time with lots of activities. And that's pretty much what I've been doing. My outer life absolutely is characterized by keeping busy and, maybe, even working. To the extent circumstances permitted it, I even was rather successful in this exterior existence of mine. One of the best pediatricians in Berlin considered me as "good," and I also received much recognition as a teacher in our circles. I met valuable, pleasant people, and even told you about the little episode that remained just that, an episode. And yet—it was just a waiting period, a waiting time, although it was quite fulfilled and thus did not lose its original character. And now I continue to wait, except much, much more impatiently and much,

much more urgently. My darling, maybe you could contact Alfred
Jospe? He made a special trip to New York some time ago in order to
find more authentic information about immigration possibilities for
his mother. Or, maybe, you could—which surely would be so much
better—go there yourself to find out from a competent entity? Dr.
Friedmann might be able to help out financially. Uncle Isiu has his
address.

Due to the age limitations, however, it may look pretty hopeless
for me. But maybe, if we belonged together officially, this would be a
possibility? I never wanted to propose this to you, and I really never
ever wanted to talk about this again. But do you remember, my
dearest one, once upon a time when you were with us in Troppau,
you asked me what I wished for, and said that you wanted to fulfill
my every wish. And then I wished so much for us to be together
forever; but I did not want to take advantage of the situation,
because I wanted you to make your own decision freely. Therefore,
I did not say anything then. But today I believe I must tell you, if you
really want me to be with you and if I did understand your last letter
correctly. Karl, I ask you not to misunderstand me! Naturally,
I would only want you to make your own free decision, even today.
But the issue seems particularly relevant today and that's why I put it
forward "for discussion."

I don't want to write much more today. I hope to be able to write
again next week. Now I have to go to my charge. He is so patient and
grateful, highly educated and very bright. Today he presented me
with an edition of "Faust." He is, however, very challenging to deal
with. Yesterday he fell straight on his face in the street, and I had to
get help in order to get him up again. He is completely helpless sitting
up and in bed, and he needs to be cared for right down to the smallest
little detail. He is such a poor guy!

Every day I am waiting for your mail! If I only had a letter
from you soon again! Please don't let me wait too long!

How is your dear mama, and how are Zilli and Karl? Please
give my regards to everyone.

> *Many, many kisses, my beloved*
> *Your Valy*

Here she has prostrated herself, *"I never wanted to propose this"*—she
has done what she promised herself she would never do, she has asked
him to marry her, to take her away from all this by making their
relationship "official." But it is 1941. A marriage, had it even been possible, had it even been what he wanted at that point, would not have
been enough to pull her from the nightmare. And yet the humiliation
is worth it, even for that sliver of a chance, even for the slightest hope
it might bring her, even in just the proposal.

Writing is the only thing that keeps her sane. And yet now her
writing has almost the quality of a fever dream:

> *10-31-41*

> *My very dearest one,*
> *. . . For the time being, thanks be to God, my situation remains*
> *unchanged. In the past I always resisted nursing work, or, at least, I*
> *was convinced that I would be really bad at it. Now it turns out that*
> *I am actually pretty good at it. At least, my charges seem very happy*
> *and wish God's blessings upon me. If their wish only were to become*
> *reality and I could already be with you! Because this is my sole and*
> *only, my great, big desire for God's blessing. Then I would be happy.*
> *I do not have any personal ambitions. Medicine means a lot to me.*
> *My station doctor used to laugh about the enthusiasm and joy with*
> *which I used to approach every new case. But you mean so much,*
> *much more to me!!! There really is no comparison—as I have often*
> *written to you, as you are the first and uppermost principle in my*
> *life. I cannot even exist alone and I don't want to be anything but a*

*part of you or something together with you. Everything else seems
meaningless to me and I am often completely desperate because what
is essential is so impossible. It would take a miracle for me to be with
you soon, and miracles do not exist!*

*My darling, I must finish now, as Friday evening supper is
about to begin. It is always a beautiful and festive occasion here with
us. On Saturdays we always have a proper religious service in our
foyer. My mother is so radiant when the people from the home show
up for the service. Hopefully, she may experience this joy for a long
time to come. And hopefully, I'll be able to confirm the receipt of a
letter from you before too long.*

A thousand kisses, darling
Your Valy

This is the first time Valy really talks about God, or religion. Her life
focus, her desire to remain a doctor, nothing seems more important
than Karl now—but is it really him? Or is it the idea that being with
him will mean she has survived all this?

For Valy, the terror that has crept into daily life is set against her
relief to finally be living alongside her mother in Babelsberg. *"Hopefully she may experience this joy for a long time to come"* is an acknowledgment of the deportations, of the unknown that hovers outside their
door, the uncertainty that cloaks them, chokes them, even more than
their cut-off emigration options.

More than half of Valy's letters were mailed from "Bergstrasse 1, Babelsberg, Potsdam." This was the address, from 1940, of her mother's
old-age home, where Valy would escape to, as often as she possibly
could, and then where she finally was able to work herself in 1941.
The district of Babelsberg itself was the center of the German film
industry before—and after—the war, with the oldest large movie stu-
dio in the world, a neighborhood marked by wealth, comfort, and

prestige. And Potsdam, in general, is a bucolic, pleasant place, a royal suburb filled with palaces and gardens to wander in, relics of Germany's aristocratic past.

I find a photo of the villa Valy wrote from at Bergstrasse 1, and there I see the cupola Valy describes in her letters. The mansion was a massive, glorious structure, a mini capitol building; it had been the home of a wealthy Jew who successfully escaped, some years before Valy arrived in Berlin. It was located in what is now—and was then— a quiet, upscale suburb of large villas, a ten-minute drive from the tourist hubbub that makes historic downtown Potsdam a popular day trip from Berlin. In April 1940, Bergstrasse 1 became a Jewish infirmary and "almshouse" under the auspices of the Reichsvereinigung. On January 16, 1943, all the Jews of Potsdam were gathered at the house; most were sent to their deaths in Theresienstadt and Auschwitz and Riga.

I took the regional train from Berlin to Potsdam and then went by cab to the street that Valy wrote from for so many months. I knew there wouldn't be much to see, exactly: the little palace she lived in had been destroyed, sometime in the 1970s. After the war, well after the conference that brought the three Allied powers together in Potsdam, even the street name, Bergstrasse, was changed, to Spitzweggasse, a combined memory suppressor as effective as anything I'd come across. No one I spoke to knew much, or anything at all, about an old-age home among the villas of Potsdam.

Online I read that—despite all the changes—there remained a tiny memorial on the site. When we arrive, I see the street is a dead end and there is no obvious memorial or marker at all, just a few quiet buildings and the woods beyond. I get out of the taxi and wander up and down the block, and the cabdriver and I are soon joined by a thirtysomething student and a sanitation worker, both of whom tell me that "if it's about Jews, it's long gone." No one quite believes me when I say that the street name was changed or that there was once a nursing home here. But the driver, interested, perhaps, in someone

willing to let his meter run, remembers that, peculiarly, he has a 1928 map of the city in his car, and with it, we confirm that this was, indeed, once named Bergstrasse. With this odd stroke of luck, I am vindicated. In the end, it is the sanitation worker who finds the plaque, rusting and covered in lichen; it is nestled—half buried, covered in leaves and branches—in the ground, an homage to the small group-home of old people who clung to one another in the last years of their lives here.

At the spot, I add a stone to a small collection on top, and all the men go away feeling good that they helped this strange American find this strange *Denkmal*, or monument.

Later, by regular mail, I receive a list of those living in the home in January 1943, provided by the Brandenburgisches Landeshauptarchiv, Oberfinanzpräsident, the Brandenburg State archives in Potsdam, and the financial archives that held all the indicators of Nazi looting during the period. It is among the papers I have requested about Valy's mother. All those who lived in the *Altersheim* Potsdam had birthdays decades before the turn of the nineteenth century—except for young Valy. All, surely, then, remembered a time when Jews were so well integrated in German life that their excision from that culture, and that life, would have seemed completely impossible, incomprehensible, as unlikely as our own separation from the lives we currently lead. Valy, by contrast, had known Germany to be only a place of incarceration, of separation, of desperation. Freedom was Vienna, Troppau, even—and the fantasy of America.

11-09-41

Darling,

Another week has come and gone, time is flying, so one grows quite dizzy, and still—it does not lead to the desired goal, at least not visibly and noticeably. My days are filled with work and cares and they pass in a jiffy. And yet, there is still no letter from you! Why do you always wait so terribly long before you write?! Darling, I have to ask you urgently to get me a visa for Cuba; and, if at all possible, also for my mother. I don't know whether it still makes sense, but we have to try everything. Please get together all your and our friends. I hope they are not going to be stingy with their money. Don't forget Dr. Friedmann and Dr. Huppert and/or their relatives. Regarding the various logistics etc. in connection with the visa, please contact Ruth Schnell, 1002 East 17th Street in Brooklyn New York. She is the sister of Elli Königsfeld who is the chief nurse of my former children's station; she got the visa for her sister Elli and will surely be able to advise and help you. She is very competent and nice. Please make sure to contact her. We very much hope that sister Elli will soon be able to travel. Maybe you will also have an opportunity to speak with Elli's friend or fiancé Dr. Proskauer. He is especially intelligent and fine. Last September he received a calling to NY University. But please,

more than anything, do write to Ms. Schnell. And, above all, write
to me!

   Farewell, darling. I think often of you and of the time when I
will be with you again. I know for sure that such a time will come. It
is often so difficult for me in the present time with all its questions to
believe in it and to get along here. But one is always reminded of that
time—it does not let itself be repressed.

Please do write! A thousand kisses

Your Valy

Some had been able to get around the quota system by being named to posts at universities. Medical doctors could be "called," as Valy puts it, as professors; it meant they were outside the visa system, they were "necessary." It might have been possible in 1939. But November 1941? To Cuba? Even if Germany had not decided to close down emigration, this was nearly impossible at this point. The Cuba option had all but completely closed; the United States was suspicious of Jews using Cuba as a stopping point to America and had helped end Jewish emigration to the island. It was also increasingly, drastically, phenomenally expensive.

The U.S. State Department was of no help either. In November, Assistant Secretary of State Breckinridge Long wrote in his personal diaries, quoting with approval the words of the (Jewish) American ambassador to Moscow, Laurence Steinhardt: "Steinhardt . . . took a definite stand on the immigration and refugee question and opposed the immigration in large numbers from Russia and Poland and Eastern Europeans whom he characterizes as entirely unfit to become citizens of this country. He says they are lawless, scheming, and defiant—and in many ways, unassibilible [sic]. He said the general type of intending immigrant was just the same as the criminal Jews who crowd our police court dockets in New York and with whom he is acquainted and whom he feels are never to become moderately decent American citizens." In a month, the United States would enter the war and make the conversation moot. But in the last weeks of Valy's efforts to get out, there was little movement at the higher diplomatic levels of the U.S. government—even for those who were "someone"—and Valy was no one, really, of import.

11-17-41

My beloved, now I have been writing a letter to you every weekend for the past six weekends. What do you think of this veritable letter barrage?! It's kind of strange to be writing letters, one after the other, without knowing how you are reacting to each of them.

I wonder how much longer I will be writing like this "into the blue"?!—You know, darling, when I am asking why a cruel destiny has separated me from you, I keep thinking that maybe the purpose of our separation is for us to become mature enough for each other, so that our togetherness will not be trite or banal, matter-of-course like, that missing each other will show us how much we really mean to one another. I, at least, do know how much you mean to me and that being together with you will be an unending feast day to me. . . . Only, I don't know when that will be.

Dearest one, do write to me! Can it really be possible that you do not write at all? I implore you to make Cuba possible. Dr. Friedmann will help financially. A couple of days ago, a notice arrived for RM [Reichsmark] 22.00 with Carl Feldschuh, Brooklyn, as the sender. What is to happen with that money?

We are doing well, considering our circumstances. There is much work to be done, but we do it gladly. During my leisure hours I read and—now you surely are going to laugh—study "Handwriting and Character" by Ludwig Klages. This is a very interesting, yet rather dry and difficult book that requires a lot of concentration. And that's good.

Darling, I have to see to my patient now. He rang for me and therefore I am quickly sending you many kisses.

Your Valy

Again, here is the address of Ms. Schnell who got a Cuban visa for her sister and who might be able to advise you as she by now knows all the ins and outs.
Ruth Schnell
1002 East 17th Street
Brooklyn, N. Y.

And then, suddenly: silence. My letters—her letters—end abruptly. After Pearl Harbor, when the United States enters the war, communication between Germany and the United States comes to a halt.

I wonder if I will ever find out anything more about where Valy went after November 17, 1941. Did she hide? Did she go underground? Or try? How hard was it to do?

Eight

BURGFRÄULEIN

After the Japanese bombed Pearl Harbor on December 7, 1941, and the United States entered the war, it became all but impossible to send letters between Germany and the United States. "Some tried [to write], via Switzerland," Barbara Scheib tells me; Scheib is a researcher of quiet do-gooders, the Germans who helped, those who fed the Jews who went underground, or who hid Jews, or who found Jews hiding places—those we commonly call "the Righteous." Mail service, she explains, along with borders and diplomatic relations, was cut off. We are sitting in the Gedenkstätte Deutscher Widerstand— the memorial to Nazi resistance, on the street named for Claus von Stauffenberg, the German army officer who was part of the plot attempt to assassinate Hitler toward the end of the war; it is the very building occupied by the German High Command during World War II. The building was preserved and it still feels, vaguely, like walking onto the set of a Nazi film, but creepier, as it is real.

Scheib and her colleague Dr. Beate Kosmala spent years working on the Silent Heroes Memorial, a project devoted to those who hid or assisted Jews in hiding. The women are of a certain type, not quite as old as my mother, but closer to her generation than mine; this material is the work of looking into their own parents' generation. Kosmala is blond and bespectacled, she walks lightly, speaks softly; her presence is unobtrusive to the point of nearly being absent. Scheib wears her dark hair short, with blunt-cut bangs. They both wear tasteful silk scarves. It is a contrast, their work, with the building we meet in—the Gedenkstätte Deutscher Widerstand is all about the big stories, heroic tales of high-ranking military brass, aristocrats, diplomats (all men), many of them disappointed Nazis, most of them anti-Semites, who tried to kill Hitler in a coup on July 20, 1944. Scheib and Kosmala are more concerned with the silent heroism of "ordinary Germans," the quiet righteous, who were just as often women.

"In the end," Scheib continues, "post was only possible through the International Red Cross. Only twenty-five words were allowed. It is a poem." Even "Aryan" Germans were annoyed by the difficulty in communicating with friends and family abroad after the war began, she says. I ask about telephone calls and they both, vehemently, shake their heads. It was prohibitively expensive to call internationally, for one, but price was secondary: Jews had been barred from owning or using phones for some time. Telegrams, too, were dearly priced. Charged letter by letter, the telegram Valy sent in the spring of 1941 would have cost her nearly a month's salary. When I look at the telegram again, I notice something I'd overlooked before: at the bottom are the words *Hilfsverein, Tzedakah*—a likely reference to the Reichs-vereinigung's emigration department. The Hilfsverein der Deutschen Juden was an organization created at the turn of the twentieth century to help poor and persecuted Eastern Jews who arrived in Germany escaping eastern pogroms—*Hilfe* means "help." But by the early 1930s, it was helping German Jews to emigrate, providing subsidies for tickets, and paying for everything that led up to getting passage to another—safer—country. The organization aided some ninety thousand Jews in fleeing the Reich; eventually its work was folded into the Reichsvereinigung. Valy's Uncle Julius mentions it in one of his missives, in 1940, when he and my grandfather were hoping to get the women visas to Chile. By 1941, charity was needed not just for tickets, but also to send a simple telegram. The desperation was that great, the need that strong.

Kosmala and Scheib tell me that while we—we Jews; we Americans; we American Jews—are obsessed with the who, how, and why of going into hiding, Germans have a flip side to that: the who, how, and why of *helping*; of eluding the system, fighting Nazism from within, of simply aiding those underground. Kosmala and Scheib want to explode the myth that it was impossible to do so, that repression was so great, the consequences so dire, that it was life threatening to step forward on behalf of Jewish neighbors. In fact, there were not always mortal consequences to aiding Jews; whereas in Poland those who aided Jews were shot, in Germany some of those who assisted their Jewish neighbors were sometimes barely punished at all. But the fear of punishment was enough to keep many out of the business of aiding their former neighbors.

At the same time, Scheib and Kosmala are quite clear that they don't want anyone left with the impression that a large percentage of the population helped—Silent Heroes is not only a project of unearthing the righteous, but also exposing the casual cruelty of bystanders who assumed helping was out of the question. Nor do they want anyone to believe that those Jews who did survive did not suffer. Indeed, they were often the worst off, psychologically, once they emerged and realized they were totally and completely alone in the world. Nor, as well, do they want me to believe it was easy for those who managed to slip into the underground system to survive day to day, let alone until the end of the war. This last, they emphasize, is important in the case of Valy. Who would have been her support, after all, given that she was a newcomer to Berlin? Who would have come to her defense, given how often she moved and how shallow her roots? Often those below ground were aided by a dozen or more people. Whom did Valy have in this cold, frantic city?

As 1941 turned into 1942, the deportations to the east picked up pace and cruelty. But first the German manufacturing world used this slave labor, drove it into the ground, complained that this skilled labor force, so cheaply acquired, so annoying to lose, was necessary. With deportations increasing in frequency, more and more people considered hiding.

For those who were successful in going underground, the stories highlighted in the Silent Heroes memorial are not remotely, let alone universally, happy. Like Alice Lowenstein, who went from hiding place to hiding place with her two daughters, aged four and six, in an exhausting run made more so by her younger girl, who had a dangerous habit of telling strangers about the men who had come to take away her father. Alice decided to get the girls as far from Berlin as she could, and in 1944, she finally found them a place on a farm, in Weimar, about 175 miles southwest of Berlin. Alice was able to write to her children for some time, but then the war and the world began to disintegrate around her and services like the mail no longer functioned; for six months or so, there was no correspondence. Alice didn't know it, but during that time the girls were denounced and the Gestapo brought them back to Berlin, back to their original home, to determine if the kids were Jews. All the tenants in their old building said they did not know the girls; that is, until the *Hausmeister*, the building superintendent, ran after the Gestapo to confirm: these girls were Jewish. With that, the Lowenstein girls were sent to Auschwitz, just months before the war ended. When their mother came to claim them, she discovered, instead, that they had been murdered.

And yet, as wrenching as Lowenstein's story is, as crushing as it reads even just on paper, her experience is considered a success. And therein lies the complexity and incomprehensibility of survival. Thousands tried to do what Alice did. Of half a million Jews living in Germany at the beginning of the war, some 270,000 to 300,000 were able to emigrate. About 180,000 Jews were deported from Germany; the remaining 15,000 or so included those in mixed-race relationships who were "protected" from immediate deportation to the ghettos and camps of the east. In Berlin itself, once a thriving center with some 160,000 Jews, some 5,000 to 7,000 Jews went into hiding and about 1,400 survived. When we think of the millions dead, of course, we include the swath of east and south—Poland, Ukraine, Romania, Hungary, Greece. But Germany itself, the heart of the Reich, had, ironically, far fewer Jews at the outset.

But before I continue to investigate what happened to those who ducked beneath the waters of legitimacy, disappearing in plain sight to blend into the world around them, those who were able to survive despite losing food rations, and beds, and family members, before I can dig deeper to see if Valy was among those illegals, before I can even ask how she might have been a part of that system and what it would have taken to survive under false identity, I am still wondering about those last years aboveground. Especially for those who, like Valy and her mother, worked for the Reichsvereinigung—work which, for a time, protected its workers.

Endlessly bothering me was this: I knew that, like many women her age, Valy did not try to flee immediately. Instead, she remained in Europe, largely, I suspected, for her mother—whose name, at first, when I found Valy's letters, I did not know, and whose life, at first, I had no clue how to penetrate beyond the small details. Unlike Valy, after all, I didn't have her mother's testimony. Over time I gathered pieces: she had been a young mother when her marriage dissolved, and then a successful businesswoman, and later the competent, caring manager of an old-age home. Perhaps, I thought, if I knew more about her, I could better understand Valy's motivations, better know Valy's story. Her name, at least in Valy's letters, was "Toni." It was clearly a nickname. It got me nowhere in official databases of the dead.

In the Yad Vashem victim database, there are 177 names of the murdered that are linked, in one way or another, with the surname Scheftel: there are alternative spellings, two *f*'s, an *a* instead of an *e*; there are children, including one born in 1940; there are the elderly. But as, finally, I turned my focus to Toni, I kept coming back to one listing: Hanna T. Scheftel, born on December 27, 1885, in Borszczow, Poland, and deported on March 12, 1943, to Auschwitz, on the 36th Ost (East) transport, from Berlin. The age of this Scheftel seemed closest to correct, and though she was deported from Berlin, not Babelsberg or Potsdam, she seemed the most likely to be the woman I wanted to know more about.

In the *Gedenkbuch Berlins: Der Jüdischen Opfer des Nationalsozialismus*—the remembrance book of the murdered Jews of Berlin—there she was again, Hanna Scheftel, née Flamm. Flamm! This was the same last name as the "Uncle" Julius writing to my grandfather. This must be her. Still, there were no clues about who she really was, let alone whether she was the woman I truly sought, how she went from Troppau to Potsdam to Berlin—and how she avoided the deportations from her own old-age home in January 1943. I wrote once more to the ITS archives at Bad Arolsen, requesting any files they might have on this Hanna or Channa Scheftel. Within a few days, I receive an e-mail with these details: "SCHEFTEL née FLAMM, Chana, born on 27.12.1885, last address: Berlin N 4, Auguststrasse 14/16." (This building, I knew, had long been controlled by the Jewish community of Berlin, and hosted various social service agencies.) "Deported from Berlin to Concentration Camp Auschwitz by the 'Geheime Staatspolizei [Gestapo] Berlin.' Category: 'Jüdin' [Jewess]."

The e-mail continued: "Apart from the transport list we mentioned, we also hold one index card made out by AJDC Berlin"—this was the American Jewish Joint Distribution Committee, the organization survivors once called "the Joint," formed in the 1910s to help Jewish refugees, and which worked, financially at least, to save Jews during the war—"and another made out by the Reichsvereinigung. Unfortunately, we have no information available on Mrs. Scheftel's further fate."

```
S C H E F T E L , Hanna Taube, geb. Flann

27. 12. 1885   Borszow -Polen        gesch.  dtsch

  jüd.      jüd.      RV. seit Geburt
  Kaufmann  Heimleiterin


Babelsberg, Bergstr. 1, Altersheim


                        024176
```

Toni's Reichsvereinigung card has a typed note indicating her address is Babelsberg, Bergstrasse 1, Altersheim (old-age home)—this is the address Valy wrote from, this was where she was the *Burgfräulein*. I am correct! This is Toni. I write to Jean-Marc, jubilant that I have connected Uncle Julius to Toni to Valy to the old-age home—I nearly shout out loud with my discovery.

On the Reichsvereinigung card, I note that under Toni's name it first says *"Kaufmann"* (merchant) and then *"Heimleiterin"* (house manager); the Babelsberg address is crossed out, and below it, on January 16, 1943, the Auguststrasse address was written down in pencil. This was the day her old-age home was disbanded, the day when all these elderly men and women were rounded up and sent east to their certain deaths, all these Germans who could well remember a time when Jews were high-standing members of society, war heroes, not pariahs. The home, by then, had become overcrowded, but Toni, Valy writes even before the vise has closed on them, had valiantly tried to keep each member feeling cared for, honored even, until the end. But there is no mention of Valy in the International Tracing Service notes on Toni at all.

Auguststrasse 14/16 is a few doors down from Clärchens, a still-working 1910s-era dance hall once frequented by Nazi officers, with a large beer garden I often biked past. It would have been a strange source of camaraderie and boisterous activity given the tragedy and desperation just a few doors down. Built in the middle of the nine-teenth century as a part of the Jewish Hospital, during the Nazi era, while there were still Jewish children in Berlin, Auguststrasse 14/16 housed a Jewish day-care center. Marion Kaplan, in *Between Dignity and Despair*, lays out the scene:

> Mothers doing forced labor brought their children to the center around 5 a.m. The children played in the courtyard, took baths, and ate their meals at the center. "They were serious children. . . . They laughed less than others, they also cried less. It was as though they wanted to make as little trouble as possible for us," reported a caretaker. They were probably also lethargic from malnourishment.

One day, in February 1943, the mothers returned to collect their children after their day of backbreaking, soul-destroying labor, and discovered their kids had been deported, without notice, without their knowledge; there were just the empty prams and scattered toys, the hurried detritus of a group of children gathered up willy-nilly and spirited away. The wailing of the mothers went on for hours.

Auguststrasse 14/16's day care was called Ahawah—"love" in Hebrew. It was one of a number of day-care centers the Nazis methodically liquidated; the old and the young were useless. Jews, despite themselves, had continued to have children, though far fewer than before the war, and, of course, there was no avoiding getting old. I stand there on the street, listening to the laughter of bicyclists commuting home from work, the sounds of a nearby gallery opening its doors for night visitors, and wonder at the incomprehensible pain this street has seen.

Auguststrasse 14/16 also served as what was then called a *Siechen-heim*, a boardinghouse for the old and infirm, as well as a way station for those factory workers who had already been listed for deportation but were deemed too important for the factory to be sent yet—a *Juden-haus* filled, I imagine, with dread and despair. The building has long been in a state of disrepair, enormous, decrepit, seemingly haunted, though recently it began to be rehabilitated, a project funded by the Jewish community.

When I realize that Toni lived here for some months, I head back to the building to look up at it. I go home just after, on the tram, riding through the busy streets of former East Berlin. I am not feeling well at all. I go straight from the train into bed, where I remain for hours, with my head aching and my eyes crossed from the lights I see when I have migraines.

The headache began from my pregnancy, but the idea of the abandoned toys of those long-ago deported day-care children did not help, especially as my little Jew tossed and kicked inside me. Pregnant women did not survive the roundups. They were deported immediately to the east, where many were murdered immediately, or died soon after. The world shimmered from my migraine auras; the pain closed me in, made me claustrophobic, terrified to be alone and terrified of the lights that made the pain worse. I tried to sleep.

Sleep won't come. Eyes closed to the swirling world around me, I mull over what I know about Toni, Valy's mother, her only friend, her albatross: I do not know much. I open my eyes in my darkened room. The Joint Distribution Committee—how did Toni have a JDC card? Did Valy have one that I didn't find? Did the JDC try to enable her—or them—to escape? The organization facilitated the emigration of about 190,000 German Jews from 1938 to 1939, and then worked to help Jews in Hungary and Romania. After the war, the Joint worked to help those who had survived.

The questions keep bubbling back up: The Babelsberg home for the aged was liquidated on January 16, 1943. Neither Valy nor her mother was sent with the group of elderly. Why were Toni and Valy spared that day? What happened to Valy that day? Where did she go? For God's sake, where is she? How did she survive? Some of the answers about who Toni was, and the work she did, come in the form of a bulky envelope from the Brandenburgisches Landeshauptarchiv Potsdam, the local state archive for Potsdam.

The archive has several records for Toni—also called "Antonie"— including a letter that spells out, in her own voice, the crushing weight of her continuous impoverishment and explains her role at the home in Babelsberg.

October 8, 1940.

In reply to your valued official communication, I politely inform you that I possess no assets with the exception of a life insurance policy, which does not mature until 1949. Since May 1940 I have been employed by the Reichsvereinigung der Juden in Deutschland in the Babelsberg Home for the Elderly, 1 Bergstrasse, and my net monthly wage, in addition to board and lodging, is RM 77.52. In the last tax year, I had no income at all and supported myself from the remaining proceeds from the closing down of my household.

It is signed:

Chane Taube Scheftel, Jewess, Place of identity: Berlin, Identity number: A 438802.

Two pages later there is another explanation of her life. "Chane Taube Sara Scheftel, date: October 7, 1940. I was born on December 27, 1885, in Borszczow, and am divorced." Her property declarations claim she has no possessions of which to speak.

She may have been completely dispossessed by 1943, but from May 1940 until January 1943—or later?—she had had a position of relative privilege within the Reichsvereinigung, running her old-age home. By the time she is moved to Auguststrasse, she earns 130 RM per month, of which 42 RM are deducted from her already extremely meager wages for her room and board. She is living in one room, with nothing.

I realize I must go backward in time again, to better understand her experience—and thus, also, Valy's—working in the Reichsvereinigung, and why they were spared for a time.

——————

A few days later, I take the train up to Hamburg to meet Dr. Beate Meyer at the Institut Für die Geschichte der Deutschen Juden (Institute for the History of German Jews) to ask her for help with my questions, the ones I know to ask, the ones I haven't yet discovered. She has been writing about the Reichsvereinigung for many years, so many that nearly everyone I ask—from the Holocaust Museum in Washington, D.C., to the various academics I consult in Berlin—says things like, "Well, you must have spoken to Beate Meyer? No? Well, then"— and so I do. She and I will meet several times, both in Germany and in the United States. She is not terribly keen to be in a story, but she is very willing to talk.

Meyer is soft spoken, with wild, white-blond hair and eyes pouched and weary, behind large glasses, from reading too much about the years of persecution. She is a bit younger than the generation that some in Europe call "'68ers," one of the generation that turned on its parents, that upended Germany, forced it to look in at itself, at its past.

"In the beginning," she says, "in the time of emigration," when emigration was still legal, before October 1941, "there were a lot of people on social welfare . . . people who remained in Germany because their relatives emigrated and they were old people, sick people, children without parents, and so on. They remained in Germany and the Reichsvereinigung had to find homes and orphanages and hospitals and hospices," she tells me. Jews needed this social welfare network when they were kicked off the mainstream system; the Reichsvereini-gung needed workers to run all those homes, and schools, and spaces. It was work, and it was better than forced labor in the factories, where any rules of health and safety and time management were purposely, cruelly, upended. The Reichsvereinigung was beholden to, really at the whim of, the Gestapo, but also tried to work for the community. That tension held, for a time.

It is a damp day, and the halls of the Institute for the History of German Jews are quiet, save the faint footfalls of the occasional stu-dent. It is an old Jugendstil building, with the feel of a hybrid hospital and university. I am hungry and tired and feeling very pregnant though I have months to go before I give birth.

I show Meyer a few of Valy's letters, especially those that come in October 1941, the moment deportations to the east started and emi-gration was cut off. When deportations began, Meyer says, Reichs-vereinigung officials "had some illusions" about who could stay and who would go. It seemed, at the time, some—possibly like Valy, and certainly like Toni—would remain "necessary" to the Reich—it's a word that carries great weight in the context of survival, and of creat-ing a hierarchy among Jews. What did they think? I ask, meaning the workers of the Reichsvereinigung, the workers like Valy who made no real decisions about their fellow Jews, but were in the system, some-where in the mix. What did they know about what it meant to be sent away? And what about the leadership? Did they know much more?

Meyer sighs, heavily. It's not an easy question—she can't *know* exactly. But she tries to give me an answer. At first, she says, "the heads of the Reichsvereinigung thought the deportations would only include a part of the Jews, that part would be evacuated and then ev-erything would [settle down] and then everything would . . . They could have community and religious life and could live life as people of . . . yes, as a second class, as underdogs. But they thought they could live [like that] in the German Reich. And they would survive. But in the end of 1941, they realized that that was an illusion—that the deportations would go on until the last Jew was included." Belatedly the Reichsvereinigung appealed to the Joint Distribution Committee to procure visas for its higher functionaries. Perhaps that explained Toni's Joint card, I thought.

Some sixteen thousand Jews were rounded up and expelled from the capital from autumn 1941 to the following fall. The social ostracism was minor in comparison to the terror of daily life. In the late fall of 1942, Jews in Berlin with access to illegal radios heard BBC broadcasts about Jews being murdered by gas. It was, quite literally, unbelievable. And yet, undeniably, people were disappearing, everywhere, most never to be heard from again.

I tell Meyer that Valy writes, desperately, about emigration up until her last letter, hopes for something to come through—to Cuba, to anywhere. I thought that was completely impossible. Meyer says I'm wrong. "Emigration from Germany was still possible until the war began," she says, despite the curbs on age, on ability to leave, despite dozens of technical obstacles. Small handfuls of people were able to flee. "There were some so-called illegal immigrations when ships were hired and people were put on the ships, but it was not clear that [refugees] could enter a country [they arrived in] or if they would get a visa for a country where they could stay." Perhaps, I realize with a start, Alfred Jospe was right. With $150 per person, maybe Valy and her mother would have made it to Chile. "The Gestapo tried to force the Jewish people to go on ships but the Reichsvereinigung hesitated," Meyer explains. "They said, 'It's too dangerous.'"

In Austria, Jews were less cautious, she says. They sought these extra-legal options—through Yugoslavia, Greece, Italy, to Palestine—sooner, and more often, than their northern neighbors. What made the difference? I ask. "The German Jewish leaders were Germans!" She laughs, a bit bitterly. "They thought everything should go in an orderly way." The Austrians just wanted out. Austrian Jews, she reminds me, had been swept under by a quick wave of institutionalized anti-Semitism that began with fury in 1938, with the Anschluss, when five years of progressive anti-Jewish legislation endured by their German neighbors was imposed on the newly incorporated Reich in a matter of weeks. In Germany, on the other hand, the "German Jewish leaders became familiar with the rising persecution," a slow sinking, a loss of footing, that took place gradually, from 1933 on. Each subsequent humiliation was endured, weathered, surmounted. "But as they delayed the chance to leave, the Reich decided that they wouldn't let them leave after all."

Not everyone delayed. More than half of Germany's Jews had left by 1938. It was the others, those left behind, the girls who had not been sent out, so their brothers and fathers could escape—as Valy tells my grandfather "only women are left"—the elderly, the infirm; it was the families that couldn't quite believe it would get any worse—when that group began to clamor to leave, the doors had closed.

Jews like Valy and Toni scrambled to remain relevant; work was literally the difference between life and deportation. Meanwhile, the Nazis prepared to liquidate the population. But that process couldn't take place all at once; extermination took time. The German manufacturing sector still needed this labor force, after all. And the camps themselves were not ready.

Meyer continued, narrating the movement from forced immigration to expulsion to extermination. "They needed trains and camps and guards," she says. "First they brought [Jews] to the ghettos for a certain time and after that they would be brought to other ghettos far in the east but nothing was prepared. Then [the Nazis] decided to murder the Jews." Murders were at a rapid clip in the east. Five hundred thousand had been killed between June and the end of 1941 by the Einsatzgruppen in the east. "But the decision to murder the German Jews, too, was made in December 1941." There is no document that confirms this, but it is the date that most historians agree was the turning point for the fate of German Jewry.

Some who remained in the Reich when the deportations began received ominous notes from the ghettos of the east with coded words like "widow" written after a name, so that those who received the message would know—a husband had died. But how? Why? That was unclear, unexplained. Those who were sent on early transports to the ghettos in Lodz and Riga had little contact with people back at home: a few letters, and a few eyewitnesses, reported conditions that seemed unbelievable—hygiene had disintegrated, food was scarce, death everywhere. In 1942, Marianne Strauss, the girl who was in the Kindergartenseminar, the subject of Mark Roseman's book *A Past in Hiding*, was able to discover a glimpse, through letters smuggled by a sympathetic—and daring—Aryan, the horrific conditions of the Izbica ghetto her lover had been deported to in Poland, along with his family.

But it was not merely the destination that was terrifying to the Jews of Berlin like Valy and her mother. The collection points in Berlin were also awful: Jewish workers in these makeshift transit camps, one based at the Levetzowstrasse Synagogue, another at an old-age home at Grosse Hamburger Strasse, were told that, under penalty of their own deportation, they could not report back what they saw; they could not pass messages back to those who remained behind. The so-called evacuations were terrifying, mortifying; a foreshadowing of deprivations to come. Inmates were subjected to body searches in front of their neighbors; rooms were locked to prevent flight; dozens upon dozens of children were packed into a room with space for, perhaps, twenty, with fetid air and endless anguish all around. "A dreadful future awaited them, and some of them already guessed this. . . . The older ones wanted to be left alone. . . . The smaller ones cried for their mothers, from whom they were cruelly separated in the same building," remembered worker Edith Dietz after the war. In the former Levetzowstrasse Synagogue, women threw themselves over the balcony to their deaths in the pews below; the sound of sobbing filled the air for hours, days, on end.

But if 1941 was dreadful, it was 1942—after Valy's letters end—when the prospects for even those with work became much, much worse. That fall, Alois Brunner arrived in Berlin. "He was the Nazi

responsible for deportations from Vienna," explained Meyer. The Gestapo in Vienna was considered more brutal, more efficient—more
effective. Brunner—at the time, all of thirty years old—was brought to
Berlin to streamline the deportations and speed them up in the goal of
a *judenrein*, or Jew-free, Berlin. Instead of random deportations, Brunner "changed the assembly camps in Berlin into a kind of prison and he
caught the Jews in the streets and in their houses." He would seal off
whole city blocks, encircle entire apartment buildings; he gave orders
to liquidate the old-age homes and orphanages. Deportations were no
longer piecemeal; now everyone in the dragnet would be taken.

No one was protected any longer; not the Reichsvereinigung
workers, not their charges. "Only the Jews who lived in privileged
mixed marriages," said Meyer. "But a normal Jewish woman who was
not a so-called *Mischling*"—a person of half-Aryan descent—"was not
able to avoid the star. Despite that fact, a lot of Jews didn't wear it
when they left their homes because they said it was dangerous to wear
it and dangerous not to wear it." With the star, they were targets in the
street—of taunting, harassment, beatings, random arrest, or worse—
but if they decided to forgo the star, woe be the man or woman who
was discovered to be a Jew defying the law. That was considered sabotage; that meant immediate deportation.

"So they avoided [the star] but they had to wear it in their working
place," Meyer continued. "There were controls by the Gestapo and
they had to wear [the star] when they left the house because non-
Jewish neighbors could denounce them for not wearing it. . . .
[Then] they would get a notice they [had been selected] for the next
deportation."

With or without the star, Valy and her mother, like all the Jews in
Berlin at this point, knew that the chance of deportation was coming
closer and closer, whatever it meant to be sent to the east; the reality
of which remained unclear. "These deportations were something
monstrous," wrote Camilla Neumann in Berlin, at the end of the war.
"It was horrible when the dark car with the SS bandits stopped in

front of the door and picked up the careworn men and women and the innocent children. . . . A large number of people from the Jewish community had to participate in the round-ups. They were authorized by the Gestapo and one had to go with them. If one resisted, they used force. They said that otherwise it would cost them their own heads. We were very distressed that Jews allowed themselves to be involved in something like that. But it did not stop with that. Finally the Jews were caught like dogs. They were rounded up from the stores, from the waiting rooms of doctors, from the streets and were loaded onto trucks. If one did not climb on quickly enough, one was shoved on."

As the existential threat of expulsion hung over them, the indignities and deprivations continued. Though Valy's letters to my grandfather had stopped, from the Brandenburgisches Landeshauptarchiv records I see that Valy and her mother work on, through the following year. But life began deteriorating at an ever more rapid clip, and those who waited for word of her—my grandfather, her uncle, her friends—heard nothing further and surely feared what they were experiencing.

In early January 1942, Valy and her mother were forced to turn in all remaining warm items to the Gestapo: wool sweaters and clothing and socks; ski boots and skis; furs. In February, they were banned from purchasing newspapers; in March, they were stripped of the right to use all public transport unless they had a necessary seven-kilometer commute—and paperwork documenting that. By summer, the shopping hour restrictions were made stricter: Jews could no longer line up before the four p.m. start time, and they would not be served if the hour ended before they had shopped, even if they had entered a shop in advance of the five p.m. end-of-shopping hour. In October, Jews were banned from buying books. Many of the restrictions were published in the *Jüdisches Nachrichtenblatt*, the Jewish newspaper controlled by the Gestapo. It got thinner and thinner as a paper and began to include practical life skills, like how to cook an omelet with no egg, liver sausages with no liver, make coffee with no coffee. The editor in chief had a heart attack and died.

On one brutal day in October 1942, leaders of the Reichsvereinigung were told to assemble staff in the building of the synagogue on Oranienburger Strasse. Once inside, they were told to select five hundred lower-level workers who were no longer "necessary" for work. "There was a terrible scene," says Meyer. "The head of the social welfare department," the woman who likely employed Valy, "had a nervous breakdown, saying, 'Take me, take me, but not my staff!' And others refused [to choose]." Two days later, the Gestapo declared that for every person selected for deportation who tried to escape, one higher-ranking official would be shot. The Reichsvereinigung members themselves went to flush out those who had evaded the edict.

That was actually the second terrible event of 1942, says Meyer. The first was when a small group of young Jews, led by a Communist, attacked an anti-Semitic and anti-Communist exhibit on the Soviet Union, wounding a handful of Nazis. The resistance fighters were sentenced to death for the bombing, their family members were deported, and the leaders of the Reichsvereinigung were forced to stand for hours on end, facing a wall, not told what their punishment was being meted out for. In the aftermath of that incident, Meyer says, five hundred were arrested and two hundred fifty shot immediately.

Eventually, Meyer emphasizes, as the Reichsvereinigung prepared list after list of Jews to be sent east, those who remained in Berlin had come to realize that they were all to be deported, and the only reason they weren't being sent at once was merely a question of infrastructure, not intention. This realization taints the image of the Reichsvereinigung and has shaped much of Meyer's work. Why did they not warn people to hide? Did Toni—eventually a "leader" in the Reichsvereinigung, at least in terms of her old-age home—did she hold any responsibility? Did Valy, who was merely placed by these Jewish leaders but did, after all, receive her salary from them? They were cogs, more than anything, worker bees in an enormous hive.

But of the chiefs? Leaders like Rabbi Leo Baeck, those who deter-mined the lists of deportations, those who heard more from the Ge-stapo? This conversation spawned half a century of debate.

Hannah Arendt unequivocally believed that the work of the Reichsvereinigung was akin to what their counterparts were forced to do in Poland, where the Gestapo strong-armed Jewish communities into forming *Judenräte*, Jewish councils, which were forced to aid the Nazi effort to destroy the Jews. Scathingly, she wrote in *Eichmann in Jerusalem*:

> To a Jew this role of the Jewish leaders in the destruction of their own people is undoubtedly the darkest chapter of the whole dark story. . . . In the matter of cooperation, there was no distinction between the highly assimilated Jewish communities of Central and Western Europe and the Yiddish-speaking masses of the East. In Amsterdam as in Warsaw, in Berlin as in Budapest, Jew-ish officials could be trusted to compile the lists of persons and of their property, to secure money from the deportees to defray the expenses of their deportation and extermination, to keep track of vacated apartments, to supply police forces to help seize Jews and get them on trains, until, as a last gesture, they handed over the assets of the Jewish community in good order for final confiscation.

Arendt believed, conclusively, that without these helper Jews, the sheer need for manpower alone would have mucked up the works of the Gestapo; that the Jews themselves smoothed the way for their own destruction. She believed that the immorality of the helpful work of the Jewish councils was as clear as the immorality of their execution-ers; that the moral breakdown of European society extended to the victims themselves. But Arendt's worldview was predicated on her knowledge of the full destruction of European Jewry, knowledge that Berlin's Jews (and Warsaw's and Amsterdam's) did not have.

I want to know: Where were Toni and Valy in that system? So, I ask Meyer, was the Reichsvereinigung culpable? But Meyer, like other scholars I read later, rejects the question, rejects the purity of Arendt's argument. The Reichsvereinigung was in an impossible situation, she says, and the leaders thought they were doing the best for the community with the tools they had in hand. "To claim that demonstrative refusal, open resistance, and a mass movement underground would have enabled a greater number of people to survive is mere speculation— and assumes that the majority of German Jews would have been prepared for this. . . . The tragedy of the Reichsvereinigung . . . is marked by the objective hopelessness of all attempts" to protect their own people. "The representatives became entangled in the Nazi policy of extermination, for which they were at the same time not responsible," she wrote in an essay she sent me that was published to accompany an exhibit on the lives of Jews in Berlin under the Reich. In other words: the killing would have gone on, with or without their cooperation.

I press her further: Were these Jews in any way responsible for their own persecution, their own destruction? In Austria, the surviving Jewish officials were later vilified, prosecuted, sometimes to a greater extent than captured Nazis. Doron Rabinovici starts his provocative book *Eichmann's Jews* with the story of Wilhelm Reisz, who was charged in 1945 by the public prosecutor's office, who singled him out for having "brought misfortune on his compatriots in order to gain advantage for himself." He was sentenced to fifteen years and three months of hard labor—a fate similar, Rabinovici points out, to that of the Nazi responsible for the deportations of the Jews of Austria, even though Reisz himself had lived with the constant fear of deportation. Reisz hung himself after his trial. But, Rabinovici says— and he will also tell me this in person, sometime later when we meet—that in Austria, as elsewhere, those Jews with some degree of power were afraid that if they left the task of organizing their cousins and community members to the Gestapo, it would be far more brutal; they were afraid, they argued later, that their own family members would be taken if they didn't cooperate. And so they became part of the system.

Part of the system or not, the work the women did, and so many of these workers were women, especially while they skated closer and closer to their own deportations, weighed heavily upon them. Women were tasked with preparing food, sandwiches, for the deportees; these snacks and water were the woefully inadequate provisions for a trip that was days long, especially as the food brigade itself was slowly decimated, its members picked off for deportations, sent off into the unknown with the drip drip drip of horrific anticipation. I imagine, simply by dint of her position, Toni may have been among these sandwich makers, these deportation preparers.

"Of some forty women who helped in the beginning, in the end there were only eight," wrote Herta Pineas in May 1945. She herself was a member of these provisions-preparing brigades. White arm-bands afforded them freedom of movement and set them apart from the unlucky. And they watched with increasing terror the manner in which the deportees were sent. "The trains were sealed before departure, and not a window was allowed to be opened!" wrote Mrs. Pineas.

> At the rear of the train there was a machine gun, and in the middle there were also Gestapo. At the station there was no food even for the smallest children; there was only cold skimmed milk, and too little of that too. And for us at the train the families with many children were the worst. The children were holding their dolls in their arms, happy to be following their grandparents, who had already "departed" ahead of them.

Children were jammed into closed, windowless furniture vans to be brought from transit camp to train station. By the end of 1942, even the meager provisions these women prepared were no longer permitted or offered. By then, if one of the women workers expressed sadness or disapproval, she, too, would be sent along. So they suppressed all emotion. Aryans, too, would watch the Jews arriving and loading at open platforms, impassively. No one spoke of what they witnessed.

Toni and Valy, it seems, were just as trapped as those who left on trains before them.

———

Meyer asks me if I'd like to take a tour of Hamburg's old Jewish quarter, filled as it is with *Stolpersteine*—literally, "stumbling blocks"—brass-topped cobblestones hewn by Gunter Demnig, an artist based in Cologne, that are laid in the ground in front of houses to mark those deported from address after address, in a project that began in 1992. There are hundreds in Hamburg, as there are, these days, across Germany and Austria. I found it enormously moving to look down with each step to see the carved words *"Hier wohnte . . ."*—"Here lived . . ." The entire former Jewish quarter is filled with them, glittering with each step. It is incredibly effective. A whisper that becomes a refrain—Lost lost lost lost lost. But the refrain is tempered: each *Stolperstein* must be purchased by an interested friend or family member; each stumbling block is requested—you must be remembered to be memorialized.

And as we walk, we talk. Meyer points out the theater where the Jewish community leaders brought sandwiches to the soon-to-be deported, a last piece of nourishment before the starvation that would come. Across the street, there is once again a "Jewish" restaurant, Café Leonar; the menu lists Jewish food, like chicken soup with matzah balls, Israeli salad. It is a bookstore café, and though it opened only in 2008, it is the first Jewish eatery to open since the war. We walk on. "This is the place where the synagogue was, and this is the ground," Meyer says as we come upon a large square, with cobblestones laid out in the shape of a bursting star. The plaza is now named for Rabbi Joseph Carlebach, the last rabbi of Hamburg. The main synagogue of

Hamburg, which stood here until 1938, was magnificent, with a cupola that soared high above the city; it burned on Kristallnacht.

Carlebach is something of a legend for having stuck by his congregation, even when he might have fled; he provided spiritual shelter to the desperate. Though five of his nine children escaped to safety in England and Palestine, the four youngest were deported with him to Riga, where all but one were murdered by bullets in the forests outside the ghetto.

———

According to the files at Yad Vashem and the notes I received from the Brandenburgisches Landeshauptarchiv, Toni worked in Berlin until March 9, 1943, when she was forced to list all of her belongings, in a property declaration that would have stripped her of each Reichsmark in property, on behalf of the Reich, if she had any property to speak of at that point. She had nothing at all by then. Her forms are nearly empty. She lived in the city until the twelfth; I know now that this was a (relatively) late date for Berlin. It is a sign she might have ranked higher in the Reichsvereinigung than, for example, the factory workers who were swept up and rounded onto trains during the last week of February 1943 in what became known as the *Fabrikaktion*—factory action—during which thousands upon thousands of Jewish forced laborers were taken away without notice, pulled directly from the factories into city-based transit camps, shoved onto trucks in just the clothes they were wearing, with no preparation, no food, no water, and with a great deal of public anxiety among the Jews—especially family members—who remained in the city.

I also knew that most of those Reichsvereinigung members not taken during the *Fabrikaktion* were given a horrible, horrible task. Hildegard Henschel, wife of one of the higher-ups in the organization, testified at the Eichmann trial that those women workers who were left were themselves roped into the effort: they were sent out to

the apartments of the factory workers, to collect the children who had
been left at home, locked in their apartments, as there was no day care
on Saturdays and their mothers were all forced laborers. The Jewish
women of the Reichsvereinigung were sent to take the kids from their
homes to the deportations centers; the overcrowded transit ways, to
these gateways of death. Eight thousand persons, the factory workers,
were detained, Henschel explained in Jerusalem. "And they began, of
course, to ask questions: 'What is happening to my children, my children are at home, and where is my husband, he works in the factory,
he is not here!' The Jewish Community began to organize its staff, in
order to gather the families together at least. The children were
brought from the homes, where some of them had been locked in by
their parents, since there was no school anymore and many people did
not know where to leave the children. Attempts were also made to
unite husbands and wives. These efforts were almost completely successful, as far as the children were concerned, but with the grown-ups
it was more difficult."

Henschel believed it was a service, that it was an altruistic effort to
reunite families. But there is something terrifically chilling in this
image, of Jews going to collect Jewish children, for delivery into the
hands of their executioners. Valy's mother, I am almost sure, though I
cannot know, was among those nurses and staff who were sent to collect the children. By this point, she was working at Auguststrasse 14/16.
She was a staff member of the Reichsvereinigung, and while she herself is spared these rounds of deportations, she might not have been
spared the job of helping—inadvertently, forcibly—to destroy the
youth of Berlin.

Beate Meyer repeats this story to me, of the taken children. "It
was a chaos, too," Meyer says. "They felt responsible for the children
and they felt children had to stay with their families and so they were
deported with the families." But could the children, I ask, have been
saved? She looks at me and shakes her head sadly. "Where could they
bring them?" she asks. "There was no place for them to go."

Sometime later I ask Meyer about why Toni was not taken with the people in her old-age home, and what she might be able to tell me about her reassignment, if it might lead me to know more about Toni's import, her role, her time in Berlin. But Meyer can't give me much more. "I went through my lists of staff of the Reichsvereinigung [Berlin] from January, April, and May 1943," Meyer tells me, "but didn't find any hint to Chana Scheftel, not in general and not in particular in connection to the Auguststrasse home. I don't know why she isn't mentioned at Auguststrasse. She should be. Auguststrasse was a *Siechenheim*, for elderly and ill people who were in need of care. In addition, it was used as accommodation for other Jews until their deportation. . . . In 1941–1942, the Reichsvereinigung tried to give the personnel from dissolved institutions jobs in other departments, mostly those ones that dealt with deportations, because this department became bigger. But in 1943 they couldn't act in that way. Sometimes the staff of a home or a hospital was deported with the inhabitants or patients. Sometimes the Reichsvereinigung needed— just in that moment, when an institution was dissolved—a qualified person for another job at another institution until it, too, was closed. Sometimes a friend or colleague heard about the deportation of a certain home and asked superiors for help." Meyer apologizes for not having a more specific answer and recommends another German historian. He writes me that he has no answers—the history of Auguststrasse 14/16, he says, is itself a book.

There is nothing further these historians can tell me, with certainty, about Toni's last days in Berlin.

But what I piece together is this: Like other middle-level Reichsvereinigung members, Toni was useful until March 12. On that day, her work no longer "necessary" to the Reich, she, too, was shoved onto a train at Grunewald station, heading east to Auschwitz. There were 899 others with Toni on that train; she was fifty-seven years old— and, emotionally, she was alone. Valy was not with her that day.

At the U.S. Holocaust Memorial Museum in Washington, I

watch video testimony from Norbert Wollheim, recorded in the early 1990s. Wollheim was deported on the same day as Toni. Somewhere in those same train cars, he, along with his wife and their small child, was shoved aboard. Of his small family, only he would survive. In his testimony, Wollheim explained that he and his family, after being picked up by the Gestapo, were driven to the transit station at Berlin's Grosse Hamburger Strasse, in Mitte. It doesn't exist anymore as a building, but there is a prominent memorial, with a garden, and a wall with an eerie series of statues of Jews waiting to leave. Wollheim recounted:

> Then the procedure of deportation started with all kinds of paperwork. . . . Even in the middle of that war, when everything was short including paper, there was enough paper for all kinds of procedures. And we had to declare our so-called funds—our possessions—and we were served with a kind of summons . . . saying we had been declared enemies of the Reich because of our behavior and that we were to be deprived of our property. And this was served on all of us, including my then-child of three and a half years, because of also his outrageous behavior toward the German Reich. After two or three days we were taken by trucks to a German freight railroad station and put on cattle cars and then this train with approximately a thousand people left Berlin. We were—in each of these boxcars there were approximately sixty to seventy people, just a bucket for sanitary purposes, no water, hardly any air because they were closed.

"Somehow, for reasons that are difficult to explain," Wollheim continued,

> we felt a certain amount of relief, because after all these weeks of waiting, and these weeks of expectations, knowing that so many trains had left Berlin already before, we thought, "It's a new

chapter," and we were actually looking forward to that chapter with optimism and hoping or believing, envisioning that we would be taken to some kind of labor camp where we could work, but survive, and wait for the end of the war. . . . We had difficulties to find out where we were going, but when we saw we were going toward the east . . . my wife . . . she and others wrote cards, postcards, because we knew it from other things, from transports which had left Berlin before, that people had thrown out these cards and these cards had been mailed. . . . We were in such a rather good mood that we even started to sing. There was a song in the youth movement, it's in Hebrew, "How nice it is when friends sit together and are together in friendship." . . . It was Friday evening after darkness fell, one of the elderly ladies remembered she had taken some candles along and she was lighting the candles and saying the prayers and we found this somehow encouraging, though it's so absolutely irrational now, it's so irrational that here, but nobody knew . . . that ninety-five percent of the people on that train would not live to see the next evening.

Surely among those who did not live to see the morning was Valy's mother. In 1943, that brutal year, women in their fifties were not often selected for work on the notorious selection ramps that divided the living from the soon-to-be-dead at Auschwitz. Surely she was shoved into the line designated for gas upon arrival at the camp. Surely she was chosen for death. But of that I can only guess. There is no further information about her; she received no number at the camp. Her story has no end. She simply disappears.

Nine

A NEW NAME

There are no brass *Stolpersteine* marking the lost in front of 43 Brandenburgische Strasse 43, the last Berlin address I have for Valy. In the files I received from the Brandenburgisches Landeshauptarchiv, I confirm that, for a year or so after the letters end, Valy's life remained in Babelsberg, Potsdam, with her mother, both women cut off by war from the outside world. And then, at some point, at the very end of 1942 or the very beginning of 1943, her time as the *Burgfräulein* comes to a close; like Toni, Valy moves back into Berlin, and out of the old-age home, just before all of its residents are sent to the east and, surely, to their deaths. The hope Valy writes of in late 1941—to hear the Shabbat morning service in the foyer for a long time to come—lasted one year.

I go back again to my box of letters to see if there is any chance I have missed something that can give me a clue as to what my grandfather and Valy were thinking or doing after Valy's letters stop—during that crucial window from December 1941 until the beginning of 1943 for which I have nothing. When I first discovered the box labeled "Correspondence, Patients A–G," I separated out a clump that seemed less immediately important. And there I see it. A letter postmarked July 21, 1942, from the Berkshire County Chapter of the American Red Cross. It is addressed to Dr. Charles (!) J. Wildman. Perhaps that was why I didn't open it originally.

"Dr. Wildman," the letter reads, "We have just received the enclosed message for you from Germany, through the offices of the International Red Cross in Washington, D.C. If you wish to send a reply, the reverse side of the form may be used. Your message must be in English, must be typewritten, and is limited to twenty-five (25) words of purely personal character. The return message must be sent through the American Red Cross. . . . We shall be glad to forward it promptly for you, as one of the Red Cross Services. Very truly yours . . ."

There is nothing else in the envelope. Valy reached out, and my grandfather, it seems, replied. It was mid-1942. He got a poem from her, he responded in kind. But the words themselves are lost. I write to the Red Cross in Geneva, to ITS, to Sweden, and I wait.

Oh, what did they say! I call the archivists at the Holocaust Museum in Washington, D.C. The librarian who answers tells me it is unlikely it contained much news—other than the very fact that she was still alive, still living in Berlin. He suggests it might be on file in Geneva, but it is unlikely. Representatives at the American Red Cross in Washington, as well as at the Pittsfield branch in Massachusetts, similarly turn up nothing for me. I open the envelope a dozen times hoping I have somehow missed something. The only piece of information I have is that they communicated, at least once, in 1942.

It is here where my grandfather's story finally fully splinters away from Valy and Toni's experience. It is unbelievably incongruous—almost unfairly so—to juxtapose what was happening for my grandfather the year that Valy's life shrank from tiny to minuscule. In 1942, his practice has finally begun to thrive. The Vienna friends he hears from now are in Philadelphia, or Brooklyn—or they are trapped in Shanghai—desperate and poor, but relatively safe. He no longer hears from those who remain in Vienna or Berlin.

Letters still surface from strange parts of the world. In June 1942, an old schoolmate, David Teichmann, writes him unhappily from Tatura, Victoria, Australia, where he has been interned in a prisoner-of-war camp for German nationals. "You may be surprised to hear from me from as far away as Australia," Teichmann writes, wearily. "Just a few weeks before I was due to leave for America from England, I was unfortunately interned and sent out here." I read that twice—he was deported, I realize, with horror, from England to Australia. "I am not too bad, but I find life in here pretty monotonous." He asks my grandfather to send him a few medical textbooks, as his own are out-of-date. Konrad Kwiet, the Australian Holocaust historian I met in Bad Arolsen, sends me a paper on these Jewish unfortunates. Some two thousand German Jews were interned in Australia, deemed potential fifth columnists, and stuck, like poor Teichmann, in camps like Tatura.

My grandfather may worry for them all, but his life is in an infinitely better—easier—place at this point. His relationship with Tonya, the girl he first dated in America, has fully ended—though she continues to write to him, to push for his attention. He is considering how to join the war effort. "It is every Jew's duty—this is the only country in which we still have some freedom," Tonya wrote that summer. And he is dating my grandmother, Dorothy Kolman, who herself seems to still be wooing him. Dorothy writes, that same month, "I came to Philadelphia yesterday and spent last evening with a southern friend of mine. . . . There, at long last I met her uncle, a young, brilliant lawyer about 27—whom I've been hearing about for years. . . . Funny thing, the family always considered us a wonderful match and were sure we couldn't resist each other's charms should we but meet. . . . When I met him all I could say to him was 'Oh you're the man I'm sure to marry!' And he said practically the same thing. He is incidentally quite fascinating, and what quick wit!" I tell my father about this letter. He says he knew of it already, that it was part of the oft-told story of their courtship—the big trip she took, the way she told Karl there

*Dorothy Wildman, née Kolman,
my grandmother, around 1941.*

would be other men, and the way he called her back and said he wanted only her, and asked her not to see any of her other suitors anymore. He may be passing messages through the Red Cross to Valy, but he is also moving on.

I have my grandmother's letters to him as she traveled to North Carolina, for a college reunion, and New York. She notes the ramp-up to war, but life is not yet defined by it. "Near Washington we had to stop for an unusually long time so I raised my window shade to investigate. To my great surprise I looked right into a train just crowded with soldiers . . ." She, too, worries, about when and whether Karl, too, will be sent overseas. His army status remains unclear. By October, they have determined their own status: they will marry. She travels to New York to look for wedding clothing and to meet with his family; she investigates for him how to strip the second *n* from Wildmann— to remove that German stain. Their lives are otherwise so very normal: "Our trip down was pleasant enough. There was no traffic and conditions were ideal for speeding but we drove 55 miles per hour as patriotic citizens should." She considers who will be in their wedding party. Cilli, Karl's sister, she writes, has declined to be a bridesmaid, she claims she is too busy running after her children. Dorothy teases Karl in an earlier letter—"Your diagnosis is correct, doctor, I miss either seeing or talking to you and hearing your deeply philosophical observations on life and love or your scintillating analysis about such weighty matters as your right shoe." But mostly she talks of how in love she is, how much she misses him when she is away. The words, at times, mirror Valy's. "I feel like kissing you but since I can't I'll just have to imagine it."

In November 1942, *The Berkshire Eagle* will run a story about Karl and Dorothy's wedding, accompanied by a lovely photo of my grandmother, her lips reddened, her face turned demurely to the side. "The bride wore white satin with a sweetheart neckline, a fitted bodice and a court train." There was a violinist, a vocalist, and an Orthodox rabbi.

The walk from the train to Valy's last address in the city is past a massive sex shop, the sort with cartoonish-looking photos of women of enormous proportions and furry handcuffs in the window. Brandenburgische Strasse 43, Wilmersdorf, is a mixed-use building from around 1910. On the ground floor I see there is a homeopathic medical practice, a lawyer, a taxi school; the upper floors are residential apartments. When a tenant enters the foyer, I slip in after him and begin to take photos. I am obtrusive. A man in his late sixties approaches and asks if I need help. I demur. But then I babble a bit: I tell him I believe the building had once been a *Judenhaus*. He looks perplexed. I feel badly, suddenly, about saying this; he was clearly born after the war, or, at the very least, had been quite young. It is an ambush. "I've been here twenty-seven years," he says. And the building, he tells me, has been standing on the same spot for over a century. He is confident I am mistaken: nothing of import took place here.

A much younger man joins us, with better English. "I'm a journalist," I explain. "A woman I know was deported from here." I pull out Valy's International Tracing Service file that I received in Bad Arolsen and show them. "You see," I say, pointing to the address listed at the top of her form. "She lived here. And was sent away from here." They seem surprised. The older man invites me to dinner, he is curious to know what I have discovered.

I have discovered, I say, that life was increasingly unbearable. Even years before deportation.

Beyond the address, the ITS file showed me something else I had not yet wanted to think about, had still not yet known how to consider. Valy's ITS file is not connected to Toni's at all. At the beginning of January 1943, seven months after she reached out to Karl through the Red Cross, Valy changed her name from Scheftel to Fabisch, after Hans Fabisch, her husband. Like Karl, Valy married.

Unfairly, I found this heartbreaking to know—I simply couldn't fathom what had changed for Valy after her final letter, which is still so filled with love and desperation—*"You know, darling, when I am asking why a cruel destiny has separated me from you."* What brought her to the point of agreeing to marry this other man?

Was she, like Karl, finally moving on? I wondered if this was a sort of final recognition that *this* was her reality, this diminished world, this life seemingly without a present; and to deny herself the only possible sliver of life, the closeness of another person, the normalcy of physical contact, was not only no longer a priority, but no longer even practical. In 1941, she wrote my grandfather that she passed up romantic opportunities for him; by the end of 1942, clearly, she no longer denied herself. Perhaps, I thought, this was a happy turn—this relationship—perhaps it gave her a bit of joy, a piece of something that could not be taken away from her. In the years since Karl fled, after all, her entire relationship with my grandfather had taken place in her mind. A romantic daydream, made more vivid, made more tangible, tactile, present by her increasing desperation, her "endless hibernation," a life lived in black and white while his continued on, far away, in Technicolor.

It was hard to know how to understand the shift because, while I knew and loved my grandmother, about Hans I knew nothing, other than that tantalizingly strange detail of his age: born in 1921, he was twenty-one to Valy's thirty-one, a gendered age gap as unusual then as it is now, if not more so. How they met, I had no clue; when she had decided to finally give up on my grandfather and marry someone else, I could not say. It seemed that, because of him, she left Babelsberg and her mother to live, once again, in Berlin. But all I knew for sure was that their names are linked beginning in late 1942.

Their names are linked not only at ITS. I look again at the two fat files that arrived in the mail for me—one from the Brandenburgisches Landeshauptarchiv and the other from the Entschädigungsamt Berlin, the indemnity agency that holds the reams and reams of paper regarding restitution and compensation cases. In the 1950s, a case was opened on behalf of Valy and Hans.

In Hans's property files I received from the Brandenburgisches Landeshauptarchiv, I see that Valy and Hans, like all Jews facing deportation, were each declared enemies of the state. The couple, then, like Toni, were required to fill out detailed property files so that the Gestapo could thoroughly loot everything that they still owned. Their assets were inventoried, and appraised, as follows:

I. I linen cupboard, coated cloth, Reichsmark (RM) 20

2. I dressing table, coated cloth, RM 20

3. 3 tables, RM 25

4. I shelf, RM IO

5. I red plush couch, 2 armchairs, RM 25

6. I narrow rug (runner), RM 20

7. I narrow rug, RM IO

8. I carpet, RM IO

9. I microscope, RM 25

IO. I ceiling lamp (3 parts), I table lamp, RM 5

About 50 books, garments, clutter [no value given]
   Total value for this page: RM I70
   Affidavit of service, January 27, I943.

Living in one room, they list very little—two chairs, one bookshelf— but I'm struck by three items declared in her handwriting, things she must have dragged from home to home for years: a red velvet couch, fifty books, a microscope. All those books! A microscope! Preserving her intellectual identity, I imagined, was a way of preserving her dignity. She writes to my grandfather of reading *Faust*; in fact, she writes of reading continuously, she quotes poetry, she writes of the time when they read together, when they were studying together—she does not say that these daydreams, that these reading projects were an act of private sabotage, a means of resistance. Yet it was, and they were: the destruction of intellectual freedom, of intellectual stimulation, was as much a piece of the Nazi project of daily deprivations as malnutrition. It was a mind-numbing stripping of stimulation, of humanity. Keeping those books was a way of staving off that starvation of the soul.

The documents continue: "October 1, 1942: notice that all the assets of Valerie Sara Fabisch née Scheffel [*sic*], born in Troppau on November 4, 1911, and of late residing in Berlin-Wilmersdorf, 43 Brandenburgischestr., are to be confiscated on behalf of the German Reich." About her—very new—husband it states that "Hans Israel Fabisch, a metal worker, a Jew," was "earning about RM 32 per week working for Siemens-Schuckert and, since August 1941, living in Berlin-Wilmersdorf at 43 Brandenburgischestr., 4th floor, c/o Striem. He has one furnished room, for which he pays RM per month to his landlady, Gertrud Sara Striem, also Jewish." Rent was paid through January 31, 1943. But an archivist tells me that Gertrude Striem— who was, apparently, a pianist—was deported on January 29, 1943, to Auschwitz.

Hans also has assets of up to 2,500 RM in the Deutsche Bank— access to which he would have long been denied, as those accounts were blocked. As for "Valerie Sara Fabisch née Scheftel, Jew, profession: nurse," her wages are listed at "RM 110 per month," and she is "employed by Reich Association of Jews in Germany at a Jewish home for the elderly in Babelsberg, residing since January 1943 at 43 Brandenburgischestr. in Berlin-Wilmersdorf." She lives in one furnished room, for which she pays RM 40 per month to her landlady, Gertrud Sara Striem, a Jew. On July 15, 1959, a request from the restitution office for the files of Hans Fabisch was filed by the same Ilse Charlotte Mayer who wrote to the International Tracing Service on his and her behalf. Correspondence with Ilse went on for years.

What did Valy and Hans *know*, when they filled out these property forms? What did they expect? Were they preparing to go underground? Did they believe, at this late date, after more than a year of deportations to the east leaving Berlin, that the east could mean anything other than terror?

Inge Deutschkron, the woman who hadn't remembered Valy from the Kindergartenseminar, tells this story, of her own incremental knowledge and her own realization that deportation would be worse than hiding: It was November 1942, and Jews in Berlin were leaving the city on train after train, headed east, though no one knew exactly what they faced when they got there. One day Emma Gumz, a laundress who had done Inge and her mother's clothing for many years, beseeched the women not to go if and when they received a notice to leave for the east. Pressed to explain, Mrs. Gumz broke down—the neighbor's son, Fritz, had come back from Poland. There he had seen terrible things done to Jews. Mrs. Gumz made the Deutschkron women promise to seek help from her and her husband and hide. Eventually they agreed.

"You don't know what she knew. All you know is what those around her knew," Marion Kaplan, the New York University professor and author of *Between Dignity and Despair*, tells me, when I start to relate Deutschkron's anecdote. We had been talking about Valy, and she was steering me back into focus. "You can't know. You're barking up the wrong tree if you say *what did she know and when did she know it*. All you can do is paint a context in which you describe that she is a little fish among big fish—and those big fish probably did know. Did she know? Maybe she might have heard people talk or maybe not. Some knew from illegal radio broadcasts from the BBC. [Also] there are always people who sort of know some information but don't absorb it for what it really means." Kaplan tells a story of a family who all had the same information—two couples—one goes into hiding, the other leaves with the deportation. Both believe they have chosen the safer route, though only the couple in hiding will survive.

As for Valy and Hans, she muses further: "Do I think they would have known by then, by the end of '42?" Meaning, would they have known that deportation might mean death. "Yes. Because they weren't getting letters or cards from the deported. Do I think the people in the *Judenrat* or the Reichsvereinigung knew? Probably? But am I positive? No. She is a little person. A nobody. Would they have told her? Who knows. But remember, the BBC is already reporting this in mid-1942."

Hans and Valy were living together at Brandenburgische Strasse 43, in Wilmersdorf, Berlin, until January 29, 1943. With a bit of sleuthing, an archivist at the Landesarchiv confirms for me that the building was filled with *Judenhäuser*, those apartment-sized ghettos, once single-family or single-person dwellings, now layered with strangers: all Jews. Eventually, fifty-four Jews were deported from number 43 Brandenburgische Strasse alone, and 765 from the entire street. Those living there now have no knowledge of what these buildings saw. The apartments once occupied by doomed Jews were absorbed back into city life, often immediately upon the exit of the condemned inhabitants.

In the middle of Valy and Hans's property files, notes indicate that Nazi officials began to clear their apartment of all the couple's remaining possessions on June 12, 1943. It is all dry and bureaucratic: They reassess and decide Hans has overestimated—it is not 170 RM worth of goods, it is 100 RM. Then they sell it. All of it. Eighty RM for the remaining worldly possessions of Hans Fabisch and Valerie Scheftel. The next page notes there are still 600 RM in Hans's account, left in Deutsche Bank, still to be requested on behalf of the Reich. In the meantime, Brandenburgische Strasse 43 once again became an apartment building like any other, with residents going about their lives, much the same as today. An immediate, purposeful fog of amnesia descended upon the street.

There is nothing further on the newlyweds. On all postwar documents, Valy is simply listed as missing after January 29. Her mother lived on in the city, alone, for another six weeks. On one page of Toni's property files, where she is asked if any family members have "emigrated," she answers affirmatively—Valerie Scheftel—*destination unknown*. After all that time trying to stay together, refusing to emigrate without her, Valy had been sent east without her mother. Had she thrown a postcard to Toni from the train, as some did? Did she try to get her mother word of what was happening? I don't know. I don't know so much. I am frustrated. I have hit another dead end. I wonder—could Valy have survived under an assumed name? Could she—like one survivor I meet—have been on a list to be taken but then slipped away? Could she have changed her appearance and her identity to live underground? Is this too fantastical to consider?

———

Sometime after I begin to parse these archival documents, I finally give birth. We name our daughter for my grandfather—his sunny worldview and cosmopolitan mien were things I was keen for my daughter to inherit. We decided our daughter's middle name would bear weight: we would give her Chaim, his given name. For her first name, "Orli" had made the early lists: "my light" in Hebrew. It fit my grandfather's unique ability to see the light, the opportunity, in every situation. It is the one characteristic everyone who remembers him recalls: his optimism.

Some months after Orli's birth, Herwig comes to visit, from Vienna, along with his girlfriend Camilla. They ask where I am in my search, and I show them Valy and Hans's files from Bad Arolsen, and the additional pieces I received from the German archives.

When I discovered Hans's existence, I tell Herwig and Camilla over dinner, I began to construct a fantasy narrative about their relationship. How did she meet, let alone marry, a man so much younger? How did she, finally, give up on my grandfather? I spun romantic fantasies. *Maybe he was a concert pianist.* Maybe they met at a bar, though those were banned, so perhaps not. Maybe they fell in love over music; maybe he swept her off her feet. She had so loved music, I think, just like everyone she studied with in Vienna.

But in speaking of them, I realize I needed to return once again to these thick files. I take them back out of their manila envelopes. In fact, I see immediately, the files easily explode the idea that it was music that brought them together. In Hans's file, I find a clue, a curriculum vitae, filled out by Hans in his own hand.

I was born on April 29, 1921, in Breslau, the son of businessman Rudolf Fabisch. After completing the seventh year of secondary school [*Obersekunda*], I spent April–October 1937 at the Gross-Breesen agricultural training school for emigrants [for Jewish youths wanting to immigrate to Palestine], in Silesia, where I was trained in market gardening and farming. I left Gross-Breesen to attend Dr. Hodurek's state-approved professional school for chemists in Breslau, which I had to leave, however, after two full semesters because of my Jewish origin. To complete my education, I attended the Rom School of Chemistry, a Jewish school, in Berlin from January through April 1939. Then I was offered the opportunity to work in the Israelitisches Krankenheim [the Jewish medical facility] in Berlin, as a trainee in the laboratory, and also spent two months working in the facility's kitchens. Since August 24, 1939, I have been working in the lab of the Jüdisches Krankenhaus in Berlin, on Iranische Strasse.

His note is accompanied by a letter from the head of the lab at the Israelitisches Krankenheim, describing Hans's responsibilities there—it is a recommendation form, really—and a letter from Dr. Fritz Israel Weinmann at the private Chemieschule Hermann Rom, telling what Hans Bernhard Jakob Israel Fabisch studied at the school. Valy and Hans may have met at the hospital.

I've been frustrated, I tell Herwig, as the trail runs cold. But as we look at the pages together, I sheepishly admit I have overlooked something else: I have not searched for the woman who beseeched the International Tracing Service for the whereabouts of Valy and Hans. Hans's sister, Ilse Charlotte Fabisch Mayer—the key to Hans, and maybe to Valy—began to look for them some twenty-five years before my birth. In part I did not look for her because I did not know where to begin. There is no listing for her in British phone books; she has, unsurprisingly, no online presence. The address she gives in London is no longer connected to her name. But I realize, as I look at the files with Herwig, in her restitution claims for her brother, she provided more information about herself than she gave to ITS in Bad Arolsen. On one page I see she listed the dates her three children were born. It's small, but it's incredibly useful. Even if she is no longer living, they likely are.

Ten

LONDON INTERLUDE

*I'm looking for descendants of Ilse Charlotte Mayer, née
Fabisch, born in Breslau September 12, 1915. Immigrated
to London. In the 1960s she lived at 181 Goldhurst Terrace,
London NW6. She had three children, one born in 1939,
one born in 1944, and one born in 1946. Frau Mayer had
a brother murdered in Auschwitz, Hans Fabisch, and in
the 1960s she searched for him and his wife, Valerie Fabisch
(born Scheftel). Any news about any member of this family
would be most welcome! Thank you!*

I find no record of Ilse, in all the ways we normally search these days,
so I do something terribly old-fashioned: I take out an ad in a British publication, the *Journal of the Association of Jewish Refugees*. The
immediate goal of the Association of Jewish Refugees, founded by and
for the German and Austrian Jews who took refuge in Britain, was to
reestablish these traumatized lives and collect—as well as reconnect—
lost family and friends; its journal is still published. More important:
there is still a section of the AJR, just as there was after the war, devoted to searches for lost loved ones.

In the immediate postwar period, a number of journals were
established by and for Jewish refugees. Lists upon lists of survivors

were published, announcements that family or friends had survived. Searches placed in the *Aufbau* (Reconstruction), the journal published in the United States, were legendary. They were classified ads, basically, but instead of looking for a car or a spouse, the ads were searching for family, for children, for friends. For years they ran, in the pre-pre-Internet era, at a time when we were, globally, remarkably unconnected, when it was possible that siblings could live across the country, or a city, from each other and never know it, and certainly could live on separate continents and never be sure the other had survived. Given the devastating impact of the Holocaust on just my grandfather's friends, such advertisements made a great deal of sense. How would one know, for example, a cousin had arrived in Lyon, or survived in hiding in Budapest? How would one know, if you'd survived the war in Shanghai, as did a number of my grandfather's friends, if your sister had made it to New York? What would her address be? The *Aufbau*— which began publishing in 1934—provided some of the first indications of deportations; it also listed the dead, in increasing numbers, as the war ended. Some of those advertisements were themselves half informed, listing family members with "location unknown" who would later turn out to be among the murdered. The circulation in the mid-1940s reached as high as a hundred thousand. My father remembers it coming to his childhood home—the *Aufbau* and *The New England Journal of Medicine* were essential reading.

In 1959, *Time* magazine ran a feature on the *Aufbau*, saying it had been "the voice of help and hope for thousands of Jewish refugees" and one of the "most influential foreign language papers in the United States." At the time, its circulation had dropped to a still-respectable thirty thousand–plus subscribers. The *Aufbau* had scooped other major papers on the announced decision of the West German government to pay out monies to victims of the Holocaust. The weekly newspaper (which went biweekly and eventually turned into a monthly magazine) remained influential for many years. In 1997, the United

States Holocaust Memorial Museum used the *Aufbau* as researchers set about trying to track down the fate of the nearly one thousand passengers of the *St. Louis*, the doomed ship filled with refugees (mostly German Jewish citizens) that set sail for Havana from Hamburg on May 13, 1939. A small group of passengers were allowed to disembark in Havana, but Cuba refused entry to the rest, and the United States (despite pleas from those on board, despite the begging of the Joint Distribution Committee) also refused to issue visas to allow the hapless Jews on board to disembark in Miami. The boat was sent back to Europe, and the passengers went on to be distributed among the United Kingdom, Belgium, the Netherlands, and France; some 254 of the original group would die in the Holocaust. The rejection of these refugees came, especially after the war, to symbolize the miserable plight of the Jewish unwanted.

The *Journal of the Association of Jewish Refugees* is a bit like a smaller, more focused *Aufbau*. Ten thousand children arrived in the UK on the Kindertransport before the outbreak of war, in a relaxing of quota restrictions that allowed some under age sixteen to flee to safety; about sixty percent of these children never saw their parents again. Around seventy thousand adult refugees came to the UK as well, before the war; more came after. Each needed services; each needed help integrating into their new life. In the aftermath of the war, the AJR took on different roles, everything from connecting families to long-lost siblings or spouses or parents, to helping victims file claims against the German state. The journal of the AJR served in that capacity as well.

AJR still publishes, though, of course, it is now online as well as a glossy newsletter. Members now publish their recollections of major events—Kristallnacht, for example—as well as place obituaries, honor anniversaries, and offer services to help with the aging, and the indigent; the population is growing very old; it is disappearing. Holocaust survivors are entitled to money for elder care from the Conference on

Jewish Material Claims Against Germany, which gives such funds to survivors. Though there remains, in the AJR, a small section devoted to searching for information about survivors or victims, not surprisingly, such searchers have taken a distant third (or fourth or fifth) place to the other activities of the magazine.

To that end, though I thought it probably a futile exercise, it was here I decided to place my ad.

———

Two months later, I flew to London for a two-day conference on Islam in the West. It is my first time away from Orli, and my breasts are still heavy with milk. I carry a pump, feel guilty, and yet am relieved to be gone. I don't exactly know who I am anymore. Immersed as I am in my own work and stress, I give no thought at all to Ilse, or her descendants.

On my third night, the conference finished, I meet Jean-Marc Dreyfus, whose work had led me to Bad Arolsen in the first place. He now teaches Holocaust studies at the University of Manchester. We arrange to go to the blockbuster Gauguin exhibit at the Tate Modern because Jean-Marc is, among many other things, an excellent museumgoer. He mostly wanders off alone, but pops up every now and again to give an insight I wouldn't have gleaned otherwise. ("Gauguin went to Bretagne when it was still seen as wild and primitive," he says at one point, as we looked at work from the 1880s. He points out the costumes, the landscape, and the hints of Post-Impressionism in the blue trees on the horizon.) When we take a break for tea, Jean-Marc berates me. He tells me that I should start writing already, that I am failing Valy once again. Valy's story, he says, his voice rising, cannot remain a collection of letters on my desk, in a box. It will do her no good. *But I still don't know what happened,* I protest. He sighs. He is not sure what it is I hope to find. "You have so much!" he insists. And then he takes a step back. "You aren't my student," he says. "I'm sorry." But no, I say, miserably. You're right. I'm failing her.

Between the museum and dinner, we stop at my hotel and I check my e-mail.

And there it is:

Dear Ms Wildman,

I have just looked through the AJR Journal and am feeling very unsettled & tearful!

I am Ilse Mayer's youngest daughter Carol, born in 1946. I am understandably extremely curious and excited to find out what information you have or what I can help you with.

Sadly my mother died 4 years ago after several years decline. My father Paul Yogi Mayer has survived her. I cannot wait to hear back from you. Please get in touch.

My daughter has googled you on slate.com and discovered your interest is about Valy, Ilse's brother Hans's wife. I look forward to the opportunity to exchange information and learn a little more about what happened.

Looking forward to your reply is a massive understatement!

Carol Levene (née Mayer)

I come back downstairs, overwhelmed. "You must e-mail her immediately," Jean-Marc says. "Maybe she lives in London?" So I reply to Carol—*I'm in London!* I tell her, and then explain I have a four p.m. flight the next day. Is there any chance you live here, I ask, and would be willing to meet? A few hours later, she calls. "Sarah, you can't imagine how emotional I am," she says. "I'll come find you wherever you are."

And so, the next morning, I am in the lobby of the Chesterfield Mayfair Hotel, greeting Carol Levene, née Mayer, the youngest child of Ilse Charlotte Mayer and Hans's niece. We embrace, and then marvel at the surreality of the moment, the sheer wonder of our meeting. She is simultaneously an apparition and an intimate. We leave the hotel and walk around the corner to Shepherd Market for a coffee. She talks the whole way, filling me in, at first, on her mother's story.

Ilse and Paul, Carol's parents, emigrated from Germany in April 1939 with Carol's brother, then only a few months old. A sister, and then Carol, were born in London. After the war, Ilse searched endlessly for Hans and for her father and mother, Rudolf and Doris, after letters stopped coming. She never forgave herself for leaving without her younger brother, or her parents.

"She could never talk about Germany or her family; she couldn't discuss it with us," Carol says, wiping tears. "It was too hard for her. In fact, we never knew enough about what happened and my father felt we shouldn't explore more if she doesn't want us to. But since she's died, I want to, I feel I have a responsibility to."

Carol is a petite woman with rosy round cheeks and straight bobbed chestnut-colored hair; she is wearing a soft oatmeal-colored V-neck sweater with black palazzo pants. She is unadorned, but well put together. Other than her melodious accent, she could be any one of my parents' friends, Jews of the baby boomer generation.

Carol tells me her mother could never hear about the war or its aftermath: if a program came on television, if ever the word "Nazi" was uttered, she simply shut down. No one asked her questions. Carol's father, Paul, encouraged the silence, feeling his wife couldn't handle the tension. "She couldn't stomach the search for restitution," Carol says, though I knew she had, in fact, pursued the case. Despite her endless sadness, and pain, "she was an unfailingly polite woman," says Carol, explaining that even in her final days of dementia, as the nurses in her home for the aged came to bathe her, Ilse would say, "Thank you very much, you're so kind. Thank you so much." Ilse had gone to a Jewish women's college in Berlin, Carol tells me; she was older than Hans, by some years. I wonder immediately if she might have known Valy herself.

Promising to introduce me to her father, now ninety-eight, on my next visit to London, Carol announces she has two things to show me. At this, wizardlike, she produces a black cloth bag.

Out first comes a page printed from a Berlin city website: two small brass cobblestones bearing the names of Hans and Valy embedded into a block of sidewalk. *Stolpersteine.* The address listed on the top of the page is Brandenburgische Strasse 43. Surprising myself, I begin to cry; the stones hadn't existed when I last visited the building; indeed, the page indicated they had been put in six weeks before my London visit. I wonder aloud who might have placed them. Carol seems shocked as well—it was not she, she assures me. She assumed, she says, that it was me.

And then, out of Carol's bag comes a letter. It is dated 1999 and it is written, in English, by a man named Ernest Fontheim.

Carol hands me the letter, and I begin to read:

Dear Mrs. Mayer,

I recently received your address from Mr. Walter Laqueur who told me that you are the sister of Hans Fabisch. As Walter probably told you, Hans and I were very good friends in a crucial period of our lives. I thought that you may be interested in my recollections of your brother and the general circumstances of his life at a time when there was no longer any postal connection between the two of you. To begin with, Hans was my best friend during the 21 months when we knew each other; in fact he was my last best (male) friend. I never had such a close (male) friend again.

It is seven typed pages, and, unbelievably, it appears, at first glance, to be a guide to Valy and Hans's attempt to go into hiding in Berlin, and their final days before deportation. It is my key to understanding everything that happened after my letters end. Ernest knew them both well. It is a detailing of Hans's life in Berlin, his work, his hopes, his adventurousness—and his relationship to Valy.

"You must take some time with this," Carol says, urging me to wait until she is gone to read. Then she adds that I might want to return: she has hundreds of letters at home, from Hans, maybe from Valy, from her grandparents, from others connected to them.

"He was my Uncle Hans's best friend, and he writes about wearing the star and trying to go into hiding," Carol says of Ernest Fontheim. They met on the first day they were both conscripted for forced labor at Siemens on April 29, 1941. Fontheim describes their days—their predawn first S-Bahn train to the factory, to the people who worked alongside them, to the total deprivation of cultural life for Jews—just as Valy wrote in her letters.

"I would like to tell you so much about me, but when I start thinking I find that, most of the time, my life is so poor as far as inner content is concerned, and thereby I mean positive experiences, that it hardly makes sense to talk a lot about it," Valy wrote in October 1941. *"It was and continues to be some kind of stupor, a type of hibernating condition, an eternal waiting for you. Somebody once said that the best and most tolerable way of dealing with a long wait is to fill the time with lots of activities. And that's pretty much what I've been doing. My outer life absolutely is characterized by keeping busy and, maybe, even working."*

Skimming quickly, I realize: Finally I have a means of understanding how Valy, ten years Hans's senior, had met and married, and when. Suddenly the shadow character of Hans, the also-ran, the man who was not my grandfather, takes shape, begins to turn into a real person, an incredible character, as drawn by his friend, dashing, mischievous, studying surreptitiously to become a doctor—he was waited for, vainly, desperately, by his older sister, who had made it to the United Kingdom. Hans, I read, had prepared papers for himself and Valy to go underground. I look at Carol. Here is this other person I hadn't known existed, who cared. Here is this whole *group* of people, rather. Carol, her father, her siblings. Suddenly there is a whole additional family for whom this story mattered.

I put the letter down for a moment. It is too long, and answered so much, and raised so many questions, I couldn't process it without taking great time.

Carol begins to talk. In the early 1990s, she interviewed her mother, along with her mother's circle of German Jewish refugees. It was a tight-knit group; the women had become family to one another during and after the war; most, if not all, had suffered tremendous loss. "All of them had come out of Germany and had met here, and became the replaced families throughout their lives. It was all through women. The men didn't have intimate relationships. I have a tape of her and her friends talking about what it was like to come to England. They talk about their kids and personal stuff." After Carol's interview, her mother announced it was time for her to return to Breslau. Carol was shocked to hear her say it.

"She had always said, 'I'm never going back to Germany,'" she explains. "I was really worried. I thought she'd be destroyed. But she came back and she was so happy! She said, 'All these years I've hung on to the pain and ghastly memories and couldn't talk about it. But I've gone back and found the happy childhood that I had. And my school and all the good things that there were as well in my younger life. It was fantastic.' She said she couldn't have done it if we hadn't had that conversation." The trip allowed her to reclaim some of the joy of a German childhood that had been comfortable, wealthy, assimilated, and, above all, joyful.

Carol has two girls, Charlotte and Jessica, in their middle and late thirties, respectively, and a toddler grandson named Leo; his photo filled up her mobile phone. Charlotte and Jess were raised only nominally Jewish. It was Jess who looked me up on the Internet, read my stories online, and told her mother, I imagine, that I was legitimate.

Paul, Carol's father, is still alive. A gifted athlete, he would have competed in the 1936 Olympics, in the decathlon, Carol tells me, had the anti-Jewish policies not been in place. The family story is that there was an "alternate" team of Jewish athletes, ready to go in the event the International Olympics Committee insisted Jews be included. No such team was called upon, but Paul remained active in athletics his entire life.

After arriving in England, Mayer enlisted in the British army, joined the SOE—Special Operations Executive—and parachuted behind enemy lines in France and Germany. After the war, he founded the Primrose Club, a youth and recreation center that helped survivor children and teens reclaim normal lives after their distinctly abnormal childhoods. In an effort to return joy and normalcy to the (mostly) boys who had survived the camps and emerged to find themselves virtually alone—their entire families, in so many cases, murdered—he introduced them to other Jewish British teens and involved them in dances and sports. Mayer was profiled in Martin Gilbert's book *The Boys*, about the unlikely convoy of survivor children—mostly teenagers, mostly boys—liberated from camps and taken to the United Kingdom in the summer of 1945. He was, all in all, generally acknowledged for having addressed the trauma of those returning from camps in ways far ahead of his time; the idea of integrating these kids in groups with those who had lived the war years relatively normally, in England, was itself revolutionary, and fantastically successful. In the 1990s, he was awarded an honorary doctorate from Potsdam University. Until recently, he lectured extensively on his life.

Carol says he has a trove of papers from Hans and the family—letters, photos, artifacts. "The next time you come," she insists, "you'll start to go through them all with me. You must come meet my father. And it has to be soon. He's ninety-eight."

"Now! Now you must write this book," pushes Jean-Marc, who, by that point, has joined us.

As I get up to pay for our coffees, I realize I am witnessing an unspooling, an interconnectedness I haven't remotely anticipated. The story is no longer just about Valy. It is a microcosm of the strange ways in which we remain connected to our history, the peculiarity in which the tragedy of the individual, amidst the greater horror, somehow allows Carol, me, our families to understand the war better, to incorporate it into not just our sense of self, but also how we internalize it, make it our own, how we relate to the past, all of us, and how we hold it, selectively, simultaneously close and at a distance.

Carol, too, has given me a tremendous gift: the opportunity to understand the rest of Valy's story. Back in America, I read and reread the rest of Ernest Fontheim's letter. But before I do, I look him up. Still alive, Fontheim lives in Ann Arbor, Michigan, where he is a professor and research scientist emeritus of physics at the university. I call the number in the phone book. His wife answers. "I'm calling about Hans Fabisch," I blurt out, realizing I have not prepared what to say. "I'll get Ernest," she says.

Eleven

THE ONLY
POSSIBILITY

Sometime in the lonely summer of 1942, Valy—bereft of even the rare letters my grandfather had provided, bereft of credible options to *get out*—sometime in those miserable months when it seemed the rest of the world had forgotten her and her mother, sometime in that period when it seemed nothing could ever shake the torpor that had settled over them, the endless waiting, the dreary sameness of their days, caring for the elderly and worrying they would lose even the small semblance of normalcy their lives still retained, by being sent, like their neighbors, *east*, whatever that meant, sometime in those months, Valy met Hans Fabisch. And as bleak as her world was, as miserable as she felt, and as hungry—and oh, they were so very hungry, food was all they thought about—suddenly there was something to wake up for again. He made her feel young, for the first time, really, since Vienna.

Hans was raffish, still a bit pudgy about the cheeks, despite malnourishment, despite entering his twenties. He had a stick of hair that stuck up in front, and a streak of noncompliance with authority, with the rules of the day, that felt, to all who met him, like opportunity. He had studied chemistry for as long as he was allowed to go to school and then he found work at the Jewish Hospital, as Valy had, but by the summer of 1942, he was a regular forced laborer, working ten-hour days on his feet in armaments at Siemens. Hans told Valy, with great confidence, his dream was to go back to school—it wasn't an idle thought. He was only twenty-one. Their ten-year age difference meant Hans had been deprived the trajectory of a normal education: having grown up under the Reich since the age of twelve, he had been able to finish high school but not to go on to university. He would, he told her, become a doctor. He firmly believed the war would end, and he would find his way into a classroom—somewhere, he hoped, other than Germany. He was so certain of this, so refreshingly optimistic about his chances of survival, he was determined to keep up with his peers in his studies. To that end, he had started to train himself, he'd collected books; he studied on his own. Valy—as she had with my grandfather so many years before—offered to tutor him, to serve as a teacher, a sounding board, to quietly resist the system by refusing to let him be undereducated. In turn, Hans introduced her to his world of Jews who were fighting to remain sane—to remain human.

It was a welcome moment of forward thinking. Working at the Jewish Hospital, and then working in her mother's old-age home, Valy had filled her days first by caring for the miserably malnourished children; speaking with the anxious parents who themselves seemed to wither away week to week, their clothes battered and patched, their spirits waning; and then trying to prop up the elderly who lived under her mother's care, to keep them going physically and mentally.

Valy sewed a star onto each of her uniforms. She hoped her shoes would not wear out; if they did, she had no recourse. The fear of being sent on the next transport dominated every conversation, every waking moment. "What could we possibly talk about?" wondered Gerda Haas, a nurse at the Jewish Hospital. "We couldn't go to a movie. We didn't [have] concerts, or any of the culture that normal people grow up with. We couldn't go shopping. We didn't have any new clothes to show off. What are we going to talk about? Transports and going

underground, and we had no
family left. We couldn't talk
about family anymore, so we
talked about that all the time. It
was like ruminating—the same
thing all the time. It was a very
unnatural life actually."

Ernest wrote:

Hans Fabisch.

> *In normal times, both of
> us would have studied at the
> university. Hans's goal was to
> become a physician, and I
> wanted to study either
> chemistry or physics. The path
> was now blocked for us. Hans
> and I were very conscious of the fact that the combination of long
> hours at hard work in the factory and total lack of any cultural or
> intellectual stimulation would lead to a complete proletarisation in a
> cultural and intellectual sense. Economically we were already
> proletarians anyway. . . . We consciously decided to fight this
> trend. . . . We got together with a circle of Jewish young people, all of
> them forced laborers in the German war machine, all of them well
> educated and intellectually curious and frustrated over not being able
> to have any intellectual stimulation. This group of young people was
> not a formal organization, which would not have been possible
> anyway because it would have run afoul of Gestapo regulations for
> Jews. Most of us had some connections to Jews of the older generation
> who had been kicked out of their professions and were frequently
> eager to give informal talks to young people. We met periodically in
> each other's apartments to listen to such lectures. . . .
>
> Hans prepared himself very seriously for his medical career. . . .
> He had several medical books for this purpose. He did some of these*

studies with the support of Dr. Valy Scheftel, a Jewish physician from
Vienna who then lived in Berlin and, of course, as a Jew could not
practice medicine. . . . Hans and Valy fell in love and got married on
January 5, 1943. Valy was several years older than Hans. She was
a lovely and very warm person, and she and I also became good
friends.

———

As soon as I return to America, I arrange to fly out to Ann Arbor to meet Ernest Fontheim—he seems excited to meet me, tells me to stay at Weber's Inn for its indoor pool and fine hospitality. We debate dates, and shyly discuss the wonder of discovering each other. He cannot see me the night I arrive, then he suggests I stay only one night; our interview will last less than a day. Despite those restrictions, I am thrilled. In the back of my mind, I have Jean-Marc's warning about not relying on ninety-year-olds, or, at least, not expecting much from ninety-year-olds, but I am too excited to know someone who knew Hans and Valy, intimately; someone who can provide answers—even to the simplest things, like where and how they lived. How they fell in love! What their love was like—and what they experienced each day, how they experienced each day, from the most minute, to the broadest expression of their time.

"As you know," Ernest wrote Ilse Mayer, "[Hans] was alone in Berlin [i.e., without his parents] and shared a furnished room with another young Jewish man of roughly the same age, Karl-Hermann Salomon, in a fifth-floor walk-up apartment in the *Hinterhaus* of Brandenburgische Strasse 43, Berlin-Wilmersdorf."

This meant the "backhouse"—these old Berlin buildings had a "front" and a "back," with a courtyard in between, or even two courtyards and more buildings, all connected to the same address. When I first visited, I hadn't known which part of the building they lived in. I had just wandered through, looking up, looking around.

They sublet the room from a Jewish widow, a certain Mrs.
Striem. I vaguely remember that Hans told me that before being
drafted to work for Siemens he went to the Chemieschule. That was a
school run by the Jewish community of Berlin where students could
learn the elementary aspects of chemistry to enhance their employment
opportunities abroad in case they could still emigrate. For many of the
students, the Chemieschule also served as a substitute university.
Hans and Karl-Hermann were not close personally, and in fact Hans
felt that KH often rubbed him the wrong way. I myself lived at
home, a few blocks away at Eisenzahnstrasse 64 where my family
(my parents, my younger sister, and I) sublet two rooms in a larger
apartment belonging to an aunt and uncle of my mother. In addition
to my family and my mother's aunt and uncle, the latter's son and
two unrelated widows [all together nine people] lived in the
apartment which originally only served my mother's aunt and uncle.
In those days all Jews in Berlin were squeezed together in so-called
Jew-houses. That was one of the great ideas of the
Generalbauinspektor für die Reichshaupstadt, Albert Speer. I had
somewhat strained relations with my parents and Hans was all alone
in Berlin. So we became each other's confidants and did many things
together in our limited free time.

At first I think, when Ernest arrives in the crisp, freezing morning to get me, crunching across the snow in practical boots and a massive jacket, Jean-Marc is wrong. Ernest is brilliant. He is rounding
past ninety, and he is stooped, held up as much by his suspenders as
his ever-sagging spine, his face craggy, his voice, within an hour of
talking, loses energy, tone, and level. He still drives, a faux-fur-lined
hunter's cap pulled down tightly over his ears, and he banters without
pause as we head from the inn into a cluster of professors' homes in the
Michigan suburbs. He is shyly pleased I have made so much effort to
meet him, makes a huge fuss over the cookies I brought to give him
and his wife. But then I am disappointed beyond reason: he is happy

The Jewish Hospital's notes on Hans, 1939. "We wish him only the best for his future."

to welcome me into his home, but also adamantly determined that he will write his own memoirs. He is guarded with me and my three recording devices, my videos; he is afraid that I will publish his story before he can. That I will take it from him; render it mine and not his. He will not, he says patiently, but intractably, reveal anything further than what I have already read in my letter—or rather, his letter to Ilse, that Carol gave me in London. He will not give me anything further, nothing beyond the story of Hans, he will offer nothing about his own miraculous saving. He has given a testimony to the Holocaust Museum, he says, and as he sees me write that down, he adds that the contents of that interview are sealed until the event of his death or the publication of his memoirs. At the end of our first two and a half hours of speaking, he says, essentially, *anything that is not about Hans is off-limits to you. I don't want my life in print before I write it myself.* I reassure him I won't take his story. I understand his determination; in fact, I admire it. It is, in a way, a version of what the former Kindergartenseminar student Inge Deutschkron said to me in Berlin—we American Jews, so anxious to scoop up these stories, to take them for ourselves, we help ourselves to them, as though they are our birthright. We try to take more than our fair share, really. And here is Ernest Fontheim, who lost his whole family—who am I to take his story, too? Who am I to steal the narrative, the one thing he retained?

And yet I am also, selfishly, terribly frustrated. I offer to write a separate book—a separate something—*I could be your interlocutor,* I say, thinking this might be a solution. *I can write your story—you can dictate it.* He smiles and says, "That's generous," but he declines.

But, as Ernest said on the phone, he is willing to talk a bit about Hans. The two men met on the first day they were conscripted for forced labor at the *Elektromotorwerk*—the electronic motor division—of Siemens on April 29, 1941, Hans's twentieth birthday. Explains Ernest, "He was almost exactly a year and a half older than I. We hit it off from the very first day. We had similar backgrounds, similar education, a similar sense of humor, and looked at life and our situation in much the same way. In many ways he was an inspiration for me." Both had been pulled from school far too young. The two young men were from an intellectual tradition, and now they were dying intellectually, banned from all cultural events and academic pursuits. It was daily agony; so together they gathered a group of young Jews, all forced laborers, all with connections to Jews banned from their professions. They set up an underground salon, in essence: after the factory shift, the older Jews gave lectures to the younger ones: an architect; a former epidemiologist, who had run the city of Berlin's epidemic response team from the city hall before 1933. For a moment, the disorienting, impoverishing, impact of all these accomplished Jews suddenly finding themselves without a perch, without their status, without their jobs, their livelihoods, was temporarily suspended. It was a respite from the desperation, and exhaustion. Someone had managed to scrounge an old phonograph, and others had saved recordings from symphonies. They played them, very, very quietly so as not to alert their neighbors, and they closed their eyes, pretending they were back in the concert halls of their youth.

Ernest and Hans began work each morning at six a.m., a shift that lasted until four p.m., with two thirty-minute breaks. To make the six a.m. clock-in, which meant a 5:45 arrival at the factory gates, Hans and Ernest would take the first S-Bahn train of the morning, which left their area of Berlin at 5:15. The streets would be as black as the inside of a closet, an unnatural urban inky hue, with streetlights darkened and apartment buildings shuttered, all prevented from emitting light so as not to attract bombers. Ernest and Hans would meet at the corner of Kurfürstendamm at a precise moment and whistle to each other. They were exhausted, constantly, and the companionship was as much motivational as it was practical. At Siemens, they were hustled into packs of Jewish workers, separated from their Aryan counterparts. Jews were not allowed to be sprinkled among the other workers, lest they perform sabotage, undermine the effort. All movement was strictly patroled. Jewish workers ate lunch standing, at their workspace—Aryans could use a cafeteria—and bathroom breaks for Jews were at nine a.m. and one p.m., in a group, led by a foreman. Visiting the toilet alone was not an option.

Hans and Ernest riveted commutators, the rotary electrical switches for motors. It was long and boring work, always on their feet. Ernest remembers forty or fifty Jewish forced laborers, men and women, old and young; the youngest were two fourteen-year-old boys. None of these laborers had ever worked in a factory before. All were hoping for a swift Allied victory. I expressed surprise he knew so many young people left in the city. But of course, he said, there were kids who were too old for the Kindertransport, or whose families had not been able to get their children on a transport (there was a strict, limited number of spaces) or had simply not opted for it, as they couldn't imagine separating themselves from their children; there were those whose entire families had tried to emigrate, but were unsuccessful, especially those who tried to leave after Kristallnacht, when the consulates were mobbed and the chances were dim. Among them was Margot, the woman who would, after the war, become Ernest's wife, and before that, the woman with whom he would go into hiding. But though he filled me in on some of the details, under Ernest's strict instructions, that story can't be told here.

As harsh as the working conditions were, the hunger was nearly as bad. From the beginning of the war, on the first of September 1939, Germany introduced rationing for all food, says Ernest, stirring a cup of tea. "Dairy. Wheat. Vegetables. Fruits were subject to rationing, and ration coupons were passed out, including to Jews. There were three levels of ration coupons. One was a general consumer—*Normalverbraucher.* Then a higher category, somewhat bigger rations for workers—*Arbeiter*—and then the highest category was heavy workers, people like miners—*Schwerarbeiter.* The work we did at Siemens would have qualified us for workers' cards, one level up from general consumer. But we didn't get that. We got 'normal consumer,' and then after some time, cards were cut below that of the general consumer. The meat and meat product ration card was totally eliminated so you couldn't buy any meat anymore, and meat also included poultry, of course. And meat products like sausages and so on. Oh, and also in addition to food, also tobacco was rationed."

So were clothing cards. They both wore the same clothes they had worn for the last two years. They could not replace them. But Ernest insists they felt only anger and indignation, not fear. They wanted to thwart the system, to thumb their noses at their overseers; they did not think of danger, they thought of escape.

To Carol's mother, Ernest wrote:

Starting on September 19, 1941, every Jew had to wear a yellow Star of David when appearing in public. That measure not only made us Jews targets of all kinds of harassment, but also enabled the government to issue a list of additional restrictions on our freedoms, which now became easy to enforce. Jews were permitted shopping only one hour per day, from 4 to 5 p.m., Monday through Friday, and no shopping at all on Saturday. Under wartime conditions, practically

all shopping consisted of food buying. In the era before supermarkets,
one had to go to the butcher, the baker, the dairy, and the greengrocer,
and in each of these stores there was always a line. If a Jew had stood
in line for, say, fifteen minutes, and it was 5 o'clock, he had to leave
the store without having bought anything. Any German had the right
to get in line in front of a Jew. Even if a merchant would have
wanted to serve the Jew after 5 o'clock, he did not dare for fear that
one of the other customers might denounce him. Most working Jews
returned from their jobs only after 4, some not until shortly before 5
(like Hans and I for example). For these people buying the meager
rations became in itself a nightmare.

Both Hans and Ernest were forced to matriculate at Jewish schools
after 1938 and that communal experience—combined with some natural teenage rebellion—meant they both felt much more Jewish than
their extremely secular, extremely assimilated parents. By the fall of
1941, they were almost defiantly eager to put on the star. That said,
everything got harder once the star came on. The curfew imposed on
Jews—eight p.m. in winter, nine p.m. in summer—was rigorously en-
forced by Gestapo spot checks, and it did not mean simply to be inside—it meant to be ensconced in the home at which you were
registered. "A classmate of mine came home ten or fifteen minutes
after curfew," says Ernest, explaining how they knew not to test these
hours. Gestapo officers were at this tardy friend's house when he arrived home. "They took him right away. For a half a year he was in
what they euphemistically called a 'work-education' camp, like a concentration camp. The inmates were brutally treated, they did hard
work, with little food." Ernest's friend was "a big sportsman, he had a
tall muscular figure, and [when] he came out from that year, he was a
terrible sight. He was emaciated and looked practically different from
how he looked before. So we knew, with that curfew, we had to reli-
giously observe the restriction in order not to have such a fate." When
Hans and his friends met for their intellectual retreats—or just to be,

vaguely, social—it would be for an hour, or two; always they would arrange to break up their meetings in time for all to get home.

The same anxiety held true for the restrictions on using public transport—it was only acceptable for those, like Hans and Ernest, traveling more than seven kilometers. But that permission had to be carried on their person at all times. And if the train or tram were used for any purpose other than an authorized work commute, and that person was discovered, he or she could be immediately listed to be sent away into the ether that seemed to mark the deportations. Special yellow cards were issued for those who worked for the Reichsvereinigung.

Hans and Ernest kept thinking of ways around the restrictions. He wrote to Ilse:

> *One month after the introduction of the star, the deportations to the east started. Initially all Jews who worked in defense plants were exempted from deportation. So we were protected. However any Jew who was discovered without a star was subject to deportation, regardless of a defense job. . . . Hans and I went to the movie theaters even though that was strictly forbidden for Jews and was therefore connected with a certain risk. Before the introduction of the yellow star, this risk was not very great provided we went to movie theaters in areas far away from our neighborhood. . . . With the introduction of the star, the situation changed drastically. Obviously it was suicidal to be seen without a star in one's house, or street or even neighborhood, and we surely could not go to the movies with the yellow star. So Hans came up with a solution to this dilemma. He bought some little metal hooks and eyes [the kind used on blouses that close at the back], filed the hooks to a sharp point, sewed a hook on each of the six corners on the back of the Star of David, and then hooked the star on his outer coat or jacket. In this way the star became easily removable. He also made a set for me. So we could leave our building and neighborhood as good Jews and, after some safe distance,*

*duck into a building entrance, remove the star, and emerge
transformed as pure "Aryans" ready to go to the movies. On the way
home we reversed this procedure.*

The truth, Ernest explains later, in one of the long phone calls we
start having after my visit (all of them beginning or ending with me
reassuring him that such conversations aren't to disrupt the integrity
of his story, but to understand what it meant to be in Berlin at that
time), was this: "Before the star, movies were also—and parks—
everything was prohibited. But since there was no way really to recognize a Jew officially, at least other than by looks, maybe it was much
easier to circumvent these prohibitions—we even went to the state
opera house on Unter den Linden [the main drag of the eastern part of
the city]! In 1940—that I remember—it was a one-week sort of guest
performance of the Rome opera at the Berlin state opera and strangely
I forgot which opera I saw there. It may have been *Rigoletto. . . .*"

After the star was introduced, Hans's star-removal system was
only used for the movies, and only when the two could get as far from
their apartments as possible. They had "a sort of sense of pride," he
explains. "I liked the fact that it was designed to suppress me," says
Ernest of the star. "I—initially at least—I felt sort of good about it.
Now it sounds crazy to me but I definitely remember that's how I felt."
But the star was a sort of ghetto in and of itself, a confining, a redis-
tricting of the social map, by separating Jews from non-Jews with the
medieval markings. They would walk for hours to skirt the streets
they were forced to avoid, like the major shopping thoroughfare,
Kurfürstendamm, and the parks they could not be seen in, like Tier-
garten, the massive park that bisects a huge chunk of Berlin's western
half.

As he tells me this, Margot flutters in the background, putting
trays of cookies and tea together for us, dropping lines like, "Hans
never seemed young, so it was not strange he was with a woman who
was not young." I ask about Valy; she was always well put together,

Ernest says, almost fashionable, to the degree that was possible in 1942.

Ernest's stories fill in the character of Hans. The man—the second love of Valy's life?—who was not my grandfather, begins to take on definite shape. He was impossibly brave, and just as smart as Valy. I ask Ernest, again and again, what did it feel like to be living through this time? What did it feel like to have friends disappear, day after day? How aware was he of what was happening in the "east"? They didn't know exactly what the east meant, he says now. But they knew they weren't hearing word back. Ernest wrote:

> *There was a feeling of complete impotence in the Jewish population. Our lecture-and-music group decided that we should do something actively. One of the most unnerving aspects of the deportations was the fact that, with few exceptions, no mail or message of any kind was ever received from any deportee. So we decided that the first person from our circle to be deported should try by any means to get a message back about the conditions at the destination. Shortly thereafter a girl from our group was deported. Nothing was ever heard from her. After that, all of us agreed that everyone should try to go underground to avoid deportation and that the time to prepare such a step was now. The term "underground" meant a change in identity and residence to that of a fictitious "Aryan."*

For men the age of Hans and Ernest, though, it meant something else as well, something equally if not more dangerous: it meant running the risk of being seen as a deserter from the German army. All men of conscription age were serving by the winter of 1942. To take off the star and go "underground" for a woman was somewhat easier. For a man it meant a dual deception. It was something that gave all the men in their group pause. There was another problem as well—underground, they would have to be fed. They would lose their ration cards. They would need help.

It takes me ages to see Hans's niece, Carol, again. I try to make arrangements, I travel again to Berlin, I try to stop in London, but Carol's father, who she'd promised would be an essential interview, falls ill soon after Carol and I first meet. He is sick for many months. I don't want to push her—or him. I wait. I interview, instead, Walter Laqueur, the historian, whom the family has known for many years. Laqueur and Hans had gone to school together in Breslau. He remembers Hans better than I might have hoped, but it is the broad outlines he recalls—Hans was short, he was sporty, he was secular. Laqueur is kind, yet skeptical. What can be said, he asks me gently, about young people who died in the war? "What is there to say about a twenty-one-year-old? What did they ever do? You'll have to write around them," he says, meaning write through their experience, using others to explain what Hans might have experienced.

I remain undeterred. Carol had mentioned she had letters from Hans. And I think—despite his youth, despite his truncated chance to really live—there is more still to know. I am determined to visit with her again and sort through Hans's own words to see if there is more to be culled about the memory of the man Valy married. I want to see if he explained to his family his relationship to this girl, so much older. More: I hope to talk to Carol's father about what Hans was like as a young man, before Carol's parents were able to flee. But then, six months after she and I first meet, Carol's father, Paul Yogi Mayer, dies in London. I have not had the chance to talk to him after all. There are dozens of obituaries published in all the major English papers; he was celebrated for his work helping reintegrate young survivors into the UK, lauded by personalities across the British spectrum. Selfishly I rue that another incredible person has been lost, lament that this generation is literally fading away before my eyes, dying as I race across the globe.

When I finally see Carol again, more than a year has passed. She invites me to spend a night at her London townhouse at the edge of the city after a conference I attend in Cambridge. I take a train down to meet her and she picks me up in a sporty little black car with a child's safety seat installed in back. She wears a kind of dark gray, striped, Moroccan caftan and a necklace of large smooth stones or seed-shells; she is enormously affable, endlessly hospitable. We eat cheese and vegetables, drink copious amounts of tea. Her home is the bottom floor of an early-twentieth-century two-family house, nestled in one of those London strips of Edwardian-era homes built between 1900 and 1910 that looks out of central casting, or the set of a BBC show: inside, a collection of antique china plates and saucers in varying pastels are perched in an antique sideboard; Persian rugs and brocade floral couches face an unused fireplace, topped by a lovely pen-and-watercolor from the early part of the last century, a portrait of a young woman, her hair in an elaborate upsweep, and a Tiffany lamp. An enormous, sprawling garden spills out the back, filled with her own plantings. And Carol, too, fits the scene, with her language peppered by words like "muddled" and "lost the plot," which sound so perfectly British to my American ear.

Carol has a collection of artifacts and documents that rivals my own, the paper detritus of a world upended: her parents' world, so similar to my grandfather's. We spend twenty-four hours sitting crossed-legged on the floor of Carol's living room surrounded by hundreds and hundreds of letters from family trapped in Germany— Hans, his parents (Carol's grandparents), her uncles. One, named Walter Raschkow, was—like Victor Klemperer—married to a non-Jew, and so, protected, survived the entire war in Germany. As he learned his Jewish family members were being deported, he became a keeper of records, saving every scrap of paper about each nephew, sibling, cousin, knowing, by 1942 at least, that he was the last relative they could contact. He takes notes about each, reminders to himself. He seems aware that they may not return.

Some of this was preserved by Walter's daughter, Ingeborg, who never married, Carol explains, as we leaf through page after page. In her old age, Ingeborg had all of the family's possessions still with her—everything Carol's grandparents had managed to store with her protected father, as well as everything her own parents had managed not to give up. But at the end of her life, she was taken care of by a man who coerced her into leaving all of it to him. The family was allowed access only to the photos and the letters. The rest—Art Nouveau works; ceramics and glassware; hints of the haute-bourgeois life the family had once led—were swept into the swindler's life and out of the Fabisch–Mayer family forever. It was a second, and final, stealing, and devastating to Carol's mother, who had already lost so much.

There must have been a great deal he took: Carol's collection includes a 1930s-era photo album Walter had kept, with family members looking sporty—and happy—at Alpine ski resorts; it is a glimpse at their life of wealthy comfort before the Reich. There is also an autograph book from Carol's mother's friends, dated 1929. Each girl writes her a note in a different language—Latin, German, Hebrew—they are so *literate*. And so modern: Carol's own parents lived together before they were married; the wedding came only when her mother was pregnant with her first child. Soon after, the three emigrated together.

Carol's father, Paul, also kept notes on each person. And now Carol has a growing scrapbook of material on everyone, each document encased in plastic sheets. There are dozens of pages on her parents, her mother's last German passport—stamped with its large red *J*, good for one trip, in one direction; her mother's class pictures from the 1930s, laughing gorgeous girls, some blurred, they are moving too fast for the photographer in their rush toward life, all with that question hanging over them, the one that presses down on every photo of every group of Jewish teens from the 1930s—it is hard not to look at these images without some dread: Who among these girls with braids or stylish wavy bobs, these casual embraces, survived the next years?

And then, finally, here are the materials from Hans; letters, endless, endless letters that begin the moment Ilse Charlotte Mayer es-

caped: some requesting help in joining his sister in the United Kingdom; others attesting to his abilities and his studies; still more requests for help securing work in the UK—and then those that detail his struggles, like Valy, when he loses job after job in Berlin, as he works to keep his parents' morale boosted, as he tries to keep his own head above the rapidly moving waters of Nazi regulations. Bits and pieces of his endless struggle—alongside his parents—to emigrate swim out at us from the morass. In July 1939, it all seems possible; he writes to Ilse and Yogi:

> *As for my humble self, my parents are far more worried about me than I am. They're not entirely wrong, however, because the difficulty is primarily my livelihood after my parents' departure and my emigration, both where and how, because I would not only have to pack all my things alone, but also deal with the authorities on my own, and first be declared legally of age so I could do that. Nevertheless, I continue to be in favor of having my parents leave as soon as possible. . . . So, it'll work out.*

He is frustrated, he writes to a friend named Lilo who seems to have passed on the letter to Ilse, that his parents refuse to leave him behind—"my parents aren't willing to leave without me and thus they are putting the whole thing in jeopardy. We all have to coax them, otherwise it will really go wrong yet." The emigration options, at first, are merely stymied by money, but somehow, one after the other, they slip away, both for him and for his parents. He remains cheerful:

> *Dear Ilse and Yogi,*
>   *. . . You surely know that I work in the kitchen now, where we, a team of three, cook the fleishik [meat] food for 100 people (as the milkhik [milk] kitchen is completely separate). From that alone you can tell that it has to do with an extremely Orthodox operation, and that is a real contrast to the lab, quite seriously, because apart from me they all come from the former [Orthodox] community, and my boss, of course, wears a sheitel. In short, one is always more pious than the next, and in the first few days I made a lot of blunders. Also, when I [mentioned] that I enjoy eating crab, my comrades, who by the way are very nice, came close to falling off their chairs. Best of all I like the food, which is really ample, even though there hasn't been any meat in this kitchen for months. . . . The work I have to do in the kitchen is not always pretty—or what would Ilse say if she had to take on 50 herrings or peel onions in great quantities? But everything is all right, though it took me a long time to get used to the herring. But there's a lot of nice work too, and I have already learned to properly peel potatoes, peel rhubarb and asparagus, and even make pancakes (always in two pans at the same time). And in the case of the herring and onions, I would like to say . . . Gam zu l'tovah! [This is also for good.]*

But his sanguinity begins to ebb. His letters become increasingly anxious. The dates are cut off but I try to organize the letters by level of worry:

Dear Yogi,

In response to a telegram that I have just received from my parents, I'm sending you enclosed my curriculum vitae, a certificate of good health, my birth certificate, and two passport photos. . . .

You're probably as just well informed about the whole matter as I am. . . . Naturally, this is one of the most unpleasant moments we've experienced in the past 6 years, but I want to ask you to keep a clear head here too, and not to expend more energy or effort or money on this matter than you can really afford, because it's better if at least you three continue to live in somewhat well-ordered circumstances, instead of all of us falling apart over this business. . . . I ask you also not to involve Ilse overly much in all these things, because we want to handle these "men's matters" among men, to the greatest possible extent.

For today, then, all the best, and warm regards.

And then:

Breslau, August 6

Dear Ilse and Yogi,

. . . A few days ago, my mother was at the information center for emigrants to request her passport and Dad's passport. But she was informed there that the passport could not be handed over until a certain amount of money was deposited for me. Then we spoke with the British Consulate in Breslau, which advised us for the time being to just send the permit, without the passport, to Berlin. This now has been done. . . . Now, finding a job will probably be the most essential thing, and I'm sure you will manage to do so somehow. . . .

Carol holds up a letter from Boots, the British pharmacy company, rejecting Hans in his application for work. They are concerned he will not be up to speed in the English language, and with English practices. She muses aloud, wondering if they know their rejection was a death sentence. There is one photo of Hans, smiling genially, tie a bit askew. Carol's daughter Jess, she says, looks eerily similar to Hans: family who knew Hans were always struck by it. "Especially round the eyes." Amid these missives, there are also reports on the family. Hans's father, it seems, has cancer and undergoes radiation therapy. Hans donates blood. There are pages and pages on his father, Rudolf, and his progress.

And then, I see, buried in the pile: bits and pieces about—and by—Valy herself—letters she has written to Uncle Walter, letters Hans has written about his girlfriend.

As we sort through the piles of decaying paper, Carol and I talk about families not talking, and of how relatively little connection her children have to these letters, how distanced they seem from their own history. I wonder—does the third generation really *need* this story as much as I think we do? What am I doing here with my fingers on seventy-year-old pages from the dead, chattering with a woman on the other side of the Atlantic, while my own daughter sits at home in America? Is it worth it? We talk about our families—Carol's husband, Eric, still legally bound to her, lives not far away but not *with* her. They remain close friends. At this point she likes her life, her cottage, her independence. In fact he comes around twice while we sort and talk, once to help with house repairs, once to come out to dinner. He is white haired and handsome. And he goes home at the end of the evening.

On a break during day two, Carol and I sit in the garden soaking up improbably nice weather, eating shortbread and drinking tea in the sun as Carol's upstairs neighbor's children shout and laugh around us. Their chatter fills the background of my tapes. We talk about her mother's collection of women friends, all survivors as well, all refugees, who all lost someone, or many. They were one another's families, she says, they watched one another's children, they stayed close throughout their lives. She talks again about her mother, how devastated she remained, how damaged she was, by whom and what she had lost.

And the collection bears that out, the massive torrent of early letters, the assurances of possibility in 1939 that give way to the Red Cross–restricted allowance of twenty-five words—*poems*, as the women of the Silent Heroes Memorial in Berlin had described them—the weak assurances that all is just fine sent from Berlin to London and back again.

But Carol's letter trove explains so much. Especially the later letters collected by Uncle Walter, the protected one. Rudolf, Carol's grandfather, writes to Hans from Theresienstadt, in December 1942, saying he is well but frightened for Hans and indicating, cryptically, that Hans's mother is "with Uncle Hermann"—who, they all knew already, was dead. Hans's mother has not survived her time in the east. And Hans, in turn, writes to his Uncle Walter that he has heard Valy will be deported with others from the old-age home where she works in Babelsberg if she is not married, immediately, to a more essential worker. As Walter is the only living, present, older relative, Hans appears to need his permission to marry Valy—to save her. He asks for their understanding and he asks them to send him his—now deceased—mother's clothing (in his letter he calls her "Mutti," like Mommy) and shoes for Valy, who has not been able to repair or replace her clothing in two years.

[Shortly before Christmas 1942]

My dear ones:

Yesterday I collected your Christmas package from the post office. As I arrived back home, your dear letter had also arrived. I don't have to tell you how happy your kind attentions, in both words and deeds made me. It is obvious that such a package would be a special great joy to me, especially since I really have such need for its content.

Everything you sent fits perfectly. The cigarettes almost took my breath away. The wonderful cakes and the . . . cookies, especially the oatmeal ones I really love.

. . . It seems that my marriage will go through now—but only if you agree. Both of us are sufficiently intelligent to see the "ifs and buts" quite clearly. Although I think it possible that we will stay together forever, the marriage at this point primarily serves practical purposes.

My future wife is called Valy (we will wed on January 5th); her full name is Dr. med Valerie Scheftel. She comes from Troppau, studied in Vienna and now works together with her very young mother in the Babelsberg Home her mother leads. Valy has asked me not to talk about her age. In any case, the difference is less than 10 years. She is exactly as tall as Mutti, but somewhat thinner. Mutti's shoes are a little too big for her, but she is able to wear them. I leave the choice of items that may be appropriate to Aunt Inge.

Now I have to stop writing in the middle of the letter as our break is over. I wish you a very Happy New Year (1943) in all respects and want to thank you yet again for your understanding attitude and for the highly nutritious proofs of your friendship!

With kindest regards, also from Valy,

Merry Christmas 1942!

Your Hans

Reading this, I am pulled up short. "Although I think it's possible that we will stay together forever, the marriage at this point primarily serves practical purposes." In the fall of 1941, Valy proposed marriage to my grandfather as a means of saving herself. She loved him, of course, or at least she believed she did (if there is a difference, I'm not sure of it), but here, with Hans, it all seems perfectly clear: the marriage was practical as much as romantic. Does this mean the love affair that Ernest was so sure of was only an elaborate means of evading deportation? I don't know. Perhaps she did love him, and he her, but that is not the emphasis here.

After a year without being able to even send real letters to Karl—a year when she watched the world disintegrate before her eyes, a year of train after train sending a thousand Jews at a time to ghettos and camps in the east, a year of terror, the city of Berlin leached of its Jews—a word like "love" may have meant, more than it ever did, "salvation" as much as it meant romance. Was Karl on her mind as they reached out to family to secure a marriage certificate? Perhaps only remaining free mattered. Marrying Hans might not have meant that she had abandoned all ideas of my grandfather, but what did that fantasy matter now?

After Hans's letter to his uncle, events progress much faster than he had anticipated. Hans moves Valy into his apartment and writes a more desperate letter, soon after his Christmas missive.

Dear Aunt Inge and Uncle Walter,

When I wrote you in my next-to-last letter concerning my girlfriend Valy, I had no idea of the things that have happened in the meantime. I need to make it as short as possible now and send all the detailed explanations later, because every hour is valuable.

The dissolution of the old-age home in which the aforementioned Valy works is imminent, and to prevent her, like the other people employed there, from being deported to the East, the only possibility is for us to get married as quickly as possible. You must believe me— first, that there really is no other way, and second, that under no circumstances can I stand here and watch as this person who is so infinitely near and dear to me goes the same way as my dear mother. I will spell all this out for you later.

Now I need, as documents for the civil registry office, the birth and marriage certificates of my parents and the birth certificates of my grandparents. Please let me know about the following questions as quickly as possible:

1) Do you possibly have the birth and marriage certificates of my parents? If so, please send them to me immediately by registered mail.

2) *Where were my maternal grandparents born?*

3) *When were they born (year and day)?*

4) *What are their full names?*

5) *What is the maiden name of my maternal grandmother (Reichenbach?)?*

6) *Did my parents marry in 1913 or in 1914?*

Please give me answers as quickly as possible. Because the notice of intended marriage must be posted before the old-age home is dissolved, everything depends on the speed with which we obtain the papers. I have written to Uncle Paul Fabisch in Breslau regarding my paternal grandparents; he probably will have the information.

The fact that this letter is written in such haste cannot be changed. The marriage problem itself has already been discussed and thought through calmly and with a number of sensible and well-informed people.

*For you, the whole matter must seem very romantic and overhasty; however, it is not so, and I beg you to understand and to keep in mind that I regard this separation as unbearable, after the emigration [*Abwanderung, *the Nazi term for deportation to an extermination camp] of my parents and the death of my mother.*

Now I will wait to hear from you.

Warmest regards,

Hans

And then there is one more:

Dear Aunt Inge and Uncle Walter,

Please don't be cross with us for not writing, but things are frantic again right now. The home in B. [Babelsberg] had to be vacated within 24 hours (!), and Valy is moving in with me today (moving in is allowed). We're up to our ears in work, and besides I

still have to go to the factory, where I'm also writing this postcard.
So, please bear with me for a while. That's all for today,

Love,
Valy and Hans

Now I know: Hans had already saved Valy from certain death once. Their marriage, be it propelled, in part or more, by romantic love, was fueled entirely by the imminent fact of her impending deportation if she weren't attached to an essential worker. Her time with the Reichsvereinigung had run out.

Among Carol's collection, I find that Valy wrote to Uncle Walter, too. Her letter is far more formal; it is a thank-you, and an apology for upending their family, for being the cause of some controversy, between her age and the—apparent—hastiness of their marriage.

Sometime after these letters arrived, Walter took notes on what he had received:

From the letters that I received from Hans Fabisch and his wife
"Valy" (Valerie Scheftel) between the time before Christmas 1942
from Berlin and January 14, 1943, I have the following personal
knowledge:

In the letter before Christmas 1942, he told me (among many
other things that do not belong here) that his marriage now was
going through and that the wedding with Dr. med. Valerie Scheftel
was set to take place in Berlin on January 5, 1943.

Dr. Scheftel, who comes from Troppau, studied in Vienna and
worked at that time in the Babelsberg Home that is managed by her
relatively young mother.

A few days later (the date is missing) Hans told me that the
Nazis had decreed that the Babelsberg Home had to be dissolved; for
this reason it had become imperative that I send him the papers that
were required for the marriage, which I still had from his parents, as

quickly as possible by registered mail. This, of course, I did
immediately.

On 12-28-1942, Dr. Valerie Scheftel, to whom we had sent
various items of clothing, wrote me a letter of thanks and apologized
for having possibly upset us by the rather spontaneous marriage
decision and other related matters. . . .

Additionally I received a [letter] . . . with a postal stamp of
January 14, 1943.

Again a small package that, as it was often the case in those
times, was returned with a notation that the recipient had moved to
an unknown location. . . .

Thereafter, I did not hear anything at all.

It was nearly, but not totally, impossible to survive in Berlin, in the
heart of the Reich. Ten to twelve thousand Jews attempted to hide in
Germany, and five thousand or so actually survived, seventeen hundred
in the capital alone. (By comparison, in 1925, there were 160,000 Jews
living in Berlin.) The numbers are minuscule. It required great effort, a
great number of people aiding you, unusually good luck—not to mention an unusually calm disposition, an ability to think on your feet, and
the wherewithal to shift goals and locations on a moment's notice.

Jews like Valy who came from other parts of the Reich, who did not
know the city well and had no friends from before—especially those
who knew no non-Jews, who had no longtime neighbors, and thus no
network—struggled. And yet they believed. And they took tremendous risks. They had no choice. It was lonely, it was awful. But what
was the alternative? Meeting Hans was a break—it was companionship, of course. Perhaps it was also love, physical, emotional, touch at a
moment that was so cold and terrifying there could be nothing to shield
you from that anxiety in the night other than your own exhaustion.

Ernest's letter refers to the time period that Valy and Hans were
writing to Walter.

> *Hans, Valy and I discussed the need to go underground. All of us*
> *were in agreement that going underground was the only way to save*
> *ourselves from deportation. At that time we did not even know the*
> *full truth about Auschwitz. As a first step, Hans and I bought forged*
> *identification papers.*

Siemens was beginning to welcome a new influx of workers. They were non-Jewish laborers brought in from the east and elsewhere. Ernest saw it as an ominous sign. His foreman told him to train the woman assigned to his same post. He was told to let her try his job, from time to time, to observe his actions. He suspected that this meant he was working to school his own replacement.

On Christmas Eve, 1942, Ernest's mother, father, and teenage sister were arrested. From the transit camp at Grosse Hamburger Strasse, his mother relayed a stark last message through one of the Jewish workers who were pressed into service by the Gestapo: those who questioned her asked a great deal about her son, who had not been taken. The worker who relayed the message to her son had been a teacher in Ernest's school; he still remembered Ernest, still cared for him. It was a stroke of luck: most of the Jewish workers were far too afraid of the consequences of passing messages to the remaining Jews in the city. The old teacher knew Ernest well enough to trust him, to care for him. Reading this I am reminded: Valy had no such person to warn her, in this city she was a virtual stranger. The message was both a warning and a love letter, a farewell kiss. With his mother's words in mind, sometime before New Year's Eve, Ernest stopped wearing his yellow star, he stopped working at Siemens; he moved out of his apartment, he carried his fake papers all the time and he moved into a temporary, and dangerous, "safe" house. It was risky to be on the street as a military-aged boy not at the front—was he a deserter? was he a Jew?—but more risky still to chance the roundups.

Ernest wanted Hans to join him underground. Hans preferred to wait. He thought that as long as he worked for Siemens, he'd be ex-

empt from deportation. Why go underground until he had to? Ernest
argued that the Gestapo would hardly advertise the moment when
their exemptions expired. But Hans was firm. He had his false papers,
he said, he could go underground at any time.

Besides, his priority was to marry. It was Valy who hesitated: she
did not want people to know their age difference. "Both of us are sufficiently intelligent to see the 'ifs and buts' quite clearly," Hans wrote
to his uncle. "Although I think it possible that we will stay together
forever, the marriage at this point primarily serves practical purposes."
And it was those purposes that finally convinced her. For Valy was
about to be out of a job: the old-age home her mother ran, and that
also employed her, had been notified it was to be liquidated; its tenants
"sent East." While Valy's mother was still useful to the Reich—she
had already been reassigned to Auguststrasse 14/16—Valy was not.
Her best means to avoid deportation, she believed, and Hans believed,
was now Hans himself. It had been seven months since Karl and Valy
wrote to each other through the Red Cross.

Hans and Valy married on the fifth of January, 1943.

"Why did they marry?" I asked Ernest, that snowy day in Ann
Arbor. "They were deeply in love," he said, without hesitating, brush-
ing aside everything else. "And they wanted to live together, and those
days it would not be acceptable to live together unmarried—but I don't
think that it was only a practical question. I think they really wanted
to be together." Did you, I wanted to know, talk about the deportations? "Yes. Lots of discussions I think I write about in that letter—we
had different strategies. I had my point of view. Hans had his."

Hans still refused to leave Siemens. "And then we had that long-
running argument; I mean he took that forged ID sort of as an insurance policy. He would go underground when no other option existed."

They still didn't exactly *know*, insists Ernest, what awaited them
in the east. "We assumed it was work under brutal conditions and living under brutal, sadistic conditions. But at that time, at least, I had
never heard of mass extermination through gas chambers."

On January 18, Ernest crept back to his parents' apartment for provisions. There he ran into an elderly woman from his old building. She told him that deportation vans were on Hans and Valy's block.

It was a bitterly cold day in the bitterest month of the year. Ernest bundled up and raced over to Brandenburgische Strasse. The furniture van used to collect Jews like a dogcatcher's vehicle was parked right in front of number 43. There were, Ernest knew, many Jewish apartments in that building, both in the front house and in the back. He knew Hans was at work, but not Valy. He had to try to reach her—otherwise, how would he ever be able to face Hans?

The apartment was on the fifth floor. He ran up the steps and rang the bell. When the door opened, a Gestapo officer stepped out. He demanded Ernest's identification papers and began questioning him. From the door, Ernest could see no one in the apartment. The officer pocketed his papers and told him to leave, but to come and see him at Gestapo headquarters the following day. Ernest tried to look past the officer—the doors were open, but he saw no one, not Valy, not her neighbors. He was sure she was out.

Back on the street, Ernest positioned himself on a corner where he could spot anyone coming or going. He planned to intercept Valy. But an hour and a half later, the van had left and there was still no sign of her. Panicked and half frozen, he ran to catch Hans on his way back from the S-Bahn train, having finished his shift for the night. The two men jogged to the building, sheltered by darkness; it was now night.

They entered the courtyard and looked up; a thin band of light beamed out from under the blackout shades of Hans and Valy's apartment. Valy, they agreed, relieved, must have come home after the vans had left, after Ernest had left his post. Together they sprinted up the stairs. At the fourth floor, suddenly, Hans paused. *Let me go on alone,* he told his friend. Wait for a signal. Then he continued, mounting the last flight of steps alone.

From his vantage point on the stairwell, Ernest saw Hans put his key in the door. But, before he could turn it, the door opened, and a tall, older man in civilian dress was in the doorway, backlit. "Who are you?" he shouted down to Ernest.

Ernest flew down the stairs three at a time, out the door, into the street. He didn't look back; he just ran and ran and ran and ran. Panting and spent, when he caught his breath, blocks from Brandenburgische Strasse 43, he realized what had just happened. He was free. No one was chasing him. And he was completely alone.

Twelve

WHAT REMAINS

Hans and Valy had the foresight to buy fake papers. They married in time to save her from the liquidation of the Babelsberg old-age home. But they waited one day too long to go underground. The Gestapo agent waiting at 43 Brandenburgische Strasse took Hans with him.

Together, Hans and Valy were held under atrocious conditions at the transit camp on Grosse Hamburger Strasse, with hundreds of others, until January 29. The deportation process had been stripped of any vestige of humanity by then. There was no longer any furniture in the building at Grosse Hamburger Strasse. Now there were only fetid mattresses on the floor, and straw for those not lucky enough to have a cushion. There were bars on each window; floodlights illuminated the grounds; armed guards with orders to shoot escapees kept constant watch. Privacy had disintegrated; doors had been removed from the few toilets. It was here, on January 27, that Hans and Valy were forced to sign over the rights to all of their property to the German Reich, a bizarre formality that would set in motion a slow-moving but well-orchestrated dismantling of their home and the careful looting of their remaining worldly possessions.

From their transit camp, Valy and Hans were taken not to Grunewald, where so many of the rest of the city's Jews had been sent before them, but to the Putlitzstrasse train station, in the Moabit area of Berlin, now known as Mitte. On January 29, along with 1,002 others, they were shoved aboard a closed cattle car bound for Auschwitz. The records the Gestapo kept of that day are very precise. On board were sixty-four children age twelve and below, fifty teenagers between ages thirteen and eighteen, 348 men and women between ages nineteen and forty-five, and 386 people between forty-five and sixty years old. The rest were the elderly and infirm. The train left at 5:20 in the afternoon and traveled for seventeen and a half hours through the German and then the Polish countryside. It arrived "on time" at the Auschwitz train station at 10:48 the following morning. Upon arrival, those who survived that terrible journey—and many died in transit, their bodies dropped to the floor beneath the feet of their former neighbors, their fellow Jews—were pushed onto what was called the Alte Judenrampe, the Old Jews' Ramp, at the Oświęcim freight station, between the Auschwitz and Birkenau camps, for the selection. (The Birkenau selection ramp so often depicted in Holocaust movies and testimonies had not yet been constructed.) The group was then marched, in columns, to Birkenau.

On the morning of January 30, 140 men and 140 women were chosen for work from Valy's train. Striped prisoner pajamas replaced clothes; hair was brutally shorn; arms were crudely tattooed with a number. Those were the fortunate. The other 724 men, women, and children who left Berlin on the 29th of January did not receive a tattoo, or camp number, or uniform. Those who had survived the journey were merely methodically stripped of their remaining earthly possessions and then immediately murdered by gas.

———

Toward the end of my first stay in Berlin, still pregnant with Orli, I took the S-Bahn train to Grunewald. The station serves the epony-

Memorial at Grunewald Station, Berlin.

mously named pretty suburb-within-the-city known for its large park. The S-Bahn 7 train rushes through every ten minutes. There is a third track, or *Gleis*, that is easily overlooked. As you descend from the S-Bahn lines, you see signs indicating Westkreuz, back toward town, or Potsdam, in the other direction, and then there is *Gleis* 17. As you ascend the stairs for 17, you see two long metal lanes and a track that seems, at first, no different from any other. But the platform is cast from steel, and every two feet is a date, a number, and a direction. It looks like this:

12.1.1943 / 1190 Juden / Berlin–Auschwitz. 12.1.1943 / 100 Juden / Berlin–Theresienstadt. 13.1.1943 / 100 Juden / Berlin–Theresienstadt.

The tracks stretch out into the distance, covered with vegetation in places but still totally visible. The memorial covers every deportation from this city; it lists the numbers sent and the days on which each of the fifty-five thousand Jews deported from Berlin was sent away. More Jews left from Berlin than from all of Belgium.

I was completely alone there that day, save for the little Jew inside me, and through the trees I watched the S-Bahn trains rushing back and forth a few yards away, the distance between normal life and terror just a few feet and sixty-five years.

But that sunny late September afternoon at the S-Bahn station in Grunewald, I didn't yet know that, as alone as Valy had been, she was not nearly as alone as I'd once believed. For twenty-four days before that train trip, she was married. For twenty-four days, she had lived with a man who cared enough to try to rescue her, who didn't want her to be alone in this pitiless city, who couldn't let her be sent away. On the twenty-fifth day, they were deported together.

———~———

After the war, when the International Tracing Service in Bad Arolsen was first set up, when Europe was still smoldering, and buildings in nearly every major city across Germany were still in ruins, Jews, weary, nearly destroyed, across the Continent, in America, from Palestine to Australia—they all tried to find one another. Valy's world, too, began to reconnect, asking if anyone knew anything about where she—or her mother—might be. Hope, tentative, uncertain, not quite crushed, remained.

At this point my grandfather was finishing his own tour of duty— he had enlisted, hoping to serve in Europe; after all, he spoke several European languages. Instead, he was sent to the Pacific theater, where he served in a MASH unit at the front. I have photos of him, standing on a temporary wood platform, afloat in a sea of mud, a pistol on his hip, outside army tents. He spent a year overseas, working as a surgeon; he wrote a paper, "Active Immunization Against Malaria." It won the Henry S. Wellcome Medal for 1946, from the Association of Military Surgeons, as the best paper on the contributions of the World War to the advancement of medicine. Dozens of letters poured in from around the country, congratulating him and asking for reprints of his scientific work. The medal, and the notes, were together with

Karl and Dorothy Wildman with Cilli and Carl Feldschuh,
my grandfather's sister and brother-in-law, around 1946.

the original box marked "C. J. Wildman, Personal." I found it the same night I discovered the letters. But, like everything else in that period of my grandfather's life, his time in the service was very vague, all broad strokes, all bright—he enlisted, rose to the rank of major, served in his own profession—medicine.

Working in a frontline hospital as a surgeon must have been grueling. There were always rumors he had been very ill at some point, though no one knew exactly from what, or where he recovered. Instead, we heard cheerful stories, like one about how he saved a young (Jewish) soldier's life in triage who turned out to be my grandmother's best friend's brother (really—the thank-you letter was also in the box). I write to the National Archives requesting information about Karl's military service and I am told my grandfather's files were burned in a 1973 St. Louis fire that destroyed thousands of army records of the era. They can offer me nothing, other than proof that he served.

As his time in the service ends, he was starting to hear from—and reach out to—his European world once again.

The letters in my "Correspondence, Patients A–G" box that came as the war began to wind down are often just as terrible to read as

those that arrived as the war began. Some are angry; some are sup-
plicating. Bruno Klein, once my grandfather's closest friend, writes
thanking him for an affidavit and letters of support he has provided;
he shyly inquires whether the embers of their youthful brotherhood
can be fanned into adult friendship.

> *Most of all, the tone of your letter pleased me very much: it*
> *brought back memories of young friendship—despite everything. I am*
> *sure that I will feel at home in the US much more quickly than I ever*
> *did in Switzerland. Do you still have contacts with "the old guard"?*
> *Probably, one has the wrong impression of the distances involved—*
> *Zwicker in Los Angeles, Bobby Weiser in New York etc.*

He sounds so tentative, so formal—but then again, it is twelve years
since they have seen each other. A lifetime. They left each other as
twenty-six-year-old recently graduated students, and here they were
thirty-eight-year-old men; they had lived through war, they had lost
everything they had ever known, they had started their lives again,
and again. My grandfather had been to the Pacific and back; Bruno
had remained a refugee in Europe. Bruno will spend his life shuttling
between New York and Switzerland, never quite at home anywhere.
They will rebuild their friendship—I have their letters stretching until
the 1980s, where the two men, at that point well into their seventies,
joke about Kurt Waldheim, the Holocaust, American Jews, pathos,
and memory.

But Bruno's hopeful overtures are nothing compared with the
letters of those who knew Valy and searched for her, back in her
hometown.

"At last peace has arrived after 6 difficult war years," begins one,
mailed October 25, 1945.

> *In spite of the beautiful word "peace," there still is no peace,*
> *the innocent and guilty equally being subjected to terrible*

paper love

*suffering. I keep waiting for our beloved Valy and her Mama.
Knowing that she is alive would be the happiest day in my life. I
would be happy to give her the items, which I safeguarded and
remained intact throughout the Russian occupation. Also, there is
one of your pictures, which I safeguarded together with the rest of
the items and pictures. It was painted by Professor Morino. I
would be delighted to hear from you. . . . 2 years nothing from
Mrs. Scheftel and Valy. Now I have let you know what's most
important.*

This was Maria Richterova, author of a half-dozen letters, written in
Sütterlin script, an old-time written German that I have to track down
special interpreters to read. She is a Sudeten German in Czechoslovakia, and a—what? A neighbor of Valy and her mother in Troppau? A
former maid? It is unclear, never explained. Maria writes, increasingly
anxiously, about her uncertain future: she is about to be expelled,
along with twelve million other ethnic Germans living in Czechoslovakia, Poland, and elsewhere; they are all about to be resettled, brutally, outside the only country they have ever known. She claims to
have held on to all of Valy's possessions that were not taken along with
her to Berlin.

Her letters are wrenching, lamenting her lost neighbors, and ruing
her current situation. "Foreign items safeguarded by locals are not supposed to be confiscated, but everything is seized anyway, and nobody
will ever see any of them again," she writes in another letter. "Therefore I am asking you, Venerable Doctor, to help me to continue safe-
guarding these items and also put in a word in favor of our things.
After all, the British and Americans are in power."

They are so sparse, her letters, and yet so full. It is as though she
wants to argue to someone—if anyone will just listen!—that she did
well by Jews, she tried, she hoped, she prayed, she kept their things,
she did not loot! she plans to return them! Was she telling the truth?
Had she really done these things out of altruism? Could Valy or her

mother—or their neighbors—have truly believed they would really return to Troppau after the war? Of this I don't know.

Maria wants to know from my grandfather what she should do, and if he can help her. "To be able to hand those over to our beloved Valy would count among one of my happiest hours, because she was the best and noblest human person whom I have ever known."

She writes again and again, her situation worsens. "Yesterday I walked 28 kilometers on foot to the district government agency asking them to release to me the items belonging to our beloved Valy, her beloved mother and you, so I would be able to take them with me during resettlement, but they bluntly refused . . . if the Venerable Doctor were to write to the district government . . ."

Perhaps Maria saw this as her own opportunity—as her letters continue, the only clear thing is her own need:

Dear Venerable Dr. Wildmann,

I just got word that the families have been informed, how much they will be allowed to take along for resettlement. It is so little, that one can carry it with one's bare hands. Dear Dr., I would be forever grateful, if you could put in a word for us and our relatives with the powers that be belonging in the victorious countries, as all of us were opposed to fascism, after all, and I would be very happy not to leave here like a pauper and be allowed to take along enough for minimum household needs.

Her naïveté put too much faith in my grandfather's abilities to negotiate, on her or anyone's behalf, with the new Czech authorities, with the occupying Allies; but her anxiety was totally justified. There were death marches of Sudeten Germans; some three million of them were not just expelled but vigorously, aggressively persecuted in the months following the war, a stain on the Czech relationship to Europe that extended until the early part of this century. Thousands died on the marches away from their homes that Maria describes. I can't find any further information on her—and her last name, I'm told, is so common as to make it nearly impossible that I ever would. Her letters are a microcosm of the Sudeten German postwar experience, a mini drama that unfolds from 1945 through 1946 and then fades away.

So I know this: in 1945 into 1946, Maria let my grandfather know that Valy had not, at the very least, returned to Troppau. But then again, no one was going "home"—if home was Troppau or Vienna. Perhaps my grandfather still held out hope that Valy and Toni were in a displaced persons camp somewhere in Germany. There were so many who were.

When I first started to think about Valy and Karl, a Holocaust historian directed me to watch an episode of *This Is Your Life* broadcast in 1953. The honoree was a young and beautiful woman named Hanna Bloch Kohner. She has a slight accent, is dressed gorgeously, like a sketch of a 1950s Chanel model, with a fitted jacket, white gloves, and full skirt. At one point in the broadcast, the announcer intones, in that distinctive voice, "Looking at you, it's hard to believe that during seven short years of a still-short life, you lived a lifetime of fear, terror, and tragedy!" At the end of the broadcast, there is a special guest—"your brother, Hanna . . . The last time you were in touch with Gottfried was in a Nazi concentration camp nearly ten years ago. Now here he is, from Israel! Your brother, Dr. Gottfried Bloch!" And Hanna begins to weep and weep, overwhelmed with an emotion well beyond the show's normal scope.

It was the first time anyone had seen a Holocaust survivor on television. The brother is the most extreme, but actually, all of Hanna's "long-lost" friends hail from her seven years of internment—in Westerbork, in Theresienstadt, in Auschwitz, in Mauthausen—and the period just after the war when she wandered Europe, stateless and in shock, until an old boyfriend, who, like my grandfather, had fled Europe in 1938, shows up at her door, in a U.S. Army uniform, a knight in shining armor. Eventually, they marry.

It is shocking to view the show now, in part because she was so very young, so lovely. Our survivors had always been wrinkled and old. But in the early 1950s, they were still young, even though terribly, terribly scarred. Hanna Block Kohner had lost so much that *This Is Your Life* did not remotely touch—her first husband was murdered, she terminated a pregnancy to save her own life. Who is assembled here for her, really? Who could the producers produce to represent her past? It is a weak, random group of the strays who survived. Not her parents, murdered in camps. Not her other friends—all are dead. And yet they describe her time from camp to camp—You were down to seventy-three pounds!—as though it were a time in finishing school.

Hanna's tragedy disguised as happiness underscores something that has hovered with me these many months: The stories of these survivors were not happy stories, there were no neatly tied-up endings, and often, there were no endings at all. Survival alone did not equal happiness—unless happiness was the path that survivors chose, obstinately, like my grandfather did.

"Correspondence, Patients A–G" offered dozens more stories from the end of the war. There are the many, many letters from the Binder family, close Vienna friends, stuck in Shanghai from 1938 to 1949 and desperate to leave for America or Palestine. They ache and scream, these letters; they are poor. Terribly poor. And they, too, want help from my grandfather: they want him to bring them to America. As awful as their experience may have been, these letters have a happier ending than some: they are scattered—a son to Palestine, a daughter to San Francisco—but they are not dead.

These postwar letters come from my grandfather's entire old Viennese world; hands that reached out to him from cousins and half siblings, friends and acquaintances, the remnants of a Viennese old guard of the 1920s and 1930s, a population that would never again reassemble. Angry, bewildered, tentative, *weary*, they wrote.

September 18, 1946

Dear Carl,

I got your address from your sister Cilli, and I'm delighted to hear about you and to know how you are!

I heard you've gotten married in the meantime and have a little boy. Please accept my warmest congratulations.

If you feel like writing, I'd like to hear from you in person and learn what you're doing and how you are. After you left, nobody heard from you, you never thought of finding out what was happening or had happened to your relatives. Don't take this as a reproach, because even if you would like to make up for it, it's already too late.

Unfortunately, we had a great many victims. Our dear parents died in concentration camps, and our dear brother Alfred in Palestine passed away a year ago.

You see, things don't seem so jolly in our family, and that's why I'm asking you to write to Regina and to me, so that we don't feel so alone in the world. You know, when husband and wife are together, you can bear everything much more easily, but Regina's husband unfortunately was traumatized by the war and is incurable. You can imagine what pain this causes my dear sister. My husband was deported three years ago, and now we have lost our oldest. Believe me, Carl, it is terrible, and I don't know whether you can understand me. That's why I'm asking you again to write us once in a while, it will make things easier for us.

I would like to have some pictures of you and your family.

With my regards and kisses to you and your dear wife and child,

Lotte

P.S. *Write to Regina, she'll be glad.*
Regina Hirschfeld, 17 Chesney Court, Shirland Road,
London W9

Lotte was the daughter of my grandfather's half brother Manele. My great-grandfather was married twice; his son from his first marriage was thirty years older than my grandfather. Lotte was somewhat younger than Karl, but she was his friend and contemporary. When they were all in Vienna, surely, given her age, she looked up to him.

My father was the boy born that Lotte mentions, and such a thing is strange for him to know—that six months after his birth, the world his father left behind was reaching out to chastise; to implore. When I read it to him, my father is fascinated but perplexed. He knew Lotte, but not that there was a rift between her and my grandfather. By the time he met her—in the mid-1950s—any rancor had long since been set aside; he remembers warmth. He certainly never knew about all that she had lost in the war.

In 1950, Lotte settled in Lyon, France, married again, and had another child. His photo is in a subsequent letter, a small boy in a tub outdoors. "Georges" is written on the back. The next letters are far more cheerful; they speak of family and visits, and they talk of meeting in Europe—my grandfather and grandmother, at that point, had begun their biannual sojourn in Europe, and they saw Lotte in France, in Switzerland, in the United Kingdom, where her sister Regina had settled. The boy in her photographs, I realize, must be about sixty now. He has the same last name that Lotte took in her second marriage—Sudarskis. I track him down and e-mail him, this Georges. He is a money manager in Abu Dhabi, he has a home in Venice. He has done well. It takes him, literally, years to respond.

But when he does, it is amazing. He is thrilled to hear from Karl's granddaughter. He remembers my grandfather well—he himself went to university in Montreal—and he would come south to swim in the lake by my grandparents' house in Massachusetts. His mother loved my grandfather very much. "I remember the tenderness with which she would speak about Karl," he says, as we chat over Skype, echoing my father's memory. He remembers once, maybe in the 1970s, meeting a son of my grandfather's who spoke French. That would be my father, I say.

He tells me his mother never spoke of the war, but as a fifteen-year-old he stumbled upon papers that suggested she had once had another name, another life. Even this is a memory he cannot quite conjure. He describes finding out she had a past husband in the way we describe events of our childhood—it is like a dream; he cannot quite remember how he knew, or what he knew, and when he knew it. He knows he confronted her, and he knows she offered only the most basic response: *Yes*, she said. *There was another marriage*. She did not invite further questioning. He thinks the first husband told her to leave Vienna without him. She traveled through Germany, to the Netherlands, and on to Paris sometime in 1939, all on her own. This much he knows for sure, it is the only thing he knows with certainty: for a very long time, she was alone.

Later I'll see that in the Yad Vashem digital database of victims' names there is that of one man, Eugene Stryks, born in Vienna in 1916, whose last name is the same as Lotte's first married name: Stryks was deported from Drancy, the transit camp outside Paris, to Majdanek, on March 6, 1943. I wonder whether this was Lotte's first husband; if it was, he made it as far as France with her when they ran.

Georges never pressed his mother about her wartime experiences. On some level, he says, perhaps he was too afraid of what he'd hear. More: he was too convinced she didn't want to speak.

"Look," he says, "you were born in America," and years after the war. "But in 1950, when I was born, it was only five years after that war, after that terrible war. And I would never ask questions, and my brother didn't ask—all the children of this generation that I know never asked questions of their parents, during this period. In a definite sense they felt it was unspeakable. And I agree. In all senses of the term—it is terrible . . . it is unspeakable." Georges, too, has never heard of Valy, never heard her name, never heard his mother mention her, though surely, in Vienna at least, Lotte and Valy would have known each other.

So then I ask about that line—the "oldest one," a boy—perhaps a son?—who seems to have died, and Georges is startled. He has no idea what I'm talking about. I read him the letter. He is shocked. Overwhelmed. I say that if Lotte lost a son—if that's what that line means, unless she is referring to her older brother—perhaps she felt it was too much of a trauma to share. He is horrified by the idea. Completely shocked. We hang up uncertain, both intimates and strangers. I have a hard time reaching him again. I'm not sure he wants to hear from me. I feel terrible about having disclosed this information to him, about having made him consider the possibility that there was something even more devastating his mother had never wanted him to know. Who was I to insert myself into this narrative? This wasn't even my story to tell.

Yet despite this transgression, I press on. I want to know—because I know Lotte and my grandfather were close—I want to know what her sons know. When I find myself in Israel for work, sometime after that Skype call, I arrange to meet Georges's brother, Gilbert, who made aliyah many years ago, from France. Gilbert explains that his father was one of a large Polish Jewish family that moved to France just before the war—a half-dozen brothers and sisters, leaving their parents behind. Those paternal grandparents, just like Lotte's parents, were murdered. He thinks Lotte and his father met sometime during the war, that she found work with his father.

I then tell this Israeli Sudarskis about Lotte's first postwar letter, and that strange, melancholy line *we have lost our oldest*—and the child I believe Lotte lost. He, too, does not quite believe it; he has never heard anything like it; his mother certainly said nothing. I tell him, too, that since my conversation with Georges, I have been able to discover more of what happened to his immediate family. But perhaps because we have just met, or because our meeting is rushed, a breakfast in the center of Jerusalem, a civilized moment of poached eggs with asparagus in the upper-middle-class posh neighborhood of Rehavia, or perhaps because he is so very happy that I reached out, I don't tell him that I have a letter from his grandparents, accusing my grandfather and great-grandmother of not helping them. It was one of the letters I first read when I began looking for Valy; it was so shocking— so devastating—my neighbor, a German journalist, who read it with me shook as he helped me decipher the impossible handwriting.

> *Vienna, June 19, 1941 To Sara Wildmann*
> *[my great-grandmother]*

> *Dear Aunt,*
> *... It is directly a story from heaven, how you left me here, sick. ...*
> *You don't think about asking us if we are still alive. I am ashamed*
> *when other people are asking if I received letters from you to say I*
> *haven't heard anything from you. And I don't get any sign of life.*
> *... I had to sell everything I have so that I can survive. ... I am*
> *here with my family and I have no clue and I am completely helpless.*
> *Dear aunt. The only thing I cannot understand is that you once had*
> *a good character. And now you have forgotten us. I am now*
> *desperate. And God should forgive our bad thoughts. And so dear*
> *aunt I ask you . . .*

It is written in a manic scrawl, with ink that bleeds through the paper. The author is my grandfather's half brother Manele, and, accusations aside, I now know he actually had a chance to leave but didn't take it.

Manele's file was among those that were found by the Viennese Jewish community—the Israelitische Kultusgemeinde Wien, or IKG—at the turn of this millennium: a collection of hundreds of thousands of pages, a strange, dusty, moldy assemblage of notes, abandoned and forgotten, in a downtown Vienna attic—desperate requests to get out of the trap that Vienna had become, official questionnaires filled out by frantic would-be émigrés, looking for exit visas and for financial assistance to leave. For over ten years, the U.S. Holocaust Memorial Museum, with the Jewish community of Vienna, worked to organize, preserve, and microfilm the material. In the summer of 2012, I was finally able to peer inside the holdings in the Austrian Jewish Archives and inquire what they had for the Wildmann family. Sure enough, there is a clear request filled out, stamped September 5, 1939, from Manele, almost exactly one year to the day after my grandfather left for New York.

Manele, I see, when I go over the file at the U.S. Holocaust Memorial Museum with the help of an Austrian-American researcher named Anatol Steck, was a grocer, a merchant. Some months later I will go to visit the home address he lists on his questionnaire. The apartment is in the heart of Vienna's posh first district, in a massive, dove-white marble building, carved with cherubs; the shop itself is nearby, on Bäckerstrasse. The grocery is now a mountaineering shop. Across the way is the Kaffee Alt Wien, which opened in 1936 as a coffeehouse. These days it is dark and smoky, with red banquettes, the walls plastered over with posters advertising past music concerts; it's a scene of cheap beers and a crowd of late-night drinkers (it stays open well into the wee hours of the morning)—but when Manele ran his shop across the street, the deep wood of the bar would have been for *ein grosser Brauner*—a large espresso—and he would have had the chance to drink there, each morning, until Jews were forbidden to enter Aryan establishments. The IKG file makes very clear what would have happened to my grandfather had he not fled when he did:

MANELE WILDMANN #38,016

Did you learn a new trade? *No.*

Do you speak other languages? *German and some Hebrew.*

What is your current economic position and income? *Not good. I'm destitute.*

Are you in a position to get all the necessary documents for the emigration? *Yes.*

Where do you want to go? *To Palestine.*

What means do you have to facilitate your immigration? *Keine Mittel. [No means at all.]*

What relationships do you have abroad, especially in the country where you want to emigrate to? *Ephraim Wildman, living in Petach Tikva. Son. Working in gastronomy—a restaurant— Worked at an orange plantation since 1932.*

Do you have a valid passport: *No.*

Relatives?

Daughter: Lotte Wildmann born in Vienna; profession Sales.

Blanka born in Vienna; also in Sales.

Then there is Josef Moses Wildmann born in Vienna, cobbler.

Wife: Chaja Sarah Wildmann. Housewife.

In his own words he continues:

I have a son in Petach Tikva who has written me that he has applied for me as well as my wife and my fourteen-year-old son to come; he believes that in October he will get the permission. But considering the fact I also have two daughters age 18 and 20 whom he cannot apply for, I am now forced to approach to ask the help and advice of the emigration department and then . . . as I'm asking the emigration department for their advice because it would only be an option if we could all go together and then my son can help us with advice and action.

I had on Bäckerstrasse a small grocery store. And that helped us to basically feed ourselves . . . but now we are able to feed ourselves only barely with a lot of distress. I have nothing to sell. I do not know whether there will be any income that might be used for the passage. We are living off our own provisions.

On the next page it is decided: Manele and Chaja have elected to send their young son, but they will not go with him.

> Name: *Josef Moses Wildmann*
>
> Number of persons to destination: *One person to Palestine. One ticket from Vienna to Palestine*
>
> Money provided by applicant: *Zero*
>
> Still to be provided: *Zero*
>
> Current living conditions: *one room, one cabinet, one kitchen. Living room bedroom and a kitchen.*

"That is where the whole family is living for 33 Reichsmark per month. That's the rent. It says they have sublet part of it," says Anatol, who is reading to me from the document.

> Family relationships: *To remain behind: the parents and one sister.*
>
> Paid by: *Hachshara Mizrachi*
>
> Notes by the community: *[Josef] Has an elementary and basic schooling Hauptschule [trade school] and then Gymnasium. He has not earned a living yet. Father of the applicant had a small grocery store until October 23, 1938. The store was closed due to lack of stock/produce. They ate it all. The father of the applicant receives 15 m every month from the Jewish community in support and receives food from the soup kitchen for the last 8 months*
>
> *6 September 1939*
>
> *He [Josef] has luggage, and one bicycle.*
>
> Connections to abroad: Certificate comes from the brother.

The Jewish community interviewer of the Wildmann family— who it so happened was the same Wilhelm Reisz who commits suicide in Doron Rabinovici's book—then adds an aside:

> *Information supplied is believable. Applicant makes a good impression.*
> *The need and the precarious situation are established by the above*
> *information. Approved 6 September 1939.*

All this means, I realize: Manele and his wife, Chaja, believed they would be able to leave, but they would have only been able to take with them Josef, the youngest one. "He was applying to the immigration department for the whole family to travel together," says Anatol. But in the end only Josef was sent to Palestine, alone. The girls, too, eventually fled. But their parents were, by then, stuck. "Often the older generation was left behind," he explains.

My grandfather probably never knew exactly what happened to his half brother and his wife. But I do: in the last few years, all of the Gestapo files of Vienna have been scanned and placed online.

Manele and Chaja were arrested on the thirtieth and thirty-first of July 1941. In the end, they were not even granted the dignity of dying together: Manele was sent to Auschwitz, where he died in November; Chaja to Ravensbrück, where she lived until the following June. Their Gestapo files, and mug shots, are on files placed online by the DÖW—the Documentation Centre of Austrian Resistance. They look ravaged, worn, far older than their years; a long metal pole holds their heads up, like specimens. Chaja's hair is messy, undone from her bun. Manele's face looks bewildered, shot with exhaustion. Their life until deportation would have been complete misery.

For his part, in 1950, Karl went to Vienna to see what—who—was left. The city was still digging out from war destruction. Did he look for Valy on that trip? I have no notes, I have no messages from him to say what he did or with whom he met, or even what his impressions were of the city he had left behind twelve years earlier. I only know that he then went to Israel and met the surviving cousins. Of that leg of the journey, I have photos; Israel looks dusty and hot; large areas of land I know now as suburbs of Tel Aviv look expansive, unbuilt.

He began to patch up old relationships, reconnect with childhood friends. By this point, he had become the successful doctor Valy had believed him to be in 1941; by 1946 and 1950, he was flush enough to be able to give out small loans and donations to relatives—including money to Josef Wildmann, the son of Manele, who was still living in Tel Aviv. Affidavits were sent from one side of the globe to the other. There was contrition, there was redemption, there was, if not forgiveness, some resolution.

It must have taken some time. There are many letters that are so angry, so bruised by what the writers have been through, that they lash out at my grandfather for having the temerity not to have experienced it beyond 1938. And they are still—unlike the letters that come later—they are still talking about the war, what they lost. It is unfair to be angry with Karl, of course, and yet what has been fair for them? And yet still, as much as I scan, no one can tell me if they have heard news of Valy or her mother.

Tel Aviv, II/XII/1950

My very dear Karl:

Finally, after waiting for such a long time, I got your letter. You are making us wait too long. I was sure that you had forgotten about us. In German one would say "Out of sight, out of heart." It has been four months. . . . I was very angry with you because you were so close to me, not just like a cousin, but more like a brother. As you know well, only little remained of our entire family. Our greatest joy is to know that somewhere, far away, on the other side of the ocean, there are close relatives of ours who show keen interest in what remains of the former large family. . . . Oh, how nice it would be to have you nearby in Palestine. That would be our greatest happiness. My advice would be to everyone to sell and liquidate everything and come to Ha'Eretz, because Israel is the only right place for Jews. . . .

You are not mentioning anything about dear Uncle Sam and the

*cousins. Are they not interested in being in touch with us by letter, or
do they not recognize us as relatives? After Hitler's war, the entire
Jewish world was trembling, and everybody was looking for relatives
and friends. Everybody wanted to know whether they were still
alive, whether they needed anything. We are not so lucky to have
relatives and close acquaintances who take an interest in how we are
living; they are our cousins, and that is very sad. As God is our
Witness,—we are not looking for any kind of [financial] support but
rather contact by letter with our own family.*

The writer is cousin Reuven Ben-Shem (born Feldschuh; Ben-
Shem was a zionification of his name). As a student in the 1920s,
Reuven lived with my grandfather in Vienna and studied psychology
with Freud. He had spent several years in Palestine, where he had
been a founder of the Kibbutz Kiryat Anavim, outside Jerusalem. He
returned to Europe in the early 1920s, when he received word his father had been murdered in a Ukrainian pogrom.

My grandfather was twelve years Reuven's junior, also orphaned,
and they were very close. Reuven went on to work in Poland—as a
journalist, as a writer, as an editor. He married a musicologist named
Pnina, and together they had a daughter named Josima, who was a
piano prodigy. Pnina encouraged them to stay in Poland, even after
the Germans invaded.

Late on a Friday night in the Tel Aviv suburb of Ramat Gan, a few
days after I met Gilbert Sudarskis, I find myself at a Shabbat dinner
with Reuven's family. The guests have moved from the table to a sag-
ging leather couch, an array of liquor lined up on the coffee table. Our
host, Kami Ben-Shem, Reuven's son born after the war to his second
wife, goes into a backroom and brings out a selection of crumbling
yellow paper. The first page, which is kept in a plastic sleeve, is an announcement for a concert. It is dated at the top "15 March 1941";
"Josima Feldschuh," it says, above the image of a rosy-cheeked girl
with a bow in her hair, sitting at a piano, and then, below her photo,

in Polish, "11 year old piano virtuoso." The program promises selections from Mozart's *Marriage of Figaro* and Schubert's Unfinished Symphony, a concert held at Rymarska 12, in the heart of the Warsaw Ghetto.

Reuven faithfully recorded everything that he saw, everything he experienced, in a diary. "The dead are naked," he wrote. "When someone had just starved, they cover him in wrapping paper and lay him down on the sidewalk, and at night his friends, or just beggars, walk out, and undress him completely, and leave him all naked with no shoes, no dress or even underwear." Josima, Kami's half sister, was smuggled to the Aryan side just before the Warsaw Ghetto uprising took the German army by surprise. Her father had feared for her safety during all his months in the ghetto.

January 1942. There's talk recently of the vandals murdering the children and the blood of all the fathers hardens in their veins as they listen to such whispers. . . . I returned home and I am all shaken. My child is sleeping, I am looking at her. My eye deceives me and I don't see her. She disappears, the bed grows empty. I was frightened. I bent over and held her so forcefully that she woke up, quizzical and afraid. She calmed down as she saw me, and her face radiated with a lovely smile. She sent me a kiss by air, turned over to her side, and fell asleep. Inside me fritters a demon of fear.

This prescient parental anxiety jolts me. We all sit and watch our children sleep, I think, reading this. We watch them and wonder how to protect them from the outside world, and our world is so much less imminently dangerous, there is no comparison.

And Reuven's anxiety was borne out: Josima died of tuberculosis some weeks after she went into hiding; soon after, her mother, Pnina, took her own life. Only Reuven survived. After the war, Reuven never spoke of Josima, but her framed photo hung like a ghostly mezuzah in the doorway to his home, so each member of Ben-Shem's new postwar family would see her as they came in and as they went out.

We, the American cousins, knew little to nothing of Josima—although we vaguely knew Reuven had lost everyone, and that he had named his postwar son Nekamiah, "Revenge of God" or "Revenge! God!" His second marriage was to another survivor, with an equally harrowing tale—this was Ruth, who saw her own sister be murdered before her eyes; she herself jumped from the train to Treblinka, leaving behind a half-dozen siblings.

My grandfather's Viennese world was so embittered, so angry—at their fate, but also at him for having missed the worst of it. He got off easy; it is the subtext of their letters. It was a bitterness that transcended generations, seeped through to our modern, easier lives.

I spent a weekend with Kami, as Nekamiah is known, his wife, Shely, and their daughter, Sharon, in Ramat Gan, when I was twenty and Sharon nineteen, she and I lying on thin twin mattresses, plotting ways to meet soldiers and then slipping out to go dancing to American music in Israeli clubs. But then I returned, some weeks later, during Pesach, and I felt the family mocked me, assumed I had no history, no knowledge of Jewish life, because of growing up in America. "Do you know what anti-Semitism is?" Kami asked during the Seder, in front of his guests; then he asked if I understood the Seder plate, if I had been to a Seder before. I didn't understand, then, that it wasn't a mocking so much as a real question. I didn't understand at all—the Israelis were chiding me in a similar way to how Karl's cohort chided him. They thought we were so smug and secure in America, while they suffered in Europe or in Israel. That we didn't help, that we had no idea how it all really happened then, what the Israelis had lived through, now, what we benefited from by their very presence in the Jewish state. They pushed me to agree to move to Israel for good, I couldn't possibly be happy, or safe, in America, as a Jew. It was too much. I went in another room and burst into tears.

Our family was *destroyed*, they said. We have *no one but each other.* But I didn't hear that; instead, I heard them mocking my Hebrew, I heard their intimations that I didn't know anything about Judaism, let alone Israel. I felt unwelcome. In my journal I write of my tears, and that I did not spend the night that night, nor would I on any subsequent night. I didn't want any part of their Israel, the Israel that seemed to look only backward, toward the persecution that had ejected us from Europe. I stopped contacting them.

But when I meet them now, a decade and a half later, I am chagrined. They are all older, the parents, the children. Sharon now has two girls of her own. It is Shely, her mother, I see first. "I remember you cried," Shely says upon greeting me, recalling that I fled the table, recalling my tears. "You were homesick I think?" And they all feel so much less threatening, and so much more important, than I had realized so long ago. "Your grandfather was so warm," Kami says to me, over dinner. "He was such a presence in my childhood." He says my grandfather came to see them, again and again, throughout the years. I was wrong in my youthful assessment of him. Kami, like me, cannot fully grasp what these men went through. We have all lived easier lives.

Sharon is chagrined that my experience with them, at twenty, was so raw. "Maybe this can be a bit of a *tikkun*, a reparation, a balm," she says of our meeting now, reconciling over the achievements of her grandfather—we meet so I can write a story about this amazing diary, this unknown document that he smuggled with him from Warsaw to Tel Aviv—and the stories of our past. We are walking on the boardwalk at Namal Tel Aviv, the Tel Aviv port. It is sunny and lovely and the sea stretches out before us. Children are everywhere, running and screaming. I am pregnant, again; it seems every other woman around me is as well. There are balloon-blowing clowns and bicyclists, and dozens of restaurants. We get pomegranate juice squeezed for us, and sit. I tell them about my search for Valy, about the photos and letters that were kept for decades, reminders, painful pressure points. And I ask Kami—*was Reuven happy?* And Kami takes a breath and looks at his wife and then at the table. He is a big man—I remember this from when I first met him—tall with a mass of curls that have grayed in the years since we last met. But the question seems to cause him to shrink. He smiles slightly when he looks back at me, and says he is not sure that his father—if any of them—was ever happy, that any of them ever could truly be.

I'm not sure. My grandfather, I think, really did live a happy life. He insisted upon happiness, almost, perhaps, as his own revenge. Nevertheless: he kept the letters that reminded him of when he was powerless. Of when there was nothing to be done.

As I sit in an open-air restaurant with Kami and Sharon and Shely, I look out over the sea. And I realize one thing is glaringly absent from these later letters, from when the 1940s turn into a new, more peaceful decade and the requests for money and for visits are met with affirmations—*Yes, I can help*, Karl writes again and again, *Yes, I will send money, Yes, I will come* to Tel Aviv, to Switzerland, to France. He hears from many, many people. But the name of Valy Scheftel is no longer mentioned anywhere. She simply disappears from the correspondence.

Thirteen

VIENNA INTERLUDE

I am back in Vienna. It's the summer of 2012 and I have an assignment from *Travel & Leisure* that fills up my days with tours of restaurants and shops, neighborhoods and activities, but in the spaces in
between, it also gives me the latitude to search—and think—a bit
more, about the city of Valy and Karl. I set out early each morning, to
walk. Crossing the plaza in front of the Rathaus, the City Hall, one
day, I am overwhelmed by a tremendous feeling of good fortune: it is
a privilege to know this city well, to have close friends here, to feel
I—if not belong, exactly, that I feel at ease here, despite everything.

In the second district, I pause and look out across the Donaukanal
toward the U-Bahn station Rossauer Lände; I have photographs of
Valy and Karl at this very spot; she is pushing her hair back and smiling into the wind, he is contemplative, their faces smooth, unworried
and young.

I walk once more to the places she mentions in her letters—
Heinestrasse, the Augarten. A Saturday farmers' market bustles in
suddenly hip Karmelitermarkt, and I wander through, sampling produce from vendors. I sip coffee in one of the newer cafés, and then
head toward my grandfather's old block on Rueppgasse. For the

first time I notice a name next to his apartment number. I debate ringing the bell, then don't.

I have a strange relationship to Vienna; I've been many, many times now and, somehow, I love it. I love the eighteenth- and nineteenth-century buildings set against the sky when the weather is fresh and clear. I love the endless number of *Kinos*, the 1960s-era cinemas, and the old coffeehouses. I love wandering the city alone at night, from the glass Palmenhaus outside the Albertina Museum through the first district, by foot or taking one of the rent-a-bikes with my friend Georg, together careening past the Museumsquartier in the seventh district. I love the ridiculous surfeit of cultural venues, the Volksoper, the Staatsoper, the Burgtheater. I have a memory connected to each—this is where I saw the Nederlands Dans Theater with Alice and Ingvild; this is where I saw some strange, avant-garde dance with Karin; this is where I stood in back for the first time, mimicking my grandfather and his friends, at the Musikverein; this is where I went to learn to waltz; this is where I sat until far into the night, over wine and cigarettes, with Sophie; this is where I danced with Andrea. And at the same time my relationship to the city remains, inevitably, fraught. I am constantly swept back up into the drama of this lost love, these lives cut short, and this unresolved pain.

In Washington, this summer, Anatol Steck, at the Holocaust Museum, the purveyor and translator of the long-lost Jewish community files, connected me to a half-dozen Viennese academics I'd never met before this trip. So, with Anatol's introductions in hand, I race across Heldenplatz, where Hitler first announced the Anschluss to adoring

Austrians. This day it is packed with a beer festival; dozens upon dozens of women are in dirndls, their breasts pushed up high, their Austrian nationalism unabashedly forthright, their hair in braids, their men in lederhosen. I am late to see Doron Rabinovici, whose book *Eichmann's Jews*, about the role Jews played, their complicity, or their lack of agency, in their own destruction in this city, has just been translated into English. He tells me about how dour he found it to move to Vienna, in the 1960s,  from Israel, where he was born, a bit like going from the Technicolor scenes of *The Wizard of Oz* into the black-and-white. Then, as we talk about dead Jews, and live Jews, and Jewish life—suddenly, as though we ourselves are in a film about Jewish Vienna—up comes Ruth Beckermann, the best-known living Viennese Jewish filmmaker, to say hello to him. There is a very, very small cast of characters in the active Jewish world of Vienna.

But it is a young academic whom Steck insists I meet, named Tina Walzer, who leaves the deepest impression. Walzer asks me to meet her at the Währinger Jewish cemetery just past Nussdorfer Strasse, on the other side of the Gürtel, the belt that rings the periphery of the city. It takes me some time to find the cemetery entrance, but when I do I am overwhelmed. I walk in alone—I am early, or she is late—and Währinger is unlike anything I've ever seen in person. It has been nearly entirely reclaimed by nature. There are branches and bushes and trees and brambles and a path—is that even a path?—packed with gray mud, cracked and dusty. Things seem to crawl up my bare legs, get inside my sandals—I need boots to be in here. But it is not the overgrowth that gets me: the graves themselves are in various stages of decay and disarray and vandalism, they are broken in two, in twelve, in hundreds of shards of clay.

There are pieces of bone on the ground—a femur, a bit of skull. There are fully open graves crawling with ivy. There are smashed headstones. Our history is often served to us so sanitized, so clean. This is decidedly unvarnished. This reminds me of a story that sent me with archaelogists in Spain to uncover Spanish civil war mass graves. It is an open wound.

Despite myself, I am overcome. My eyes, my throat, burn. When Walzer arrives I have tears running down my face. I say, "I didn't realize it would be so bad," which I immediately wish I could retract, as she has worked hard to better this space. On my tape I can hear my sniffling, my hurried attempt to pull myself back together.

Walzer explains that the cemetery was opened in 1784 and closed in 1885—it was open to all Jews, not just prominent ones—and it once encompassed a far larger area—she points to high-rise white buildings a few hundred feet away, public housing, she says, that stands on what was hallowed ground. "There were thirty thousand graves," she tells me, "but you only see about eighty-five hundred tombstones now."

A very prominent garden architect was employed here just after World War I, and this was once a marvelous place, a park. "It was well kept until 1938—until the National Socialists took over. Then the gardener was killed and no one ever showed up again. No one else was interested. It was totally forgotten."

I ask about the desecration—the split stones, the open graves, the bones. Walzer says all this stems from just after the Anschluss. It took place while Karl and Valy were still here. The graves were exhumed, in part, after Hitler spoke to the adoring masses at Heldenplatz; the Naturhistorisches Museum took the skulls from these graves for racial

profiling, to display the differences in the Jewish skeleton. Further: this holy land was sold off in parcels when the Jewish community was forced to raise money for their own deportation. Money raised in these fire sales was used to pay for the trains that took the Jews to Auschwitz and Ravensbrück, among other camps.

Walzer points to a building in the distance. Twenty-five hundred graves were once on that land, she says. A bulldozer "went into the cemetery and took the soil—with the bones—and this soil and bones were used to repair the streets of Vienna and around Gürtel Strasse, all in front of Westbahnhof—the train station. I want a marker there, because when you get out of the train, what do you step on? The cemetery."

When I marvel that it has remained so overgrown, that the bones and the open graves still stand there, as though we have stepped back in time, she sighs. "In fact it is relatively well kept now," she says. "I had to clean the whole place on my own. No one was willing to pay for that." There is not enough money, the Jewish community has struggled with infighting, with what to do with this destroyed space. They are stuck: to totally clean up the desecration will take away the visual impact of seeing the destruction wrought by the Nazi occupation. But to leave the cemetery as it is renders it unsafe for the general public to enter, ensures it will stay hidden, forgotten, forever. Walzer regrets, in some ways, having taken on the task at all, and yet I can see what drew her here, what made her feel someone had to do something.

I ask her how she started this project—Why her? Why this?—and she tells me that throughout her childhood, she felt, somehow, peculiarly connected to the period of German occupation. When she studied the war in high school, and her class was shown the images, the films, from the opening of the camps, "I had the feeling this has something to do with me. It was very strange." Her mother refused to speak of the period. "She said, 'Go talk to your grandmother.'"

With that, at age fifteen or so, Tina discovered her mother and grandmother—and therefore she herself—were Jewish. Her grandfather, she learned, had been deported, in the early years of the war, and her grandmother then fled east, to Shanghai. Before she did, uncertain of whether she would survive the journey, she placed Tina's mother, then a toddler of one year, with a Viennese Christian family. In 1946, Tina's grandmother returned and took her now-six-year-old daughter—Tina's mother—away from the only family she had ever known. Her mother never forgave her grandmother for not taking her to Shanghai. "It must have been terrible," says Tina. "And my grandmother didn't understand why my mother was not grateful for saving her life. So, no one ever wanted to talk about this and my mother didn't want to speak of anything—of being Jewish or Judaism or anything." It was, yet again, the story of an unhappy survival.

Such secrets aren't uncommon in my generation. Perhaps Tina's is more extreme than some—a lost grandfather? A purposely suppressed Jewish past?—but is it really so different from the ways all families tell stories and create their own narratives? That night I go out with Herwig and Georg and we talk of family secrets, the things we have discovered as we have grown older, about our own grandparents—their hidden lives. We talk again about the history we have all come to live through, to investigate, even as we move forward.

———

The following day, outside Café Sperl, the nineteenth-century *Kaffeehaus* that hugs a corner of Gumpendorferstrasse, all soaring windows, velvet banquettes, and surly service, and so iconic it was used in the filming of *Before Sunrise*, that Ethan Hawke–Julie Delpy movie about love and connections and youthful optimism, I meet another historian, Ingo Zechner. He has read my original series of stories on Valy and my grandfather, and I have the feeling he feels he knows me somehow and, as a result, that we are already intimates. He is young— or, at least, only slightly older than I—but he was involved in the incredibly belated efforts to compensate Jews for their lost property, and their (monetary) claims of victimization, starting in 2000. We talk about why he abandoned Carinthia, his childhood home, the area of Austria long sullied by racist leaders, why he became a historian, why he works so deeply in the history of the Holocaust, how he has been affected and directed by the history of Austria.

Many months later, in Washington, D.C., Ingo will show me a series of films taken in Vienna just after the Anschluss that have only just begun to be analyzed. They are home movies, amateur videos, taken by bystanders in March 1938. They show Jews scrubbing the streets, surrounded by pulsating, massive, jeering crowds, and storefronts defiled by anti-Jewish graffiti. They highlight the unbelievable number of flags and swastikas that appear suddenly from one day to the next in the streets. Indeed, these shorts reveal the takeover of the city in a way so tactile, so brutal, so visual, they underscore how deeply personal the Nazification of the city must have felt. In one film that I ask Ingo to play for me again and again, I see Karl's precious University of Vienna appear on screen—the steps in front of one of the lecture halls are filled with goose-stepping Nazis singing *"Deutschland, Deutschland, über alles."*

By the time I see those films, I have given birth again, to another girl. This is the second daughter I have grown and birthed while I searched for Valy. My friends in Austria are having children now, too—Georg and his girlfriend, Ana, have a daughter just a week before my partner, Ian, and I do. We exchange messages, gifts, photos, promises to get the families together. Next summer, we say, we'll climb the Rax mountain range, just as Valy and Karl once did. Do these girls need these stories, too? How can we impart this history without the burden?

Fourteen

ENTZÜCKEN

Years ago my father told me that the most jarring moment for him at the Holocaust Museum in Washington wasn't seeing the cattle car that visitors are invited to walk through—though that was, as it is meant to be, emotionally manipulative, deeply evocative, and disturbing—but instead encountering a photo that museumgoers are presented with at the beginning of the permanent exhibit. The image, at first, appears to reveal very little: a line of women and men, hundreds long; they could be waiting for anything.

It is a photograph of Jews seeking exit visas in Vienna in the weeks after the Anschluss. My grandfather was on that line.

Recently, a new document was added to that section of the permanent exhibition. It is a massive flow chart tracing the steps Jews had to take before they could flee Vienna, drawn up, in 1938, by the Jewish community itself. It was only discovered, in an attic, after the turn of this millennium. There was a horrifically complicated system of looting and subjugation that each frantic Jew had to go through—my grandfather, of course, included: each step toward emigration cost a fee, a tax of sorts, and with each payment, a stamp was received. At the end, once all the stamps were presented to a final office, a passport

and transit papers may or may not have been issued—all of which had
to be used within a tiny window of time, or the whole thing would
expire and the process would start again. That any Jew was able to
winnow his way through that morass, to come through to the other
side, was in and of itself heroic, improbable.

The first time I came across the box of letters in my parents' basement,
"Correspondence, Patients A–G," that very first time I pawed through
it, I pulled out a folded, deeply yellowed sheet of paper with Valy's
basic information on it—her birth date, her address at the Babelsberg
old-age home, her full name—Dr. Valerie Scheftel. It was dated 1943,
and it was a request to HIAS, the Hebrew Immigrant Aid Society; my
grandfather had scrawled notes on it. He was already married, he was
already in the army, and he was looking for Valy. But HIAS didn't
have any information for him.

I can find no further information about what happened to Valy
after she boarded the 27th Ost Transport from Putlitzstrasse train station in Berlin Moabit to Auschwitz. She may have died en route. She
may have been gassed upon arrival. I know only that she had no number assigned to her, and the vast majority of those who arrived in
Auschwitz and received no number were those deemed, immediately,
expendable. Extinguishable. If she survived the seventeen-and-a-half-
hour journey, crammed up against her fellow Jews, crushed into that
breathless space, she would have emerged onto the freezing platform
into what seemed, that terribly cold year, to be an endlessly sleeting
rain. She would have been bewildered, thirsty, exhausted. Immediately there would have been shouting. The Gestapo beat the prisoners
with sticks, with rubber truncheons. Everyone was screaming at the
selections—from the prisoners to the SS guards barking orders—
Remove watches! All valuables removed! Valy would have been told
to move to the left, and Hans to the right. Perhaps they cried out;
perhaps they grasped hands, perhaps they tried to remain together.

But of this I can only guess. I can find no eyewitness accounts of those moments, of that particular day. And try as I might, I have not found a single person who heard from her after January 29, 1943. She disappears.

Some time ago, on one of my visits to her apartment, Tonya, my grandfather's first girlfriend in America, whispered to me that she'd heard Valy was an "angel" in the camps, a "Florence Nightingale" nursing the inmates. She was sure she'd heard that Valy had lived in Auschwitz for a very long time and tended to those who fell ill. I can't possibly know if there's even an inkling of truth to this, but it is fascinating. It speaks to what we want to believe as much as what we do believe; it speaks to the myth that built up around Valy in the wake of my grandfather's love and guilt and anger that, occasionally, it seems, spilled out when he mentioned her. As much as I loved my grandmother, and, of course, without her I would not be here, the myth of Valy's ghostly campside nursing skills seems a part of that vague sense all those who knew of her held on to—that something beautiful was lost when she was left behind.

Hans, unlike his wife, has a death certificate. It is dated February 15—just over two weeks after their arrival in Auschwitz. He was among the 140 men selected for work on January 30, but he died soon after. The cause of death recorded was *Pleuropneumonie*—pneumonia.

Ernest Fontheim, Hans's best friend, believes that his quick death was of a broken heart, or a suicide, not illness. Ernest is sure that Hans wouldn't have wanted to live without Valy, that he threw himself on an electrified fence, or got himself shot, out of sorrow. He is sure that Hans was too strong to die so fast, too quick-witted not to survive the camps. To die so soon of pneumonia seems unlikely to me, too—but then again, it was deep winter, and there was no means of recovery, no antibiotics, no one who would have tried to nurse him back to health.

I don't know for sure that Hans's death was as romantic as Ernest believes. The truth is stark: not a single person returned from the 27th transport to the east. Not one of the 1,004 ever found his or her way back to Germany. So whether Hans was murdered immediately, by bullet or, later, by electrocution or deprivation, is less important than the very fact that Hans, like every other person on that train, was murdered, whatever the cause of death listed may claim.

Ernest still regrets Hans's and Valy's disappearance. "I have gone over the events of that day innumerable times," he wrote Hans's sister, Ilse, in 1999. "It was a monumental tragedy. There is no doubt in my mind that Hans had the intelligence, stamina, strength of character, and ability to adapt himself quickly to changed, unexpected circumstances, all of which were necessary for surviving underground."

To me he said the same: in some ways he has never forgiven himself for not saving them. He spent that January day in 1943 trying to protect Valy, and in the end, he believes, Hans protected him. "I have gone over that day again and again since—in the last what is it? Almost seventy years. Sixty-seven years . . . I don't know. [The Gestapo was] going through the entire street, they went door to door with the furniture van used to pick up Jews to take them to the transit camp on Grosse Hamburger Strasse. In many apartments there must have been someone missing: people were out at work like Hans was, or were out visiting someone, or God knows where else."

Ernest fears that the Gestapo specifically placed an agent in that apartment to trap him, as much as to trap his friends; he worries that his efforts to save Valy actually endangered Hans, maybe endangered them both. In Ann Arbor, the afternoon I spent with Ernest, I was sure it couldn't possibly be the case.

Months after my visit, I received a scan of Hans's Siemens work card from the archivists at the International Tracing Service. The card was typed; listed first are his name, birth date, and address. A line gives his "entry date," the day he started work, as April 29, 1941. At the next line, designated "exit date," someone typed—or stamped— "__.2.43"; the font is heavier, the ink darker than for the other typeface on the card. A space was left for the date in February to be filled in. I can't know with absolute certainty, but it appears that

Hans's expected departure was February 1943. But then, by hand, "2.43" is carefully crossed out in red pen. Written alongside it, in the same red pen, is "1.18.43," the last day he actually worked.

Hans, it seems, was *not meant to leave Siemens in January*. That his overseers assumed he'd be leaving in February indicates they may have anticipated him being swept up in the February *Fabrikaktion*, when so many workers were taken, en masse, from the factories themselves. I looked at the card dozens of times; I might be wrong, of course. They might have simply filled in all dates for Jewish workers in advance. They might have assumed all Jews would be taken in February. Yet it appears possible that Hans was captured before he was meant to be deported. But either way: that he was going to be taken was never in question.

Ernest partly blames himself, but surely Hans would have balked if Valy had been arrested first and he had been spared. After all, Hans had already saved her once. He had already given Valy a few extra weeks of life when he rescued her from Babelsberg by rushing to marry her. And, really, the idea of blame here has no meaning.

———

When the war ended, Ernest returned to Berlin. Newsreels of the end of the war show a city nearly razed to the ground, the population stumbling over the detritus of what was once the center of the Thousand Year Reich. All around were shells of buildings, the dead, and the haunted eyes of the survivors, perpetrator and victim side by side in search of their loved ones. Ernest spent hours upon hours walking in those early weeks, from one end of town to the other, searching for news. Of his group of friends, none who were deported to the east returned. Only he and those who had gone into hiding were left. Everyone else was missing.

"At the Jewish community, a running registry was kept of people who returned either from living underground," like Ernest, "or from concentration camps," Ernest told me when I visited him in Ann

Arbor. "And of course I was looking for Hans and Valy, as well as my parents and sister, and a few other relatives and friends. I went there at least once a month. The registry was kept initially in the Jewish Hospital in Iranische Strasse and I lived in Tempelhof, across Berlin, and the first few months after the end of the war there was no public transportation, so I had to walk from Tempelhof. It was a tremendously long walk, through streets strewn with rubble and, initially, with dead corpses and so on.

"But nobody of the people that I was looking for ever appeared."

———

Ernest has sought, for decades, for a way to memorialize Hans and Valy—and his parents and his sister. His experience is, in some ways, the photonegative of my grandfather's; he did not leave in time, and his time in the Reich has shaped his life, shaped his sense of guilt, or at least his sense of loss, in ways that my grandfather did not share—in part because Karl did not see the full extent of the horror, and in part because of their distinctly different personalities. Ernest watched almost everyone he'd ever loved taken from him. My grandfather, at least, had his sister, his mother, his brother-in-law, and his nephew. Eventually, too, he had three of his closest friends. And, of course, he had my grandmother. She wasn't European born, but she was his intellectual match. It was not the world of his youth, or his father's, but it was more than enough to begin life anew in America.

I don't even know if my grandfather tried to memorialize those lost to him—but then, in 1990 when he died, such memorials were less common—and he had my grandmother to consider. Someone who might not have appreciated a grand gesture for the lover he'd left behind.

———

Valy's story, and my grandfather's, became a part of my blood and bones in the last few years. What once appeared to be a simple legacy—a grandfather who escaped, who created a better life away from the European killing fields—became a story of a world upended, a life set aside, a narrative rerouted.

"*My very dearest Bruno,*" my grandfather wrote on March 28, 1977. I was two years old.

> *I attended a UJA [United Jewish Appeal] meeting last night— film, narrator, Israeli songs and dances, Mauthausen, Tel Aviv, El Al, Jerusalem, many emotions, reflexes, pathos, pride and vows. In all this and in spite of all this, I can't get rid of the feeling that for whatever reasons—and there are many and varied ones—America has indeed produced a homo novus, immensely attractive in his naivete, Unbefangenheit and Heiterkeit [impartiality and serenity], yet missing that emotional dimension which alone lends substance to a concept, to a feeling, to a commitment, indeed, to being. Somehow there is a hollow ring to the American pathos and an emotional ignorance of the identity of the Jew, the significance of Israel and the meaning of history.*

There is something to this—the way the Holocaust has been thrown in, to lists, to our consciousness, we beat our breast and weep, we turn the channel. How much easier it will be going forward, to do so, with no survivors left to talk to us. Now those we can speak to were the very youngest survivors—the children—who themselves often lost all touchstones to their identity, who often were coached to forget.

I wish I could say I found Valy, that she was living in Brussels or Budapest or Brooklyn. I wish I could say that she had survived at all. I wish I could say that I know the truth about her life. But I can't. But then again, what is the truth of someone's life? As Aubrey Pomerance, the head of the archives at Berlin's Jewish Museum, said to me, "There is no collection that documents a person's life from moment of birth to moment of death. But you can cull a lot of information from one single document." And cull I have tried. And talk.

Instead of Valy, I found dozens of other individuals whose lives were affected or imploded by the terror of the Nazi years. I found cousins of my grandfather, scattered from Venice to Melbourne to Queens. I found dozens of my counterparts, from my generation, whose lives were shaped by the past—these are the other grandchildren, those who, like me, remain drawn in by our grandparents' stories, what they survived, what they lived through, that enabled us to be who we are, that enabled our very existence.

We aren't alone in our desire to know more, to pass something on. I have looked for Valy through the birth of two children now; it is hard not to wonder at the privilege of that opportunity.

And yet—they are all dying, our eyewitnesses. Our connections.

We, the grandchildren, have these stories we have all collected. What will our own children know of these stories? What do we want them to know? It is not the same as hearing it from the witnesses themselves. But it will have to be something. It is important that we have one another. It's not possible to remember alone.

———

My grandfather would not have survived, sanity intact, let alone thrived, if he had spent the postwar decades of his life looking backward. And yet the past was never past, merely suppressed. There were always secrets, always stories, always rumors. There was always a sense of remove, a distance from the world he had adopted, that had adopted him, a sense that only those who had gone through it with him, who had known whom he'd known, had understood those differences, could really understand what the twentieth century had wrought.

Often in these last few years I have gone back many times to the one letter I have that he wrote to her: *"I believe that you once read a book that begins with the words: 'I want to write of a generation that was destroyed by war, although it may have escaped its cannons.'"*

But of course she did not escape its cannons—and that generation he describes was really himself, his own, his life. It was he who escaped the cannons, turned his back on death, and embraced a version of life that, if not entirely truthful, became his truth. Sometimes I wonder if my grandfather hoped someone would find these letters, thus ensuring that he didn't let Valy die twice. By doing so—purposefully or not—he enabled one woman not to be disappeared.

And yet, there are no happy endings to these stories—indeed, often, and most discomfortingly, there are often no endings at all. There are still mysteries in Valy's story; mysteries I think my grandfather lived with his whole life. Surely after the war, he looked further, surely he at some point discovered—if not specifically that she went to Auschwitz—that she was gone. When I went back to look again at that photo album I found so many, many years ago, the one that prompted my grandmother's devastating comment about true love, I was bowled over by the number of her photos it contains. He kept them out of love, I imagine, but also out of guilt, and out of sorrow— for her, for his childhood, for everything that was lost.

June 30, 1986

My dear Bruno,

. . . My question remains—does unlimited freedom to come and go, to stay or leave, to attend or ignore, to eat or starve, to read or dream, create a vacuum or is it paradise at last?

It seems to me we have to remember the dreams of yesteryear. We have to reach back about 60 years to sense again our appetites, to feel again our budding egos, to define again our identities. . . .

Yesterday I went out in a canoe . . . by myself along the shoreline and across the Lake. I had an Erlebnis [experience] which I hadn't had for 50 years. For half a century I was racing by in a speed-boat or water skiing. In this half a century I saw the shoreline 1000 times but I had no concomitant inner experience. It was meaningless, empty adventure.

Yesterday's Erlebnis connected so wonderfully with the water, the shoreline the little houses I had known as a young man. There was meaning, there was an echo—strange people greeted me. There was an exhilarating sense of self in this wide world, a self I used to know—a marvelous antidote to deadening routine.

We have to stop racing and all that it implies: that there is a future, that tomorrow is more important than today. . . . We have to assign overwhelming importance to the day and to our act, our performance on this day. We have to summon our accumulated experience and our accumulated resources to fashion a day that we can live with Entzücken [delight]. Please Try!

Once when I was six years old, I went out on that canoe with my grandfather. My grandparents lived on Pontoosuc Lake in summer, strangely only about five miles from their "town" house, in the Berkshires, so close because my grandmother's father had bought the land years before the war. It was the first time I was in a canoe alone with my grandfather. I wore a life vest, but I couldn't help paddle, and at some point, along the way, he grew tired. We were stuck, pushed into a cove by the wind, or lack of wind, I can't remember exactly, and he stood and waved to a passing motorboat to tow us in. As he did so, he tipped our canoe and I was trapped underneath. I remember the light of the water and gasping for air, though there was plenty of air trapped with me. I was already a decent swimmer, but I did not know—or know how—to take off my life vest and so I bobbed there, terrified and trapped, until I felt him, powerful, pull me out from under the boat in one fell swoop, through the water. "I was always there," he said. And he laughed. We were brought back to my grandparents' house by motorboat, me shivering in my wet clothes, my mother angry, upset. *But we are fine,* he assured her. *It was nothing.* And I was wrapped up in the towels printed with butterflies that were kept near the guest room in the basement, past the sketches that my grandparents had brought back from Haiti, and brought up to sit on the porch, overlooking the water, and I saw he was right. It was fine. After a time

I went down to the hammock strung between a massive oak and a solid wood pillar, just over the water. I lay there, dozing, listening to the murmur of adult conversation on the hillside above me, and feeling safe. It is still one of my most favorite, most calming spots, to be today.

It was Ernest who purchased the *Stolpersteine*, the brass memorial stumbling blocks, that are now nestled into the sidewalk at 43 Bran-

denburgische Strasse. I have gone now, twice, to see them there, glittering underfoot.

Here lived Valerie Fabisch née Scheftel, says one. *Born 1911. Deported on 29 January 1943 to Auschwitz. Murdered.* Alongside hers is one for Hans Fabisch. The other fifty-two Jews deported from the building, thus far, have no marker.

Acknowledgments

I have worked to make this book as factually accurate as possible. In the interest of readability, my own timeline has been compressed—for example, multiple visits to cities have sometimes been condensed, in the narrative, into a single trip—but this has no impact on the veracity of the story or the events of Karl's or Valy's life. I have changed only one name for privacy reasons, that of my roommate in Vienna.

I have been able to tell Valy's story with the help of a small army of supporters.

My agent, Sydelle Kramer, pushed me (and pushed me) to get this story into the world; she shepherded it, nurtured it in ways above and beyond all reasonable expectation, and deflected my (not-inconsiderable) neurosis. Sarah Stein, my editor at Riverhead, fell in love with Valy back when she was a few pixels in a *Slate* story. Sarah stayed with Valy, and me, from idea to proposal through manuscript, gently guiding me along the path of the best story we could tell. She carefully midwifed this process, and I'm forever in her debt for believing in Valy—and me. Jean-Marc Dreyfus has been a confidant, mentor, and, above all, friend, for more than a decade now. Without his insistence, this story would never have made it to the page.

Without his eleventh-hour readings, I would have made dreadful mistakes in the text. I am so lucky to have met him, on a sunny Paris day, so many years ago.

The Milena Jesenská Fellowship at the Institut für die Wissenschaften vom Menschen in Vienna provided essential time to learn to love that city, as my grandfather once did. The Arthur F. Burns Fellowship (and the Holbrooke Research alumni grant), as well as the ACG Journalism Grant from the American Council on Germany, gave me essential opportunities to live and work in Berlin, and, later, the chance to travel to the Czech Republic. The Pulitzer Center on Crisis Reporting funded my time in Israel. The German Marshall Fund of the United States awarded my original work on Valy with the Peter R. Weitz Prize for reporting in Europe, an acknowledgment that gave me a much-needed confidence boost. The International Reporting Project at Johns Hopkins School of Advanced International Studies sponsored my first six weeks of reporting abroad and then, nearly a decade later, became my home while I wrote this book as a Visiting Scholar there. IRP's John Schidlovsky has been a supporter and friend from the beginning.

Valy's letters would not have been accessible to me without the help of Ulrike Wiesner, who first translated—gorgeously—Valy's words and the words of many of the other people who wrote to my grandfather. Ulli brought Valy to life, explained her cultural references, and brought out how very literate she was; Ulli was a generous giver of time, consultation, and expertise. Kathleen Luft stepped in as a translator late in the game and was always available, even in the wee hours, with the smallest of questions about everything from individual sentences in a letter to skimming official documents written with 1930s-era German legal vocabulary. Her work was crucial to getting this story right. Radovan Pletka helped with the Czech aryanization papers. Karin Isbell came in to help with the Sütterlin script.

Dozens upon dozens of academics and others whose life work centers on this period were incredibly generous to me with their time, opinions, and research. At the risk of leaving someone out, I must thank: Konrad Kwiet, Richard Breitman, Marion Kaplan, Beate Meyer, Barbara Schieb, Beate Kosmala, Aubrey Pomerance, Wolfgang Benz, Hermann Simon, Laurel Leff, Gudrun Maierhof, Ingo Zechner, Doron Rabinovici, Tina Walzer, and Walter Laqueur. Jeremy Zwelling of Wesleyan University invited me to speak there after the original series ran. For nearly twenty years now, I've had the privilege to call upon him for advice.

Daniel Silver opened his home and personal archives to me. Daniel Necas, at the University of Minnesota Immigration History Research Center, provided essential files on my grandfather. Herbert Posch, at the University of Vienna, unearthed my grandfather's and Valy's school records, fielded my calls, met me more times than he needed to, and took me around the university, all in an effort to help me understand better their experience on campus. The archivists at the International Tracing Service in Bad Arolsen have been endlessly available and helpful, submitting to my requests on numerous occasions.

At the U.S. Holocaust Memorial Museum I have been fortunate to often consult with and be advised by Jürgen Matthäus, Radu Ioanid, Paul Shapiro, and Anatol Steck, each of whom always cheerfully accepts my calls, e-mails, and visits. The library and archives at the museum were infinitely more accessible with the help of Michlean Amir, Vincent Slatt, Ronald Coleman, and Peter Lande.

Linda Kinstler and Mimi Dwyer made sure that every piece of this story was as factually correct as possible. Claire Winecoff went through the galleys with a fine-tooth comb. All errors introduced are therefore entirely my own.

Spending time away would have been a lonely project had it not been for the friends I have in these cities. In Vienna, I am so very lucky that IWM introduced me to Georg Maißer, Sophie Loidolt, Herwig Czech, Andrea Roedig, and Thomas Szanto—a group I now count among my closest friends anywhere in the world. I'm always happy to return to Berlin to see Ralf Neukirch, whose friendship draws me firmly into the present. Also in Berlin, Carolyn Mimram rescued me when I was extremely pregnant, got me packed and on a plane and has been my hero ever since. In Kassel, Ulrich Brinkmann and Urte Helduser offered me housing and camaraderie. In the Czech Republic, Kate Treveloni was a much-needed friendly face.

Without Pavel Kuča, I would still be wandering the Czech countryside lost; I never would have found my way to understanding Valy's life in Troppau. Pavel took my hand, literally, and led me around the country. In Israel, Laurence Weinbaum and my Ramat Gan family, Shely and Kami Ben-Shem and Sharon Ben-Shem Da Silva, brought me Reuven Ben-Shem's part of the story. Toby Ticktin Back makes Jerusalem another home. From Madrid to Berlin to San Sebastián, Baruc Corazón has been a constant friend.

In London, Carol Levene opened her home, her heart, and her cache of letters. She gave me the incredible gift of understanding the fullness of this story. Ernest Fontheim, in Ann Arbor, Michigan, agreed to revisit a very sad chapter of his life with me, and welcomed the chance to celebrate Hans.

Back in America, I am forever grateful for the friendship, support, and love of Stephanie Handel, Madeleine Remez, Jonathan Becker, and Zeenat Rahman. Wendy Blum, my other mother, has been a shoulder, a shelf, and, above all, a friend since I was in the womb. Morgan Fahey, Diego Salazar, Shola Olatoye, Miguel Aguilar, and Shayla Harris were supporters from afar to whom I often turned for advice. Elsa (Marleny) Diaz cared for my children when I was holed up with my computer or far away around the globe. My in-laws Mishele and Kenneth Halpern were always quick with support, cheerleading, child care, and a kind word when I needed one.

I am grateful to Noam Scheiber, Shar Taylor, Cathy Alter, and Jeanette Buck for reading various confused versions of this book, providing essential feedback and editorial recommendations, at all hours of the day and night. To say this book would be poorer without their input is an understatement. Sacha Z. Scoblic and Lisa Goldman generously took time to read my ideas for the book proposal years ago; notes they provided then have finally borne fruit.

Valy's story owes everything to June Thomas and David Plotz at *Slate*, who agreed to run the first ten thousand words about my search. June's editorial eye on the *Slate* series made all the difference to its success.

My parents, Joseph and Margot Wildman, kept these letters for me when I was traveling around the world, and, of course, believed in me from the beginning and nurtured my (sometimes unfathomable) obsession with the past. My father's interest in Jewish history in particular was clearly contagious (and his meticulous eye saved this text from numerous errors). My mother's humor and levity considerably lighten what might have been a sad process. It's impossible to thank them enough. My aunt Judy Wildman is always available for a question, and advice. My sister, Rebecca Wildman Repetti, and my brother-in-law, Michael, make my world a better place.

More than anyone, this book would simply, full stop, not have been possible without the support of Ian Halpern, my partner, whose unflappable belief in me long after I stopped believing in myself sustained me and this project these many years. He has read this book nearly as many times as I have, offered advice, an editorial eye, a calming hand, borne the brunt of child care, and given me more love, latitude, and superhuman patience (so much patience) than any one woman deserves.

Finally, for my two wonderful girls, Orli and Hana, the two little Jews who grew during the long gestation of this project. Pregnancies and book writing are not natural companions, but they kept me looking toward the future, even when I was so deeply mired in the past. I only regret they did not arrive soon enough to meet my *saba*, C. J. Wildman, without whom, obviously, this book would not exist.

Notes and Sources

Other than the letters between Karl and Bruno, nearly all correspondence with my grandfather was in German. Valy's letters were translated by Ulrike Wiesner, with the exception of August 1939; this was translated by Kathleen Luft. Letters from Hans, Lotte, and Uncle Julius were divided between Luft and Wiesner. Letters from other friends—including Alfred Jospe, Paula Holländer, Reuven, and files from Vienna school friends were translated by Wiesner. Karin Isbell translated the letters of Maria Richterova.

Introduction: In the Beginning

8 **"If not, then not" in Valy's folded note:** The line in German is: *"Wenn nicht, den nicht"*; the lyrics of "Der Eine Allein" are by Hermann Löns, translated by Kathleen Luft.

Chapter One. Situation Excellent

30 **"The National Committee for Resettlement of Foreign Physicians was organized more than two years ago":** David L. Edsall, N. C. Tryon, and Tracy J. Putnam, "The Émigré Physician in America, 1941: A Report of the National Committee for Resettlement of Foreign Physicians," *Journal of the American Medical Association* 117, no. 22 (November 29, 1941), p. 1881.

30–32 **National Committee for Resettlement of Foreign Physicians:** Information comes from Laurel Leff's paper "Combating Prejudice and Protectionism in American Medicine: The Physicians Committee's Fight for Refugees from Nazism, 1939–1945," *Holocaust and Genocide Studies* 28:2 (Fall 2014).

CHAPTER TWO. THE WONDERFUL CITY

50 **rumor of Jabotinsky holding up a suitcase and shouting in the packed Konzer-
    thaus, "Run, Jews, run!":** George E. Berkley, *Vienna and Its Jews: The Tragedy
    of Success, 1880–1980s* (Lanham, MD: Madison Books, 1988), p. 246.

51 **"in the early years of the twentieth century Vienna *was* Europe":** Tony Judt,
    Postwar: A History of Europe Since 1945 (New York: Penguin, 2005), p. 2.

53 **Milena Jesenská:** See Margarete Buber-Neumann, *Milena: The Story of a
    Remarkable Friendship*, trans. Ralph Manheim (New York: Schocken Books,
    1977).

55 **an extraordinary book about three forgotten slave labor camps:** Jean-Marc
    Dreyfus and Sarah Gensburger, *Des Camps dans Paris: Austerlitz, Lévitan, Bas-
    sano, Juillet 1943–Août 1944* (Paris: Fayard, 2003).

58 **the Ephrussi banking family:** Edmund de Waal, *The Hare with Amber Eyes:
    A Hidden Inheritance* (New York: Picador, 2011).

63 **The interwar years in Vienna:** See Berkley, *Vienna and Its Jews*, p. 172; and
    Steven Beller, *Vienna and the Jews: 1867–1938* (Cambridge, England: Cambridge
    University Press, 1989).

64–65 **The immediate time around the Anschluss:** See George Clare, *Last Waltz
    in Vienna: The Rise and Destruction of a Family, 1842–1942* (New York: Henry
    Holt, 1989).

66 **the best short narration of the horrific pre-Nazi-period violence:** Benno
    Weiser Varon, *Professions of a Lucky Jew* (Cranbury, NJ, and London: Cornwall
    Books, 1992).

CHAPTER THREE. SEARCH NUMBER 557 584

81 **Postwar casualty and war-lost numbers:** Judt, *Postwar*, pp. 28, 29.

87 **Conan and Rousso present the problem of opening historical material:** Éric
    Conan and Henri Rousso, *Vichy: An Ever-Present Past*, trans. Nathan Bracher
    (Hanover, NH, and London: University Press of New England, 1998).

87 **Bad Arolsen and ITS:** See Jean-Marc Dreyfus, "À Bad Arolsen, dans la
    Forêt des Archives Nazies," *La Vie des Idées*, September 11, 2008, http://www
    .laviedesidees.fr/A-Bad-Arolsen-dans-la-foret-des.html; and Sarah Wildman,
    "Paper Love: Inside the Holocaust Archives," January 2009, http://www.slate
    .com/articles/news_and_politics/dispatches/features/2009/paper_love_inside_
    the_holocaust_archives/50_million_mysteries.html.

CHAPTER FOUR. WHO SHE WAS

113 **This much I know:** Information in this chapter comes from: Marcin Wodziński
     and Janusz Spyra, eds., *Jews in Silesia* (Kraków: Księgarnia Akademicka, and
     Wrocław: University of Wrocław, Research Centre for the Culture and Lan-
     guages of Polish Jews, 2001); Livia Rothkirchen, *The Jews of Bohemia and Mora-
     via: Facing the Holocaust* (Lincoln: University of Nebraska Press, and Jerusalem:
     Yad Vashem, 2005); and Jiri Fiedler, *Jewish Sights of Bohemia and Moravia*
     (Prague: Sefer, 1991).

130 **By the early 1930s, smart girls like Valy were sent to Vienna to study:** See Harriet Pass Freidenreich, *Female, Jewish, and Educated: The Lives of Central European University Women* (Bloomington: Indiana University Press, 2002).

132 **"The Third Reich will win again":** Victor Klemperer, *I Will Bear Witness: A Diary of the Nazi Years*, vol. 1, *1933–1941* (New York: Modern Library, 1999), p. 268.

138–39 **Valy's mother's file:** Toni Scheftel's aryanization papers translated for the author by Ulrike Wiesner.

CHAPTER FIVE. BERLIN

149 **Before my grandfather had even left Europe:** Statistics here are from Wolf Gruner, "Poverty and Persecution: The Reichsvereinigung, the Jewish Population, and Anti-Jewish Policy in the Nazi State 1939–1945," www.yadvashem .org/odot_pdf/Microsoft%20Word%20-%203214.pdf; and Gruner, *Judenverfolgung [Jewish Persecution] in Berlin, 1933–1945* (Berlin: Stiftung Topographie des Terrors, 2009), translated for the author by Kathleen Luft.

152 **women were often seen as having needs secondary to those of men:** Marion A. Kaplan, *Between Dignity and Despair: Jewish Life in Nazi Germany* (Oxford: Oxford University Press, 1998), pp. 138–141.

152 **"The emigration problem demanded our greatest labors":** Testimony of Alfred Schwerin, in Richarz, *Jewish Life in Germany*, pp. 401–402.

153 **Kindergartenseminar:** Gudrun Meierhof, "The Jewish Seminar for Teachers in Kindergartens and After-School-Care Facilities, 1934–1942," translated for the author by Ulrike Wiesner. Unpublished manuscript provided by author.

153 **the League of Jewish Women, a remarkable feminist organization:** Lara Daemmig and Marion Kaplan, "Juedischer Frauenbund (The League of Jewish Women)," Jewish Women's Archive, http://jwa.org/encyclopedia/article/ juedischer-frauenbund-league-of-jewish-women.

153 **Marianne Strauss:** See Mark Roseman, *A Past in Hiding: Memory and Survival in Nazi Germany* (New York: Picador, 2002).

154 **Only works by Jews could be performed:** Testimony of Alfred Schwerin, in Monika Richarz, ed., *Jewish Life in Germany: Memoirs from Three Centuries*, trans. Stella P. Rosenfeld and Sidney Rosenfeld (Bloomington: Indiana University Press, 1991), pp. 401–402.

155 **the population of Jews under age thirty-nine decreased by nearly eighty percent:** Kaplan, *Between Dignity and Despair*, p. 143.

156 **I pick up historian Wolf Gruner's book:** Gruner, *Judenverfolgung [Jewish Persecution] in Berlin, 1933–1945*.

159 **she later wrote a book—called *Outcast* in English:** Inge Deutschkron, *Outcast: A Jewish Girl in Wartime Berlin* (New York: Fromm International, 1989).

165 **"My registration number is very high":** Hertha Feiner, *Before Deportation: Letters from a Mother to Her Daughters, January 1939–December 1942*, ed. Karl Heinz Jahnke (Evanston, IL: Northwestern University Press, 1993).

168 **Germany's numbers, officially, weren't actually all that low:** Author interview with Professor Richard Breitman, August 8, 2012.

Chapter Six. Three Hundred Dollars

176 **the deportation of the Jews of Stettin:** Christopher Browning with Jürgen Matthäus, *The Origins of the Final Solution: The Evolution of Nazi Jewish Policy, September 1939–March 1942* (Lincoln: University of Nebraska Press, 2004), p. 64 and preceding pages.

176 **"Men, women, children and even the inmates of the local Jewish home for the aged":** From the Jewish Telegraphic Agency, February 19, 1940, "Koenigsberg Jews Slated for Expulsion; Stettin Deportees Put at 1,500," http://www.jta .org/1940/02/19/archive/koenigsberg-jews-slated-for-expulsionstettin-deportees -put-at-1500.

184 **In January, Jews had been denied legumes:** Kaplan, *Between Dignity and Despair*, p. 151.

189 **"Solveig's Song" lyrics:** Translated from the Norwegian with the help of Ingvild Torsen, Eli Nilsen, and Nancy Aarsvold.

190–91 **"The successes in the West are prodigious":** Klemperer, *I Will Bear Witness*, pp. 337–338.

194–95 **Earlier that spring . . . thirty thousand people had applied:** Richarz, *Jewish Life in Germany*, pp. 410–411.

Chapter Seven. The Vise

199 **In January 1941, Jews are denied the right to repair their shoes:** Kaplan, *Between Dignity and Despair*, p. 170.

204 **Gerda Haas, giving testimony to the Holocaust Museum:** United States Holocaust Memorial Museum interview with Gerda Haas, June 12, 1995, www .ushmm.org.

204 **"we are convinced that in reality America wants to help":** Richarz, *Jewish Life in Germany*, pp. 412–424.

206 **the Jewish Hospital in Berlin, founded in 1756, was kept open:** See Daniel B. Silver, *Refuge in Hell: How Berlin's Jewish Hospital Outlasted the Nazis* (New York: Mariner Books, 2004).

213 **James G. McDonald, who served as high commissioner for refugees:** Quoted passages here are from Richard Breitman, Barbara McDonald Stewart, and Severin Hochberg, eds., *Refugees and Rescue: The Diaries and Papers of James G. McDonald, 1935–1945* (Bloomington: Indiana University Press, 2009), pp. 200–205, 214, 239, 245.

214 **"We can delay and effectively stop":** Memo from Assistant Secretary of State Breckinridge Long to the State Department, June 26, 1940, www.pbs.org/wgbh/ amex/holocaust/filmmore/reference/primary/barmemo.html.

215 **"I wish to say . . . that if I had my way":** Breitman, Stewart, and Hochberg, *Refugees and Rescue*, p. 248 (and *Congressional Record*).

216 ***The New York Times* published a front-page story blaring:** "U.S. Ruling Cuts Off Means of Escape for Many in Reich," *The New York Times*, June 19, 1941, retrieved online January 14, 2013.

216 **"Bars have now been raised":** Editorial, *The New Republic*, August 18, 1941.

216 **Otto Frank, Anne's father, was tripped up:** Patricia Cohen, "In Old Files, Fading Hopes for Anne Frank's Family," *The New York Times*, February 15, 2007.

225 **"Rabbi Wise always assumes such a sanctimonious air":** Breckinridge Long diary, quoted in Breitman, Stewart, and Hochberg, *Refugees and Rescue*, p. 257.

226 **Levetzowstrasse Synagogue:** See Roger Moorehouse, *Berlin at War* (New York: Vintage, 2011), p. 161.

228 *"And I remembered Storm's 'Oktoberlied'":* Valy refers to the German poet Theodor Storm (1817–1888). The lyrics to "October Song" (translated by Ulli Wiesner) are as follows:

The rising fog, the falling leaves:
to wine we are beholden!
The grayish day no longer grieves:
it's golden, yes, it's golden!

And if all madness be unfurled
(by church or temple polished),
this world, this most amazing world,
can never be demolished.

And even if the heart should smart
let glasses sound the meeting!
For all we know, a righteous heart
will never stop its beating.

The rising fog, the falling leaves:
to wine we are beholden!
The grayish day no longer grieves:
it's golden, yes, it's golden!

Though it is fall, wait just a while,
just wait and keep consuming!
The spring arrives, the sky is blue,
the violets are blooming.

The days of blue shall be at hand,
and ere they all shall leave us,
we'll let the wine, my noble friend,
reprieve us, yes, reprieve us.

231 **20,000 Jews to be deported to Lodz and Washington knew:** George Warren (later adviser on refugees and displaced persons) files, Breitman, Stewart, and Hochberg, *Refugees and Rescue*, p. 258.

232 **"I have the impression even the Jewish Council":** Jürgen B, in Donald L.

Niewyk, ed., *Fresh Wounds: Early Narratives of Holocaust Survival* (Chapel Hill: University of North Carolina Press, 1998), pp. 260–261.

CHAPTER EIGHT. *BURGFRÄULEIN*

244 **On the Hilfsverein der Deutschen Juden:** See the Central Archives for the History of the Jewish People, https://cahjp.huji.ac.il, A/176 Jewish Virtual library. Also Yad Vashem, Shoah Resource Center, www.yadvashem.org/yv/en/holocaust/resource_center/index.asp.

246 **some 270,000 to 300,000 were able to emigrate . . . In Berlin itself . . . some 5,000 to 7,000:** Kaplan, *Between Dignity and Despair*, chapter 8, "Life Underground," and p. 228.

250 **Ahawah day-care center:** Its story is told in Kaplan, *Between Dignity and Despair*, p. 176.

253 **the role of the Reichsvereinigung:** Information comes from author interviews with Beate Meyer, and from her essays "Between Self-Assertion and Forced Collaboration: The Reich Association of Jews in Germany, 1939–1945" and "The Fine Line Between Responsible Action and Collaboration," in Beate Meyer, Hermann Simon, and Chana Schütz, eds., *Jews in Nazi Berlin: From Kristallnacht to Liberation* (Chicago: University of Chicago Press, 2009).

257 **In 1942, Marianne Strauss . . . was able to discover a glimpse:** Roseman, *A Past in Hiding*, chapter 7, "Report from Izbica."

257 **"A dreadful future awaited them":** Interview with Edith Dietz, quoted in Meyer, "The Fine Line Between Responsible Action and Collaboration," p. 320.

258 **On the increasing difficulty for even Jews in mixed marriages:** See Martin Doerry, *My Wounded Heart: The Life of Lilli Jahn, 1900–1944*, trans. John Brownjohn (New York: Bloomsbury, 2004).

258 **"These deportations were something monstrous":** Camilla Neumann, quoted in Richarz, *Jewish Life in Germany*, pp. 435–436.

259 **In early January 1942, Valy and her mother were forced to turn in:** All Berlin Jews must turn in warm items per Wolf Gruner; see Gruner, *Judenverfolgung*.

261 **"To a Jew this role of the Jewish leaders":** Hannah Arendt, *Eichmann in Jerusalem*, in *The Portable Hannah Arendt*, ed. Peter Baehr (New York: Penguin, 2000), pp. 348–349.

262 **"To claim that demonstrative refusal, open resistance":** Meyer, "The Fine Line Between Responsible Action and Collaboration," pp. 346–347.

262 **the story of Wilhelm Reisz:** Doron Rabinovici, "Prologue," *Eichmann's Jews: The Jewish Administration of Holocaust Vienna, 1938–1945* (Cambridge and Oxford, England: Polity, 2011).

263 **"Of some forty women who helped in the beginning":** Herta Pineas, in testimony of Hermann Pineas, in Richarz, *Jewish Life in Germany*, pp. 449–455.

265 **Hildegard Henschel, wife of one of the higher-ups:** Hildegarde Henschel's Eichmann trial testimony is retrieved from www.nizkor.org/hweb/people/e/eichmann-adolf/transcripts/Sessions/index-02.html.

268 **video testimony from Norbert Wollheim:** United States Holocaust Memorial Museum interview with Norbert Wollheim, recorded 1992, www.ushmm.org.

CHAPTER NINE. A NEW NAME

277 **the property files and Gestapo materials:** I'm grateful to the Brandenbur-
gisches Landeshauptarchiv, Potsdam, for copying files and sending them to me.
I relied on Rep. 36 A Oberfinanzpräsident Berlin Brandenburg (F 1701) and (II)
(Nr. 35551), as well as Rep. 35 A Staatspolizeistelle Potsdam (Nr. 13), regarding
Valy's mother, Toni Scheftel, geb. Flamm. The files on Hans Fabisch come
from the Brandenburgisches Landeshauptarchiv as well: Landesarchiv Berlin A
Rep. 092 Nr. 8636. The Compensation files on Fabisch are from the Landsamt
für Bürger- und Ordnungsangelegenheiten Abt. I Entschädigungsbehörde,
Reg. Nr. 303 696. All of the above were translated for the author by Kath-
leen Luft.

CHAPTER TEN. LONDON INTERLUDE

286 **Searches placed in the Aufbau (Reconstruction):** Debórah Dwork and Robert
Jan van Pelt, *Flight from the Reich: Refugee Jews, 1933–1946* (New York: W. W.
Norton, 2012), p. 353.

286 **"the voice of help and hope for thousands of Jewish refugees":** "Refugees' Best
Friend," *Time*, November 23, 1959.

294 **Mayer was profiled:** Martin Gilbert, *The Boys: The Story of 732 Young Concentration Camp Survivors* (New York: Henry Holt, 1997). Mayer was himself the
author of *Jews and the Olympic Games—Sport: A Springboard for Minorities*
(London: Vallentine-Mitchell, 2004).

CHAPTER ELEVEN. THE ONLY POSSIBILITY

298 **"What could we possibly talk about?":** United States Holocaust Memorial
Museum interview with Gerda Haas, June 12, 1995, www.ushmm.org, p. 23.

302 **photo of the Jewish Hospital's notes on Hans:** Personal collection of Carol
Levene. Translated by Kathleen Luft.

304 **Margot, the woman who would, after the war, become Ernest's wife:** See "Ann
Arbor's Ernest Fontheim," *Washtenaw Jewish News* (Feb./March 2004), http://
www.slowtale.net/writing/0204_WJN_Fontheim.pdf, and "Wallenberg Medal
Honors Officer Who Hid Family, Refused to Join Nazis," *The University Record
Online*, http://www.ur.umich.edu/0405/Oct04_/04/05.shtml.

CHAPTER TWELVE. WHAT REMAINS

328 **the transport of January 29, 1943:** Information comes from the Yad Vashem
website, www.yadvashem.org.

328 **The Birkenau selection ramp so often depicted:** See, for example, Götz Aly,
Into the Tunnel: The Brief Life of Marion Samuel, 1931–1943, trans. Ann Millin
(New York: Metropolitan Books, 2004), p. 77.

342–45 **The IKG file:** Files for Manele Wildmann were translated for the author by
Anatol Steck.

347 **Reuven Ben-Shem:** See Laurence Weinbaum, "'Shaking the Dust Off': The Story of the Warsaw Ghetto's Forgotten Chronicler, Ruben Feldschu (Ben Shem)," *Jewish Political Studies Review* 22, no. 3–4 (Fall 2010), http://jcpa.org/article/shaking-the-dust-off-the-story-of-the-warsaw-ghettos-forgotten-chronicler-ruben-feldschu-ben-shem/#sthash.Rlbr761D.dpuf. Also Sarah Wildman, "Our Lost Warsaw Ghetto Diary," *Tablet*, April 18, 2013, http://www.tabletmag.com/jewish-arts-and-culture/books/129585/our-lost-warsaw-ghetto-diary.

348 **"The dead are naked" and "January 1942. There's talk recently of the vandals":** Translation and notes from Reuven Ben-Shem's diary are from Weinbaum, "'Shaking the Dust Off': The Story of the Warsaw Ghetto's Forgotten Chronicler, Ruben Feldschu (Ben Shem)."

CHAPTER FOURTEEN. *ENTZÜCKEN*

364 **Hans's Siemens work card, along with his files and those of Valy:** These were provided by the International Tracing Service in Bad Arolsen, Germany. Translated by Kathleen Luft.